Network Technology Foundations:
Self-Study Guide

President

James Stanger, Ph.D.

Vice President, Publishing

Todd Hopkins

Senior Content Developer

Kenneth A. Kozakis

Managing Editor

Susan M. Lane

Editor

Sarah Skodak

Project Manager/Publisher

Tina Strong

Customer Service   ComputerPREP
Certification Partners, LLC
1230 W. Washington St., Ste. 111
Tempe, AZ 85281
(602) 275-7700

Network Technology Foundations

Developer

Kenneth A. Kozakis

Contributors

James Stanger, Ph.D., Patrick T. Lane and Irina Heer

Editor

Susan M. Lane

Publisher

Tina Strong

Project Managers

Todd Hopkins and Tina Strong

Trademarks

Disclaimer

Copyright Information

Table of Contents

List of Labs

List of Activities

List of Optional Labs

List of Quizzes

List of Figures

List of Tables

Course Description

Network Technology Foundations teaches essential networking technologies and skills, including TCP/IP, stable network creation, wireless networking and network troubleshooting. You will learn to use various network components and protocols that enable users to share data quickly and easily. You will explore the different types of transmission media, and will learn how network architecture and topologies provide for efficient and secure communication. In addition, you will learn about the OSI reference model and its relationship to packet creation, and you will compare and contrast the OSI model with the Internet architecture model.

You will study the functions and features of internetworking server types, and learn about the benefits of implementing a Content Management System (CMS). You will also achieve competency in performing basic hardware and operating system maintenance procedures. In addition, you will learn about mobile computing devices and the importance of RFC documents.

You will also learn about the importance of routing, and will explore IP addressing, IP address classes and subnet masks. Finally, you will explore essential network security concepts, Internet-based challenges facing today's users, and methods you can use to secure networks and network transmissions, including authentication, encryption and firewalls.

All CIW Foundations courses offer Case Studies about real-world skills applications, and job-related topics such as project management and the relationship between technology and business operations. The CIW Foundations courses prepare you to take the CIW v5 Foundations certification exam.

Guided, step-by-step labs provide opportunities to practice new skills. You can challenge yourself and review your skills after each lesson in the Lesson Summary and Lesson Review sections. Additional skill reinforcement is provided in Activities, Optional Labs and Lesson Quizzes that are included in the coursebook and on the companion CD-ROM.

The companion CD-ROM contains the lab files used in the course. To practice the skills presented in the coursebook, refer to the Course Setup Guide And System Requirements section for information about system requirements and using the lab files.

Series

Network Technology Foundations is the third course in the CIW Foundations series. CIW Foundations consists of the following courses:

- Internet Business Foundations

- Site Development Foundations

- *Network Technology Foundations*

Prerequisites

No prior experience using the Internet, developing Web pages or configuring networks is necessary. However, you should be familiar with an operating system such as Microsoft Windows Vista before taking this course. The CIW Foundations courseware does not provide entry-level computer literacy. Rather, it builds upon computer literacy training and certifications such as Microsoft Office Specialist (*www.microsoft.com*) and IC3 (*www.certiport.com*).

Certification

The CIW Foundations series of courses prepares you to take the high-stakes CIW Foundations certification exam. If you pass the CIW Foundations exam, you will earn the highly respected CIW Associate certification, which is recognized throughout the industry as validating essential Internet skills for the workplace. The CIW Associate certification proves that an individual has evolved from being an Internet consumer to an Internet producer, capable of producing real-world Internet applications. A CIW Associate certificant can use common Internet-ready applications, can create properly formed HTML/XHTML documents, knows database essentials, understands project management concepts and can troubleshoot networks. For information about taking the Foundations exam, visit *www.CIW-certified.com*.

Self-Study Courseware

This coursebook was developed for self-directed training. Along with comprehensive instructional text and objectives checklists, this coursebook provides easy-to-follow hands-on labs and a glossary of course-specific terms. It provides Internet addresses needed to complete some labs, although due to the constantly changing nature of the Internet, some addresses may no longer be valid. The coursebook also includes margin notes that provide additional tips and commentary to supplement course narrative, and that direct you to material relating directly to specified CIW Foundations exam objectives. Each course lesson includes practice, study and assessment materials such as preview and review questions, Case Studies, Application Projects, pen-and-paper-based Activities, Optional Labs and Quizzes.

The coursebook includes a companion CD-ROM that provides files needed to complete labs. The companion CD-ROM also includes an appendix listing the CIW v5 Foundations certification exam objectives and locations of corresponding material in the coursebook. The companion CD-ROM provides all answers to Activities, Optional Labs and Lesson Quizzes. Lesson Quizzes are provided as study and self-assessment resources only; success on these materials in no way guarantees a passing score on the CIW v5 Foundations certification exam.

After you have finished the course, you will find this coursebook to be a valuable resource for reviewing labs at home or in the workplace and applying the skills you have learned.

Additional online resources

In addition to the material found in the coursebooks, you can visit CIW Online at *www.certification-partners.com/cciivv/CIW-Online/index.html* to help you prepare for the CIW v5 Foundations certification exam. CIW Online provides a variety of online tools you can use to supplement the Official CIW Courseware, including:

- **Practice Exam questions** — The CIW Certification Practice Exams help measure proficiency on specific topics or the full range of CIW skills objectives. With nearly 700 exam questions, this powerful tool can be used to pre-assess certification aptitude, to prepare for the high-stakes exam environment, and to identify skills gaps and additional study needs. Visit *www.CIW-certified.com/training/practice-exams.asp* or call (602) 275-7700 for product and purchase information about currently available CIW Certification Practice Exams.

- **Course review questions** — The course review questions consist of more than 1,300 multiple-choice questions that cover numerous topics throughout the Foundations course material, not just those topics addressed by the CIW exam objectives. The questions are completely integrated with material from the book and can be used to assess your understanding of the course material.

- **Interactive exercises** — These activities consist of fill-in-the-blank, true-or-false, categorizing, matching and crossword puzzle exercises. The self-testing exercises provide immediate scoring and feedback after completion, allowing you to focus on topics that require additional study. The exercises are based on Foundations content and prepare you to excel in tests and quizzes that feature multiple-choice questions.

- **Online flashcards** — Over 400 glossary flashcards test your vocabulary of important Foundations terms. The interactive flashcards show a vocabulary term on one side and the definition on the other. You may move through the flashcards as necessary for extra review.

Course Objectives

After completing this course, you will be able to:

- Identify convergence networking, the client/server model, network topologies and major network operating systems.

- Describe the packet creation process and explain the Open Systems Interconnection (OSI) reference model.

- Discuss local area networks (LANs), wide area networks (WANs), Internet Exchange Points (IXPs) and common network components.

- Compare and contrast the functions of network protocols, and describe network transmission media and types, including wireless network technologies.

- Describe IEEE LAN standards and discuss the benefits of virtualization.

- Describe the Internet architecture model, Internet protocols, the routing process, routing protocols and port numbers.

- Explain IP addressing, IP address classes, default subnet masks and the use of private IP addresses.

- Use diagnostic tools for troubleshooting TCP/IP networks.

- Identify and describe the functions and features of various internetworking server types.

- Describe the functions and benefits of implementing a Content Management System (CMS).

- Identify maintenance issues for common system components.

- Identify the benefits and security risks of mobile computing devices.

- Describe the characteristics of file system types and use file system management tools.

- Identify and suggest corrective measures for operating system boot problems and application failures, and identify methods to remotely manage workstations.

- Identify essential network security concepts and network attack types, and identify various methods of defeating network attacks and securing network transmissions, including authentication, encryption, VPNs and digital certificates.

- Discuss issues of Internet privacy and identify Internet-based challenges that face today's users.

- Describe firewall topologies and security zones you can set up to protect your internal trusted network from an outside untrusted network, such as the Internet.

Course Setup Guide and System Requirements

In order to implement this course, you will need to set up your computer based on the hardware, software and connectivity requirements listed in the following sections. However, you may want to use additional software to further explore network interaction or related technologies.

Hardware requirements

The following table summarizes the hardware requirements for all courses in the CIW program.

Note: The CIW hardware requirements are similar to the minimum system requirements for Microsoft Windows Vista Business implementation.

Hardware Specifications	Minimum Requirements
Processor	1 GHz 32-bit (x86) or 64-bit (x64) processor
L2 cache	256 KB
Hard disk	40 GB with at least 15 GB of available space
RAM	At least 1 GB
CD-RW	32X
Network interface card (NIC)	10BaseT or 100BaseTX (10 or 100 Mbps)
Sound card/speakers	Required for movie clips and labs that use sound
Video adapter	Support for DirectX9 graphics with: • WDDM Driver • At least 128 MB of graphics memory • Pixel Shader 2.0 in hardware • 32 bits per pixel
Monitor	Super VGA (1024 x 768)

Software requirements

If you are taking all three CIW Foundations self-study courses sequentially, there is no need to reformat your computer for each course. The recommended software configurations for computers used to complete the labs in this book series are as follows.

Internet Business Foundations

To be installed before starting the course:

- **Microsoft Windows Vista Business** (typical installation)
- **Microsoft Internet Explorer 8.0** (typical installation)

To be installed during course labs:

- **Firefox 3.0.5** (binary provided in the C:\CIW\Internet\Lab Files\Lesson03 folder)
- **Google Chrome 1.0** (binary provided in the C:\CIW\Internet\Lab Files\Lesson03 folder)
- **Ogg Codecs** (binary provided in the C:\CIW\Internet\Lab Files\Lesson04 folder)
- **Aethera** (binary provided in the C:\CIW\Internet\Lab Files\Lesson06 folder)
- **Thunderbird 2.0** (binary provided in the C:\CIW\Internet\Lab Files\Lesson06 folder)
- **TightVNC**, **Bzip2** and **Bunzip2** (binaries provided in the C:\CIW\Internet\Lab Files\Lesson07 folder)
- **Audacity** and **Windows Live Messenger** (binaries provided in the C:\CIW\Internet\Lab Files\Lesson08 folder)
- **Ad-AwareAE** (binary provided in the C:\CIW\Internet\Lab Files\Lesson09 folder)
- **GanttProject** (binary provided in the C:\CIW\Internet\Lab Files\Lesson10 folder)

© 2009 Certification Partners, LLC — All Rights Reserved.   Version 2.0

Site Development Foundations

To be installed before starting the course:

- **Microsoft Windows Vista Business** (typical installation)
- **Microsoft Internet Explorer 8.0** (typical installation)
- **Firefox 3.0.5** (typical installation)

To be installed during course labs:

- **Lynx** (binary provided in the C:\CIW\Site_Dev\Lab Files\Lesson01\Lab_1-2\Lynx folder)
- **FormMail** (binary provided in the C:\CIW\Site_Dev\Lab Files\Lesson07\FormMail folder)
- **KompoZer** (binary provided in the C:\CIW\Site_Dev\Lab Files\Lesson10 folder)
- **XAMPP** (binary provided in the C:\CIW\Site_Dev\Lab Files\Lesson11\Lab_11-1\XAMPP folder)
- **Audacity** (binary provided in the C:\CIW\Site_Dev\Lab Files\Lesson11 folder)

Network Technology Foundations

To be installed before starting the course:

- **Microsoft Windows Vista Business** (typical installation)
- **Microsoft Internet Explorer 8.0** (typical installation)
- **Firefox 3.0.5** (typical installation)

To be installed during course labs:

- **uTorrent** (binary provided in the C:\CIW\Network\Lab Files\Lesson01 folder)
- **FileZilla_v3.0.2.1** (torrent file provided in the C:\CIW\Network\Lab Files\Lesson01 folder)
- **7-Zip** (binary provided in the C:\CIW\Network\Lab Files\Lesson01 folder)
- **FineCrypt 10.1** (binary provided in the C:\CIW\Network\Lab Files\Lesson05 folder)

Installing and configuring Microsoft Windows Vista Business

The three CIW v5 Foundations self-study courses can be completed without reinstalling the operating system for each course. Install Windows Vista Business with the default settings. The only requirement is that your system must be able to access the Internet in order for you to perform the hands-on labs in all CIW v5 Foundations self-study courses.

Note: If you have already installed Windows Vista Business and have Internet access, you can skip this section.

The instructions for installing Windows Vista Business are as follows:

1. Obtain a valid license for your copy of Windows Vista Business.

2. Begin setup by setting the boot sequence for your computer so that it will boot from the CD drive, then insert the Windows Vista Business CD-ROM and reboot.

3. When prompted, specify your installation language, time and currency format, and keyboard type.

4. When prompted, enter your 25-digit product key.

5. Accept the license terms.

6. Specify to conduct a Custom (advanced) installation. Use the following parameters to perform a custom installation of Windows Vista Business.

When This Information Is Required	Use
Phase 1	
Partition Location	Default (C:)
Partition Size	Entire hard disk drive
Phase 2 (after Windows formats and installs files to your hard disk drive)	
User Name	Your name
Type Administrator Password	*password* (all lowercase letters)
Confirm Password	*password* (all lowercase letters)
Windows Protection Method	Specify: *Use Recommended Settings*
Date, Time and Time Zone Settings	Customize for your location

Configure Windows Vista Business for use in these courses by specifying the following settings:

Specify a valid IP address

1. Log on as Administrator.

2. Select **Start | Control Panel**, then double-click **Network And Sharing Center**.

3. Click the **View Status** link next to *Local Area Connection*, then click the **Properties** button to display the Local Area Connection Properties dialog box.

4. In the list box, click **Internet Protocol Version 4 (TCP/IPv4)**, then click **Properties** to open the Internet Protocol Version 4 (TCP/IPv4) Properties dialog box.

5. Select **Use The Following IP Address**, then manually enter the IP address information specific to your system. You can use DHCP if you prefer; however, prepare the system for networking.

   Note: Do not enter DNS configurations; you will configure DNS during the labs.

6. Click **OK**, then close all open dialog boxes and windows.

Specify the CLASSROOM workgroup

1. Select **Start | Control Panel**, then double-click **System** to open the System window.

2. In the Computer Name, Domain, And Workgroup Settings section, click the **Change Settings** link to display the Computer Name tab of the System Properties dialog box. Click the **Change** button.

3. In the Member Of section, click **Workgroup**, type *classroom* in the Workgroup field, click **OK**, enter your name and password when prompted, then restart your computer.

Disable the Windows Vista Business firewall on your system

1. Select **Start | Control Panel**, then double-click **Windows Firewall** to open the Windows Firewall window.

2. Click the **Change Settings** link to display the Windows Firewall Settings dialog box. Select **Off (Not Recommended)**, then click **OK**.

3. Close all open windows.

When you are finished configuring Windows Vista Business, verify that your system is working and that it can communicate with other systems on the Internet.

Connectivity requirements

Internet connectivity is required for this course. You will experience optimal performance with a dedicated Internet connection (e.g., a cable/DSL modem or a T1 line). However, you can complete the course using a slower connection (e.g., 56-Kbps modem).

CIW v5 Foundations Self-Study Kit Companion CD-ROM

Each coursebook includes a companion CD-ROM. The files on the CD-ROM are referenced and used throughout the course.

When you insert the CIW v5 Foundations Self-Study Kit Companion CD-ROM, you will see a list of courses. Select the appropriate course, and you will be prompted to unzip an executable file. This executable file will create a directory of all supplemental materials for the course. You can choose to download the directory to the default location, which is C:\CIW\[*Course_Title*]. Optionally, you can select another location. After you choose the location and unzip the file, a directory will be created on your hard disk drive. All supplemental files for the course will be downloaded to this directory. You can then create a shortcut to this directory on your Desktop. As you conduct the course labs, you can use this shortcut to access your lab files quickly.

CIW v5 Foundations Movies

The CIW v5 Foundations courses offer movie files from LearnKey that discuss selected technology topics. To view the movies, log on to the CIW Online Campus at *http://www.certification-partners.com/ciw-online/*. Use the coupon provided with your materials to register for the movies and view them online. If you have any questions, please contact Product Support at (866) 370-3511 or *support@certification-partners.com*.

To view the movies, you need the following programs:

*   Microsoft Internet Explorer 5.5 (or later) browser (*www.microsoft.com*), or Mozilla Firefox 3.0 (or later) browser (*www.mozilla.com*)

*   Windows Media Player 9 (or later) and all necessary codecs

*   Windows Update, to obtain the latest updates for the versions of Internet Explorer and Media Player you have installed on your computer

Note: You will install Windows Media Player and Mozilla Firefox software on your system during labs in the Internet Business Foundations course.

Consider the following points about the CIW v5 Foundations Movies:

- The movies provide supplementary instruction in a multimedia format, and enhance the coursebook narrative and labs. However, movie content does not comprehensively address CIW Foundations exam objectives and is not intended to replace coursebook content.

- CIW Foundations coursebooks include a Movie Time appendix that indicates appropriate points at which to view the supplemental movies.

- The coupon provided allows you access to the CIW Online Campus to view the movies. Do not distribute the coupon to unauthorized users.

Conventions and Graphics

The following conventions are used in this coursebook.

Terms   Technology terms defined in the margins are indicated in **bold type** the first time they appear in the text. However, not every word in bold type is a term requiring definition.

Lab Text   Text that you enter during a lab appears in ***italic bold type***. Names of components that you access or change in a lab appear in **bold type**.

Notations   *Notations or comments regarding screenshots, labs or other text are indicated in italic type.*

Program Code or Commands   Text used in program code or operating system commands appears in the `Lucida Sans Typewriter` font.

The following graphics are used in this coursebook.

 Tech Notes point out exceptions or special circumstances that you may find when working with a particular procedure. Tech Notes that occur within a lab are displayed without the graphic.

 Tech Tips offer special-interest information about the current subject.

 Warnings alert you about cautions to observe or actions to avoid.

 This graphic signals the start of a lab or other hands-on activity.

 The Movie Time graphic signals appropriate points in the course at which to view movie clips. All movie clips are © 2009 LearnKey, Inc.

 Each lesson summary includes an *Application Project*. This project is designed to provoke interest and apply the skills taught in the lesson to your daily activities.

 Each lesson concludes with a summary of the skills and objectives taught in that lesson. You can use the *Skills Review* checklist to evaluate what you have learned.

↘ This graphic indicates a line of code that is completed on the following line.

Lesson 1: Introduction to Networking

Objectives

By the end of this lesson, you will be able to:

- 3.1.1: Define basic data and telephony network concepts, including convergence, Voice over IP (VoIP), AC/DC requirements for telephony and data equipment.

- 3.1.3: Identify basic network topologies (e.g., ring, mesh).

- 3.1.4: Define the Open Systems Interconnection reference model (OSI/RM) in terms of packet creation.

- 3.1.5: Define the nature, purpose and operation essentials of Transmission Control Protocol/Internet Protocol (TCP/IP).

- 3.1.6: Define local area network (LAN) and wide area network (WAN).

- 3.1.7: Identify the core components of the current Internet infrastructure and how they relate to each other, including routers, Internet Exchange Points (IXPs), backbone networks.

- 3.1.8: Identify the components of a Network Operations Center (NOC).

- 3.2.1: Distinguish among common cable types used in networking (e.g., CAT 5, CAT 6, crossover).

- 3.2.2: Identify hardware and software connection devices and their uses, including network interface card, modem, cable/DSL modem, hub, router, switch, firewall.

- 3.2.3: Distinguish between Ethernet and Token Ring networks.

- 3.9.1: Distinguish between ad-hoc and infrastructure mode.

- 3.9.2: Identify the function of a wireless access point (AP).

- 3.9.3: Connect wireless networks to standard wired LANs.

- 3.9.4: Identify benefits and drawbacks of Wired Equivalent Privacy (WEP).

- 3.9.5: Use a Secure Set Identifier (SSID) and describe its purpose.

- 3.9.6: Identify the purpose of MAC address filtering.

✒ 3.9.7: Identify security issues with wireless networks.

✒ 3.9.8: Evaluate the practicality of a wireless LAN in an organization.

✒ 3.9.9: Troubleshoot wireless connectivity.

✒ 3.10.1: List elements of virtualization (e.g., virtual machines, host operating system, virtualization software, RAM, processor speed, and disk space).

✒ 3.10.2: Identify benefits of virtualization, including reduced consumption of electricity, less heat generation, conservation of space, more efficient use of hardware.

Pre-Assessment Questions

1. Which network topology provides multiple communication paths so that an alternative path may be used if a connection fails?

    a. Ring
    b. Bus
    c. Star
    d. Mesh

2. Which category of twisted-pair cable includes four twisted pairs, is typically used for 100BaseT Ethernet, and supports transmission rates of up to 100 Mbps?

    a. Category 2
    b. Category 3
    c. Category 4
    d. Category 5

3. A packet consists of what three elements?

    _____

Overview of Networks and Protocols

infrared
A spectrum of light used for communication between various network-enabled devices.

A network can be defined as two or more connected computers that share data by way of a transport medium. This configuration can include a small business network in one room, two Personal Digital Assistants (PDAs) that communicate by means of **infrared,** or a worldwide network such as the Internet that connects millions of users.

Networks have become extremely popular because they allow users to share data quickly. In the past, users had to place files on a floppy disk or print them, and deliver them to the destination in person or by mail. Networks allow information to be distributed easily and quickly through a system of protocols, cables and other hardware.

network interface card (NIC)
A circuit board within a computer's central processing unit that serves as the interface enabling the computer to connect to a network.

To communicate efficiently, networks require a standard, or protocol. Network protocols are established rules that enable data to flow from one **network interface card (NIC)** to another. Network protocols correspond (roughly, in some cases) to the **Open Systems Interconnection (OSI) reference model**.

Local area networks (LANs) and wide area networks (WANs) are the basis of networking and internetworking. The two systems can work together to allow companies to transmit data internally and externally.

Open Systems Interconnection (OSI) reference model
A layered network architecture model of communication developed by the International Organization for Standardization (ISO). Defines seven layers of network functions.

In this lesson, you will learn about networking basics, network protocols, and LANs and WANs.

Telephony and Convergence Networking

OBJECTIVE
3.1.1: Convergence networks

Before examining specific types of computer networks, we will turn our attention to one of the oldest existing networks — the public switched telephone network (PSTN). The PSTN has connected millions of users for decades, and remains a cornerstone in internetworking today. In the following sections, we will discuss how the PSTN and data networks have been combined to create convergence networks that enable unified communications.

Traditional telephone network

NOTE:
Watch the "Warriors of the Net" video, located at *www.warriorsofthe. net,* at least once during the first two lessons of this course. The video explains how the Internet works. It is available in various resolutions and languages.

Since the inception of the telephone, voice has been carried over circuit-switched connections of the PSTN. Originally, all phone service was analog. Today, however, the network is entirely digital except for the portion that extends from the central office of the local telephone company to the user.

Typically, to exchange data over the public telephone network using a dial-up connection, a modem is necessary. A modem (modulator/demodulator) is a device that translates, or modulates, a digital signal coming from your computer into an analog signal that can be carried over the phone line. A modem attached to the receiving computer demodulates the analog signal back into a digital one.

Today, the PSTN is a hybrid network. About two-thirds of today's telephone users begin a telephone conversation in their homes using analog technology (the other one-third uses mobile phones). The signal is then converted into a digital signal at the central office, and this digital signal is sent across a major portion of the telephone network. As necessary, signals are converted back into analog at the central office, to which the destination telephone is linked.

Internet Service Provider (ISP)
An organization that maintains a gateway to the Internet and rents access to customers on a per-use or subscription basis.

The PSTN is still an integral part of the Internet infrastructure because it furnishes most of the long-distance connections. Most **Internet Service Providers (ISPs)** pay long-distance providers for access to telephone lines.

IP telephony and Voice over IP (VoIP)

Internet Protocol (IP) telephony is a technology that uses packet-switched connections to exchange voice, fax and other forms of data that were previously carried on circuit-switched connections. (You will learn about packets later in this lesson.) Using the Internet, the packets of data are sent over shared lines. IP telephony enables users to avoid the tolls charged on telephone company lines because most ISPs absorb this cost.

Voice over IP (VoIP)
A technology that converts voice into data packets for transmission over a packet-switched IP network. Allows the use of the Internet for real-time voice and video traffic.

Voice over IP (VoIP) involves the use of a data network to deliver voice information, instead of the traditional circuit-switched lines of the PSTN. Most local and long-distance providers, cable TV companies and ISPs now offer IP telephony services. Many companies also use VoIP solutions rather than traditional voice services in order to provide more services. The term *convergence technology* is often used to describe the combination of voice, video and data all on one data network.

Unified communications (UC)

unified communications (UC)
A business trend that seeks to simplify and integrate all forms of communication. Also, a set of technologies that enable voice to be converted into text, and vice versa.

Convergence has given rise to **unified communications (UC)**, in which voice can be converted into text and vice versa. Your e-mail inbox is capable of receiving faxes, even if they are sent via a traditional fax machine. Your e-mail inbox can also receive voicemail recordings. Unified communications technology seeks to eliminate communication latency (the amount of time between the moments when any form of communication is sent and received) as much as possible to make communication more efficient.

Presencing and mobile communication

presencing
The ability for a device to automatically track and report the user's location and availability.

Presencing is the ability for devices to automatically track and report your location and availability. For example, when a user signs in to an instant messaging (IM) service, his status (e.g., online) is advertised (or published) to the people on his contacts list. A user's presence information, or presence state, is provided to a presence service via a network connection. Presencing requires collaboration among a number of devices (for example, mobile phone, electronic calendar, IM client, GPS) and the presence services with which each of them is connected. Google Latitude (*www.google.com/latitude/*) is an example of presencing.

Mobile communication (or mobile computing) refers to a person's ability to use technology while "on the go." Devices that enable a user to engage in mobile communication include:

- Laptop computers.

- Mobile phones and smartphones (e.g., BlackBerrys, iPhones, etc.).

- Personal digital assistants (PDAs), such as PalmPilots, etc.

These devices are useful because they are portable, can connect to each other via the Internet, allow data storage, and contain enough processing power to perform tasks that you can also perform using your computer. You will study mobile computing and devices further in a later lesson.

Networking Evolution

Originally, networks were operated on a centralized, or mainframe, model, which usually limited networks to large, well-funded institutions such as universities and Fortune 500 companies. By the late 1980s, however, many business networks adopted the client/server model, which uses a more modular approach and allowed small to medium-sized businesses to create powerful networking solutions. The advent of the Internet led to another shift to Web-based, increasingly decentralized and more affordable networking.

Mainframe

Mainframe (or centralized) computing provided the first practical network solution. This centralized approach used central servers, or mainframes, and remote terminals. Usually, these terminals were diskless, or "dumb," stations that could only request information. Most information processing occurred on the "back end" (the server), not on the "front end" (the client).

Retrieving information from mainframes

Obtaining information from a mainframe traditionally involves a great deal of processing by the mainframe. A terminal sends an information request to the mainframe, which in turn processes the query and obtains the desired information from a database or other source. After this processing is finished, the mainframe structures the information and returns it to the terminal. You will see how the client/server model differs somewhat from this model. Figure 1-1 shows a mainframe model.

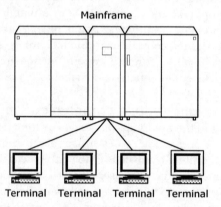

Figure 1-1: Mainframe model

Mainframe liabilities

The mainframe-computing model has two main liabilities. The first is that the mainframe must handle all the processing work. The second is that the request and response packets sent between the terminal and the mainframe occupy a relatively large amount of the network's bandwidth. In large, heavily used networks, these two liabilities create unacceptable network congestion.

front end
A client that acts as an interface to a collection of servers (for example, mainframes or PC-based servers). A Web browser is a typical front-end client.

back end
A series of systems that fulfill requests made by a client. Back-end systems can include mainframes and servers containing information databases.

The future of mainframes

Owing to the overwhelming investment in mainframes over the decades by universities, businesses and other institutions, the mainframe model is still quite prevalent and will not disappear soon. However, with the advent of the Web and more sophisticated computing technologies, Web-based interfaces and other bridging technologies will replace, or at least greatly modify, the traditional "dumb terminal" and mainframe environment. Furthermore, fewer institutions are investing in the traditional mainframe model, opting instead for client/server and Web-based solutions. Often, mainframes remain in use, but users will not interact with them directly. In many cases, you will be using client/server technologies on the **front end** to gain access to information, but will in fact be accessing mainframes that perform some of the work on the **back end**.

Mainframes and cloud computing/Software as a Service (SaaS)

cloud computing
A computing paradigm in which users are able to access software and services over the Internet instead of from their desktops.

The term **cloud computing** (also known as Software as a Service [SaaS]) refers to the use of Web browsers to access sophisticated applications that reside on a remote series of servers. In many ways, cloud computing is a modern implementation of mainframes. The primary differences, though, are that today's server systems and clients are far more robust, there is more bandwidth available, and the Web browser is capable of doing far more work than a standard dumb terminal. Nevertheless, it is somewhat accurate to see today's cloud computing and SaaS model as a modern revamp of the mainframe model.

Cloud computing and Software as a Service (SaaS) are discussed in detail in the CIW Internet Business Foundations course.

Client/Server Model

client
An individual computer connected to a network. Also, a system or application (such as a Web browser or user agent) that requests a service from another computer (the server) and is used to access files or documents.

The client/server model, also called distributed computing, attempts to reduce network slowdown by dividing processing tasks between the **client** (the front end) and the **server** (the back end). The back-end computer is generally more powerful than the front end, and is responsible for storing and presenting information. A client/server example is illustrated in Figure 1-2.

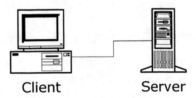

Client   Server

Figure 1-2: Client/server model

server
A computer in a network that manages the network resources and provides, or serves, information to clients.

Client/server model databases and SQL

The client/server model contains two types of databases:

bottleneck
A point in network communication at which information is processed more slowly. Also, any element (a hard drive, I/O card or network interface card) that slows network connectivity rates.

- **Single database servers** — information storage on one central computer system.

- **Distributed databases** — information storage across several computers, while still allowing searches and transactions to occur as if the information were stored centrally.

The primary advantage of the distributed database approach is that it divides the task among several powerful computers and network connections. Such distribution tends to decrease the number of network **bottlenecks**.

NOTE:
This example refers to a specific server-based application example.

Databases store information in an organized, tabular format. To enable transactions between these databases and users, the client/server model must translate human-readable language into machine-readable code. Thus far, the most efficient way to accomplish this task is by using the Structured Query Language, or SQL (pronounced "sequel").

SQL allows users to phrase queries on the front end that can be understood by the back end. Requesting data from a server in SQL involves the following process:

data
Information being stored, usually in a database.

1. The user requests **data**.

2. The client computer translates the request into SQL.

3. The client sends the request to the server.

NOTE:
TPC/IP and ODBC provide a framework for interoperability, but do not guarantee that the systems will be able to work together. Appropriate applications and, possibly, custom client software are also required.

4. The server processes the request, which might involve communicating with a remote database or server.

5. The server delivers the response to the client.

6. The client delivers the response to the computer screen.

The key difference between this retrieval model and the one used by mainframes is that the client processes much of this request.

Client/server advantages

In addition to shared task processing, client/server benefits include a modular approach to computing. Because the client/server model allows you to add new system components, you are not limited to one solution. At one time, network administrators had to choose between one system and another. However, with the advent of open standards such as Transmission Control Protocol/Internet Protocol (TCP/IP) and Open Database Connectivity (ODBC), heterogeneous systems can work together more efficiently. For example, UNIX and Windows servers that use TCP/IP can work together, allowing businesses to scale solutions according to customer demand. The client/server model is scalable because it gives you the ability to adjust to new demands. The client/server model also allows users more control over their own files.

NOTE:
Multi-tier computing models are typically referred to in the context of an enterprise application model rather than a networking model. Microsoft's COM+ and .NET framework are examples.

Two-tier, three-tier and n-tier computing

Traditional client/server relationships are similar to two-tier computing in that both computers are responsible for part of the processing task. In two-tier computing, one computer is responsible only for formatting the information on the screen. The other computer is responsible for both the process logic and the data storage. Client/server relationships distribute the task more evenly between the two computers. Client/server and two-tier computing are often considered **legacy models**.

legacy model
A model that, because of its age, may not support modern technologies without manipulation or upgrades.

business logic
The coding (usually in SQL) necessary to create relationships in the data stored in a database.

Developers and networking professionals have cooperated further to create more efficient models, which separate **business logic**, **presentation responsibilities** and data into at least three separate levels, called tiers:

- **Three-tier** — In a common three-tier model, a Web server contains the business logic, a Web browser is responsible for presentation, and a database server contains the data.

- **N-tier** — An n-tier model uses multiple systems to divide responsibilities further. It is a more sophisticated version of three-tier computing in which many different individual systems help process information.

presentation responsibilities
The forms in which the data and business logic are presented on your screen. Presentation responsibilities include XHTML and HTML forms, and application-specific interfaces such as Web browsers.

Whenever you perform a transaction on a site such as eBay or Amazon.com, you are using either the three-tier or the n-tier model. Cloud computing is an example of n-tier computing.

Advantages of three-tier and n-tier computing

Separating these responsibilities into at least three different tiers provides the following benefits:

- **Flexibility** — It is possible to upgrade or change components in one tier without necessarily having to change components in the other two (or more).

- **Increased speed** — Because responsibilities are divided among at least three tiers, each tier can concentrate on only certain data to speed information processing. This division of responsibilities can reduce network latency.

Sometimes, three-tier/n-tier networking is referred to as Web-based networking because clients often use a Web browser to access network services.

Network Operations Center (NOC)

A Network Operations Center (NOC) is a specific location, usually a dedicated room, from which a network is managed, monitored and maintained. The term originally was used in relation to telecommunications networks, but is now used widely in relation to data networks. As data and telephony networks continue to converge, distinctions among equipment types will probably disappear as they relate to NOCs.

The NOC is the central point for network maintenance and troubleshooting. It contains workstations that are configured to display all activities and functions of the networks being monitored. For example, workstations are configured with packet sniffers and monitoring software that allow NOC administrators to quickly identify anomalous traffic (for example, worms, viruses, traffic spikes and downed networks). These workstations also contain management software, including firewall and router configuration software, and ways to control workstations remotely.

Application Service Provider (ASP)
A company that provides applications and services (over the Internet) to individual or enterprise subscribers that would otherwise need to provide those applications and services on their own servers.

NOCs also generally include multiple, redundant network connections and redundant power supplies to help ensure communication and power. Most NOCs for larger companies also have dedicated telephones from a separate provider, as well as mobile phones, to ensure that they can communicate with the company and all ISPs and **Application Service Providers (ASPs)** in an emergency or in case the company's standard telephone provider experiences problems.

Networking Categories

All networks consist of the same three basic elements, as follows:

- **Protocols** — communication rules on which all network elements must agree. You will learn about networking protocols later in this lesson.

- **Transmission media** — media that enable all networking elements to interconnect. You will learn about transmission media later in this lesson.

- **Network services** — resources (such as printers) that are shared with all network users. You will learn about network services later in this course.

Aside from these similarities, two basic types of networks exist:

- Peer-to-peer networks
- Server-based networks

Peer-to-peer network types

Peer-to-peer networks are subdivided into the following two types:

- **Microsoft peer-to-peer** — a legacy model in which Microsoft-based systems communicate with one another without using a centralized system to control authentication and access.

- **P2P (peer-to-peer)** — a modern model that supports many thousands of simultaneous users who can download and upload files on a worldwide network.

Microsoft peer-to-peer network

Microsoft peer-to-peer networks tend to be less expensive and easier to work with than server-based networks. However, they are less secure, support fewer users (no more than 10) and experience more problems with file system management. Figure 1-3 illustrates a Microsoft peer-to-peer network.

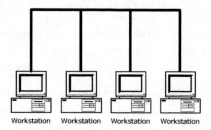

Workstation   Workstation   Workstation   Workstation

Figure 1-3: Peer-to-peer network model

Various Microsoft operating systems support peer-to-peer networking, including Windows XP and Windows Vista.

P2P network

A modern P2P network is created when a workstation uses add-on software to participate in large, decentralized networks that are usually located on the Internet. First popularized by the now-defunct free version of the Napster network, P2P networks include:

- LimeWire (*http://limewire.com/*).

- Gnucleus (*www.gnucleus.com/Gnucleus/*).

- Freenet (*http://freenetproject.org/*).

- JXTA (*https://jxta.dev.java.net/*).

- KaZaA (*www.kazaa.com*).

 WARNING! *Do not download files (for example, MP3s or unauthorized software) from these networks. Doing so may be illegal and can result in punitive action against you. Discussion of P2P networks should never be misconstrued as support for them or as an encouragement to use them.*

These networks are often used to illicitly share copyrighted information (for example, audio files and software). However, these networks can be used for legitimate purposes. Following are the two types of P2P networks:

- **Centralized** — This type of network requires logging on to a central server, which maintains a database of all attached peer clients. Because logging on to a central server is required, this type of network is not a true peer-to-peer network. Napster is an example of this type of network. The fact that a group of central servers was used to maintain the database of remote clients allowed the service to be shut down easily.

- **Decentralized** — This type of network consists of groups of clients/servers that communicate with one another to create a network that has no single central database. The KaZaA network is an example.

Server-based network

node
Any entity on a network that can be managed, such as a system, repeater, router, gateway, switch or firewall. A computer or other addressable device attached to a network; a host.

host
A computer that other computers can use to gain information; in network architecture, a host is a client or workstation.

A server-based network is a configuration of **nodes**, some of which are dedicated to providing resources to other **hosts** on the network. Dedicated nodes that make their resources available are called servers. These resources can include printers, applications and documents.

Server-based networks offer user security because a central database can track the resources that users can access. However, dedicated servers can be expensive. They may also require a full-time network administrator.

Figure 1-4 illustrates a server-based network.

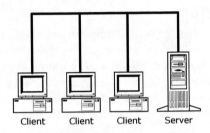

Figure 1-4: Server-based network model

Examples of server nodes include:

- Print servers.

- File servers.

- Mail servers.

- Web servers.

- Database servers.

Client nodes can access these resources over the network. Examples of common network operating systems include:

- UNIX/Linux.

- Microsoft LAN Manager.

- Microsoft Windows 2003 Server/2008 Server.

Authentication

authentication
The process of verifying the identity of a user who logs on to a system, or the integrity of transmitted data.

Network resources require users to authenticate before accessing resources. Server-based networks enable **authentication** in the following two ways:

- **Centralized** — In this mode, users access a single server or set of servers and present authentication information (for example, a user name and a password, or biometric information).

- **Decentralized** — In this mode, users access each individual server and present authentication information.

Centralized authentication has become increasingly popular because it simplifies the administration of users and user credentials.

Network Topologies

OBJECTIVE
3.1.3: Network
topologies

Topologies are basic configurations that information systems personnel use to wire networks. They are the basic design of any network. Topologies used to connect computer networks include bus, star, ring and hybrid.

Bus topology

Bus topology networks require that all computers, or nodes, connect to the same cable. When a computer sends data, that data is broadcast to all nodes on the network. Generally, traditional bus topologies are not used in modern networks.

Star topology

NOTE:
Star is the most
common topology
in new network
installations. 10BaseT
and 100BaseT are
common examples.

Star topology networks connect network nodes through a central device, usually a hub or a switch (you will learn about hubs and switches later in this course). Because each computer's network connection terminates in the hub, this arrangement greatly reduces the risk of an entire network failure. For instance, if a cable breaks or a node fails, only that cable segment or node will be affected. The rest of the network will continue to function. Figure 1-5 illustrates a star topology.

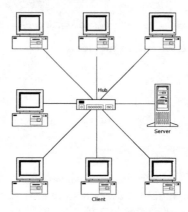

Figure 1-5: Star topology

NOTE:
From an electronic
and traffic
management
standpoint, many
star topology
implementations
are operationally
the same as bus
topology
implementations.

Network administrators can troubleshoot networks far more easily in a star topology because the failure is usually isolated. Following are the advantages and disadvantages of star topologies:

- **Advantages** — The network is usually not affected if one computer fails. Network expansion and reconfiguration are relatively simple. Network management and monitoring can be centralized.

- **Disadvantages** — If the hub (or centralized connection point) malfunctions, the entire network can fail.

Ring topology

Multistation Access
Unit (MAU)
The network device
that is the central
connection point for
Token Ring
networks.

NOTE:
The most common
example of ring
topology is Token
Ring.

Ring topologies do not have a central connection point. Instead, a cable connects one node to another, until a logical "ring" is formed. When a node sends a message, the message is processed by each computer in the ring. If a computer is not the destination node, it will pass the message to the next node, until the message arrives at its destination. If the message is not accepted by any node on the network, it will travel around the entire ring and return to the sender. Token Ring networks are connected using a **Multistation Access Unit (MAU)**. Generally, ring topologies are now used mostly in large metropolitan networks. Token Ring networks are considered obsolete.

Hybrid network

Larger networks combine the bus, star and ring topologies. This combination allows expansion even in enterprise networks. Two common examples are star ring and star bus. In a star ring network, two or more star topologies are connected using a Multistation Access Unit as a centralized hub.

In a star bus network, two or more star topologies are connected using a bus trunk. The bus trunk serves as the network's **backbone**. Figure 1-6 illustrates a star bus network.

backbone
The highest level in the computer network hierarchy, to which smaller networks typically connect.

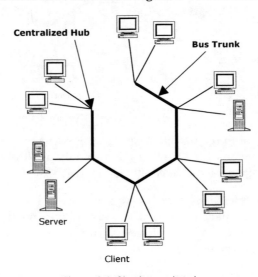

Figure 1-6: Star bus network

media
Any material that allows data to flow through it or be stored on it; includes hard and floppy disks, wire, cable, and fiber optics.

Note that each star network contains two nodes that are connected to a centralized hub, and that the hubs are connected by linear bus trunks. This topology is excellent for larger companies because the backbone can implement **media** that support high data transmissions. Following are further advantages and disadvantages of star bus topologies:

- **Advantages** — Network expansion is relatively simple. The network is usually not affected if one computer fails.

- **Disadvantages** — If the hub malfunctions, computers on that hub will be unable to communicate. Connections between the malfunctioning hub and other hubs will fail.

Mesh topology

Mesh topologies connect devices with multiple paths so that redundancies exist. Messages sent on a mesh network can take any of several possible paths from a source to a destination. Mesh networks differ from other topologies in that the component nodes can all connect to each other via multiple hops (that is, by going through intermediate nodes along the way).

There are two types of mesh topology: full mesh and partial mesh. In a partial mesh topology, some nodes are organized in a full mesh, but other nodes are connected to only one or two other nodes in the network. Partial mesh is less expensive to implement and is usually found in peripheral networks connected to a full mesh backbone. Figure 1-7 illustrates a partial mesh topology.

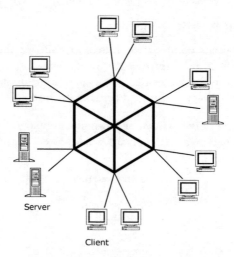

Figure 1-7: Partial mesh topology

Notice that in the partial mesh network shown in the preceding figure, each node can communicate with any other node even though the source and destination nodes are not directly connected to each other.

Because full mesh networks are expensive to implement, partial mesh networks have become popular. A partial mesh network has much of the redundancy of a full mesh network, but costs less. However, with that cost savings you lose the benefit of a truly reliable network.

In a full mesh topology, all devices are cross-connected so the best path can be chosen at any given moment. A full mesh is very expensive but is the most reliable because it provides the greatest amount of redundancy. If one node fails, network traffic can be redirected to any of the other nodes. Full mesh is generally reserved for backbone networks supported by public carriers such as the phone company.

The advantages and disadvantages of mesh topologies are as follows:

- **Advantages** — Mesh topologies are the most fault-resistant network type. If one connection is terminated, another can be chosen to deliver the data to the destination.

- **Disadvantages** — Additional hardware can make private mesh topologies expensive.

 Many P2P networks use a mesh topology. This approach is not necessarily expensive because it relies on the Internet, which has already been created. However, private mesh topologies are more expensive to build.

Network Operating System

network operating system (NOS)
An operating system that manages network resources.

A **network operating system (NOS)** manages resources on a network, and offers services to one or more clients. A NOS can manage multiple users on a network; provide access to file and print servers; provide services such as Web access, File Transfer Protocol (FTP) and e-mail; and implement network security. Network operating systems such as Microsoft Windows Server 2003/Server 2008 and UNIX/Linux are very popular.

A NOS enables clients to access remote drives (those not on the user's computer) as if the drives were on the client's own computer. A NOS also allows servers to process requests from a client and decide whether that client can use a particular resource.

NOTE:
Systems in a peer-to-peer network are commonly referred to as peer servers or member servers, depending on the operating system that they are running.

Similar to a client/server relationship, part of the NOS must run from the client and part of it must run from the server. In a peer-to-peer network, each client can serve as both the client and the server.

This section will discuss two of the most popular network operating systems:

- Microsoft Windows

- UNIX/Linux

Interoperability

interoperability
The ability of one computer system to communicate with another; often refers to different operating systems working together.

All major network operating systems (Microsoft Windows, UNIX/Linux) can operate with one another. This feature, called **interoperability**, makes it easier for corporations with various clients and servers to create a network, even though the clients and servers all use different operating systems. Figure 1-8 illustrates how network operating systems can interoperate with their clients and servers.

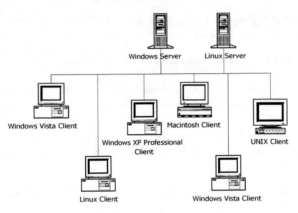

Figure 1-8: NOS interoperability

In most cases, software must be installed on the server and client for interoperability. The following sections explain the fundamentals of the two major network operating systems.

Microsoft Windows Servers

NOTE:
Optional Lab 1-2: Reviewing network operating systems provides a brief additional introduction to Windows networking.

Microsoft Windows New Technology (NT) is a family of network operating systems that began in 1993. It quickly became known for its support of high-performance servers, advanced workstations, and client/server computing.

The Windows 2000 Server family, released in 2000, introduced new management technologies, the Microsoft Active Directory service, and a high-performance Web server featuring Active Server Pages (ASP). The server versions are as follows:

- Windows 2000 (introduced in 2000)

- Windows Server 2003 (introduced in 2003)

- Windows Server 2008 (introduced in 2008)

The Windows 2000 Server family uses TCP/IP as the default network protocol and includes the software necessary for Microsoft's .NET program. This technology provides a ready-made networking platform that allows companies to transfer information by means of various types of servers (for example, Web, database and e-mail).

For in-depth experience with network operating systems, such as modern Windows servers and Linux, you should enroll in the Master CIW Administrator track.

UNIX/Linux

kernel
The essential part of an operating system; provides basic services; always resides in memory.

UNIX was developed by AT&T's Bell Telephone Laboratory (now part of Lucent). In 1969, Ken Thompson, Dennis Ritchie and others worked on a team for AT&T in developing a mainframe computer system called MULTICS. This team created an alternative operating system that could work well on relatively small computers. This alternative was named UNIX, as a pun on MULTICS. Since the 1970s, many versions of UNIX have evolved from the original **kernel**. However, there is no single version of UNIX. Instead, several different versions, known as "flavors," of UNIX have been developed over the years. Each flavor is based on the following basic platform strategies:

- **System V** — a version of UNIX developed by AT&T.

- **Berkeley Systems Distribution (BSD)** — the version of UNIX developed by students at the University of California, Berkeley.

Some of the more popular flavors of UNIX today are as follows:

NOTE:
Visit any Linux vendor. In addition, visit a popular open-source software site: *www.freshmeat.net* or *www.sourceforge .net.*

These sites offer Windows, Linux-based and UNIX-based software.

GNU's name is an acronym for "GNU's Not UNIX." However, GNU has been developing UNIX-like software for some time, and has effectively become associated with the UNIX name.

- **Linux** (which contains elements of both System V and BSD) — This flavor was developed by Linus Torvalds, the GNU organization (*www.gnu.org*) and the open-source community. Various flavors of Linux exist, including Slackware (*www.slackware.com*), Red Hat (*www.redhat.com*), Mandriva (formerly Mandrake; *www.mandriva.com/en*), SuSE (*www.novell.com/linux/*) and Ubuntu (*www.ubuntu.com*).

- **Sun Solaris** (based on System V) — Traditionally the premier version of UNIX, Sun Solaris (*www.sun.com*) runs primarily on non-Intel systems.

- **BSD** — This flavor includes FreeBSD (*www.freebsd.org*), which was the first BSD-based operating system that was free and available on various platforms. Apple's OSX, available on all newer Macintosh systems, is based on FreeBSD, NetBSD and OpenBSD. NetBSD (*www.netbsd.org*) was a redesign of FreeBSD that provided additional stability and ease of use as a server. OpenBSD (*www.openbsd.net*) was a thorough redesign of FreeBSD with a better-than-average security record.

UNIX systems have been tried and tested for years, and are widely considered the workhorses of the Internet. The majority of Web, e-mail, FTP and database servers still run one form of UNIX or another. When properly configured, UNIX systems have a reputation for stability and efficient use of resources. However, they often require a knowledgeable administrator and more administration time; an improperly configured UNIX server can be difficult to administer and can cause security problems.

shell
A command-based interface that allows a user to issue commands.

As with any operating system, UNIX systems consist of at least one kernel, a file system and a **shell**. UNIX systems are often associated with a shell because you must usually enter commands from a command line rather than from a graphical user interface (GUI).

x.org
A windowing system used with UNIX and all popular operating systems.

Because there are hundreds of UNIX commands, GUIs were developed to simplify UNIX operations. The most popular UNIX GUI is the **x.org** system, which consists of the following:

- **Server** — provides access to the computer; provides the actual interface.

- **Font server** — provides fonts for use in GUI windows and menus.

- **Client** — attaches to the server.

- **Window manager** — provides borders and menus.

The X Window server, font server and client often reside on the same computer, although they need not necessarily do so.

UNIX uses TCP/IP as its native core networking protocol. Additional protocols can be installed if necessary.

Linux

NOTE:
Linux can be thought of as an open-source, work-alike "clone" of UNIX.

As you have already learned, Linux was developed by Linus Torvalds, the GNU organization and the open-source community. The Linux kernel is copyrighted to Linus B. Torvalds under the terms of the General Public License (GPL), which states that the source code must be freely distributed and that anyone is allowed to make copies for their own use, or to sell or give to other people (with a few restrictions). If any changes are made to the kernel, then these changes must be made freely available.

Linux can operate as a client or as a server and supports all of the most common Internet protocols, including TCP/IP, SMTP, POP, NNTP, Telnet, HTTP, FTP, IRC, DNS and more.

Linux is an excellent choice for LANs, regardless of the combination of clients — including Macintosh, DOS, Windows, OS/2 — which can all use their own native communication protocols. Linux also includes a free X Window Graphical User Interface (GUI), allowing most X-based programs to run under Linux without any modification. Windows programs can run inside X Window with the help of an emulator called Wine.

Various flavors of Linux exist, and they are distributed by several commercial and non-commercial organizations that enhance the basic functions of the operating system. SuSE Linux, for example, is a distribution of Linux that has features of the core Linux kernel plus enhancements, which are specific to that distribution.

The Need for Protocols

NOTE:
Think of the network protocol as the "language" that a computer speaks to communicate with other computers. Two computers must have at least one protocol in common to be able to communicate, but a common protocol alone does not guarantee communication.

Earlier, you learned that network protocols are established rules that enable data to flow from one NIC to another. Unless you understand the specific rules applied to network communications, you will not be able to administer a network efficiently. You need protocols so that systems developed by various vendors can communicate with one another.

Various protocols are mapped to specific layers of the OSI reference model (often called the OSI/RM). Without the OSI/RM standard, and without standardized protocols, network communication would be haphazard at best.

OSI Reference Model

OBJECTIVE
3.1.4: OSI reference model

The OSI/RM was defined by the International Organization for Standardization (ISO) in 1983 (see *www.iso.org*). The OSI/RM has three practical functions, as follows:

- It gives developers necessary, universal concepts so they can develop and perfect protocols that can work with operating systems and network products developed by other vendors.

- It explains the framework used to connect heterogeneous systems. In other words, it allows clients and servers to communicate even if they are using different applications and operating systems; all they need is a common protocol, such as TCP/IP.

- It describes the process of packet creation. You will learn more about packet creation shortly.

The OSI/RM allows systems from various vendors to communicate with one another; significant deviance from the OSI/RM will result in communication failures.

Networks are built using the OSI/RM, just as a building is constructed from a blueprint. For instance, Microsoft Windows and UNIX refer to the OSI/RM when creating their networking software. The OSI/RM provides a common framework that allows these network operating systems to interoperate.

The OSI/RM is an example of a protocol-layering model because protocols are mapped to various layers in the model. For example, whenever protocols such as IP are discussed, they are usually linked to the network layer (Layer 3) of the OSI/RM. Several other networking models exist. While few manufacturers follow the OSI/RM guidelines exactly, most models closely parallel the OSI standard.

The OSI/RM consists of seven layers, described in Table 1-1. We will review each layer carefully because they help explain how information is sent over a network.

Table 1-1: OSI/RM layers

Layer Name	Layer Number	Description
Application	7	The interface to the user in a networking environment. Networking applications such as file transfer and e-mail function here. The first layer is used when a packet is being created in a system.
Presentation	6	Provides useful transformations on data to support a standardized application interface and general communications services. For example, it converts text from American Standard Code for Information Interchange (ASCII) format into Extended Binary Coded Decimal Interchange Code (EBCDIC). Encryption occurs at this layer, and codecs operate here as well.
Session	5	Responsible for describing how protocols build up and tear down connections (or sessions). Also adds traffic flow and synchronization information.
Transport	4	Provides reliable, transparent transport between end points (the source and destination hosts). Also supports end-to-end error recovery and flow control. This layer is responsible for the accuracy of data transmission.
Network	3	Responsible for logical addressing. Organizes data into packets. Provides reliable addressing services among hosts and networks. Ensures that packets are forwarded and routed to their destinations.

Table 1-1: OSI/RM layers (cont'd)

Layer Name	Layer Number	Description
Data link	2	Defines how data is formatted for transmission and how access to the network is controlled. Frames are created and transmitted with the necessary synchronization, error control and flow control. In short, the data link layer prepares the information so it can be placed on the transmission medium, such as a copper wire. In the IEEE 802 series of LAN standards, the data link layer is divided into two sublayers: - Logical Link Control (LLC) sublayer - Media Access Control (MAC) sublayer
	LLC sublayer	The Logical Link Control (LLC) sublayer is responsible for separating network layer protocols from the underlying network technology. It provides Service Access Points (SAPs) between the MAC sublayer and the network layer protocols. A SAP identifies which network layer protocol (such as IP) generated and is to receive the frame. The LLC is also responsible for error and flow control.
	MAC sublayer	The Media Access Control (MAC) sublayer defines the network adapter interface options and the access method used on the network. The MAC sublayer is responsible for placing data on the transmission medium.
Physical	1	Associated with transmission of unstructured bit streams (electrical impulses, light or radio signals) over a physical link (such as copper wire or fiber-optic cable). Responsible for the mechanical, electrical and procedural characteristics that establish, maintain and deactivate the physical link. This layer controls how data is transmitted and received across the media.

The OSI/RM provides the concepts and nomenclature you need to be able to discuss packet creation and networking protocols.

OSI/RM layers and communication

NOTE:
Layers cannot be skipped. Communication flows from layer to layer. For the application layers on two systems to communicate, the data must pass through all layers on both systems.

Like any other networking model, the OSI/RM describes how systems communicate with one another. For Host A to "talk" to Host B, Host A must encapsulate its data and send it over the network to Host B. Host B must then de-encapsulate the data. That is, an application on Host A may pass a request down through the layers of the OSI/RM to the physical media, and an application on Host B will pull that request up from the physical media through the layers of the OSI/RM in order to process the request.

For example, if a client sends a request to a server, the request might begin with a mouse click by a user on a Web page hyperlink. The mouse click occurs at the client's application layer. The request travels down the OSI/RM layers until it reaches the data link layer, where it is placed onto a copper wire, or whatever transmission medium is used (the physical layer).

The client's request travels across the wire until it reaches the server. The server's data link layer pulls the request off the wire (physical layer) and sends it up the server's OSI/RM, as illustrated in Figure 1-9. When the request arrives at the server's application layer, the request is processed. The server then returns a response to the client, using the same method.

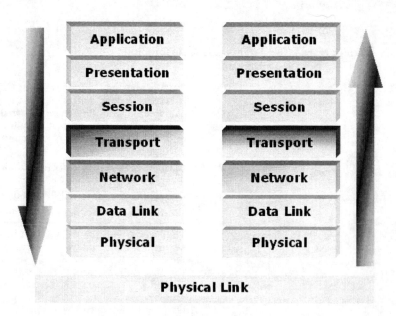

Figure 1-9: OSI model layers

In the preceding figure, the left column contains the seven OSI/RM layers that exist on the client. The right column contains the same seven layers that exist on the server. The upper four layers are used whenever a message passes to or from a host. The lower three layers are used whenever a message passes through a host. If the message is addressed to the particular host, the message is passed to the upper layers. If the message is addressed to another host, it is not passed to the upper layers, but is forwarded to another host.

If the client sends a request to the server, the request might begin with a mouse click by the user on a Web page hyperlink. The mouse click occurs at the client's application layer. The request travels down the OSI/RM until it reaches the data link layer, where it is placed onto a copper wire, or whatever transmission medium is used (the physical layer).

The client's request travels across the wire until it reaches the server. The server's data link layer pulls the request off the wire (physical layer) and sends it up the server's OSI/RM. When the request arrives at the server's application layer, the request is processed. The server then returns a response to the client, using the same method.

Data Encapsulation

The process of passing information through the layers of the OSI/RM is called encapsulation or packetization. A Protocol Data Unit (PDU) is a packet of information that is created by a computer and passed from one layer of the OSI/RM to another. A PDU contains information specific to each layer. Each layer adds a header to the data being passed through it to prepare it for transfer. At the end of the encapsulation process, a frame is formed.

Packet creation: Adding headers

The packet creation process begins with Layer 7 (the application layer) of the OSI/RM, and continues through Layer 1 (the physical layer). For example, when you send an e-mail message or transfer a file from one computer to another, this message or file undergoes a transformation from a discrete (i.e., complete) file into smaller pieces of information (packets). Beginning with the application layer of the OSI/RM, the file continues to be divided until the initial discrete message becomes smaller, more manageable pieces of information sent at the physical layer.

As shown in Figure 1-10, each layer adds its own information (the header) to the packet. This information enables each layer to communicate with the others, and also allows the receiving computer to process the message. Keep in mind that each layer considers whatever has been passed down to it from an upper layer to be "data." It treats the entire higher-layer message as a data payload. It does not concern itself with what was added by the upper layers.

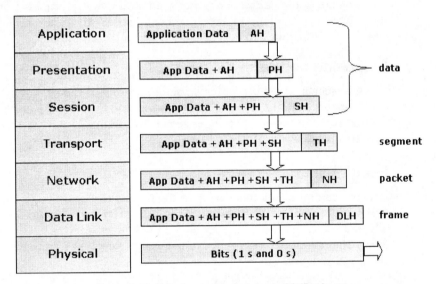

Figure 1-10: Headers added at each OSI/RM layer

Data, segments, packets and frames

The terms data, segment, packet and frame are the protocol data unit names assigned to information at specific points in the encapsulation process. That is, they refer to information at the application (and presentation and session), transport, network and data link layers, respectively. An item of information is considered data as it is generated and passed down through the upper three layers of the OSI, which are often collectively known as the application layer.

Data: The application, presentation and session layers

Data is passed down to the transport layer, where it is encapsulated to include source and destination port numbers that identify the applications (such as FTP or e-mail) between which the data should be passed. At this point, the data is considered a segment.

Segment: The transport layer

A segment is passed down to the network layer, where it is encapsulated and given source and destination IP addresses. At this point, the segment becomes a packet.

Packet: The network layer

A packet is passed down to the data link layer, where it is encapsulated and given source and destination MAC addresses, and an error-checking mechanism called a cyclical redundancy check (CRC). At this point, the packet becomes a frame.

Frame: The data link layer

Frames are passed down to the physical layer, where they are sent across the medium as a bitstream.

NOTE:
If you think of a packet as a box that contains articles, the CRC can be considered a packing slip or bill of lading.

Cyclical redundancy check (CRC)

A cyclical redundancy check (CRC) is a mathematical calculation that allows the receiving computer to verify whether a packet is valid. When a sending host transmits a packet, it calculates a CRC by summing all the ones in the payload and storing this sum as a hexadecimal number, which is then stored in the trailer. When the receiving host reads the packet, it runs its own CRC, then compares it with the CRC stored in the trailer. If the two match, the packet is not damaged, and the receiving host processes the packet. If the CRCs do not match, the receiving host discards the entire packet. The CRC occurs at OSI Layer 2 (the data link layer).

Removing headers

When a receiving host processes a packet, it reverses the packet-creation process and de-encapsulates or removes each header, beginning with Layer 1 and ending with Layer 7. All that is left at the end of this process is the original, unaltered data, which the host can then process.

Peer layers

Network communication is based on the principle of peer layers. In a single system, each OSI layer has one or two adjacent layers (the layer above it and the layer below it) with which it interacts. For example, the data link layer receives packets from the network layer. The data link layer encapsulates the packets into frames and then passes them to the physical layer.

On the receiving end of a communication is another system. Within that receiving system, any given layer communicates only with that same layer on the sending system. That is, when the network layer on the sending system adds information (such as a destination IP address), that information will be of use only to the network layer (its peer) on the receiving system.

Packets

NOTE:
Internal packet structure, format and contents vary among different protocols. Packets created by one protocol cannot be directly interpreted by another protocol. Therefore, two systems cannot communicate unless they have at least one protocol in common.

Although a unit of information technically becomes a packet when it passes through Layer 3 of the OSI/RM, the term packet is loosely used to describe any fixed piece of information sent across a network. Whenever you send information across any network, you begin the packet creation process. A packet consists of the following three elements:

- A header (OSI/RM layer information)

- The actual data (for example, the client request or server response)

- A trailer (often contains techniques ensuring that errors do not occur during transmission)

Many networking professionals use the terms "packet," "datagram" and "frame" interchangeably. Although this usage is accurate most of the time, "packet" is a generic term for any piece of information passed through a network. A datagram is a packet at the network layer of the OSI/RM. A frame is a packet at the data link layer (used to traverse an Ethernet network). Even though the concepts are slightly different, these terms are used synonymously.

As shown in Figure 1-11, the header contains several different pieces of information, such as addressing information and an alert signal to the incoming computer.

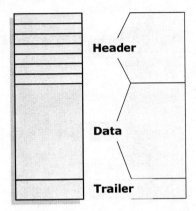

Figure 1-11: Packet structure

The packet also contains the original data (also called a payload) sent by the application, such as a page request sent by a Web browser. The trailer contains information signifying that the end of the packet has been reached, and also usually contains information that validates the packet. For example, it could contain cyclical redundancy check (CRC) information.

OSI/RM Protocol Examples

Various protocols, as well as network components, are mapped to particular layers of the OSI/RM. Many protocol suites (also called protocol stacks) overlap the borders of the seven-layer model because they operate at multiple layers (for example, several application-layer protocols overlap into the presentation and session layers). Most protocols map to the application, transport and network layers.

The application layer allows applications to speak to one another across networks. The transport layer provides reliable data delivery, and the network layer provides addresses used on a network and rules for particular networks. Protocols do not map to the physical layer; the physical layer affects hardware.

The networking protocols listed in Table 1-2 are examples of common protocols that operate within the OSI/RM layers. The protocols listed in the first row of the table are those found in the upper layers of the OSI/RM, which are the application, presentation and session layers. No specific section is available for the presentation and session layers because these layers include the upper-layer protocols.

Table 1-2: OSI/RM protocol examples

Layer(s)	Corresponding Protocol	Protocol Description
Application (upper layer) **Presentation** **Session**	Simple Mail Transfer Protocol (SMTP)	Used to send e-mail messages
	Post Office Protocol 3 (POP3)	Used to allow clients to log on to a remote server and obtain e-mail messages
	Internet Message Access Protocol (IMAP)	Used to allow clients to access and manage e-mail messages without first downloading them
	Hypertext Transfer Protocol (HTTP)	Used to interconnect Web pages
	Server Message Block (SMB)	Allows files to be shared on a Microsoft network
	Network file system (NFS)	Allows files and printers to be shared on a UNIX network
Transport	Transmission Control Protocol (TCP)	Part of the TCP/IP protocol suite; provides reliable delivery and manages sessions
Network	Internet Protocol (IP)	Part of the TCP/IP protocol suite; responsible for addressing hosts and routing packets in any network running TCP/IP
Data link	Ethernet	A LAN protocol that was created by Xerox, Digital Equipment Corp. and Intel; the most popular LAN technology
	Token Ring	A LAN protocol that was created by IBM to provide more reliability than Ethernet; not as commonly implemented

You will learn more about the TCP/IP protocol suite throughout this course.

Connection-oriented (stateful) and connectionless (stateless)

NOTE:
Connection-oriented protocols operate with a broadcast and acknowledgment. The receiving system acknowledges the packets it receives. Acknowledgments are not used with connectionless protocols. The packets are broadcast without expecting a reply.

Some network protocols require that a host establish a connection, or session, before they transfer information. Because of this requirement, session-oriented (or connection-oriented) protocols are often called stateful protocols. A state is the name given to a session. Connection-oriented protocols are considered more reliable because they first gain a system's attention, then prepare it to receive information, and then send the information in a process commonly known as "handshaking." However, connection-oriented protocols require more system overhead, and are not always appropriate for certain networking tasks. An example of a connection-oriented protocol is TCP.

Other network protocols do not require a previously established session; they rely on a "best-effort" technology that sends the information, hoping that it will reach the other system. This type of protocol is called connectionless, or stateless. An example of a stateless protocol is IP, which provides addresses for the TCP/IP suite. Many connectionless protocols send information by means of short messages called datagrams.

You might assume that a connection-oriented protocol is more important or reliable, but this is not necessarily true. Each protocol type has its own place in a network.

Routable and non-routable protocols

Some protocols can travel through LANs and WANs and beyond because they can pass through a router. TCP/IP is a routable protocol.

NOTE:
DLC has become less common as more printers directly support TCP/IP.

Non-routable protocols use predefined, or static, routes that cannot be changed. Some protocols are non-routable because they do not use the functions of the OSI/RM network layer. Non-routable protocols include Local Area Transport (LAT) and the Data Link Control (DLC) protocol. You will learn more about routing later in the course.

To use a non-routable protocol effectively, you can add a bridge (bridges are discussed later in this lesson) to your network or encapsulate the non-routable protocol within a routable protocol, such as TCP/IP. Encapsulation is also called tunneling.

TCP/IP

OBJECTIVE
3.1.5: TCP/IP

On January 1, 1983, the major networks that make up the Internet adopted the TCP/IP suite as the Internet's official protocol. One reason for the Internet's rapid growth and powerful communication ability is its adoption of this suite, which was originally developed in Berkeley, California.

The TCP/IP suite is the current *de facto* standard for both local and wide area networking. Most operating systems include TCP/IP support as a default selection for installing and configuring network support, including current Windows family operating systems and all flavors of UNIX. Windows XP and Windows Vista, for example, install only TCP/IP on a default Windows installation. In addition to being used as a communication protocol on private networks, TCP/IP is required for Internet access.

TCP/IP is used as the primary or sole communication protocol on nearly all new computer network installations. In addition, most existing networks either have converted or are converting to TCP/IP. TCP/IP is a routable protocol that can be used in nearly any LAN or WAN configuration.

NOTE:
TCP/IP version 4 is commonly referred to as IPv4. Windows Vista provides support for IPv6, primarily for application development purposes and testing.

Currently, the Internet fully supports TCP/IP version 4. However, TCP/IP version 6 (known as IPv6) is expected to gain full support in the coming decade. TCP/IP is not tied to any one vendor, and therefore allows heterogeneous networks to communicate efficiently.

A collection of protocols

TCP/IP is a collection of protocols that includes Transmission Control Protocol (TCP), Internet Protocol (IP), User Datagram Protocol (UDP) and many others that will be discussed later in this course. Each of these protocols has a specific function. This lesson will discuss only TCP, UDP and IP.

NOTE:
TCP provides sequencing, acknowledgment, socket identifiers and data integrity checks.

TCP

TCP ensures reliable communication and uses ports to deliver packets. It is a connection-oriented protocol. TCP also fragments and reassembles messages, using a sequencing function to ensure that packets are reassembled in the correct order. In TCP, a connection must be built using a handshake process before information is sent or received. All e-mail protocols (for example, SMTP, POP3 and IMAP) are TCP-based.

UDP

UDP is a connectionless protocol: It allows information to be sent without using a handshake process. It is often used to transfer relatively small amounts of information.

IP

IP is a connectionless protocol responsible for providing addresses of each computer and performing routing. TCP/IP version 4 uses 32-bit addresses. The address scheme falls

NOTE:
IPv4 uses 32-bit
addresses. IPv6 uses
128-bit addresses.

into five classes, only three of which are available for standard network addressing. The original plan was to assign Class A addresses to large networks, Class B addresses to medium-sized networks, and Class C addresses to smaller networks. Class D addresses are used for multicasting, and Class E addresses are experimental. You will learn more about these classes later in this course.

IP also includes Internet Control Message Protocol (ICMP), which is used for troubleshooting connectivity between systems, as well as sending error and control messages between routers and switches. Thirty-two-bit IPv4 addresses are divided into halves: the network portion and the host portion. The subnet mask helps determine which bits form the network and host portions.

IPX/SPX

Novell, Inc., developed Internetwork Packet Exchange/Sequenced Packet Exchange (IPX/SPX), the once-dominant LAN and WAN protocol. Like TCP/IP, IPX/SPX is a protocol suite rather than a single protocol. UNIX systems support IPX/SPX. Microsoft also supports IPX/SPX, although the corporation has renamed it NetWare Link (or NWLink). Microsoft uses an emulation protocol rather than IPX/SPX because IPX/SPX is a proprietary Novell protocol.

You will typically need to install NWLink support only when configuring Windows family systems for use on a legacy NetWare network or when the user needs to communicate with systems running IPX/SPX as the only protocol. A limited number of legacy applications use SPX communications. NWLink is required when supporting these applications.

NOTE:
Very old networks
may still use IPX/SPX
instead of TCP/IP.

Currently, IPX/SPX can be found primarily on legacy systems and has been completely eclipsed by TCP/IP as the standard enterprise protocol.

IPX

IPX is a connectionless protocol that resides at the network layer of the OSI/RM. The function of IPX in IPX/SPX is similar to that of IP in TCP/IP. IPX is responsible for network addressing and forwarding packets to their destination, a task known as routing.

SPX

SPX is a connection-oriented transport-layer protocol that uses services provided by IPX. The function of SPX in IPX/SPX is similar to that of TCP in TCP/IP. SPX provides reliability to IPX: It ensures that packets arrive intact at their destination. Because this protocol resides at the transport layer, it ensures reliable data delivery and manages sessions.

Binding Protocols

Whenever you use a protocol such as TCP/IP, you must attach, or bind, it to your NIC. To create a network, you must first obtain and install a NIC, use a compatible NIC driver, and choose a protocol.

In UNIX systems, you perform this attachment by reconfiguring the kernel because the UNIX kernel incorporates all drivers and protocols. Whenever you want to change a driver or protocol, you must incorporate it directly into the kernel.

In Windows Vista, however, you bind a protocol to the NIC using the Local Area Connection Properties dialog box, shown in Figure 1-12.

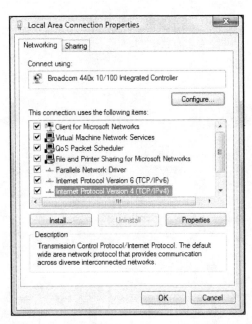

Figure 1-12: Windows Vista Local Area Connection Properties dialog box

Protocols and binding order

If you are using multiple protocols, the binding order determines the first protocol that the system will use to send information. If the first protocol is unavailable, the system will use the second protocol to deliver the packets.

Incoming packets are compared with bound protocols in binding order until a matching protocol is found. The protocol that is used for most of the computer's traffic should be bound as the first protocol.

Many operating systems, including Linux, Windows 2000, Windows XP, Windows Vista, Windows Server 2003 and Windows Server 2008, allow you to choose the binding order of network protocols.

Local Area Network (LAN)

**local area network
(LAN)**
A group of
computers
connected within a
confined
geographic area.

A **LAN** is a group of computers connected within a confined geographic area. Figure 1-13 illustrates a LAN.

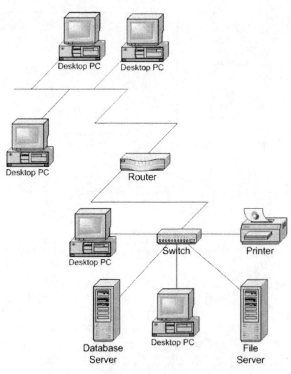

Figure 1-13: LAN example

NOTE:
This configuration is representative. Routers are not required in all LANs.

hub
A device used to connect systems so that they can communicate with one another.

switch
A device that connects either individual systems or multiple networks. A Layer 1 switch connects individual systems.

router
A device that routes packets between networks based on network-layer addresses; determines the best path across a network. Also used to connect separate LANs to form a WAN.

OBJECTIVE
3.1.6: LANs and WANs

wide area network (WAN)
A group of computers connected over an expansive geographic area so their users can share files and services.

LANs allow users to share files and services, and are commonly used for intra-office communication. They can extend over several hundred feet and generally represent one locale, such as a corporate office in Phoenix, Arizona, for example. You would use a **hub** or a Layer 1 **switch** to connect computers so that they create a LAN. Modern LANs are structured around distributed computing, and often consist of workstations and servers. In large LANs, networked computers and devices may be subdivided into subnetworks, or subnets. **Routers** can be used to connect subnets.

Wide Area Network (WAN)

A **WAN** is a group of computers connected over an expansive geographic area, such as a state or country, allowing users to share files and services. Figure 1-14 illustrates a WAN. A WAN often connects two LANs using the communications lines of a public carrier, such as the PSTN. The connection is called a WAN link. You will learn about various types of WAN links later in this course.

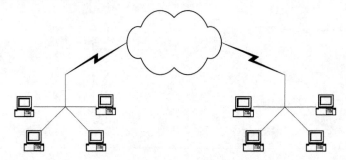

Figure 1-14 WAN example

The primary difference between a LAN and a WAN is the fact that a WAN involves two separate networks. Either a router or a switch is required to create these two networks.

In many ways, the Internet is an extremely large, complex WAN. You will learn more about network components such as routers and switches later.

Internet Exchange Point (IXP)

OBJECTIVE
3.1.7: Internet infrastructure

You have already learned that the Internet is a series of interconnected networks. An Internet Exchange Point (IXP) is a junction between one high-speed network and another. IXPs were originally known as network access points (NAPs) and are still sometimes referred to as such. As shown in Figure 1-15, the three key IXPs in the United States are in New York, Chicago and San Francisco. All these IXPs are run by telephone companies. These three exchange points, plus Washington, D.C., are the four original IXPs in the United States.

Figure 1-15: Three key U.S. IXPs

IXP connections are usually made by either a router or a switch. These high-speed networks are called Internet backbones because they provide essential connectivity for the rest of the Internet. Backbones can cover long or short distances, and smaller networks typically connect to them.

The backbone network connected by an IXP is known as a very high-speed Backbone Network Service (vBNS). Most of the IXPs in use today run in excess of 1 gigabit per second (Gbps), and are designed to reduce congestion from increasing Internet use.

Throughout most of the Internet's history, regional and governmental agencies were responsible for providing the physical connections. Beginning in 1995, commercial ISPs began to fund the Internet. This group of ISPs is called the National Research and Education Network (NREN). It uses IXPs for connectivity.

To learn more about IXPs, visit the following sites:

- Wikipedia article (*http://en.wikipedia.org/wiki/Internet_exchange_point*)

- List of IXPs (worldwide) by size (*http://en.wikipedia.org/wiki/List_of_Internet_Exchange_Points_by_size*)

- European Internet Exchange Association (*http://www.euro-ix.net/ixp/list*)

- Article in PCMAG.COM (*www.pcmag.com/encyclopedia_term/0,2542,t=IXP&i=45530,00.asp*)

Segment

A **segment** is any piece or part of a larger structure. On the Internet, a segment can be the part of the backbone that connects San Francisco to Chicago, as shown in the previous figure. On a smaller scale, a segment can be the connection between your company's network and its IXP. The term segment also describes subnetworks in a LAN (see the *Bridges* and *Routers* sections later in this lesson).

Common Network Components

Computer networks usually require a great deal of equipment to function properly. LANs and WANs typically include network interface cards, hubs, bridges, routers, brouters and switches. These devices affect the way traffic is controlled and moved throughout a network. Before investigating the individual devices, you should be familiar with the following terms that are associated with network traffic:

- **Collision domain** — a logical area in a computer network where a group of Ethernet devices compete for access to the media. In traditional Ethernet networking, only one device can transmit at any one time. When two devices transmit at the same time, the simultaneously transmitted frames collide and are destroyed. The more collisions there are, the less efficient the network is.

- **Broadcast** — a transmission from one node that is intended for transmission to all other nodes on the network. Whenever a device needs to send out information but does not know which device to address it to, it sends out a broadcast. Broadcasts are vital to the function of a network, but they generate a large amount of traffic and must be handled wisely to keep a network running efficiently.

- **Broadcast domain** — a logical network segment in which any connected device can transmit to any other device in the domain without having to go through a routing device. Broadcast traffic is limited to the confines of a broadcast domain.

Equipment configuration for a typical network is shown in Figure 1-16.

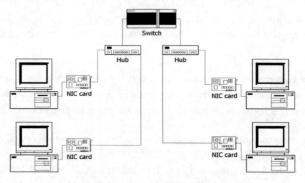

Figure 1-16: Networking components

Network interface card (NIC)

Each node in a network contains a NIC, often called a network **adapter** card. The NIC is the interface between the computer and the network (that is, it is the physical connection between the computer and the network cabling), as shown in Figure 1-17.

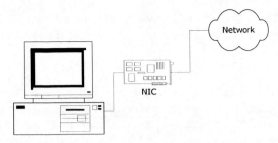

Figure 1-17: Network interface card (NIC)

NOTE:
Many PCs include NIC hardware built into the system hardware rather than implemented as a separate adapter card.

Networks transmit data serially, or one bit at a time. The network adapter converts the data from the computer into a format appropriate for transmission over the network. A NIC generally resides in the motherboard expansion slot and communicates with the computer through a NIC device driver. Networking cable connects the NIC to the network. NICs vary for Ethernet and token-ring networks, which you will learn about in a later lesson. NICs operate at the data link layer of the OSI/RM.

A NIC requires a device driver, which is specialized software that must be installed on the system to enable the NIC to function properly.

transceiver
A device that transmits and receives digital or analog signals.

Most NICs contain a **transceiver**, a network device that transmits and receives analog or digital signals. The term is short for transmitter-receiver.

In LANs, the transceiver places data onto the network wire, and detects and receives data traveling across the wire. Some network types require an external transceiver. Most NICs have more than one transceiver. Each transceiver is attached to a different connector available on the back of the card.

NICs and wireless NICs can be attached to a computer by any of the following:

- **Peripheral component interconnect (PCI) card** — a standard method for attaching any internally attached system card.

- **Universal Serial Bus (USB) device** — a method for attaching external interfaces, including NICs. Two USB standards exist, 1.0/1.1 and 2.0. USB 1.0 cards support data rates of up to 12 megabits per second (Mbps). USB 2.0 cards support data rates of up to 480 Mbps. The USB 3.0 standard is in development and will be available in 2010. USB 3.0 "SuperSpeed" cards will be able to support data rates of up to 5 gigabits per second (Gbps).

- **IEEE 1394 (FireWire) device** — similar to USB, although the original USB 1394 standard supports speeds of up to 400 Mbps. Commonly found on Macintosh systems, but increasingly found on IBM-compatible systems. IEEE 1294 cards have connectors for both internal and external devices. The Institute of Electrical and Electronics Engineers (IEEE) is an organization that creates standards for computers and communications. You will learn more about IEEE standards later in this lesson.

- **Industry Standard Architecture (ISA) card** — considered a legacy standard for connecting internal cards. Largely superseded by PCI cards, although still in use.

Most new NICs are PCI Ethernet cards with an RJ-45 port to connect to unshielded twisted-pair cable. Older NICs included an RJ-45 port and a BNC port, which was used to connect the PC to legacy Thinnet (10Base2) coaxial cable.

Media Access Control (MAC) address
The hardware address of a device connected to a network.

Every NIC has a physical, or **Media Access Control (MAC)**, address that identifies an individual machine on a network. While the NIC's interface itself is defined at the physical layer (Layer 1) of the OSI model, the physical address of the adapter, as well as its drivers, are located at the MAC sublayer of the data link layer (Layer 2).

Hub

A hub connects computers in a star-configured network so they can exchange information. It has several ports, each connected to a single node. By interconnecting the nodes, a hub serves as the concentration point for a network. Most hubs are called active hubs because they regenerate electronic signals. Figure 1-18 illustrates a hub.

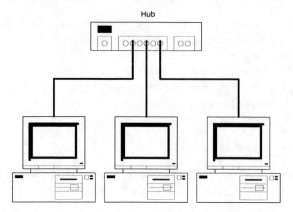

Figure 1-18: Hub connecting workstations

Hubs operate at the physical layer (Layer 1) of the OSI/RM. They can be connected to other hubs, or "daisy-chained," to provide more ports for a larger network. You can also connect hubs to switches or routers to increase the number of network nodes.

In technical terms, a hub connects multiple devices into the same collision domain and allows frame collision. Hubs do not divide a network into discrete segments the way switches do; a hub takes a signal coming from any node and passes it on to all the other nodes on the network.

This traditional Ethernet topology is often called shared Ethernet, because all hosts must share the bandwidth, only one can transmit at a time, and each host is responsible for collision detection and retransmission. A shared Ethernet network provides for only half-duplex transmission (data can be transmitted in only one direction at a time). Hubs have been replaced widely by switches in modern networks.

Bridge

Bridges are devices that filter frames to determine whether a specific frame belongs on a local segment or another LAN segment. Because bridges operate at Layer 2 of the OSI/RM, they use hardware addresses to determine which segment will receive the frame. Bridges can reduce network traffic by dividing one network into two segments, thereby creating two separate (smaller) collision domains.

Router

Routers are conceptually similar to bridges, except that they operate at the network layer (Layer 3) of the OSI/RM. Instead of using MAC addresses, routers forward and control network protocols, such as IP. They forward, or route, data from one network to another, instead of only to network segments. Thus, they are efficient tools for creating discrete network segments, which can help reduce network traffic.

Routers direct data packets between networks. They identify the destination computer's network address, and then determine the most efficient route for transmitting data to it. As a result, routers do not forward broadcast traffic (unless they are specifically configured to do so). Routers limit broadcast domains at the network layer (Layer 3).

Figure 1-19 illustrates a router connecting two networks.

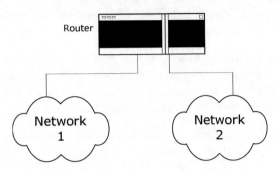

Figure 1-19: Router connecting networks

Suppose a computer on Network 2 sends data to another computer on Network 2. In this case, the router will not pass the data to Network 1. This filtering process conserves network bandwidth. You can measure a router's capability by its packets per second (PPS) rate.

Routers are protocol-dependent: They rely on the address system defined by the protocol used (IPX, IP and so forth). Different types of routers work with different protocols. For example, IP routers operate with the inherent IP 32-bit address structure. To use the IPX addressing protocol, a router that supports IPX is required. Routing will be discussed in more detail later in this lesson.

Routing table

Routers often need to communicate with one another in order to keep their information current. Routers store network information in files called routing tables. Whenever a router needs to update another router's routing table, routing protocols are used. As you will see later in the course, interior and exterior routing protocols are used, depending on the location of the router.

Switch

On a network, a switch directs the flow of information directly from one node to another. There are several different types of switches, as you will learn shortly. A Layer 2 switch, also called a LAN switch, provides a separate connection for each node in a company's internal network.

A switch segments a collision domain into as many segments as there are connections between nodes. That is, the collision domain is reduced so that only the two nodes in any given connection coexist within each collision domain. Essentially, a LAN switch creates a series of instant networks that contain only the two devices communicating with each other at that particular moment.

Switches provide full-duplex communication. A switch cross-connects all hosts connected to it and can give each sender/receiver pair the line's entire bandwidth, instead of sharing the bandwidth with all other network nodes. A switch can handle multiple simultaneous communications between the computers attached to it, whereas a hub can handle only one communication at a time. Switches forward broadcast traffic.

By definition, a switch operates at the data link layer (Layer 2) of the OSI/RM; however, there are several types of switches that operate at various OSI layers.

Types of switches

Layer 2 switch
A device that forwards traffic based on MAC addresses.

Switches can operate at several layers of the OSI/RM. A Layer 1 switch, called a switching hub, has replaced the much slower and less efficient traditional hub. A **Layer 2 switch**, also called a LAN switch, forwards traffic based on MAC addresses and is much faster than a bridge.

Layer 3 switch
A device that connects networks.

A **Layer 3 switch** forwards traffic based on Layer 3 information, and is called a routing switch if it supports network protocols, such as IP and IPX. These switches are much faster than routers because they can act on Layer 2 information as well as Layer 3 information, and are replacing routers in many installations in the core network.

Layer 4 switches make forwarding decisions based on Layer 4 information (such as the specific TCP/UDP port that an application uses), as well as on Layer 2 and 3 information.

Packet switching

A LAN switch establishes a connection between two network segments just long enough to send the current packet. This process is called packet switching. An incoming frame contains an IP packet as the payload with a header that includes the MAC address information for the source and destination. The MAC address in the frame's header is read and compared to a list of addresses maintained in the switch's lookup table. Switches can use store-and-forward or cut-through methods for forwarding traffic:

- **Store-and-forward** — The switch saves the entire packet in its buffer and checks it for CRC errors before forwarding it. Packets that contain errors are discarded.

- **Cut-through** — The switch reads the MAC address as soon as the frame begins to enter the switch. After reading the destination MAC address, the switch immediately begins forwarding the frame. This method provides no error detection or correction.

Many switches combine the two methods for forwarding traffic.

Benefits of using switches

Switches offer the following benefits for networks:

port
A logical opening in an operating system or protocol stack that allows the transfer of information. Not the same as a TCP or UDP port.

- **Simple installation** — For many bridges and hubs, installing a switch requires you to unplug connections from existing devices and plug the connections into the switch **ports**.

- **Higher speeds** — Switches have high-speed backplanes (the connections within the switch itself) that allow full bandwidth between any two users or segments. This feature eliminates the switch as a potential network bottleneck.

- **Bandwidth control** — Using a switch, it is possible to control the bandwidth available to a client or server.

virtual local area network (VLAN)
Logical subgroup within a LAN created with software instead of hardware.

- **Creation of logical computer groupings** — You can create a group of systems called a **virtual LAN (VLAN)**. A VLAN allows you to organize systems according to their logical function on the network, as opposed to their physical location. For example, a VLAN can allow systems residing in New York, Bangalore and London to all belong to the same group, in spite of their obviously different physical locations. Network hubs allow you to group systems only by their physical location.

- **More default security** — Using a VLAN, you can isolate individual systems. Also, it is slightly more difficult to "sniff" (examine data traveling over a network) network connections in a switch-based network than in a standard hub-based network, because each connection made in a switch is dedicated; in a hub-based network, any one system can see all connections made on the network.

Figure 1-20 illustrates a routing switch that connects two networks.

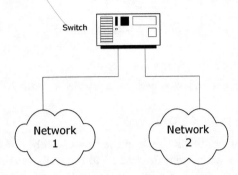

Figure 1-20: Switch connecting networks

OBJECTIVE
3.2.2: Hardware/ software connection devices

Channel Service Unit/Data Service Unit (CSU/DSU)

A Channel Service Unit/Data Service Unit (CSU/DSU) is a device that converts data from digital telephony-based lines, such as a T1 or a T3 line, into data that a network connection used by traditional network equipment (such as a router, switch or firewall) can recognize.

OBJECTIVE
3.2.2: Hardware/ software connection devices

Modem

A modem is a device that enables a computer to communicate with other computers over telephone lines by translating digital data into audio/analog signals (on the sending computer) and then back into digital form (on the receiving computer). This type of modem is called a traditional or analog modem.

NOTE:
Most modems can auto-detect connectivity settings, so detailed configuration is usually not required.

The term modem is widely used, but does not always denote an analog-to-digital translation. For instance, cable, DSL and Integrated Services Digital Network (ISDN) modems are used on all-digital networks — no translation to analog is required. The term modem has been used to describe any device that adapts a computer to a phone line or cable television network, whether it is digital or analog.

Firewall

OBJECTIVE
3.2.2: Hardware/ software connection devices

A firewall is a secure computer system placed between a trusted network and an untrusted one, such as the Internet. A firewall acts as a barrier against potential malicious activity, while still allowing a "door" for people to communicate between a secured network and the open, unsecured network.

A network firewall is most commonly placed between a corporate LAN and the Internet. By connecting to the Internet through firewalls, no computer on the corporate LAN is actually connected to the Internet, and any requests for information must pass through the firewall.

You will study firewalls in detail later in this course.

Transmission Media

NOTE:
Keep in mind that transmission media might refer to any communication path.

To transmit data, a medium must exist, usually in the form of cables or wireless methods. The following section explains the most common cable types:

- Twisted pair

- Coaxial

- Fiber optic

It concludes with a discussion of wireless media.

Twisted-pair cable

Twisted-pair cable is perhaps the most widely used cabling system in Ethernet networks. Two copper wires are intertwined to form the twisted-pair cable. Depending on the category, several insulated wire strands can reside in the cable. Cable categories will be discussed later in this lesson.

NOTE:
Twisted-pair cable is the most common choice for implementing new network installations or updating existing networks.

A twisted-pair segment cannot exceed 100 meters. Twisted-pair cable is used for many types of network standards. For example, 10BaseT Ethernet networks use twisted-pair cable; the name "10BaseT" denotes a network running at 10 Mbps, using baseband transmission and twisted-pair cable.

Twisted-pair cable is available in two basic types:

- **Shielded twisted-pair (STP)** — Shielded twisted-pair copper wire is protected from external electromagnetic interference by a metal sheath wrapped around the wires; STP is harder to install and maintain than UTP.

- **Unshielded twisted-pair (UTP)** — Unshielded twisted-pair cable is the most common type of twisted-pair wiring; it is less expensive than STP, but it is less secure and is prone to electromagnetic interference. This course focuses on UTP.

STP and UTP are available with two varieties of wire:

- **Stranded** — the most common type; flexible and easy to handle around corners and objects.

attenuation
The weakening of a transmission signal as it travels farther from its source.

- **Solid** — can span longer distances without as much **attenuation** as stranded wire, but is less flexible and will break if bent multiple times.

OBJECTIVE
3.2.1: Networking cable types

Six twisted-pair standards, or categories, are specified by the Telecommunications Industry Association/Electronic Industries Alliance (TIA/EIA) 568 Commercial Building Wiring standard. An additional level, Category 7, is commercially available, but is not standardized. Categories 1 through 4 are considered legacy standards in terms of today's converged networks. Category 1 is not considered an acceptable medium for network data transmissions, but does support low-speed serial communication such as connections to dial-up lines. Category selections are made according to network data transmission requirements.

Table 1-3 outlines Categories 5 through 7 only. As you study this table, consider the designations megabits per second (Mbps) and megahertz (MHz) for Ethernet cabling. The phrase "(mega)bits per second" refers to the speed at which information can be transferred across a wire. Standard Ethernet, for example, operates at 10 Mbps. Fast Ethernet can transmit (or push) bits across a wire at 100 Mbps. Alternatively, the term "hertz" describes the number of times a signal cycles in one second. The MHz value of a wire should be considered because Ethernet transmissions do more than simply push bits across a wire. They also transmit a particular signal. Standard Ethernet requires a cable that supports at least 10 MHz (signals that cycle 10 million times in one second). Fast Ethernet requires a cable that can support signals of 100 MHz (signals that cycle 100 million times in one second).

Table 1-3: TIA/EIA 568 twisted-pair cable categories (Categories 5 through 7)

NOTE:
You need to know Categories 5 through 7 and the implementations in which they are used.

Cable Grade	General Use	Bandwidth	Specific Network(s)
Category 5	Data	100 Mbps. Can sustain rates up to 100 MHz	A popular implementation; 10BaseT and 100BaseTX networks
Category 5e	Data	1,000 Mbps. Can sustain rates up to 100 MHz	Gigabit Ethernet and other high-speed networks
Category 6	Data	10 Gbps. Can sustain rates up to 250 MHz	Supports networks of up to 10 Gbps. If you want to upgrade a Category 5 network and still use wires, consider using this category of cable.
Category 6E	Data	10 Gbps. Can sustain rates up to 550 MHz	10-Gbps (and faster, more powerful) networks
Category 7	Data	10 Gbps. Can sustain rates up to at least 600 MHz	Proposed standard

NOTE:
For more about crossover cables, see the Data Communications Cabling FAQ at *www.faqs.org/faqs/ LANs/cabling-faq.*

Registered Jack-45 (RJ-45) connector

Registered Jack-45 (RJ-45) connectors are commonly used on certain types of Ethernet and token-ring networks, which you will learn about later in this lesson. The connector holds up to eight wires, and is used with twisted-pair wire. To attach an RJ-45 connector to a cable, the connector must be crimped using a tool called a crimper.

OBJECTIVE
3.2.1: Networking cable types

Crossover cable

A crossover cable for Ethernet networks is a specialized cable that allows you to connect two computers directly without using a hub. The crossover cable reverses, or crosses over, the respective PIN contacts. Crossover cables can be used in various situations, including the following:

- You want to connect two workstations together to transfer information quickly between them, and you do not have a hub or switch available.

- You need to connect a router to certain cable modems. If connecting a standard Ethernet cable to the cable modem does not work, try a crossover cable.

coax
Short for coaxial cable. High-capacity two-wire (signal and ground) cable; inner wire is the primary conductor, and the metal sheath serves as the ground.

Coaxial cable

Coaxial cable, known as **coax** (pronounced "co-axe"), is a high-capacity cable used for video and communication networks. Coaxial cable has remained in common networking use because cable companies are often a preferred choice for high-speed Internet access.

plenum
Space between building floors; usually contains air and heating ducts, as well as communication and electrical wires.

Coaxial cable contains a signal wire at the center, which is either stranded or solid, surrounded by a metallic shield that serves as a ground. The shield is either braided or solid, and is wrapped in plastic. If a cable travels through a **plenum**, it is coated in a fire-safe material such as Teflon.

Several types of coaxial cable exist for different purposes. For instance, coaxial cable is designed for baseband, broadband and television networks.

Table 1-4 lists common coax types.

Table 1-4: Common coaxial cable types

Cable Type	Use	Impedance
RG-6	Cable television, video, some cable modems; often for short distances (e.g., 6 feet)	75 Ohms
RG-8	Thick Ethernet (10Base5); maximum segment length of 500 meters	50 Ohms
RG-11	Broadband LANs	75 Ohms
RG-58	Thin Ethernet (10Base2); maximum segment length of 185 meters	50 Ohms
RG-59	Television	75 Ohms
RG-62	ARCnet	93 Ohms

You will notice an impedance value listed for each of the cable types. Impedance is a measure of a cable's resistance to a changing signal.

BNC connector

The British Naval Connector, or Bayonet Neil-Concelman (BNC) connector, is commonly used to connect coaxial cable to NICs, hubs and other network devices. The BNC connector is crimped to the cable using a bayonet mount. The bayonet mount technique connects the two wires (signal and ground) in the coaxial cable to the connector. The connector is then inserted into another connector and turned, which causes the bayonet mechanism to pinch several pins into the BNC's locking groove. A BNC connector is illustrated in Figure 1-21.

Figure 1-21: BNC connector

Fiber-optic cable

Fiber-optic cables consist of two small glass strands: One strand sends and one receives. These strands are called the core, and they are sometimes made of plastic. Each core is surrounded by glass cladding. Each core and cladding element is wrapped with a plastic reinforced with Kevlar fibers. Laser transmitters send the modulated light pulses and optical receivers receive them.

Fiber-optic cable can accommodate data transmissions much faster than coaxial or twisted-pair cable. Fiber-optic lines can transmit data in the gigabits-per-second range. Because they send data as pulses of light over threads of glass, the transmissions can travel for miles without a signal degradation. No electrical signals are carried over the fiber-optic line, so the lines are free of electromagnetic interference and are extremely difficult to tap.

Following are the two major types of fiber-optic cable:

- **Single-mode** — uses a specific light wavelength. The cable's core diameter is 8 to 10 microns. It permits signal transmission at extremely high bandwidth and allows very long transmission distances (up to 70 km, or 43 miles). Single-mode fiber is often used for intercity telephone trunks and video applications.

- **Multi-mode** — uses a large number of frequencies (or modes). The cable's core is larger than that of single-mode fiber, usually 50 microns to 100 microns, and it allows for the use of inexpensive light sources. It is used for short to medium distances (less than 200 m, or 656 feet). Multi-mode fiber is the type usually specified for LANs and WANs.

Fiber-optic cable is expensive, and installation can be tedious and costly. Attaching connectors to fibers used to involve a tedious process of cutting and polishing the ends of the glass strands, and then mounting them into the connectors. Modern tools and newer connectors cut and polish in one step.

Wireless Network Technologies

Wireless network connections have become extremely popular, both in enterprises and in homes. Wireless networking is usually implemented in a hybrid environment, in which wireless components communicate with a network that uses cables. For example, a laptop computer may use its wireless capabilities to connect with a corporate LAN that uses standard wiring.

The only difference between a wireless LAN and a cabled LAN is the medium itself: Wireless systems use wireless signals instead of a network cable. A standard system that uses a wireless NIC is called an end point. Following is a discussion of various media used to enable wireless networks.

Wireless networking media

spread spectrum
Technologies that consist of various methods for radio transmission in which frequencies or signal patterns are continuously changed.

Wireless communications use **spread spectrum** technologies. In spread spectrum technologies, a signal is generated by a system (for example, a computer with a wireless NIC), and then sent (i.e., spread) over a large number of frequencies to another system. That system then reassembles the data. Wireless networks can use the following types of spread spectrum transmissions:

- **Orthogonal Frequency Division Multiplexing (OFDM)** — OFDM splits a radio signal into smaller subsignals that are transmitted simultaneously on different frequencies. IEEE 802.11a and 802.11g networks can use OFDM. The 802.11a DSSS networks can operate at 54 Mbps at 5.4 GHz.

wideband
A large set of frequencies capable of carrying data at higher rates (for example, 1.544 Mbps). Usually carries digital signals. Includes DSL and cable Internet access.

- **Direct Sequence Spread Spectrum (DSSS)** — Rather than hopping from one frequency to another, a signal is spread over the entire band at once through the use of a spreading function. For this reason, DSSS is considered a **wideband** networking method. DSSS is used by 802.11b and 802.11g networks. The 802.11b (WiFi) networks communicate as fast as 11 Mbps at 2.4 GHz, and 802.11b NICs have been available in stores for years. The 802.11g NICs and networks are becoming increasingly common, and can operate at rates between 20 and 54 Mbps at 2.4 GHz. The 802.11g wireless networks are backward-compatible with 802.11b networks.

narrowband
A specific set of
frequencies
established for
wireless
communication
(usually for voice).
Communicates at
lower rates than
broadband.

- **Frequency Hopping Spread Spectrum (FHSS)** — Originally developed during World War II, FHSS is a **narrowband** transmission technology that involves changing the frequency of a transmission at regular intervals. Signals move from frequency to frequency, and each frequency change is called a hop. Both the client and the server must coordinate the hops between frequencies. That is, they retune at regular intervals during the transmission. FHSS is ideal for networks in which interference is a problem. However, FHSS networks are slower than DSSS networks, achieving speeds between 2 Mbps and 3 Mbps. Even though FHSS networks use hop sequences, they do not make connections any more secure than those found in DSSS networks. It is possible for 802.11 networks to use FHSS, but FHSS has not been as widely adopted.

The 802.11b networks have the same frequency as standard 2.4-GHz cordless phones, Bluetooth networks and even equipment such as microwaves. As a result, wireless networks can interfere with transmissions or be interfered with by other equipment.

Wireless networking modes

OBJECTIVE
3.9.1: Ad-hoc and
infrastructure mode

The following two types of wireless modes exist for 802.11a, 802.11b and 802.11g networks:

NOTE:
If possible, look at a
wireless NIC and the
software used to
configure a NIC.

- **Ad-hoc** — in which systems use only their NICs to connect with one another. Ad-hoc mode is useful when two or more systems need to communicate with one another for only a short time. This mode is also known as peer-to-peer mode.

- **Infrastructure** — in which systems connect via a centralized access point, called a wireless access point (AP). Infrastructure mode is a preferred method because a wireless AP allows some centralized access control and network protection. Also, a wireless AP can be used to connect a wireless network to a wired network. When the AP is plugged into a standard hub, wireless and wired systems can communicate with one another if they are on the same IP network.

Software provided with the NIC allows the system administrator to choose between infrastructure and ad-hoc mode.

Figure 1-22 illustrates the two types of wireless networks.

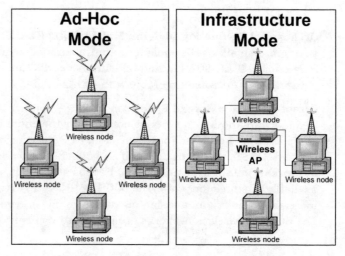

Figure 1-22: Ad-hoc vs. infrastructure mode

Wireless access point (AP)

OBJECTIVE
3.9.2: Wireless
access points (APs)

As you just learned, a wireless AP is a device that acts much like a standard hub or switch in that it allows wireless systems to communicate with one another, as long as they are on the same network. It is possible to attach a wireless AP to a standard Ethernet hub or switch, and thus extend your network without having to lay down wires, which can be inconvenient. It is also possible for a wireless AP to include a router, which enables multiple wireless and wired networks to communicate with one another.

Wireless cell

A wireless cell is a collection of wireless clients around a specific wireless AP. The farther a client is from a wireless AP, the less that client is inclined to belong to a particular cell because the AP beacon becomes too weak, and interference results.

 Resources often call a wireless cell a "sphere of influence" that is generated by a specific wireless AP.

If multiple cells exist in close proximity, a client may reside in several wireless cells at one time. Because of the nature of wireless networks, a mobile client (for example, a laptop computer) can be moved from one wireless cell to another. As a result, people can move from one wireless cell to another to gain (sometimes illicit) access to a wireless network and its resources. Resources can include files, printers and other networks, such as the Internet.

Basic Service Set Identifier (BSSID)

A Basic Service Set Identifier (BSSID) is provided by a wireless AP, and has one function: to differentiate one wireless cell from another. The BSSID does not contain authentication information. In fact, it is most often the MAC address of the wireless AP.

OBJECTIVE
3.9.5: Secure Set
Identifier (SSID)

Service Set Identifier (SSID)

A Service Set Identifier (SSID) is a unique name for each wireless cell (or network). A SSID (pronounced "Sid") is used to control access to a particular wireless cell. Usually, a SSID is a simple text string entered into a wireless AP, although a SSID can also be established by hosts participating in an ad-hoc wireless network. After a wireless AP has a SSID entered, this AP immediately becomes differentiated from other wireless cells. SSID values are case-sensitive and can be up to 32 characters long. They can also be encrypted.

 A SSID is not the same as a BSSID.

Common default wireless AP SSIDs include the following:

- ANY (in lowercase and/or uppercase letters).

- The vendor name (for example, Linksys®, Belkin — also in uppercase and/or lowercase). Cisco Aironet® cards use the word "tsunami."

Some cards default to a blank SSID. To begin to secure your system, change default SSID settings.

Figure 1-23 shows the configuration interface for a common wireless AP.

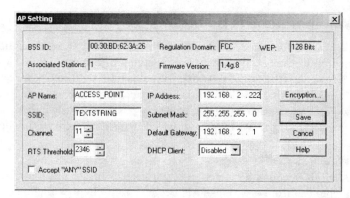

Figure 1-23: Configuration interface for common wireless AP

Notice that values exist for the BSSID as well as the SSID. It is also possible to configure a wireless AP so that it has its own IP address information. The default channel is often 11.

Wireless AP security features

OBJECTIVE
3.9.7: Wireless
network security
issues

A wireless AP provides centralized control and security features, and acts as a hub. Such measures are important because many hackers take advantage of wireless networks by placing their wireless systems in open mode, in which their systems search for all access points. Hackers then drive through a neighborhood or business district, trying to discover unsecured wireless networks. This practice is called "war driving." Both wireless APs and wireless routers provide the following features to help stop war driving:

OBJECTIVE
3.9.4: Wired
Equivalent Privacy
(WEP)

- **Wired Equivalent Privacy (WEP)** — WEP encryption can be in 64-bit, 128-bit and 256-bit keys. Today, WEP is not considered to be secure. It is a weak form of encryption because the 64-bit and 128-bit symmetric keys used to encrypt the network transmissions have been cracked. Today, acceptable forms of encryption and authentication for wireless networks include the WiFi Protected Access (WPA) standards.

OBJECTIVE
3.9.6: MAC address
filtering

- **MAC address filtering** — This feature enables the device to allow only certain MAC addresses to access the network. In MAC address filtering, a wireless AP is configured so that it allows only certain system MAC addresses to communicate with the rest of the network. MAC address filtering can be performed using either of two policies: Exclude all by default, then allow only listed clients; or include all by default, then exclude listed clients. MAC address filtering is also problematic from a security standpoint because hackers are able to forge MAC addresses. Forged (or spoofed) MAC addresses can then be used to fool an access point's filtering features.

NOTE:
You will learn more
about spoofing in a
later lesson.

Both WEP and MAC address filtering are useful tools that help systems administrators keep illicit users from attaching their systems to the network. Illicit systems that attach to the network are often called rogue systems.

Wireless management software

A wireless AP can accept programming to enable WEP, MAC filtering and other features. A standard end point uses software to control the following:

- **The end point's NIC** — Software must be loaded onto the end point's system to enable it to configure its own NIC in order to use a specific wireless channel, use WEP, monitor the connection strength and use other features.

NOTE:
After a wireless AP is
fully configured,
wired and wireless
systems can
manage it. It is best
not to depend on
wireless systems to
manage the AP
because one simple
misconfiguration in
the AP software can
cause the wireless
systems to be
disconnected from
the network. Thus,
they will be denied
access to the AP.

- **A wireless AP's or wireless router's configuration** — Software must be loaded onto an end point so that this end point can configure the wireless AP device. Generally, this type of software is capable of conducting a scan to locate the device. After the software finds the device, you can enter a password and begin configuring the device.

Following is a summary of what you can configure and/or manage on a wireless AP:

- Set the administrative password.

- Configure WEP and MAC address filtering.

- Set the AP device's IP address, which can allow it to be managed by both wired and wireless systems.

- Upgrade the device's firmware (in other words, its operating system).

- Configure the device to become a Dynamic Host Configuration Protocol (DHCP) client.

The wireless AP or wireless router will have a default IP address. To change this address so that you can configure it, you must first configure a wireless system to access this IP address. You can then reconfigure the device to use the IP addresses for your network.

Suitability of a wireless LAN

OBJECTIVE
3.9.8: Wireless LAN
practicality

You must consider several factors when evaluating the practicality of a wireless LAN in your organization. Using wireless may be less expensive than installing new cable, especially in an old building. However, if your network is spread across a wide geographic region, you must consider how many access points you will need.

You should also consider the following issues when considering incorporating a wireless LAN:

- **Security** — Wireless security presents certain challenges. Will WEP and/or MAC address filtering be sufficient? How will you control or limit the exchange of sensitive data over your wireless LAN? Will you need to update your existing network policies and procedures? Will you need to train employees in the secure use of wireless technology?

- **Learning curve** — Your Information Technology (IT) staff may require time to learn how to implement and maintain wireless technologies. IT employees may be accustomed to working with office hardware only. Wireless devices are mobile and can be in use anywhere. Other employees, too, may need time to learn how to use wireless technologies effectively.

- **Network management** — The addition of wireless LANs often complicates the management of the existing wired network. For example, will you have enough ports in which to plug in the access points? What new equipment or software might you need to secure the wireless network?

Attaching a wireless AP to a wired network

OBJECTIVE
3.9.3: Wireless to
wired LANs

NOTE:
See **Optional Lab 1-
4: Implementing a
wireless network**.

In addition to providing centralized wireless client access, a wireless AP also has an RJ-45 plug that allows you to attach it to a standard, wired Ethernet network. After you attach a wireless AP to a hub or a switch, all wireless clients will be able to access all the services available to standard Ethernet clients (for example, Internet access, intranet access and company e-mail). Figure 1-24 illustrates how a wireless AP attached to a hub allows wireless clients access to the standard Ethernet network, which itself has access to the Internet.

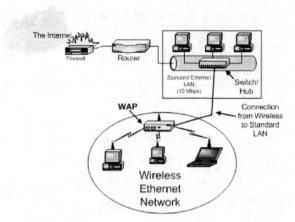

Figure 1-24: Wireless AP attached to Ethernet hub or switch

Without the connection to the standard network, these wireless clients would be able to communicate only with one another and not with the rest of the network or the Internet.

OBJECTIVE
3.9.9:
Troubleshooting
wireless connectivity

Troubleshooting wireless connections

As you work with wireless connections, consider the following issues:

- **Power** — Make sure that the wireless AP has power; technicians periodically assume that a problem exists with a particular workstation or laptop, but find that the AP was unplugged. If the AP is attached to a standard Ethernet hub or switch, make sure that all equipment is plugged in and powered on.

- **Encryption** — Make sure that all clients are using the same level of encryption as the wireless AP.

- **SSID** — One minor change in a system's SSID may cause the wireless connection to fail.

- **MAC address filtering** — Check the wireless AP to see whether filtering settings are blocking your system from the network. You may need to add your system's MAC address, or you may need to remove your system's MAC address from the AP's filtering list.

Configuring a wireless network

NOTE:
You will need two different types of software:
-Software to configure the wireless AP
-Software to configure each NIC.

Also, the AP and the NICs can be different makes or models.

Following are the steps necessary for configuring a wireless network.

1. **Plug in the wireless AP** — An obvious step, but one that is sometimes inadvertently omitted.

2. **Configure the wireless AP's SSID, encryption level and shared key** — You must use the software that ships with your wireless AP. This software can be installed on any computer supported by the vendor. Microsoft-based programs are most often provided. Choose a SSID for your AP; never use the default value. Use the highest encryption that all clients can use. When choosing a shared key, use one that is not easily guessed. Make sure that you record all information so that you can enter the correct values in each wireless NIC that connects to the AP.

3. **Insert the wireless NIC into the computer** — Wireless NICs come in various forms, including PCI, USB and Personal Computer Memory Card International Association (PCMCIA). You may need to repeat this step on multiple computers.

4. **Choose a networking protocol and configure the protocol for each client** — A logical choice may be TCP/IP, but use a protocol that is appropriate. If you choose TCP/IP, make sure that each NIC is configured so that it participates on the same network; failure to ensure that each NIC is configured to participate on the same network may cause you to mistake a problem specific to TCP/IP for one specific to the wireless NIC or the AP.

5. **Configure each computer's wireless NIC to use the wireless AP** — Insert the appropriate values (for example, SSID, encryption level and the shared key) using management software that ships with each NIC.

6. **Troubleshoot the connection** — Verify that the wireless NICs and wireless AP are functioning by making sure that the computers can communicate.

7. **Configure additional security features** — After you have verified basic connectivity, further secure the wireless network. Measures can include MAC address filtering, as well as encryption and authentication supplements.

8. **Plug the wireless AP into a wired network (optional)** — If you want to provide Internet access, attach the wireless AP to a wired network using the AP's RJ-45 jack.

Next-generation (3G) wireless

Next-generation (3G) wireless networks are not IEEE 802.11 networks. Rather, they are networks dedicated to personal devices, including PDAs and mobile telephones. Next-generation wireless networks are called 3G networks because they represent the third iteration of personal wireless technology.

First-generation (1G) wireless networks included the crude mobile phones used in the 1970s as well as analog mobile phones used in the 1980s and early 1990s.

NOTE:
Multiplexing is the placement of multiple signals on the same channel. Multiplexing allows for more efficient use of bandwidth.

Second-generation (2G) wireless networks included the introduction of digital phones as well as the use of Code-Division Multiple Access (CDMA), which is a set of protocols that allow multiplexing of signals onto one channel. This multiplexing allows both voice and data to be used on cellular networks. The original CDMA version 1 had a capacity of 14.4 Kbps, and only one channel. However, an extension allows the use of eight channels, and a top speed of 115 Kbps.

Cellular networks are often required to process an increasing amount of data traffic. Devices such as mobile phones and PDAs are providing video and data ports and technologies. To accommodate these demands, 3G networks use additional access protocols for multiplexing, including the following:

- **CDMA 2000** — has data rates of 144 Kbps to 2 Mbps. Adopted by the International Telecommunication Union (ITU).

- **Wideband CDMA** — supports speeds between 384 Kbps and 2 Mbps. When this protocol is used in a WAN, the top speed is 384 Kbps. When it is used in a LAN, the top speed is 2 Mbps. Also adopted by the ITU.

All 2G and 3G networks are digital in nature, which makes the transfer of data more efficient because modulation and demodulation of data are not necessary.

NOTE:
Security has become an increasing concern with the advent of 3G networks.

Third-generation technology allows a mobile phone or PDA user to have access to networks throughout North America, Europe and Japan, and to have access to voice and data at 2 Mbps. With the maturity of 3G networks, once-incompatible devices will be able to work together, and data should become even more available in various formats and places.

Transmission Types

After a network is in place, the data must be transmitted across the cable. This section will discuss several data transmission concepts, including:

- Asynchronous transmission
- Synchronous transmission.
- Data transmission flow.

Synchronous transmission

With synchronous transmission, the access device and network device share a clock and transmission rate. The transmissions are synchronized.

Data is exchanged in character streams called message-framed data. A start-and-stop sequence is associated with each transmission. The access and network devices need to be synchronized so that the entire message is received in the order in which it was transmitted. T1 lines use synchronous transmissions (you will learn about T-carrier services later in this lesson).

Asynchronous transmission

Asynchronous transmission is characterized by the absence of a clock in the transmission media. The access device is not synchronized with the network device. However, the transmission speeds must be the same. Therefore, data is transmitted as individual characters. Each character is synchronized by information contained in the start (header) and stop (trailer) bits. Dial-up modems use asynchronous transmissions.

Data transmission flow

NOTE:
Dial-up modems also use half-duplex communication.

The three methods of circuit operation are as follows:

- **Simplex** — Data travels in only one direction, similar to a public address (PA) system.
- **Half duplex** — Data travels in two directions, but in only one direction at a time, similar to a walkie-talkie. Ethernet uses half-duplex transmissions.
- **Full duplex** — Data travels in two directions simultaneously, similar to a phone conversation. Full-duplex Ethernet, an extension of Ethernet, supports full-duplex transmissions in a switched environment.

IEEE LAN Standards

As you learned earlier, the IEEE is an organization of professionals that creates standards for computers and communications. The IEEE 802 series of standards specifies various LAN technologies. See the IEEE Web site at *www.ieee.org* for more information.

Carrier Sense Multiple Access/Collision Detection (CSMA/CD)
The LAN access method used by Ethernet. Checks for network access availability with a signal.

A distinguishing factor among LAN technologies is their access methods. Access methods refer to the way data is placed on the physical wire for transmission. The IEEE 802 series includes the **Carrier Sense Multiple Access/Collision Detection (CSMA/CD)**, Token Ring, and demand priority access methods. Each method will be discussed shortly.

This section discusses the following IEEE 802 network standards:

- IEEE 802.2

- Ethernet/IEEE 802.3

- IEEE 802.3u — Fast Ethernet

- IEEE 802.3z and 802.3ab — Gigabit Ethernet

- IEEE 802.3ae — 10-Gigabit Ethernet

- IEEE 802.5 — Token Ring

- IEEE 802.11 — Wireless Ethernet

NOTE:
Keep in mind the importance of the IEEE 802 standards.

IEEE 802.2

All standards in the IEEE 802 series use the 802.2 standard. The 802.2 standard divides the OSI/RM data link layer into two sublayers:

- **Logical Link Control (LLC)** — This sublayer provides connection-oriented and connectionless services at the data link layer, which manages transmissions and can provide flow control.

NOTE:
Regardless of the upper-level protocol used, packets addressed to a specific computer will include a MAC address.

- **Media Access Control (MAC)** — The MAC sublayer provides:

    o   Access to the LAN media. The MAC sublayer is responsible for placing the data on the wire.

    o   The MAC address (also called a hardware address, physical address or Ethernet address).

Although Ethernet does not technically use the 802.2 standard, Ethernet is compatible with it and shares several important elements with the standard, such as the MAC sublayer.

NOTE:
In a routed network environment, the MAC address is used to send the packet from the router connected to the destination network to the final computer destination.

MAC addresses

MAC addresses are unique addresses that are burned on a NIC. The terms MAC-48 and EUI-48 (Extended Unique Identifier) are also used for MAC addresses. Each address is burned by the manufacturer and used to identify a computer on a network.

MAC addresses are called physical addresses, as opposed to logical addresses. Logical addresses are found at the network layer (Layer 3), and include IP and IPX addresses. Logical addresses are used to send data over internetworks to a remote destination. Physical addresses are found at the data link layer (Layer 2), and are often part of the physical interface. Physical addresses are used only to send data between two devices on a single network link.

hexadecimal
A base-16 number system that allows large numbers to be displayed by fewer characters than if the number were displayed in the regular base-10 system. In hexadecimal, the number 10 is represented as the letter A, 15 is represented as F, and 16 is represented as 10.

byte
A measurement of memory needed to store one 8-bit character.

NOTE:
You need to understand the MAC address format and be able to identify the vendor and serial number portions. Vendors are responsible for serial numbers. The combination of the vendor code and serial number will be unique.

OBJECTIVE
3.9.6: MAC address filtering

MAC addresses use 12 **hexadecimal** digits to form a 48-bit address (6 **bytes**). Each half of the address is used for a different purpose, as shown in Figure 1-25.

$$\underbrace{00 - 80 - 5F}_{\text{Vendor Code}} - \underbrace{EA - C6 - 10}_{\text{Interface Serial Number}}$$

Figure 1-25: MAC address components

The vendor code is identified in the first 24 bits (3 bytes). The vendor code in Figure 1-34 is for Compaq. Other vendor codes include Sun (08-00-20) and Cisco (00-00-0c). The vendor code is also known as the Organizationally Unique Identifier (OUI).

The interface serial number is identified in the last 24 bits. Determined by the vendor, the serial number is always unique to that vendor. In theory, no two MAC addresses are identical.

Even in a routed network environment — in which IP addresses determine where a packet will be sent — the MAC address is used to send the packet to its final destination once that packet has reached the local network segment on which the destination system resides.

In the following lab, you will view the MAC address on your system. Suppose you are troubleshooting a wireless system and you want to make sure that your system's MAC address is not being filtered out by the wireless network's security settings. You can view the MAC address to verify address components.

 Lab 1-1: Viewing the MAC address on your system

In this lab, you will use the *ipconfig* command to view the MAC address on your system.

1.   Select **Start**, type **cmd** in the Start Search text box, then press **ENTER**.

2.   In the command prompt window, enter the following command:

     ipconfig /all

     *Note: In Linux, you would use the **ifconfig** command, without any options or arguments.*

3.   Press **ENTER**.

4.   You will see a printout of all information relevant to your system's NIC.

5.   Look for the following parameter:

     Physical Address

6.   The Physical Address parameter records your system's MAC address. Write your system's MAC address in the space provided:

     _____

7.   Underline the vendor code portion of the MAC address.

8. The *ipconfig* command should tell you about the NIC vendor. Sometimes, however, this information is not available. The *ipconfig* command may not reveal this information, or you might be using another operating system that is less informative. If you have Internet access, open a browser and go to a search engine such as Google or AltaVista.

9. Type the vendor code portion of the MAC address in the browser's search text box.

   Note: You might also want to use the words "vendor code" (in quotation marks) in your search.

10. Write your NIC's vendor in the space provided:

   _____

11. Close your command prompt.

   *Tech Note: In Windows Vista, you can also view the MAC address by displaying the **Local Area Connection Status** dialog box, then clicking the **Details** button.*

   In this lab, you used the *ipconfig* command to view your system's MAC address.

Ethernet/IEEE 802.3

Ethernet is one of the most successful LAN technologies and is a predecessor to the IEEE 802.3 standard. Ethernet is a broadcast system for communication between systems. It uses the 10Base2, 10Base5 or 10BaseT wiring standards. It can also use fiber-optic cabling.

Even though Ethernet and IEEE 802.3 are supported together and used interchangeably, Ethernet does not totally comply with the 802.3 standard.

The differences between IEEE 802.3 and Ethernet do not hinder hardware manufacturers because IEEE 802.3 and Ethernet both support MAC addresses and the same physical layer. In addition, software that differentiates between the sublayers is available.

Ethernet/IEEE 802.3 access method

All networks that use Ethernet/IEEE 802.3 (including IEEE 802.3u, IEEE 802.3z and IEEE 802.3ab) use CSMA/CD. A station must make sure that no other transmission is already in progress. If no other station is transmitting, the sender can begin immediately. Collisions occur when two or more stations sense the channel is idle and begin to transmit simultaneously. If a collision occurs, all transmission ceases while the colliding stations are notified. The colliding stations then wait a random amount of time before transmitting.

Transmissions are broadcast to all stations. Only the destination system responds; all other systems discard the transmission. This process can create heavy traffic on a network. Therefore, it is important to divide larger Ethernet networks into segments (using a router, for example).

IEEE 802.3u — Fast Ethernet

NOTE:
Most newer Ethernet
NICs are 10/100
cards, supporting
both 10-Mbps and
100-Mbps Ethernet
and automatically
configuring
themselves online
based on the traffic
detected on the
network.

Fast Ethernet is a faster version of IEEE 802.3. It was originally developed by vendors such as 3Com, Cabletron, SynOptics, Digital, Grand Junction Networks and Intel. The IEEE 802.3 committee is responsible for Fast Ethernet. The major objective of the Fast Ethernet standard is to promote the use of Ethernet at 100 Mbps using the same access method, CSMA/CD.

Fast Ethernet supports the 100BaseTX and 100BaseT4 wiring standards, which require Category 5 UTP wiring to support 100 Mbps. It can also use 100BaseFX, which is fiber-optic cabling. Vendors support Fast Ethernet cards that use data rates of both 10 Mbps and 100 Mbps.

Many network administrators are upgrading their 10BaseT networks to 100BaseTX or 100BaseT4. In many cases, this upgrade can be accomplished by replacing 10BaseT NICs with 100BaseTX or 100BaseT4 NICs, and upgrading hubs to support both 10BaseT and 100BaseTX or 100BaseT4. This process is usually less expensive than upgrading to a 100BaseFX or16-Mbps token-ring network.

Table 1-5 displays the key differences between Ethernet and Fast Ethernet.

Table 1-5: Ethernet vs. Fast Ethernet

Category	Ethernet	Fast Ethernet
Speed	10 Mbps	100 Mbps
IEEE standard	IEEE 802.3	IEEE 802.3u
Access method	CSMA/CD	CSMA/CD
Topology	Bus/star	Star
Cable support	Coax/twisted pair/fiber	Twisted pair/fiber
UTP link distance (maximum)	100 meters	100 meters

IEEE 802.3z and 802.3ab — Gigabit Ethernet

Gigabit Ethernet, which offers a tenfold increase in data rates over the previous standard, is used primarily for network backbones. The Gigabit Ethernet standard transfers data at 1,000 Mbps using the CSMA/CD access method over either twisted pair or fiber optic.

The two types of Gigabit Ethernet are IEEE 802.3z and 802.3ab.

802.3z

The 802.3z standard is specified for the following two types of fiber-optic cable:

* **1000BaseLX** — uses a long wavelength laser. Will work over distances of up to 2 km over single-mode fiber (although many manufacturers guarantee distances of up to 10 km or 20 km). Over multi-mode fiber, the maximum cable length is 550 m.

- **1000BaseSX** — uses a near-infrared light wavelength over multi-mode fiber. Maximum cable length is 220 m. Popular for intra-building links in large corporations.

Cost must be considered when determining which fiber standard to implement.

802.3ab

The 802.3ab standard specifies Gigabit Ethernet over UTP cable.

- **1000BaseT** — requires Category 5 cable at a minimum, according to the standard, but a minimum of Category 5e is strongly recommended. Category 6 cable can also be used. Maximum segment length is 100 meters.

Unlike slower versions of Ethernet, 1000BaseT wiring uses all four pairs of wires.

IEEE 802.3ae (supplement) — 10-Gigabit Ethernet

The 10-Gigabit Ethernet standard (10GbE) is the fastest of the Ethernet standards, offering data rates of 10 Gbps (10 times faster than Gigabit Ethernet). The standard provides for transmission over the following types of fiber-optic cable:

- **10GBaseSR** — used for short distances (26 m to 82 m) over multi-mode fiber. Also supports 300 m over new multi-mode fiber.

- **10GBaseLRM** — used for distances up to 220 m on multi-mode fiber.

- **10GBaseER** — used for extended ranges of up to 40 km over single-mode fiber.

- **10GBaseLX4** — supports distances between 240 m and 300 m over multi-mode fiber using four separate laser sources operating on unique wavelengths. Also supports distances of 10 km over single-mode fiber.

NOTE:
Cat 7 cable is being designed for home use. It runs at 600 MHz, and because it can support cable TV, it will eventually replace coaxial cable.

802.3an amendment

The IEEE 802.3an amendment specifies 10-Gigabit Ethernet over twisted pair:

- **10GBaseT** — provides 10 Gbps over twisted pair using Category 6 or Category 7 cable and RJ-45 connectors. With Cat 6 cabling, the maximum cable length is 56 m. An augemented Category 6 cable specification "6a" designed to reduce crosstalk between UTP cables is expected to extend the length to 100 m. Maximum cable length for Cat 7 is 100 m.

OBJECTIVE
3.2.3: Ethernet vs. Token Ring

IEEE 802.5 — Token Ring

NOTE:
Token Ring use has become less common with the growth of star-topology Ethernet.

The Token Ring network is specified in the IEEE 802.5 definition. Token Ring was initially developed by IBM for its mainframe environment, and the IEEE 802.5 standard complies with the corporation's original development.

IEEE 802.5 access method

token passing
The LAN access method used by Token Ring networks. A data frame, or token, is passed from one node to the next around the network ring.

Whereas Ethernet uses the CSMA/CD access method, Token Ring networks use the **token passing** access method. Instead of sending broadcasts, as Ethernet does, a Token Ring network passes a token in one direction around the network. Each node processes the token to determine the destination. The node accepts the packet or places it back on the network ring. One or more tokens can circle the ring. With token passing, collisions do not occur; it is similar to a one-way street without cross traffic.

IEEE 802.11 — Wireless Ethernet

NOTE:
You should already understand the media required for creating a Wireless Ethernet network.

The 802.11 specification was introduced in 1997, and standardizes wireless LAN equipment and speeds. Such equipment is often called Wireless Ethernet equipment, and has become popular in homes, small businesses and large enterprises.

IEEE 802.11 wireless specifications

NOTE:
See **Activity 1-1: Reviewing IEEE 802.11 wireless standards.**

The 802.11 specifications are part of an evolving set of wireless network standards known as the 802.11 family. The particular specification under which a wireless network operates is called its "flavor." Following is a summary of the most common Wireless Ethernet specifications:

- **802.11 (WiFi)** — the original specification for wireless networking. Initially provided for data rates of 1 Mbps or 2 Mbps in the 2.4-GHz band using either FHSS or DSSS. At one time, the term WiFi applied only to products using the 802.11b standard, but today it applies to products that use the 802.11 standard.

NOTE:
Following are additional IEEE 802.11 specifications:

802.11c — specifies the use of MAC bridges, which are used to connect networks.

802.11d — for international wireless networks.

802.11e — quality of service standards for backbone networks. Can be used in 802.11a and 802.11b networks.

802.11f — standardizes wireless AP communication between different vendors.

802.11h — allows wireless networks to use the 5-GHz band, making them acceptable in Europe.

- **802.11a** — operates at up to 54 Mbps in the 5-GHz band. 802.11a uses OFDM for transmitting data. It also offers stronger encryption and more authentication features than 802.11b, and includes Forward Error Correction (FEC) to guard against data loss. 802.11a offers the same speed as 802.11g but offers higher capacity. 802.11a networks also allow the use of different channels, which helps avoid conflicts. The 802.11a standard was ratified after 802.11b and is not backward-compatible with 802.11b or 802.11g.

- **802.11b** — although not the first wireless standard, traditionally the most popular implementation. Operates at 11 Mbps (but will fall back to 5.5 Mbps, then to 2 Mbps, then to 1 Mbps if signal quality becomes an issue) in the 2.4-GHz band. Uses DSSS only. Because it operates in the 2.4-GHz band, it is subject to interference from microwave ovens, cordless phones and Bluetooth devices, which also operate in this band. The 802.11b standard also uses weak encryption and authentication, but is inexpensive and easy to install.

- **802.11g** — operates at speeds of up to 54 Mbps in the 2.4-GHz band. Backward-compatible with 802.11b. An 802.11g network card will work with an 802.11b access point, and an 802.11g access point will work with an 802.11b network card but only at speeds up to 11 Mbps. To achieve 54-Mbps throughput, you must use 802.11g network cards and access points. The 802.11g standard uses OFDM or DSSS. These networks provide security features similar to those provided by 802.11a networks.

- **802.11i (also known as WPA2)** — specifies security mechanisms for wireless networks. The specification provides improved encryption for networks that use 802.11a, 802.11b and 802.11g.

IEEE 802.11n wireless standard

NOTE:
As of this writing, the 802.11n standard is in its draft stage and is scheduled to be ratified by the IEEE in December 2009.

IEEE 802.11n is the most current wireless standard. It enables high-bandwidth applications such as streaming video to coexist with wireless VoIP. Compared to the previous wireless standards, 802.11n enables you to build bigger, faster wireless networks that deliver better reliability and capacity with more built-in security.

The 802.11g standard was ratified by the IEEE in 2003 but is becoming less adequate as applications become more complex and require more bandwidth. For example, the use of streaming video is difficult with 802.11g products, which have a theoretical maximum throughput speed of 54 Mbps. However, real-world speeds are generally in the 22 Mbps to 24 Mbps range, which is inadequate for video.

The 802.11n standard uses new technologies to give WiFi increased speed and range. These technologies are:

- **Multiple Input, Multiple Output (MIMO)**— uses multiple antennae to direct signals from one place to another. Instead of sending and receiving a single stream of data, MIMO can simultaneously transmit three streams of data and receive two. This technique enables more data to be transmitted in the same period of time. It also increases the range, or distance over which data can be transmitted. 802.11n equipment typically delivers more than twice the range of 802.11g equipment. The increased range of 802.11n also can mean fewer "dead spots" in coverage.

- **Channel bonding** — a technique in which two separate non-overlapping channels can be used at the same time to transmit data. This technique also increases the amount of data that can be transmitted.

- **Payload optimization (also known as packet aggregation)** — a technique that enables more data to be included in each transmitted packet.

You can periodically check the IEEE 802.11 Working Group for WLAN Standards site at www.ieee802.org/11/ for the latest information about wireless LAN standards.

IEEE 802.11 access method

The access method for the IEEE 802.11 specifications is **Carrier Sense Multiple Access/Collision Avoidance (CSMA/CA)**. CSMA/CA specifies that each node must inform other nodes of an intent to transmit. When the other nodes have been notified, the information is transmitted. This arrangement prevents collisions because all nodes are aware of a transmission before it occurs.

In the following lab, you will research IEEE LAN standards. Suppose that your IT supervisor has asked for the latest information on IEEE 802.11n. Where would you find this information on the Web?

Lab 1-2: Researching IEEE LAN standards

In this lab, you will use your favorite search engine to find more information about various IEEE LAN standards.

1. Open your Web browser and access your favorite search engine.

2. Enter a text string for a LAN standard — for example, "IEEE 802.11n" — and explore the various results.

3. Search for several LAN standards to gain a better understanding of the concepts, principles and speed ratings.

4. Close your browser.

Remember that information about standards and new technologies can be found all over the Web. Some resources may be more reliable than others. Spend some time researching this information.

T-Carrier System

NOTE:
You need to know the T-carrier bandwidths.

The T-carrier system is a North American digital transmission format that provides dedicated and private-line services for digital voice and data transmission at rates of up to 45 Mbps. T-carrier services are usually used to connect a LAN to a WAN, such as a company network to the Internet.

Table 1-6 shows common T-carrier system data transfer rates.

Table 1-6: T-carrier transfer rates

T-Carrier	Data Transfer Rate
T1	1.544 Mbps
T2	6.312 Mbps
T3	44.736 Mbps
T4	274.176 Mbps

A single 64-Kbps line is known as a DS0 line. A T1 line supports 24 DS0 channels. Each of the 24 channels in a T1 circuit can carry voice or data transmission. Japan uses the J-carrier system. This system has the same speeds as the T-carrier system.

Fractional T1

Fractional T1, also called FT1, allows customers to lease the 64-Kbps channels individually instead of the full T1 line.

Connecting a T1 line to a LAN

To connect a T1 line to a LAN, you need the following systems:

- **Channel Service Unit (CSU)** — the first point of contact for the T1 wires; it diagnoses and prepares the signals on the line for the LAN.

- **Data Service Unit (DSU)** — connects to the CSU and converts LAN signals into T1 signaling formats.

- **Multiplexor** — provides a mechanism to load multiple voice and data channels into the digital line.

- **Router** — provides the interface between the LAN and the T1 line.

E-Carrier System

NOTE:
Be careful not to confuse the T-carrier and E-carrier bandwidths.

The E-carrier system is a European digital transmission format similar to the North American T-carrier system. Each transmission speed is a multiple of the E1 format, which operates at 2.048 Mbps. Table 1-7 lists the five E-carrier speeds.

Table 1-7: E-carrier transfer rates

E-Carrier	Data Transfer Rate
E1	2.048 Mbps
E2	8.448 Mbps
E3	34.368 Mbps
E4	139.264 Mbps
E5	565.148 Mbps

E-carrier and J-carrier lines use the same equipment to connect LANs (for example, CSU/DSUs and multiplexors).

SONET/SDH

Synchronous Optical Network (SONET) is a high-speed fiber-optic system that is used by telecom companies and carriers. The European counterpart is the Synchronous Digital Hierarchy (SDH). SONET/SDH is primarily used for network backbones, such as the Internet backbone, because of its ability to transmit at high speeds (for example, 39.813 Gbps).

SONET implements a ring architecture with at least two data paths. If one path fails, the system uses the other path. Because of this feature, SONET/SDH is called a self-healing ring architecture. It uses TDM to simultaneously transmit multiple data streams.

Optical carrier (OC) refers to the optical signal, which defines the transmission in the SONET/SDH specification. The optical carrier levels are often called **OCx**.

In SDH, the term Synchronous Transport Module (STM) is used to describe the bandwidth provided. Table 1-8 provides common SONET and SDH data transfer rates. Notice the absence of an equivalent for OC-1 in SDH.

Synchronous Optical Network (SONET)
High-speed fiber-optic system used as a network and Internet backbone. The European counterpart is the Synchronous Digital Hierarchy (SDH).

OCx
Optical carrier levels; defines the transmission speeds used in SONET/SDH.

Table 1-8: SONET/SDH system data rates

SONET Service	Data Transfer Rate	SDH Service	Data Transfer Rate
OC-1	51.84 Mbps	**No equivalent**	N/A
OC-3	155.52 Mbps	STM-1	155.52 Mbps
OC-12	622.08 Mbps	STM-4	622 Mbps
OC-48	2488.32 Mbps	STM-16	2.488.32 Gbps
OC-192	9953.28 Mbps	STM-64	9.953 Gbps
OC-768	39813.12 Mbps	STM-256	39.813 Gbps

Downloading Files with BitTorrent

BitTorrent
A peer-to-peer file sharing protocol used for distributing large amounts of data.

BitTorrent is a peer-to-peer (P2P) protocol that you can use to download large files quickly. BitTorrent allows a file provider to make his or her file (or files) available to the network via a central server, called a tracker. The initial file is called a seed. Other users, called peers, can then connect to the tracker and download the file. Each peer who downloads a seed makes it available to other peers to download. After the file is successfully downloaded by a peer, he or she can continue to make the data available to others, thereby creating additional seeds.

BitTorrent's strength lies in the fact that peers can download a seed from another peer, and, at the same time, upload parts or all of the seed for other peers to access. In other words, different parts of seeds can be distributed in chunks and then reassembled on the receiving machine. This ability allows a large number of peers to be supported simultaneously and the tracker bandwidth to be utilized as efficiently as possible. Relative to standard Internet hosting, the use of BitTorrent significantly reduces the original provider's hardware and bandwidth resource costs.

Peers often use BitTorrent to distribute large files, such as video games, movies or software applications, because it is much cheaper, faster and more efficient to distribute files using BitTorrent than via a regular download. In contrast to other file transfer protocols, BitTorrent works better as the number of peers downloading and uploading a particular file increases.

NOTE:
See **Optional Lab 1-1: Using BitTorrent to download files.**

In order to download files from BitTorrent, you must install a BitTorrent client on your computer. A BitTorrent client manages file downloads and uploads using the BitTorrent protocol. Popular BitTorrent clients include the following:

- BitTorrent (the original client) (*www.bittorrent.com*)

- uTorrent (*www.utorrent.com*)

- BitLord (*www.bitlord.com*)

- BitComet (*www.bitcomet.com*)

- BitTornado (*www.bittornado.com*)

- Vuze (*www.vuze.com*)

- Transmission (for Mac OS X) (*www.transmissionbt.com*)

- ABC (*http://pingpong-abc.sourceforge.net/*)

In addition to a BitTorrent client, you also need a "torrent" file to download content. A torrent file is a small file that contains the necessary information to download the content you want. This is generally obtained from a torrent Web site. Many sites offer torrents as one method of downloading files.

NOTE:
When you research torrent Web sites, be careful of sites that contain inappropriate or objectionable content.

Following are some sites you can explore to find torrents:

- *www.legaltorrents.com*

- *www.legittorrents.info*

- *http://linuxtracker.org*

- *www.tuxdistro.com*

- *http://newteevee.com/2007/03/03/ten-sites-for-free-and-legal-torrents/*

When using BitTorrent, you should be careful that you are not illicitly copying and distributing copyrighted material. Some unscrupulous users use BitTorrent for this purpose in an attempt to obtain something for free that they should otherwise pay for. This is particularly true for music and movie files. BitTorrent users generally use the protocol to obtain files because:

- The data is free.

- They are unable to purchase the data elsewhere.

- They want to "try before they buy."

- They want to download content that was intended to be freely distributed by the creator.

To learn more about BitTorrent, visit *www.bittorrent.com.*

Virtualization

virtualization
A software technology that enables you to run multiple virtual operating systems and applications on a single physical computer.

In regular computer usage, most computers use a single operating system, such as Windows, Linux or Macintosh, and you can launch any applications compatible with that operating system. **Virtualization** allows you to run multiple virtual operating systems and applications on a single physical computer. The operating systems and applications share the resources of the single computer across multiple environments.

Virtualization software transforms the hardware resources of a physical computer, such as the CPU, RAM, hard disk and network devices, to create a fully functional virtual computer that can run its own operating systems and applications.

OBJECTIVE
3.10.1: Elements of virtualization

Examples of virtualization software include the following:

- VMware (*www.vmware.com*)

- Parallels (*www.parallels.com*)

- VirtualBox (*www.virtualbox.org*)

Virtualization software creates a thin layer of software in a special environment called a virtual machine. The virtual machine contains an unmodified operating system and all of its installed software, and runs on top of your existing operating system. The virtual machine is completely compatible with all standard operating systems, applications and device drivers.

The physical computer is the "host" and the virtual machine is the "guest." Most of the guest's code runs unmodified, directly on the host computer. The guest operating system operates as if it is running on the physical computer because it has access to the hardware components and features of the physical computer. You can safely run several guests concurrently on a single computer, with each having access to the resources it needs, when it needs them. By using virtual machines, you can run a Linux guest and a Macintosh guest on a Windows host, for example.

Requirements for virtualization

Because the virtual machines are sharing the resources of the physical computer, it is important that you consider the amount of RAM and disk space you have available, and your computer's processing speed. For example, you may have several guests that take up 25 MB of hard disk space and use a considerable amount of your computer's available memory. If you want to open several such guests, you need to make sure that your host system is able to accommodate the guest's resource consumption.

OBJECTIVE
3.10.2: Benefits of virtualization

Benefits of virtualization

There are many benefits to virtualization:

- You can run multiple operating systems on a single computer.

- You can run software written for one operating system on another without the need to reboot your computer.

- You can reduce the number of computers needed and reduce capital costs by placing many virtual machines onto a few powerful hosts.

- Energy efficiency is increased because the consumption of electricity is reduced and less heat is generated.

- Because fewer computers are needed, you will be able to conserve physical space and make more efficient use of existing hardware.

- You can take "snapshots" of existing states, so that you can restore a previous version of the virtual machine without the need to make backups.

- You can set the virtual machines to non-persistent states. This is useful in a training environment in which you want the operating system to be restored to its pre-training state before the next session.

In the following lab, you will learn more about virtualization. Suppose your company's development staff needs to create training materials that demonstrate applications that run on various operating systems. In an attempt to stay within your department's budget, your IT supervisor has asked you to evaluate several virtualization clients to determine whether installing guest environments would allow the developers to accomplish their goals without the need to purchase additional hardware.

 Lab 1-3: Evaluating virtualization applications

In this lab, you will visit three Web sites to learn more about how you can use virtual machines to run multiple operating systems on the same physical computer.

1. Open your browser and go to ***www.vmware.com*** to access the VMware site. In the Understanding Virtualization section at the left side of the page, click various links, and download any demos or podcasts that you find to learn more about virtualization and VMware.

2. In your browser, go to ***www.parallels.com*** to access the Parallels site. In the top navigation bar, click **News & Events**. On the News And Events page, you will find links for **Webcasts** and **Videos**. Click each of these links to view Webcasts and videos for topics in which you may be interested to learn more about virtualization and Parallels.

3. In your browser, go to ***www.virtualbox.org*** to access the VirtualBox site. Click the **Screenshots** link in the left navigation pane to take a tour of the VirtualBox features. Click other links of interest to learn more about virtualization and VirtualBox.

4. Close the browser window.

Now that you have researched the Web sites of three popular virtualization applications, is it easier for you to see how beneficial virtualization can be?

Case Study

Proper Protocol

Elena is a networking consultant. Three customers have asked her which protocol(s) would be best to implement their changing network requirements.

- Customer 1 is currently using IPX/SPX. The customer uses the network to access a database, receive e-mail and transfer files. This customer now wants to use a P2P application, browse the Web and check Internet e-mail (SMTP and IMAP). Customer 1 wants Elena to recommend a new protocol that will enable her to create a WAN.

- Customer 2 has asked Elena to configure 10 Windows Vista systems to use TCP/IP so that they can communicate with NetWare servers that have existed since 1996. Elena installed NWLink on the Vista systems, yet they cannot communicate with the NetWare servers. However, these Windows Vista systems can communicate with one another.

- Customer 3 is designing a new network that will include Windows Server 2008 and Linux servers. All the servers will need to support Windows Server 2008, UNIX, Linux and Macintosh clients. The network will be implemented as a WAN with more than 2,000 nodes located in different areas of the United States. All systems will need to access the Internet. This customer wants Elena to install any and all necessary protocol(s).

Elena responded as follows to these three customers:

- For Customer 1, Elena recommended TCP/IP. This protocol supports routing and can be used with other protocols that the client wants to use. Although P2P applications may exist for IPX/SPX, the ones that use TCP/IP are typical.

- For Client 2, Elena checked the frame type on the older system and adjusted the frame type setting on the Vista systems.

- For Client 3, Elena installed TCP/IP as the only protocol. All servers and clients listed support TCP/IP. Also, the fact that the network will be implemented as a WAN means that a routable protocol is required.

*   *   *

Consider the following questions for each of Elena's solutions.

- Is the solution effective?

- What alternatives, if any, might also work for this customer?

Lesson Summary

Application project

Does your company use both LAN and WAN technologies? To your knowledge, is your network an Ethernet, Token Ring, Fast Ethernet or Gigabit Ethernet network? Could any of the technologies you learned in this lesson improve your current network's performance?

The costs of using fiber optics and switches are becoming more affordable for many organizations. Do you think these technologies might soon completely replace traditional hubs, routers and copper-wire-based networks? Visit the Cisco Web site (*www.cisco.com*) and identify products discussed in this lesson, such as routers, switches and wireless access points.

Next, access the Nortel Networks Web site (*www.nortel.com*) and identify its competing products.

Search the Internet to locate several other companies that offer LAN and WAN devices. Locate pricing information for an Ethernet 16-port 10/100 switch. How does it compare with the price of a 16-port 10/100 hub? Are the additional network speed and manageability worth the price difference?

Skills review

In this lesson, you learned about basic networking concepts, networking models, networking categories and network topologies. You received an overview of the major networking operating systems. You learned about the OSI reference model, packet creation, and the fundamentals of key network protocols, such as TCP/IP.

You also acquired a basic understanding of LANs and WANs and studied the communication devices involved, including NICs, hubs, routers and switches. Transmission media types were introduced, such as twisted-pair, coaxial and fiber-optic cable, as well as wireless media. You also studied transmission types and learned about network standards, such as IEEE LAN standards.

Finally, you learned how to download large amounts of data using BitTorrent, and you studied the benefits of creating virtual machines to run multiple operating systems on the same physical computer.

Now that you have completed this lesson, you should be able to:

✓ 3.1.1: Define basic data and telephony network concepts, including convergence, Voice over IP (VoIP), AC/DC requirements for telephony and data equipment.

✓ 3.1.3: Identify basic network topologies (e.g., ring, mesh).

✓ 3.1.4: Define the Open Systems Interconnection reference model (OSI/RM) in terms of packet creation.

✓ 3.1.5: Define the nature, purpose and operation essentials of Transmission Control Protocol/Internet Protocol (TCP/IP).

✓ 3.1.6: Define local area network (LAN) and wide area network (WAN).

✓ 3.1.7: Identify the core components of the current Internet infrastructure and how they relate to each other, including routers, Internet Exchange Points (IXPs), backbone networks.

✓ 3.1.8: Identify the components of a Network Operations Center (NOC).

✓ 3.2.1: Distinguish among common cable types used in networking (e.g., CAT 5, CAT 6, crossover).

✓ 3.2.2: Identify hardware and software connection devices and their uses, including network interface card, modem, cable/DSL modem, hub, router, switch, firewall.

✓ 3.2.3: Distinguish between Ethernet and Token Ring networks.

✓ 3.9.1: Distinguish between ad-hoc and infrastructure mode.

✓ 3.9.2: Identify the function of a wireless access point (AP).

✓ 3.9.3: Connect wireless networks to standard wired LANs.

✓ 3.9.4: Identify benefits and drawbacks of Wired Equivalent Privacy (WEP).

✓ 3.9.5: Use a Secure Set Identifier (SSID) and describe its purpose.

✓ 3.9.6: Identify the purpose of MAC address filtering.

✓ 3.9.7: Identify security issues with wireless networks.

✓ 3.9.8: Evaluate the practicality of a wireless LAN in an organization.

✓ 3.9.9: Troubleshoot wireless connectivity.

✓ 3.10.1: List elements of virtualization (e.g., virtual machines, host operating system, virtualization software, RAM, processor speed, and disk space).

✓ 3.10.2: Identify benefits of virtualization, including reduced consumption of electricity, less heat generation, conservation of space, more efficient use of hardware.

Lesson 1 Review

1. What is the purpose of a Network Operations Center (NOC)?

   _____

   _____

   _____

   _____

   _____

2. Your company is using P2P technology to distribute software. Where is this software stored?

   _____

3. Name at least three products that are often called flavors of UNIX.

   _____

4. What three elements are common to all networks?

   _____

5. List the seven OSI/RM layers, beginning with Layer 7.

   _____

   _____

6. Why is it important for operating system vendors to consider the OSI/RM when developing networking software?

   _____

   _____

7. What is the difference between routable and non-routable protocols?

   _____

   _____

8. Name the two types of twisted-pair cable, and the two varieties of wire available for each.

   _____

   _____

9. What are the two major types of fiber-optic cable?

   _____

10. A network administrator suspects a security problem on a wireless network, and has changed the SSID on the wireless access point. How will existing wireless network clients be affected?

_____

_____

_____

11. What is virtualization?

_____

_____

_____

Lesson 1
Supplemental Material

This section is a supplement containing additional tasks for you to complete in conjunction with the lesson. These elements are:

- **Activities**
  Pen-and-paper activities to review lesson concepts or terms.

- **Optional Labs**
  Computer-based labs to provide additional practice.

- **Lesson Quiz**
  Multiple-choice test to assess knowledge of lesson material.

Activity 1-1: Reviewing IEEE 802.11 wireless standards

In this activity, you will match each IEEE 802.11 wireless standard with its correct description.

1. 802.11 (WiFi)

2. 802.11a

3. 802.11b

4. 802.11g

5. 802.11i (WPA2)

6. 802.11n

A. The most popular wireless implementation. It uses weak encryption and authentication, but is inexpensive and easy to install.

B. The original specification for wireless networking. It provides for data rates of 1 Mbps or 2 Mbps in the 2.4-GHz band using either FHSS or DSSS.

C. The most current wireless standard. It enables high-bandwidth applications such as streaming video to coexist with wireless VoIP.

D. Specifies security mechanisms with strong encryption for wireless networks that use other 802.11 specifications.

E. Operates at up to 54 Mbps in the 5-GHz band. It uses OFDM for transmitting data and includes Forward Error Correction (FEC) to guard against data loss.

F. Operates at speeds of up to 54 Mbps in the 2.4-GHz band and uses OFDM or DSSS.

 ### Optional Lab 1-1: Using a BitTorrent client to download files

In this optional lab, you will use a BitTorrent client to download a torrent. The torrent is supplied on the companion CD-ROM and contains a compressed version of the FileZilla FTP client. At the end of the lab, you will have a new compression utility, 7-Zip, and a new FTP client, FileZilla, at your disposal.

Tech Note: If you are behind a firewall, you may not be able to perform this optional lab because many firewalls block BitTorrent traffic.

1. Open **Windows Explorer**, navigate to the **C:\CIW\Network\Lab Files\Lesson01** folder, then double-click **utorrent.exe**. Click **Run** in the Security Warning dialog box that appears, then follow the instructions to install uTorrent. When the installation is finished, the uTorrent window will appear.

   Note: You can visit the uTorrent home page (www.utorrent.com) for tips, instructions and user guides about using uTorrent.

2. **uTorrent:** In the uTorrent window, select **File | Add Torrent** to display the Select A Torrent To Open dialog box.

3. Navigate to the **C:\CIW\Network\Lab Files\Lesson01** folder if necessary, double-click **FileZilla_v3.0.2.1.torrent**, then click **OK**. The torrent file contains all of the information necessary for the BitTorrent protocol to download the FileZilla FTP client.

4. The uTorrent window should reappear containing the FileZilla_v3.0.2.1.torrent file. The torrent file should start downloading automatically. If no activity occurs after a few seconds, click the **Start** button in the toolbar.

   Note: The torrent file may take a considerable amount of time to begin downloading.

NOTE:
Consider the percentage value in the Done column indicating how much of the file has been downloaded; the time estimate to complete the download in the ETA column; and the Pieces bar in the bottom pane illustrating how non-contiguous chunks from different seeds are being assembled in order to piece the file together.

5. When the download operation commences, the uTorrent window will display information about its progress. Click the torrent file to select it. Notice that additional information about the download displays in the bottom pane of the window, as shown in Figure OL1-1.

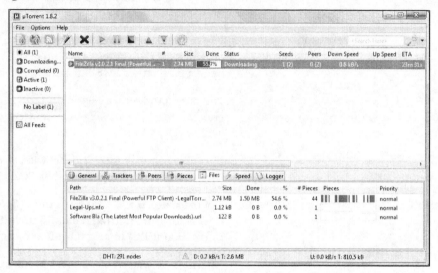

Figure OL1-1: uTorrent download — in progress

6. **Explorer:** While you are waiting for the torrent file to download, double-click **7z465.exe** in the Lab Files\Lesson01 folder and perform the necessary steps to install the 7-Zip application. 7-Zip is an open-source compression utility that you will use to unzip the compressed FileZilla application later in this lab.

7. **Browser:** If the torrent file is still downloading, you can browse the following Web sites to learn more about BitTorrent while you wait:

   • *http://computer.howstuffworks.com/bittorrent.htm*

   • *http://answers.yahoo.com/question/index?qid=20090329065748AAllU9a*

   • *www.wisegeek.com/what-is-bittorrent.htm*

   • *www.explainthatstuff.com/howbittorrentworks.html*

NOTE:
The download can take anywhere from several minutes to over an hour to complete.

8. **uTorrent:** If the torrent file is taking an inordinate amount of time to download, click the **Stop** button in the toolbar to suspend the process. You will not be able to complete the remaining steps in this lab. If the file downloads successfully, proceed to the next step.

9. **uTorrent:** Right-click the torrent and select **Open Containing Folder**. This action opens the folder containing the downloaded FileZilla torrent.

10. **Explorer:** Right-click the **FileZilla v3.0.2.1 Final (Powerful FTP Client) – LegalTorrents.rar** file, then select **7-Zip | Open Archive**. This action starts the 7-Zip compression utility and extracts the FileZilla binary.

11. Double-click **FileZilla_3.0.2.1_win32-setup.exe** and perform the necessary steps to install FileZilla.

12. **uTorrent:** With the torrent file still selected, click the **Remove** button in the toolbar, then click **Yes**. This action removes the FileZilla torrent file from uTorrent. As long as the torrent file remains in uTorrent, you are seeding it to other peers who may be trying to download FileZilla via BitTorrent.

13. Select **File | Exit**, then click **Yes** to exit uTorrent.

14. Close the remaining open windows.

15. Select **Start | All Programs | FileZilla Client | FileZilla**. The FileZilla application will open, which is an open-source FTP client you can use to transfer files over a network.

16. Close the **FileZilla** window.

17. Did you think that uTorrent was easy to use? Can you think of legitimate uses of BitTorrent to help you at work or in school?

In this optional lab, you used the uTorrent client to download a torrent and install the resulting application.

 Optional Lab 1-2: Exploring network operating systems

The purpose of this optional lab is to introduce you to some fundamental information about the network configurations being used in this course.

1. Restart your system and watch the startup process. Your operating system will be identified during startup. What operating system are you running? Is it a network client or a network operating system? Write your responses in the space provided:

    _____

    _____

2. Select **Start | Control Panel**, then click the **Classic View** hyperlink (if necessary) to display the classic Windows 2000 interface.

3. Double-click the **System** icon to display the System window.

4. Review the information in the Computer Name, Domain And Workgroup Settings section. Is your computer configured as a member of a workgroup?

    _____

5. Close all windows and return to your Desktop.

Even though operating systems such as Windows Vista are technically considered network operating systems, they can also be deployed in peer-to-peer (or workgroup) network environments. When deployed in a workgroup, the server is typically referred to as a stand-alone server.

Optional Lab 1-3: Implementing a wireless network

In this optional lab, you will implement a wireless network.

1. Obtain a wireless AP.

2. Obtain two wireless NICs.

3. Configure the wireless AP to use a SSID such as ciw-certified (lowercase, as SSIDs are case-sensitive). Do not configure the AP to use encryption at this point.

4. Configure the wireless NICs to use infrastructure mode. Do not enable encryption on the NICS.

5. Configure the NICs to use the same SSID as the AP.

6. You should now have basic connectivity. Troubleshoot the connection if problems occur. Troubleshooting tools can include:

   - Verifying settings in the software that configures the wireless AP.

   - Verifying settings in the software that configures each wireless NIC.

7. Plug the wireless AP into a standard hub and try to get the wireless systems to communicate with standard wired clients. If the hub is attached to a router with Internet access, try to configure the wireless systems to communicate on the Internet (set a default gateway).

In this lab, you configured a wireless network.

Lesson 1 Quiz

1. A server is:

    a. a computer connected to a mainframe.
    b. a computer that acts as a mainframe.
    c. a computer that shares resources with other computers on a network.
    d. a front-end computer.

2. What is a packet?

    a. A protocol that enables information to be sent across a network
    b. Another name for an e-mail message
    c. A protocol that sends e-mail messages
    d. A fixed piece of information sent across a network

3. Which OSI layer is responsible for the reliability of the data sent between hosts?

    a. Transport layer
    b. Presentation layer
    c. Network layer
    d. Application layer

4. A local area network (LAN) is:

    a. a group of computers connected over an expansive geographic area.
    b. another name for a peer-to-peer network.
    c. a group of computers connected within a confined geographic area.
    d. another name for a server-based network.

5. Wireless networks are specified in which of the following IEEE standards?

    a. IEEE 802.2
    b. IEEE 802.3
    c. IEEE 802.5
    d. IEEE 802.11

Lesson 2: TCP/IP Suite and Internet Addressing

Objectives

By the end of this lesson, you will be able to:

- 3.1.5: Define the nature, purpose and operation essentials of Transmission Control Protocol/Internet Protocol (TCP/IP).

- 3.2.4: Explain the routing process, including static routing versus dynamic routing, interior versus exterior routing protocols.

- 3.2.5: Identify common TCP/IP network parameters, including IP address (static versus DHCP), subnet mask, default gateway, DNS information.

- 3.3.1: Explain IP addressing and the concept of uniqueness, including IP address, subnet mask.

- 3.3.2: Define IP address classes used on the Internet and determine valid IP addresses.

- 3.3.3: Identify the uses of public and private IP addresses.

- 3.3.4: Determine default subnet masks and describe the ANDing process.

- 3.3.5: Define Classless Interdomain Routing (CIDR).

- 3.3.6: Identify basic IPv6 concepts.

- 3.6.1: Identify issues to consider when troubleshooting IP-enabled systems, including DNS/name resolution, correct default gateway and subnet mask, hosts file configuration, DHCP versus static IP configuration.

- 3.6.2: Identify when to use various diagnostic tools for troubleshooting and resolving Internet problems, including ping, ipconfig, route, arp, traceroute, netstat, network analyzers (packet sniffers).

- 3.6.3: Distinguish between client-side problems and server-side problems when troubleshooting common services (e.g., e-mail and Web client connectivity issues).

- 3.6.4: Troubleshoot cable and ADSL modem connectivity.

Pre-Assessment Questions

1. Which of the following protocols in the TCP/IP suite is categorized as an application-layer protocol?

    a. PPP
    b. TCP
    c. UDP
    d. FTP

2. What is the port number most often associated with HTTP?

    a. Port 21
    b. Port 25
    c. Port 80
    d. Port 443

3. What is a network analyzer?

    _____

Introduction to TCP/IP

OBJECTIVE
3.1.5: TCP/IP

NOTE:
Remember that TCP/IP is considered the *de facto* standard for LAN and WAN implementations. A complete understanding of TCP/IP concepts is critical.

Transmission Control Protocol/Internet Protocol (TCP/IP) allows computers from different vendors with various operating systems and capabilities (from mainframes to desktop computers) to communicate. Since its implementation in 1983 by the major networks that made up the Internet, TCP/IP has far exceeded expectations. Today, it is the most widely used networking protocol suite in the world, and it is the language of communication on the Internet.

For one computer to communicate with another computer over a TCP/IP network, it must know the other computer's Internet address. Each computer, or node, has its own 32-bit Internet address, called an Internet Protocol (IP) address. The IP address uniquely identifies and distinguishes a node from any other node on the Internet.

This lesson will discuss the Internet architecture, common protocols used on the Internet, and Request For Comments (RFC) documents that define and reference Internet protocols. It will also cover IP addressing, address classes, addressing rules, reserved addresses and subnet masks. The lesson will conclude with a discussion of diagnostic tools used to troubleshoot TCP/IP networks.

Internet Architecture

Similar to other networking models, the Internet architecture divides protocols into layers. Each layer is responsible for specific communication tasks. The Internet architecture consists of four layers, each coinciding with layers in the OSI/RM. Figure 2-1 illustrates the Internet architecture, and Table 2-1 displays the OSI/RM and the Internet architecture equivalents. Please note that several Internet architecture models exist, each slightly different from the others. A four-layer version was selected for this course.

Application Layer
Transport Layer
Internet Layer
Network Access Layer

Figure 2-1: Internet architecture

Table 2-1: OSI/RM and Internet architecture layer equivalents

OSI/RM Layer	Internet Architecture Equivalent
Application	Application
Presentation	
Session	Transport
Transport	
Network	Internet
Data Link	Network Access
Physical	

Network access layer

NOTE:
Refer back to the
OSI/RM, if
necessary, to help
you understand that
model.

The network access layer of the Internet architecture corresponds to the physical and data link layers of the OSI reference model. The network access layer accepts higher-layer datagrams and transmits them over the attached network, handling all the hardware details of interfacing with the network media. This layer usually consists of:

• The operating system's device driver.

• The corresponding network interface card.

• The physical connections.

For Ethernet-based LANs, the data sent over the media are called Ethernet frames, which range in size from 64 to 1,518 bytes (1,514 bytes without the Cyclical Redundancy Check).

Internet layer

The Internet layer of the Internet architecture corresponds to the network layer of the OSI model. It is responsible for addressing and routing packets on TCP/IP networks. A packet received from the transport layer is encapsulated in an IP packet. Based on the destination host information, the Internet layer uses a routing algorithm to determine whether to deliver the packet locally or send it to a default gateway.

Following are the protocols used at the Internet layer:

• Internet Protocol (IP)

• Internet Control Message Protocol (ICMP)

• Internet Group Management Protocol (IGMP)

• Address Resolution Protocol (ARP)

• Reverse Address Resolution Protocol (RARP)

Transport layer

NOTE:
The Internet-layer,
transport-layer and
application-layer
protocols are
discussed in more
detail later in the
lesson.

The transport layer of the Internet architecture corresponds to the transport and session layers of the OSI/RM. The transport layer accepts application-layer data and provides the flow of information between two hosts using the following two different transport protocols:

• Transmission Control Protocol (TCP)

• User Datagram Protocol (UDP)

The transport layer also divides the data received from the application layer into smaller pieces, called packets, which you were introduced to earlier. Each packet is passed to the Internet layer.

NOTE:
Unlike most other
connectionless
protocols, UDP does
support error
checking through
CRC.

 The transport layer is also known as the host-to-host layer, the end-to-end layer, or the source-to-destination layer.

Application layer

The application layer of the Internet architecture corresponds to the presentation and application layers of the OSI/RM. The application layer interacts with the transport-layer protocols to send or receive data.

Telnet
The Internet standard protocol for remote terminal connection service.

Users can invoke application programs and protocols, including **Telnet**, File Transfer Protocol (FTP), Simple Mail Transfer Protocol (SMTP) and Simple Network Management Protocol (SNMP), for access to nodes on the Internet.

 The application layer is also called the process layer.

Requests for Comments (RFCs)

Request for Comments (RFC)
A document published by the IETF that details information about standardized Internet protocols and those in various development stages.

Requests for Comments (RFCs) are published documents of interest to the Internet community. They include detailed information about standardized Internet protocols, such as IP and TCP, and those in various stages of development. They also include informational documents regarding protocol standards, assigned numbers (for example, port numbers), host requirements (for example, data link, network, transport and application OSI layers) and router requirements.

NOTE:
You need to know the function of RFCs for the CIW v5 Foundations exam.

RFCs are identified by number. The higher the number, the more recent the RFC. Be sure you are viewing the most recent RFC during your research. A recommended RFC reference site is located at *www.rfc-editor.org/rfc.html*.

 If an RFC has been updated, the index listing (in other words, the RFC editor query results) will state the replacement RFC number.

Protocol states

Before a protocol becomes a standard, it passes through four maturity-level protocol states: experimental, proposed, draft and standard. If a protocol becomes obsolete, it is classified as historic. To progress through the steps, the protocol must be recommended by the Internet Engineering Steering Group (IESG) of the Internet Engineering Task Force (IETF).

Maturity-level protocol states

Following are descriptions of the four maturity-level protocol states:

- **Experimental** — protocols that should only be used in a laboratory (or experimental) situation. They are not intended for operation on systems other than those participating in the experiment.

- **Proposed** — protocols that may be considered for future standardization. Testing and research are encouraged, optimally by several groups. These protocols will probably be revised before progressing to the next stage.

- **Draft** — protocols being seriously considered by the IESG to become Internet standards. Testing is encouraged, test results are analyzed and feedback is requested. All feedback should be sent to the IESG. Changes are often made at the draft stage; the protocol must then return to the proposed stage.

- **Standard** — protocols determined by the IESG to be official standard protocols on the Internet. Standard protocols are of two types: those that apply to the entire Internet, and those that apply only to certain networks.

Additional protocol states

Following are descriptions of additional protocol states:

- **Historic** — protocols that have been replaced by more recent ones or that never received enough interest to develop. Historic protocols are highly unlikely to become Internet standards.

- **Informational** — protocols developed outside the IETF/IESG (for example, protocols developed by vendors or by other standardization organizations). These protocols are posted for the benefit of the Internet community.

RFC STD 1

Documents at the draft stage usually become standards after a lengthy review process. The IETF recognizes the importance of remaining aware of draft RFCs that become standards. To ensure that everyone can readily discover when an RFC becomes a standard, the IETF has created the STD 1 document (often known as STD 0001). The STD 1 document is a live document (in other words, one that is being continually updated). Whenever an RFC becomes a standard, the STD 1 document is updated, often on a quarterly basis. You can obtain the STD 1 document at the RFC Editor site at *www.rfc-editor.org*. Search for the number 1, and you will find the latest STD 1 document. The actual document is published as a new RFC (for example, RFC 3300) whenever enough changes warrant an update.

Internet Protocols

NOTE:
Activity 2-1:
Reviewing TCP/IP protocols provides additional practice in identifying TCP/IP protocols.

Each layer of the Internet architecture involves protocols. The next section briefly describes common protocols, by layer, used on the Internet. Each protocol is listed with its respective RFC(s). Figure 2-2 illustrates these relationships within the Internet architecture. These protocols will be discussed in detail throughout the course.

HTTP	FTP	Telnet	NNTP	Gopher	SMTP
SNMP	DNS	BOOTP	DHCP	SIP	H.323

Application Layer

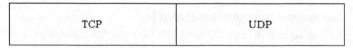

TCP	UDP

Transport Layer

ICMP		IGMP
ARP	IP	RARP

Internet Layer

Media

Network Access Layer

Figure 2-2: Internet protocols and Internet architecture

Network access layer

The protocols used at the network access layer of the Internet architecture can vary considerably, depending on which technologies are responsible for placing data on the network media and pulling data off. Examples of these technologies include:

- **LANs** — Ethernet, Token Ring and FDDI.

- **WANs** — frame relay, serial lines and ATM.

Internet layer

NOTE:
You need to be familiar with the protocols, but do not need to know the RFCs or Internet standards.

The following protocols are used at the Internet layer of the Internet architecture:

- **Internet Protocol (IP)** — the basic data-transfer method used throughout the Internet. It is responsible for IP addressing and performs the routing function, which selects a path to send data to the destination IP address. IP is defined in RFC 791.

NOTE:
Several TCP/IP utilities, including *tracert*, use ICMP.

- **Internet Control Message Protocol (ICMP)** — the troubleshooting protocol of TCP/IP. It allows Internet hosts and gateways to report errors through ICMP messages. If a problem occurs on a TCP/IP network, an ICMP message will probably be generated. ICMP is specified in RFC 792.

- **Internet Group Management Protocol (IGMP)** — used for multicasting, in which one source sends a message to a group of subscribers (multicast groups). For multicast delivery to be successful, members must identify themselves and the groups that interest them to local multicast-enabled routers. IGMP allows users to join and maintain membership in multicast groups. IGMP is defined in RFC 1112.

NOTE:
ARP is used internally by communication applications. ARP results are cached locally by the computer issuing the resolution request.

- **Address Resolution Protocol (ARP)** — translates Internet addresses to physical addresses. For example, it uses your IP address to discover your computer's Ethernet address. ARP is specified in RFC 826.

- **Reverse Address Resolution Protocol (RARP)** — performs the reverse function of ARP. It uses a node's hardware address to request an IP address. RARP is generally used for diskless workstations and X terminals. RARP is defined in RFC 903.

Transport layer

The following protocols are used at the transport layer of the Internet architecture:

NOTE:
UDP is often referred to as an unreliable protocol. UDP does not build a connection before sending data, as does TCP. Any protocol that first builds a connection before sending data is considered reliable.

- **Transmission Control Protocol (TCP)** — provides session management between the source and destination systems. It ensures that data is delivered, that it is in sequence and that no duplicate data is sent. Two computers must contact each other through a TCP connection (in other words, a session must be established) before transferring data. TCP is defined in RFC 793.

- **User Datagram Protocol (UDP)** — provides a simple datagram form of communication. One UDP packet is created for each output operation by an application, and a session is not necessary. UDP does not provide congestion control, use acknowledgments, retransmit lost datagrams or guarantee reliability, as does TCP. UDP is defined in RFC 768.

Application layer

NOTE:
Consider HTTPS, which is a variation that supports secure transfers.

The following protocols are used at the application layer of the Internet architecture:

- **Hypertext Transfer Protocol (HTTP)** — used to transport HTML documents (Web pages) across the Internet. HTTP requires a client program on one end (a browser) and a server on the other, both running TCP/IP. HTTP establishes a Web server connection and transmits HTML pages to a client browser. HTTP 1.0 establishes a new protocol connection for each page requested, which creates unnecessary Internet traffic. HTTP 1.1 uses persistent connections, which allow multiple downloads with one connection. Both the client and the server must support HTTP 1.1 to benefit. HTTP is defined in RFCs 1945 and 2616.

<table>
<tr><td>

NOTE:
Communication applications will often use FTP internally. Users need an FTP client to use FTP.

</td><td>

- **File Transfer Protocol (FTP)** — a system for transferring files between computers on a TCP/IP network. FTP offers an efficient and quick way to transfer files because it does not have the overhead of encoding and decoding data, such as sending files as e-mail attachments. FTP is specified in RFC 959.

- **Trivial File Transfer Protocol (TFTP)** — used for initializing diskless systems. It works with the BOOTstrap Protocol (BOOTP). TFTP uses UDP, whereas FTP uses TCP. Because TFTP is simple and small, it can be embedded in read-only memory (ROM), which is ideal for diskless workstations or routers seeking configurations upon initialization. TFTP is specified in RFC 1350.

</td></tr>
<tr><td>

NOTE:
Telnet is typically used to emulate "dumb" terminal connections.

</td><td>

- **Telnet** — a terminal emulation protocol developed for ARPANET. It allows a user at one site to log on and run programs from a remote system. Telnet is specified in RFC 854.

- **Network News Transfer Protocol (NNTP)** — allows sites on the Internet to exchange Usenet news articles, which are organized into topics such as "programming in C++" or "international trade issues." To use newsgroups, you must have access to an NNTP server with which you are authorized to read and post news. NNTP is specified in RFC 977.

</td></tr>
</table>

- **Gopher** — a menu-based program used to find resources on the Internet. It is very similar in concept and practice to today's Web. Users follow links from site to site in search of information. It was one of the first tools developed to pull the Internet together so users could access the entire Internet rather than just one site. Gopher servers have been largely replaced by Web servers. Gopher is specified in RFC 1436.

- **Simple Mail Transfer Protocol (SMTP)** — the Internet standard protocol for transferring e-mail messages from one computer to another. It specifies how two mail systems interact. SMTP is often used in conjunction with Post Office Protocol version 3 (POP3), which is a standard Internet mail service. POP3 stores incoming e-mail until users authenticate and download it. POP3 is defined in RFC 1939 and STD 53. SMTP is specified in RFC 821. POP3 is not considered part of the TCP/IP suite, but is integral to e-mail use.

- **Simple Network Management Protocol (SNMP)** — used for managing TCP/IP networks. It is a standardized management scheme that vendors can support. Thus, all SNMP-compliant network devices can be centrally managed by an SNMP manager. SNMP also offers low resource requirements, portability and wide acceptance. SNMP is specified in RFC 1157.

fully qualified domain name (FQDN)
The complete domain name of an Internet computer, such as *www.CIW-certified.com*.

- **Domain Name System (DNS)** — a mechanism used on the Internet to translate host computer names into Internet (IP) addresses. It is one of the most universal methods of centralized name resolution. For example, when a user requests the **fully qualified domain name (FQDN)** *www.companyname.com*, DNS servers translate the name into the IP address 201.198.24.108. DNS is defined in RFCs 1034 and 1035.

NOTE:
In a routed network environment, it may be necessary to enable BOOTP routing on network routers.

- **BOOTstrap Protocol (BOOTP)** — an alternative to RARP. Additionally, it provides a method for diskless workstations and X terminals to determine their IP addresses. A single BOOTP message specifies many items needed at startup, including the diskless computer's IP address, the address of a gateway (router) and the address of a particular server (such as a DNS server). BOOTP is specified in RFC 951.

- **Dynamic Host Configuration Protocol (DHCP)** — based on BOOTP. It is designed to assign Internet addresses to nodes on a TCP/IP network during initialization. It can also assign the address of a gateway (router) and the address of a particular server. Like BOOTP, it saves administrators a great deal of time because client systems do not require manual TCP/IP configuration. DHCP is defined in RFC 2131.

soft phone
A software application that enables a PC or PDA to function as a telephone using VoIP technology.

- **Session Initiation Protocol (SIP)** — initiates and manages sessions (or connections) between two or more participants. It is a signaling protocol only — SIP does not deliver media streams, nor does it control the delivery of media streams. SIP's primary function is to set up, modify and tear down a connection. SIP is modeled after HTTP and uses the same format for its message headers as HTTP. SIP is generally considered to be an easier implementation than its competitor, H.323. SIP uses fewer resources, and its text-based messaging and addressing scheme make it friendly. Many convergence devices such as Cisco IP phones and **soft phones**, as well as PCs and personal digital assistants (PDAs) use SIP. SIP is defined in RFC 3261.

Note: Skype is an example of an Internet telephony service provider that freely distributes a soft phone application that allows users to make calls over the Internet using their PCs.

- **H.323** — a competitor to SIP. H.323 provides consistency in audio, video and data packet transmissions over IP networks, and defines the components, procedures, protocols and services for multimedia communication over LANs and WANs. The H.323 standard allows customers to use multimedia applications on existing infrastructure without upgrading their networks. It is used on a variety of devices including Cisco IP phones, PCs, soft phones, video phones and multi-port gateways. H.323 is defined in RFC 3508.

Demultiplexing

Demultiplexing is the method that a destination computer uses to process the incoming packet. Figure 2-3 illustrates the demultiplexing process. You can refer to this diagram throughout the course.

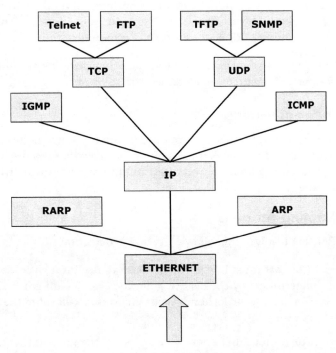

Figure 2-3: Demultiplexing of protocols

Introduction to Routing

OBJECTIVE
3.2.4: Routing
processes

NOTE:
If you need to
review the OSI/RM,
refer to Lesson 1.

Routing is an extremely important function of IP. It is the process of choosing a path over which to send packets. The device that performs this task is called a router, which forwards packets from one physical network to another. (You were introduced to routers earlier in the course.) Your knowledge of IP will enable you to see the correlation between IP and routing.

The Internet layer, or OSI/RM network layer (Layer 3), performs the routing function. A packet, or datagram, carries sufficient information for routing from the originating host to the destination host using the IP address. Packets may traverse several networks before reaching their destination host.

Packets are routed transparently, and not necessarily reliably, to the destination host. The term "transparent," when applied to routing, means that after the routing hardware and software are installed, changes are undetectable by users because the routing process is largely automated. The complexity of routing is not visible to the user. The transport or application layer is responsible for reliability, which ensures that the data arrives at the other end.

Routing can be summarized as:

- The process that determines the path that packets will travel across networks.

- One of the most important IP functions.

Routing can be divided into two general classifications: direct and indirect.

Direct routing

NOTE:
Packets having a
source and
destination on the
same network are
typically not
referred to as being
routed because no
router is involved.
Any router attached
to the network will
ignore local
packets.

If two computers on the same physical network need to communicate, the packets do not require a router. The computers are considered to be on the same local network. In an IEEE 802.3/Ethernet TCP/IP network, the sending entity encapsulates the packet in an Ethernet frame, binds the destination Internet address to an Ethernet address, and transmits the resulting frame directly to its destination. This process is referred to as direct routing. ARP is an example of a direct routing protocol.

The destination system is on the same physical network if the network portions of the source and destination addresses are the same.

Indirect routing

NOTE:
Indirect routing is
commonly referred
to simply as
"routing."

If two computers that are not on the same physical network need to communicate, they must send the IP packet to a router for delivery. They are located on remote networks. Whenever a router is involved in communication, the activity is considered indirect routing.

Routing process

Routing involves the following two key elements:

- The host must know which router to use for a given destination; the router is determined by the default gateway. The default gateway is the IP address of the router on your local network; this router will route the packet to the destination network.

- The router must know where to send the packet; the destination is determined by the router's routing information table.

Routing information table

hop
One link between two network devices; the number of hops between two devices is considered a hop count.

A routing information table is a database maintained by a router. The table contains the location of all networks in relation to the router's location. When a packet arrives at the router, the router examines the packet's destination network, and then checks its own routing information table. It determines the next router to which to send the packet, and forwards the packet to that router. This part of the journey is considered a **hop**. In some cases, the destination network is attached to the router, in which case the packet has reached its destination network. Figure 2-4 illustrates a simplified routing information table that will help you understand the basic process.

NOTE: You need a general understanding of how routing works, but do not need the details of how to manually manage a routing table.

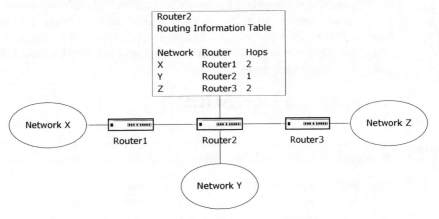

Figure 2-4: Routing information table

OBJECTIVE
3.2.4: Routing processes

Static vs. dynamic routing

Static routers contain routing information tables that must be built and updated manually. If a certain route does not exist in the static routing information table, the router will be unable to communicate with that network.

A dynamic router communicates with other dynamic routers to calculate routes automatically using routing protocols such as Routing Information Protocol (RIP) and Open Shortest Path First (OSPF). Dynamic routers can exchange information about routes of known networks. When a route changes, the routers automatically update themselves by recalculating routes.

Routing Protocols

Earlier, routing was defined as the process of selecting a path on which data will travel across networks. Routing also requires routing protocols, which determine how routers share information and how they report routing information table changes to one another. Routing protocols enable networks to dynamically change without the need to enter static routing information table entries for each adjustment.

OBJECTIVE
3.2.4: Routing processes

Interior vs. exterior routing protocols

Following are the two basic types of routing protocols:

- **Interior routing protocols** — used within an organization's network. Examples are RIP, RIP version 2 (RIPv2) and OSPF.

- **Exterior routing protocols** — used outside an organization's network. Exterior Gateway Protocol (EGP) and Border Gateway Protocol (BGP) are examples of such protocols (further discussion of exterior routing protocols is beyond the scope of this course).

An autonomous system is managed by a single organizational entity, which includes all networks and routers managed by that entity. If routers belong to different autonomous systems and they exchange routing information, the routers are considered exterior gateways. Routers within an autonomous system are called interior gateways.

Routing Information Protocol (RIP and RIPv2)

NOTE:
RIP is the more efficient choice in small networks with a relatively static structure and few alternative routes.

RIP is commonly implemented on small to medium-sized LANs. RIP maintains only the best route to a destination. Old route information is replaced by new route information, causing network topology changes that are reflected in routing update messages. Routing update messages cause routers to update their tables and propagate the changes. Two versions of RIP are used: RIPv1 (RFC 1058) and RIPv2 (RFC 2453). RIPv2 retains RIP's simplicity, but is more efficient.

Open Shortest Path First (OSPF)

NOTE:
OSPF is typically the best choice in larger networks with multiple alternative routes available.

A disadvantage of RIP is that routes are selected on the basis of the closest path (fewest hops) between the source system and the destination system. No emphasis is placed on factors such as available bandwidth, multiple connections or security.

The OSPF routing protocol is an interior gateway routing protocol that overcomes many of RIP's shortcomings. Additional versions of OSPF include OSPFv2 (RFC 2328) and OSPFv3 (RFC 5340). OSPFv3 has recently become an Internet standard protocol.

OSPF contains the following practical features:

NOTE:
The difference in traffic during routing information table updates can be significant on a large network with slower WAN links.

- **Routing information table updates** — Updates occur when necessary, rather than at regular intervals. This irregular frequency reduces traffic on the network and saves bandwidth.

- **Various types of service routing** — OSPF makes it possible to install multiple routes to a given destination. Each route can be defined on the basis of a service, such as high bit rate and/or security.

- **Load balancing** — If multiple routes exist to a given destination and all routes cost the same, OSPF distributes traffic evenly over all routes.

- **Network areas** — OSPF provides the ability to partition a network into areas, allowing growth and organization. Each area's internal topology is hidden from other areas.

- **Authenticated exchanges** — All exchanges between routers using OSPF are authenticated. OSPF allows the use of various authentication schemes. This arrangement is important because only trusted systems should propagate routing information.

- **Defined route support** — OSPF allows the definition of host-specific or network-specific routes.

Port Numbers

After an IP packet has arrived at the destination host using the IP address (you will learn about IP addressing later in the course), the packet is passed to the transport layer. The transport layer determines which service the packet is using by examining the packet's destination port number.

NOTE:
In a routed network environment, it may be necessary to enable BOOTP routing on network routers.

TCP and UDP headers contain both source and destination port numbers. These port numbers are addresses by which processes can be identified. Each port number is a 16-bit integer value that identifies a communication channel to a specific user process. For example:

- FTP = Port 21

- HTTP = Port 80

- DNS = Port 53

- SMTP = Port 25

To view many of the services and the ports associated with them, examine the services file located in the *etc* directory for Windows or UNIX. For Windows Vista, the path is C:\\Windows\\System32\\drivers\\etc. The purpose of the services file is to map each port number to the name of the service associated with that port. In addition, you can visit the RFC Editor site at *www.rfc-editor.org* to review the latest database entries.

At one time, RFC 1700 contained the latest entries. According to RFC 3232, RFC 1700 is obsolete, and has now been replaced by an online database. The entity responsible for assigning port numbers was at one time the Internet Assigned Numbers Authority (IANA). Today, however, this responsibility has been given to the Internet Corporation for Assigned Names and Numbers (ICANN).

NOTE:
The URL for IANA's current assignments (*www.iana.org/assignments/port-numbers*) may change over time. You may need to search for the new location. Remember that the ICANN is now responsible for assigning port numbers. The URL for the ICANN is *www.icann.org*.

As of this writing, the current port assignments list is at the following location: *www.iana.org/assignments/port-numbers*.
To search the entire database, go to the IANA Protocol Registries page at *www.iana.org/protocols/*.

Classifying port numbers

According to IANA, the following three ranges of port numbers exist:

- **Well-known** — ports between 0 and 1023

- **Registered** — ports between 1024 and 49151

- **Dynamic (private)** — ports between 49152 and 65535

Although Port 0 is rarely used, it is still a designated port. Many references tend to refer to Ports 1 through 1023. Also, many references tend to use the term "well-known" for all ports ranging from 0 to 1023. They also tend to use the terms "dynamic" or "ephemeral" for any port ranging from 1024 to 65535.

Following is a discussion of each range.

Well-known port numbers

Also called reserved port numbers, well-known port numbers range from 0 to 1023 and are controlled by the ICANN (previously the IANA). Well-known port numbers are used by TCP and UDP to identify well-known services that a host can provide. No process is allowed to bind to a well-known port unless its effective user ID is 0 (a user account with unlimited access privileges, such as root [on UNIX], superuser [on UNIX] or administrator [on Windows]).

Registered port numbers

Registered port numbers range from 1024 to 49151 and are considered non-privileged. Therefore, any process can use them. Administrative permissions are not required. ICANN registers these port numbers and IANA's Web site lists them, but ICANN does not formally assign them in the same manner as well-known ports. These ports are often used by specific services as contact ports. Contact ports are often necessary when a server must communicate with a remote system.

Ephemeral (short-lived or transitional) port numbers are unique port numbers typically assigned to client processes. The server process determines the ephemeral port number from the TCP or UDP header, and thereby knows the process with which to communicate at the remote system.

NOTE:
See **Optional Lab 2-1: Viewing port number assignments.**

IANA allows companies to petition ICANN and IANA to create either a well-known or a registered port number for a specific service. See the following URL for more information: www.iana.org/protocols.

Dynamic port numbers

Also called private ports, dynamic port numbers range from 49152 to 65535, and are not controlled or registered in any way by ICANN. Client-side applications open these ports randomly when accessing remote systems.

Internet Addressing

OBJECTIVE
3.3.1: Unique IP addressing

To ensure that each user on the Internet has a unique IP address, the ICANN issues all Internet addresses. The previous controlling organization, the IANA, was funded and overseen by the U.S. government. The ICANN is a private, non-governmental organization that performs the same tasks, such as Internet address space allocation. To learn more about the ICANN, visit *www.icann.org*.

Most Internet addresses contain a network portion and a host portion. The network portion precedes the host portion:

NOTE:
Each system used to communicate on the Internet will have an address unique to the Internet. When communicating on a private intranet, the system's address must be unique to the LAN, but is not necessarily valid on the Internet.

network portion, host portion

Internet addresses are specified by four fields, separated by periods:

field1.field2.field3.field4

Each field represents one byte of data. Internet addresses are typically written in dotted decimal notation. Each field has a value ranging from 0 to 255, as demonstrated by the following Internet address:

208.157.24.111

In the preceding example, the network portion is 208.157.24, and the host portion is 111.

Subnet Mask

Each system in a TCP/IP network must be configured with an IP address and a subnet mask. As you have already seen, the IP address is expressed in a four-part dotted decimal format, such as:

192.162.102.221

The subnet mask determines which part of the address is used as the network address and which is used to identify a specific host on the network. For example, your subnet mask might resemble the following:

255.255.255.0

The network address identifies a general location on the network and the host address identifies a specific system. You can compare these elements to the address on a letter. The network address works like the city and state address, identifying a general location. The host address is analogous to the street name and house number, identifying a specific location.

Subnet masks serve the following two main purposes:

- Distinguishing the network and host portions of an IP address

- Specifying whether a destination address is local or remote

First, the subnet mask distinguishes network and host portions of an IP address. Because the system does not know which bits in the host field should be interpreted as the subnetwork part of the Internet address, it refers to the subnet mask. The subnet mask tells the system which bits of the Internet address should be interpreted as the network, subnetwork and host addresses.

Subnet masks also specify whether a destination address is local or remote. Note that the subnet mask is used to "mask" the network address, so only the host address remains. In routing, this masking is extremely important. It allows a computer to determine whether a destination address is intended for a computer on the same (local) network, or a different (remote) one.

If the destination address is on the same network, the information can be transmitted locally. If the destination address is on a different network, the information must be sent to a router, which can locate the remote network.

The subnet mask identifies whether the destination address is local or remote through a process called ANDing.

ANDing

The network portion of an Internet address can be determined by using the Boolean AND operation with the Internet address and the subnet mask. This process is internal to TCP/IP, but its function is important.

When the computer is initialized, it uses the ANDing function with its local IP address and local subnet mask. Whenever it sends information to a destination address, it uses the ANDing function again with the destination address and the local subnet mask. If the value matches the initial ANDing function result, it is a local destination. If the value is different, it is a remote address.

To use the ANDing function, convert your local IP address and subnet mask into binary form. For the following example, your IP address is 131.226.85.1 and your subnet mask is 255.255.0.0.

Calculate each corresponding bit using the following rules:

- 1 and 1 = 1

- Any other combination = 0

NOTE:
A router still sees the address as consisting of a network portion and host portion only. The concept of a subnetwork portion is a convenient concept for teaching custom subnetting, which is an advanced procedure not covered in this course.

NOTE:
All TCP/IP network-connected devices will be configured with at least an IP address and subnet mask.

OBJECTIVE
3.3.4: Subnet masks

NOTE:
Do not spend too much time on ANDing; you only need to understand that systems automatically AND the subnet mask and the IP address to determine whether an address is local or remote.

When your computer initializes, the ANDing process calculates the following result:

Local IP address	*10000011 11100010 01010101 00000001*
Local subnet mask	*11111111 11111111 00000000 00000000*
First ANDing result	*10000011 11100010 00000000 00000000*

By converting the ANDing result to decimal value, the process reveals that the network portion of the address is 131.226.

Your computer uses the ANDing result from the initialization process to determine whether all future destination addresses are local or remote. For example, you are sending information to the destination address 131.226.50.4.

Destination IP address	*10000011 11100010 00110010 00000100*
Local subnet mask	*11111111 11111111 00000000 00000000*
Second ANDing result	*10000011 11100010 00000000 00000000*

The network address found is 131.226. Compare the first and second ANDing results. Because they are the same, the data is sent locally, and the router will not be used. If they were different, the data would be sent through a router to the remote network.

Internet Address Classes

OBJECTIVE
3.3.2: IP address classes

Without a classification system, the 3,720,314,628 possible Internet addresses would have no structure. To provide structure, IP addresses are categorized into classes. Classes can be determined by looking at the first byte of an Internet address.

NOTE:
Be aware of the importance of knowing these address classes, especially being able to recognize class A, class B and class C addresses.

Internet addresses are divided into five classes: A, B, C, D and E. The IP address range for each class is shown in Table 2-2. The characteristics of each class are detailed in this section.

Table 2-2: IP address classes

Address Class	IP Address Range
Class A	0.0.0.0 to 127.255.255.255
Class B	128.0.0.0 to 191.255.255.255
Class C	192.0.0.0 to 223.255.255.255
Class D	224.0.0.0 to 239.255.255.255
Class E	240.0.0.0 to 247.255.255.255

Class A

Class A addresses typically use the first byte for the network portion and the last three bytes for the host portion. Class A addresses range from:

0.0.0.0 to 127.255.255.255

The first byte can range from 1 to 126 (0 is a special-case source address and 127 is a reserved loopback address, which you will learn about later in this lesson). Class A addresses provide the potential for 126 networks with 16,777,214 hosts each.

The following is an example of a Class A address (the first byte is the network address):

121.1.1.32

Class B

Class B addresses typically use the first two bytes for the network portion and the last two bytes for the host portion. Class B addresses range from:

128.0.0.0 to 191.255.255.255

The first byte can range from 128 to 191. Class B addresses provide the potential for 16,384 networks with up to 65,534 hosts each.

The following is an example of a Class B address (the first two bytes are the network address):

168.100.1.32

Class C

NOTE:
You will probably work exclusively with Class C addresses unless using reserved IP addresses on a private network.

Class C addresses typically use the first three bytes for the network portion and the last byte for the host portion. Class C addresses range from:

192.0.0.0 to 223.255.255.255

The first byte can range from 192 to 223. Class C addresses provide the potential for 2,097,152 networks with up to 254 hosts each.

The following is an example of a Class C address (the first three bytes are the network address):

205.96.224.32

Class D

NOTE:
A host can have a unique Class A, Class B or Class C IP address and still be identified by a Class D address for multicasting.

Class D addresses support multicasting (which was introduced earlier). With multicasting, a packet is targeted to a group that is identified by a network address only. No host portion exists in the address. The first byte can range from 224 to 239. The following is an example of a Class D address (all four bytes are the network address):

230.5.124.62

Class E

Class E addresses are reserved for future use. The first byte can range from 240 to 247.

OBJECTIVE
3.3.4: Subnet masks

Default subnet masks for IP address classes

NOTE:
See **Activity 2-3: Determining default subnet masks.**

As you have already learned, all hosts with an IP address also use a subnet mask that helps a system determine the network to which it belongs. The simplest type of subnet mask is the default subnet mask. By default, each 8-bit field is turned on (255 — all binary ones) or off (0 — all binary zeros), depending on the address class (A, B or C).

Table 2-3 describes the three IP address classes in common use, as well as their standard subnet masks. Class D and E addresses do not have hosts, and therefore do not require subnet masks.

Table 2-3: Standard IP classes and subnet masks

Class	Address Range	Standard Subnet Mask
Class A	1.0.0.0 to 126.0.0.0	255.0.0.0
Class B	128.0.0.0 to 191.0.0.0	255.255.0.0
Class C	192.0.0.0. to 223.0.0.0	255.255.255.0

For more information about Class A, B and C IP addresses, consult RFCs 790 and 1366, as well as the following sites:

- http://en.wikipedia.org/wiki/IP_address

- http://computer.howstuffworks.com/question549.htm

Private IP addresses

OBJECTIVE
3.3.3: Public and
private IP addresses

Many companies and organizations do not use standard IP address ranges that can be used on the Internet. To save money, these companies purchase only a limited number of Internet-addressable addresses, and then use private IP addresses.

The ICANN suggests that companies use private IP addresses on their networks if either of the following situations is applicable to them:

- The host does not require access to other enterprise or Internet hosts.

- The host's Internet needs can be handled by mediating gateways (for example, application-layer gateways). For example, the host may require only limited Internet services, such as e-mail, FTP, newsgroups and Web browsing.

Table 2-4 provides a list of private IP addresses.

Table 2-4: Private IP addresses

Class	Private IP Address Range	Subnet Mask	CIDR Notation
Class A	10.0.0.0 to 10.255.255.255	255.0.0.0	10/8
Class B	172.16.0.0 to 172.31.255.255	255.240.0	172.16/12
Class C	192.168.0.0 to 192.168.255.255	255.255.0.0	192.168/16

Notice that the Class B and Class C address ranges do not use standard subnet masks. Frequently, systems administrators will use standard Class B and Class C subnet masks, but this is not specifically recommended by RFC 1918.

Notice also that the preceding table includes CIDR notation, which will be discussed shortly.

Private IP addresses and Network Address Translation (NAT)

NOTE:
Using private
addresses protects
LAN hosts from
Internet clients
because the hosts
cannot be reached
from the Internet.

The IP address ranges indicated in the preceding table are called private IP addresses because they have no global meaning and cannot be sent across Internet routers. Internet routers are expected to reject (filter out) routing information about them (the rejection will not be treated as a routing protocol error). However, private network addresses can be sent across company routers. In order for computers with these IP addresses to use the Internet, they must use Network Address Translation (NAT). NAT allows a router or firewall to alter the IP packet and replace the private IP address with one that can be routed across the Internet. You can also use a proxy server, which will act as a mediator between the private network and all other public networks.

The benefits of using private network addresses include the following:

- Conservation of globally unique IP addresses when global uniqueness is not required

- More flexibility in enterprise design because of large address space

- Prevention of IP address clashes when an enterprise gains Internet connectivity without receiving addresses from the ICANN

Classless Interdomain Routing (CIDR)

OBJECTIVE
3.3.5: Classless
Interdomain Routing
(CIDR)

Today, IP addresses are no longer assigned based on address classes. They are assigned according to specific ranges of addresses. Each range given will be assigned a specific subnet mask presented in Classless Interdomain Routing (CIDR) notation. CIDR notation has the following format:

address block/prefix

In this format, the address block is given, and a number is given for the prefix. The prefix designates the number of bits used by the subnet mask. For example, a range of addresses from 55.66.77.88 to 55.66.88.99 with the subnet mask of 255.255.255.0 would be noted as follows:

55.66.77.88-55.66.88.99/24

Notice in the preceding example that what would previously have been considered a Class A IP address can be used with a Class C subnet mask. This capability enables the ICANN to assign a custom subnet mask to any range of addresses. Using CIDR notation in this way allows the conservation of IP addresses because the ICANN can assign a specific number of addresses instead of a set range.

Internet Protocol Version 6 (IPv6)

OBJECTIVE
3.3.6: IPv6 concepts

With Internet use growing so rapidly, the current addressing scheme is in danger of depleting the limited number of available IP addresses. It is also creating unmanageable routing tables for the Internet's backbone routers. Although this course assumes the use of IP version 4 (IPv4), which is the standard version of IP, IPv4 has several shortcomings, including the following:

- **Limited address space** — IPv4, the current version, provides enough addresses for slightly more than 4.2 billion address assignments. Although this number seems large, it does not provide enough IP addresses to support all the IP-enabled devices that will be used in the future. Consider the fact that networked computers, mobile phones, PDAs and other devices that must be Internet-enabled all use IP addresses.

encryption
A security technique designed to prevent access to information by converting it into a scrambled (unreadable) form of text.

- **Lack of security** — IPv4 does not provide native **encryption** or authentication mechanisms, which has enabled unscrupulous individuals and groups to wage attacks and gain unauthorized access to sensitive information.

- **Speed problems** — IPv4 is highly dependent on network routers to break down transmissions, which can increase network traffic and slow transmission speed.

- **Configuration problems** — IPv4 address configuration can be automated, but the process must still be simplified.

IP version 6 (IPv6) solves these problems and will allow the Internet to function effectively well into the future. Not only does it solve addressing and routing-table problems, but it also improves the protocol. For example, it is more efficient and requires less administrative overhead than IPv4.

NOTE:
Following is a hierarchical list of large number measurements, complete with North American powers:
million (10^6)
billion (10^9)
trillion (10^{12})
quadrillion (10^{15})
quintillion (10^{18})
sextillion (10^{21})
septillion (10^{24})
octillion (10^{27})
nonillion (10^{30})
decillion (10^{33})
undecillion (10^{36}).

IPv6 provides a practically unlimited number of IP addresses because it uses a 128-bit address. As a result, it provides 340 undecillion addresses. Whereas 4 billion addresses would be 4 multiplied by 10^9, 340 undecillion addresses would be 340 multiplied by 10^{36}, which allows for a significantly larger address pool.

IPv6 is less dependent than IPv4 on routers, which helps reduce the likelihood that routers will become overburdened (in other words, congested). For more information about IPv6, visit the IPv6 Information Page (*www.ipv6.org*).

IPv6 is being implemented now, even though as of 2008, it still accounts for only a small fraction of the used addresses. IPv6 and IPv4 will probably coexist for several years, although some forecasts expect IPv4 addresses to be exhausted by as early as 2011.

System Configuration and IP Addresses

OBJECTIVE
3.2.5: TCP/IP network addressing

Systems can be configured to use IP addresses in the following two ways:

- **Static address assignment** — The systems administrator manually enters IP address information.

- **Automatic address assignment** — The systems administrator configures a client to obtain IP address information automatically from a server. This method uses DHCP (which you learned about earlier) and Automatic Private IP Addressing (APIPA).

You will learn more about DHCP and APIPA shortly.

Default gateway

OBJECTIVE
3.2.5: TCP/IP network addressing

Most IP-enabled systems are also configured with a default gateway, which is an IP address that specifies a routing device (for example, a router or firewall). After a network host is configured with a default gateway, the host will be able to communicate with a remote network, if permitted by the routing device. A default gateway is often referred to simply as a gateway.

Loopback address

NOTE:
Testing the loopback address with the ping utility verifies that the computer's TCP/IP stack has loaded and initialized properly. In other words, TCP/IP is working.

The loopback address 127 cannot be used as an Internet address. Any IP address that begins with 127 is a loopback address (12.7.0.0.0 to 127.255.255.255). This address allows a client and server on the same host to communicate with each other. The loopback address is ideal for testing and troubleshooting. For example, if your computer hosts a Web server and you type *http://127.0.0.1* in your Web browser's address text box (as a client), you will access the Web site. The loopback address can also be used to test local TCP/IP functionality by using the packet Internet groper (ping) program, which you will learn about shortly.

hosts file
A file that contains mappings of IP addresses to host names.

For UNIX and Windows systems, the loopback address is listed in the **hosts file** and is typically 127.0.0.1 with the assigned name localhost.

Broadcast address

Broadcast addresses send messages to all network hosts, and are used only as destination addresses. The network and/or host portions of an IP address cannot use the broadcast address 255 (all binary ones). Following are the four broadcast address types:

- **Limited broadcast (255.255.255.255)** — This type is used for configuring hosts when they start up. For example, a computer without an IP address can broadcast this address to obtain an IP address (from a DHCP or BOOTP server, for example).

- **Net-directed broadcast (netid.255.255.255)** — This type is used to broadcast to all hosts in a network. For example, if the network portion of your IP address is 192.34.200 and the host portion is 12, your computer can broadcast messages to all network hosts by using the destination address 192.34.200.255.

- **Subnet-directed broadcast** — If a network is divided into several subnets, a broadcast can be limited to the hosts within a subnet. You will learn about subnets later in this lesson.

- **All-subnets-directed broadcast** — If a network is divided into several subnets, a broadcast can be sent to all hosts within all network subnets. This type of broadcast is obsolete; multicasting (see Class D addresses) is preferred.

Network and special-case source addresses

NOTE:
See **Activity 2-2: Determining classes and valid IP addresses.**

The network and/or host portions of an IP address can contain zeros, but the entire network or host portion of the address cannot be entirely zeros. For instance, the Class C address 198.168.3.0 is a network address and cannot be assigned to a node.

The special-case source IP address of a computer is all zeros (0.0.0.0) when it initializes and requests an IP address (from a DHCP or BOOTP server, for example). Although the computer broadcasts the request for the IP address, its source address is initially 0.0.0.0, until it is assigned a network IP address. The special-case source address can also specify a host on the network during initialization. For instance, the network portion of a Class C address can be all zeros, and the host portion can be 11, which is 0.0.0.11. These addresses cannot be used as valid IP addresses for a node.

Normal TCP/IP workstation configuration

OBJECTIVE
3.2.5: TCP/IP network addressing

A network host must have at least an IP address and a subnet mask to communicate on a network. WAN communication requires at least an IP address, a subnet mask and a default gateway. Following are the basic configuration parameters for a workstation on a TCP/IP network:

OBJECTIVE
3.6.1: Troubleshooting IP-enabled systems

- **IP address** — the 32-bit IP address that is unique to your workstation on the network. If you enter the IP address manually, it is considered a static IP address.

- **Subnet mask** — the 32-bit number used to distinguish the network and host portions of your IP address; also used to calculate whether a destination address is local or remote.

NOTE:
Remember that a default gateway is required only in routed networks.

- **Default gateway** — the local computer's IP address (usually a router). If your computer calculates that a destination address is remote, your computer will send the packet to the default gateway. The router will send the packet to the remote network.

- **DHCP client** — If you are a DHCP client, your TCP/IP configurations will automatically be sent to your computer when you initialize your system, which is the easiest way to configure clients on a network. Obtaining an IP address from a DHCP server is the alternative to entering a static IP address.

TCP/IP services

Table 2-5 lists some of the TCP/IP services you may encounter when working with systems on a TCP/IP network.

Table 2-5: TCP/IP services

Service	Description
Domain Name System (DNS)	A name resolution service. The primary means of resolving names on a network. Resolves names to IP addresses. A system can query a DNS server with a host name and receive the host's IP address as a response. A DNS server may also be configured to provide a host name when queried with an IP address.
Dynamic Host Configuration Protocol (DHCP)	Supports automated TCP/IP host configuration. When a DHCP client starts up, it will send a query requesting configuration information. It will be given an IP address and subnet mask and may be given additional configuration information such as a primary DNS server IP address.
Automatic Private IP Addressing (APIPA)	If a modern Windows client fails to obtain an address from a DHCP server, the client will use APIPA, which causes a private IP address (an address that cannot be used on the Internet) to be assigned to the adapter. If you see a system with an IP address that begins with 169.254 and has a subnet mask of 255.255.0.0, assume that the address was assigned through APIPA.

When configuring a system for use on a TCP/IP network, you may be required to enter the IP address for one or more DNS servers. You do not need to provide the IP address for a DHCP server, but you must identify any systems that will be receiving their IP addresses and other configuration information through DHCP.

The hosts file

As mentioned earlier, the hosts file maps DNS host names to IP addresses. It is installed whenever you install the TCP/IP suite (or stack). You can edit this file and create entries using the following syntax:

        IPAddress   hostname

For example, if you want to create a manual host entry for a system with the IP address 192.168.2.4 so that it had the name of james, you must enter the following:

        192.168.2.4   james

DNS configurations

You can configure your computer to use DNS. Following are several important configuration parameters:

- **Host name** — You must specify the name of your computer, which is the host name. Your computer will be identified by this name (for example, student11) on the network.

- **Domain name** — You must specify the domain name (for example, *yourcompany.com*) to which your computer belongs.

- **DNS server** — You must identify the DNS servers that will provide you with the DNS service.

Dynamic Host Configuration Protocol (DHCP)

As you learned earlier, DHCP assigns IP addresses automatically on a TCP/IP network. Because DHCP automatically assigns IP addresses, it has become a central part of large-enterprise LANs and WANs. DHCP can save a great deal of time for the IT department because it frees IT personnel from having to manually configure each computer on the network.

DHCP assigns more than just an IP address, subnet mask and default gateway. It can also assign DNS server information and almost any other TCP/IP configurations needed by network clients.

With DHCP, a client system receives its TCP/IP configurations automatically at startup. DHCP assigns these configurations on a lease basis. The lease contains all the TCP/IP configurations for a system. For example, the leased IP address your computer receives may expire after 24 hours. After the address expires, it can be leased to another computer on the network or renewed by the same computer. If the client system is removed from one network and connected to another, it will automatically relinquish its old lease and be assigned a new one when connected to the new network.

The DHCP server has a pool of IP addresses that it can assign to network computers. This pool of addresses consists of a range of IP addresses that the network administrator enters into the DHCP server. The DHCP server then distributes these addresses to the network computers. The addresses might be private IP addresses or addresses assigned to the company from an ISP.

DHCP is based on BOOTP, an older protocol that assigned IP addresses and other parameters to diskless workstations, or "dumb terminals.". DHCP is more powerful than BOOTP because it allows reusable addresses and additional configuration options. DHCP users can communicate with BOOTP systems.

In the following lab, you will reconfigure your computer with a reserved IP address. Suppose you are the systems administrator for a small bank branch, and you need to reconfigure the vice president's computer with a reserved IP address. Which address class is suitable for this task? How would you manually enter an IP address?

Lab 2-1: Reconfiguring your computer with a reserved IP address

OBJECTIVE
3.6.1:
Troubleshooting
IP-enabled systems

In this lab, you will reconfigure your computer with a Class C reserved IP address.

1. Select **Start | Control Panel**, click **Classic View** if necessary, then double-click **Network And Sharing Center**. Click the **View Status** link to the right of Local Area Connection, and click the **Properties** button. Select the TCP/IP protocol that is bound to your NIC, as shown in Figure 2-5.

NOTE:
If you want to retain the ability to access the Internet, skip this lab or set your system back to the original settings.

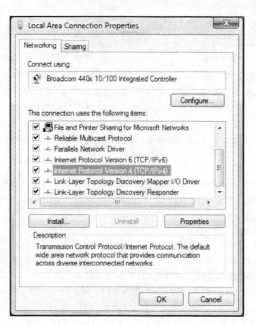

Figure 2-5: TCP/IP component

2. Click the **Properties** button. This step displays the General card of the Internet Protocol Version 4 (TCP/IPv4) Properties dialog box, as shown in Figure 2-6.

Figure 2-6: Internet Protocol Version 4 (TCP/IPv4) Properties dialog box

3. Click **Use The Following IP Address** to specify that you will manually enter an IP address.

4. Consider the following reserved Class C address range.

    The Class C network address is:

    192.168.3.0

The Class C default subnet mask is:

255.255.255.0

The Class C address range (last byte, or octet) is from:

1 – 254

An example Class C address is:

192.168.3.6

5. Enter your IP address (192.168.3.X, where X is a number between 1 and 254) and subnet mask (255.255.255.0) in the General tab of the Internet Protocol Version 4 (TCP/IPv4) Properties dialog box. For example, if your *class.com* e-mail address is student6@class.com, you can use "6" in place of "X" in the IP address, as shown in Figure 2-7.

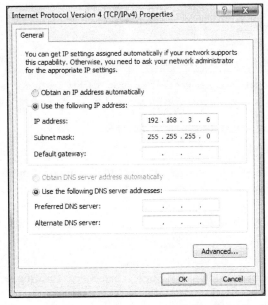

Figure 2-7: Specifying reserved IP address

6. You will configure only your IP address and subnet mask in this lab. Click **OK**, and then click **Close** to save the new settings. Then close any open windows.

7. Your computer is no longer configured to access the Internet because you are using a reserved IP address. You can contact only computers that use the same Class C address and subnet mask.

You will test for connectivity with another computer in the next lab using the *ping* command. Note that you need only an IP address and a subnet mask configured to access a network.

OBJECTIVE
3.6.2: Diagnostic
troubleshooting
tools

NOTE:
You need to
understand the
basic capabilities of
each utility and
when it should be
used, and be able
to recognize the
command's output.

Diagnostic Tools for Internet Troubleshooting

Now that you are familiar with IP addresses, you can learn how certain diagnostic tools use IP addresses to discover information within a TCP/IP network. This section will introduce tools that are used regularly by system administrators to troubleshoot TCP/IP networks. Use the following TCP/IP tools and commands to assist with general network troubleshooting:

- *ping*

- *tracert* and *traceroute*

- *route*

- *netstat*

- *ipconfig* and *ifconfig*

- *arp*

- Network analyzers

The *ping* command

The packet Internet groper, or ping, utility tests connectivity between source and destination systems. The command syntax is as follows:

    ping ip_address or host_name

In this format, *ip_address* or *host_name* identifies the remote system. Options will vary depending on the operating system. The *ping* command uses two of the most important ICMP types — echo request and echo reply.

 You can read more about ICMP types at the following location:
www.iana.org/assignments/icmp-parameters.

Using Windows, you can open a command prompt and enter the following:

    ping 128.143.22.122

This command yields the following result:

    Pinging 128.143.22.122 with 32 bytes of data:

    Reply from 128.143.22.122: bytes=32 time=100ms TTL=247
    Reply from 128.143.22.122: bytes=32 time=100ms TTL=247
    Reply from 128.143.22.122: bytes=32 time=100ms TTL=247
    Reply from 128.143.22.122: bytes=32 time=100ms TTL=247

Because a reply was received, a connection exists between your computer and the computer with the IP address 128.143.22.122. To stop *ping* replies at any time, simultaneously press the CTRL and C keys.

To test communication with another system by name, you can enter the following:

    ping www.blakearchive.org

You would see a result similar to that in Figure 2-8.

```
Administrator: C:\Windows\system32\cmd.exe

Microsoft Windows [Version 6.0.6000]
Copyright (c) 2006 Microsoft Corporation.  All rights reserved.

C:\Users\LocalUser>ping www.blakearchive.org

Pinging blakearchive.org [152.2.176.89] with 32 bytes of data:

Reply from 152.2.176.89: bytes=32 time=83ms TTL=51
Reply from 152.2.176.89: bytes=32 time=84ms TTL=51
Reply from 152.2.176.89: bytes=32 time=80ms TTL=51
Reply from 152.2.176.89: bytes=32 time=83ms TTL=51

Ping statistics for 152.2.176.89:
    Packets: Sent = 4, Received = 4, Lost = 0 (0% loss),
Approximate round trip times in milli-seconds:
    Minimum = 80ms, Maximum = 84ms, Average = 82ms

C:\Users\LocalUser>
```

Figure 2-8: Ping results — Windows command prompt

Generally, you should ping an IP address first to ensure that you have connectivity. You can ping a host name to ensure that DNS is working properly.

 Ping gives you a way of testing DNS name resolution if you know a host's name and IP address. If you can ping the host by IP address but not by host name, a problem exists with name resolution. If you cannot ping the host by either method, a problem exists with network communication.

NOTE:
Make sure you understand that the *ping* command accepts arguments.

The *ping* command has several options, including the following:

- *-n* — specifies the number of echo request packets to issue. The default is 4.

- *-l* — allows you to send larger packets than the default size of 32.

- *-a* — provides the host name if you know only the IP address.

You can read about additional ping options by entering the following at any command prompt:

>   *ping /?*

Note: You may be unable to ping systems outside your LAN if you are behind a firewall. Many systems administrators turn off a network's ability to issue or respond to ping requests at the firewall. In addition, you will be unable to ping a particular system if that system's ability to respond to ping requests has been disabled.

The ability to test connectivity among computers on a network is extremely important if problems occur.

In the following lab, you will test connectivity using the *ping* command. Suppose you work at home as a contractor. Your computer must be able to access the company's VPN so that you can use network resources and files. You are having trouble accessing the VPN, even though you are using the correct user name, password and login domain information. How could you use the *ping* command to see whether your computer is actively returning *ping* requests? How could you use the *ping* command to test your own TCP/IP configuration?

Lab 2-2: Testing connectivity using the *ping* command

In this lab, you will use the *ping* command to test connectivity.

Note: You can perform Step 3 of this lab only if you have a friend or family member with whom you can use the ping *command to test connectivity. Both you and your partner will need to be able to perform the lab steps concurrently. If you do not have a friend or family member with whom you can perform this lab, skip Step 3. Your partner must also have completed Lab 2-1 to reconfigure his or her computer with a reserved IP address using the same Class C network address as did you. For example, your partner must also have specified an IP address of 192.168.3.X (where X is a number between 1 and 254, but different from the number you specified) and a subnet mask of 255.255.255.0.*

1. Select **Start**, type **cmd** in the Start Search text box, then press **ENTER** to open the command prompt.

2. Test your own TCP/IP configurations by pinging the loopback address. Enter:

    ping 127.0.0.1

    You should receive a successful reply, similar to that shown in Figure 2-9.

```
Administrator: C:\Windows\system32\cmd.exe

Microsoft Windows [Version 6.0.6000]
Copyright (c) 2006 Microsoft Corporation.  All rights reserved.

C:\Users\LocalUser>ping 127.0.0.1

Pinging 127.0.0.1 with 32 bytes of data:

Reply from 127.0.0.1: bytes=32 time<1ms TTL=128
Reply from 127.0.0.1: bytes=32 time<1ms TTL=128
Reply from 127.0.0.1: bytes=32 time<1ms TTL=128
Reply from 127.0.0.1: bytes=32 time<1ms TTL=128

Ping statistics for 127.0.0.1:
    Packets: Sent = 4, Received = 4, Lost = 0 (0% loss),
Approximate round trip times in milli-seconds:
    Minimum = 0ms, Maximum = 0ms, Average = 0ms

C:\Users\LocalUser>
```

Figure 2-9: Successful loopback reply using ping command

3. Test connectivity with your partner's computer by pinging your partner's IP address. If you do not know your partner's IP address, have your partner type **ipconfig** at the command prompt to find out, then return to this lab. For example, if your partner's IP address is 192.168.3.7, enter:

    ping 192.168.3.7

    You should receive a successful reply, similar to that shown in Figure 2-10.

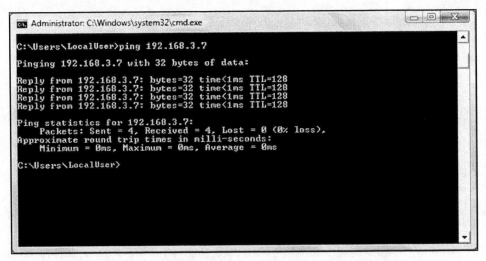

Figure 2-10: Successful connectivity test using ping command

Important: If your computer is configured with a different subnet mask from that of your partner's computer, you will be unable to ping or communicate with him or her. However, the loopback ping will succeed, because it is testing only your own local system.

4. Close the command prompt window.

5. If you completed Lab 2-1, reset your computer to its original TCP/IP configurations.

NOTE:
The *tracert* command can be used with either an IP address or a host name.

The *tracert* and *traceroute* commands

The traceroute utility can determine the path between the source and destination systems. This command also provides information on round-trip propagation time between each router and the source system.

The *tracert* command syntax for Windows is as follows:

        tracert host_name or ip_address

In this example, *ip_address* identifies the remote system.

The *traceroute* command syntax for Linux/UNIX is as follows:

        traceroute ip_address

NOTE:
You need to know how the *tracert* command is used and be able to recognize the command output.

Sometimes problems located far from your local network can compromise your network's performance. For example, if a company router or gateway fails, your Internet access may be interrupted. This disruption may cause name service failure, loss of e-mail service or complaints from users who cannot access the Web. The traceroute program can locate such failures.

Following is an example of output returned by the *tracert* command on a Windows computer (Linux/UNIX uses the *traceroute* command and has a slightly different result format):

```
tracert www.CIW-certified.com

Tracing route to www.CIW-certified.com [74.206.104.14] over a maximum of 30
hops:

1    2 ms    1 ms    2 ms    192.168.1.1
2   13 ms    9 ms   12 ms    10.160.64.1
3   10 ms   11 ms   11 ms    68.2.9.21
4    9 ms   10 ms    8 ms    68.2.13.166
5    9 ms   12 ms   13 ms    68.2.13.30
6   27 ms   16 ms    9 ms    chnddsrj02-ae2.0.rd.ph.cox.net [68.2.14.5]
7   32 ms   24 ms   20 ms    langhbr01-ae0.r2.1a.cox.net [68.1.0.232]
8   21 ms   25 ms   25 ms    eqix.lsan.twtelecom.net [206.223.123.36]
9   18 ms   18 ms   24 ms    66.192.251.26
10  40 ms   33 ms   35 ms    core-01-so-0-0-0-0.phnx.twtelecom.net [66.192.7.17]
11  36 ms   42 ms   39 ms    hagg-01-ge-0-3-0-510.phnx.twtelecom.net
[66.192.247.73]
12  40 ms   43 ms   45 ms    206-169-207-8.static.twtelecom.net [206.169.207.8]
13  44 ms   51 ms   42 ms    www.CIW-certified.com [74.206.104.14]

Trace complete.
```

NOTE:
This is an example of the Windows *tracert* command and not the Linux/UNIX *traceroute* command. The primary difference is that the *traceroute* command lists the host name and IP address before the time statistics.

The output from *tracert* shows the sequence of routers that the packets cross on the route from the local machine to the specified destination machine. In this case, the packets are traveling from Queen Creek, Arizona, to a machine named *www.CIW-certified.com*. In this example, the path from Queen Creek to *www.CIW-certified.com* involves 13 hops.

NOTE:
See **Optional Lab 2-2: Determining a local or remote destination node** and **Optional Lab 2-3: Using the tracert utility.**

The tracert program tries each stage of the path three times and reports the round-trip time for each stage.

The *route* command

The *route* command is used to display and manually configure the routes in a routing table. It is available on many operating systems, from Linux to Windows Vista and Windows Server 2008. Following is an example of the output from the Windows Vista *route* command:

```
c:\>route print
===========================================================================
Interface List
0x1 .......................... MS TCP Loopback interface
0x1000003 ...00 e0 98 76 80 65 . Linksys EtherFast 10/100 USB Network Adapter
===========================================================================
===========================================================================
Active Routes:
Network Destination        Netmask          Gateway       Interface  Metric
        0.0.0.0          0.0.0.0      192.168.2.1   192.168.2.101       1
      127.0.0.0        255.0.0.0        127.0.0.1       127.0.0.1       1
    192.168.2.0    255.255.255.0    192.168.2.101   192.168.2.101       1
  192.168.2.101  255.255.255.255        127.0.0.1       127.0.0.1       1
  192.168.2.255  255.255.255.255    192.168.2.101   192.168.2.101       1
255.255.255.255  255.255.255.255    192.168.2.101   192.168.2.101       1
Default Gateway:        192.168.2.1
===========================================================================
Persistent Routes:
  None

c:\>
```

Review the preceding output. Notice the default gateway, as well as information about how packets are routed locally. The *route* command provides additional options that allow you to add and delete routes on your system.

The *netstat* command

The *netstat* command is available in all IP-enabled operating systems. It is designed to provide information about the following:

- The services that are listening on your system. All services use ports. A port can be either a TCP port or a UDP port (there are 65,536 TCP and UDP ports). For example, the Microsoft World Wide Web Publishing Service (the IIS Web server) listens for requests on TCP Port 80. Whenever a Windows system shares a network folder, it will listen on TCP Port 139, among others. To list all listening ports, use the *netstat -a* command.

- The connections made from other systems. For example, if a remote host connects to your system's Web server, you can use the *netstat* command to determine the port that this remote client opened to connect to your Web server. Usually, a remote client will open a random port above 1023 to access Port 80 at your server. After the remote client opens a port to your server, a socket is established.

socket
The end point of a connection (either side), which usually includes the TCP or UDP port used and the IP address. Used for communication between a client and a server.

The *netstat* command displays the contents of various network-related data structures, such as the state of **sockets**. More specifically, this command displays information about packets processed by your system on the network. The command syntax is as follows:

```
netstat    options
```

Options will vary depending on the operating system. To learn about options for commands, open the command prompt and enter the following:

```
netstat -?
```

NOTE:
Some TCP/IP utility options are case-sensitive, unlike MS-DOS or Windows family command-line commands.

By itself, the *netstat* command displays only established active connections on the system. This command results in the following response:

```
Active Connections
  Proto    Local Address        Foreign Address        State
  TCP      student13:1037       192.168.3.13:1040      ESTABLISHED
  TCP      student13:1041       192.168.3.13:1050      ESTABLISHED
  TCP      student13:1046       192.168.3.13:1040      ESTABLISHED
  TCP      student13:1050       192.168.3.13:1050      ESTABLISHED
  TCP      student13:1599       207.199.11.24:ftp      ESTABLISHED
```

In the preceding response, four TCP connections have been established between student13 and a server with IP address 192.168.3.13. Another TCP connection has been established with an FTP server at 207.199.11.24. These TCP connections use the registered TCP port numbers 1037, 1041, 1046, 1050 and 1599. The FTP connection also uses the reserved TCP port number for FTP, which is 21.

The *ipconfig* command — Windows

The Windows *ipconfig* (Internet protocol configuration) command is used to display the Windows IP configuration. You have already used the *ipconfig* command to determine your physical address in a previous lesson. By default, this command displays only the IP address, subnet mask and default gateway.

The command syntax is as follows:

```
ipconfig   options
```

To view all the IP-related configuration information, use the */all* option. This option displays additional information, such as the hardware address. Following is an example of using the *ipconfig* command with the */all* option:

```
ipconfig  /all
```

This command yields the following results:

```
Windows IP Configuration:
    Host Name                    student13
    Primary DNS Suffix           class.com
    Node Type                    Broadcast
    IP Routing Enabled           No
    WINS Proxy Enabled           No
    DNS Suffix Search List       class.com

Ethernet adapter RTL80291:
    Description                  Novell 2000 Adapter
    Physical Address             00-00-1C-3A-62-BD
    DHCP Enabled                 Yes
    IPv4 Address                 192.168.3.13
    Subnet Mask                  255.255.255.0
    Default Gateway              192.168.3.1
```

The *ipconfig* command also renews and releases IP addresses from a DHCP server. If no adapter name is specified, all IP leases will be released.

For example:

```
ipconfig  /release adapter
ipconfig  /renew adapter
```

In the following lab, you will use the *ipconfig* command to analyze your computer's IP address configuration. Suppose your child must complete an after-school project in which she must post her work to a moderated online forum specially set up by her teacher. Your computer, which is using a newly installed NIC, is unable to access the Internet, and you suspect the problem may be in the TCP/IP configuration. You want to determine the MAC address of your network card. How would you use the *ipconfig* command to do so? What other configuration data can you view by using *ipconfig*?

 Lab 2-3: Identifying IP configuration and MAC address information

In this lab, you will locate your computer's IP address configuration and MAC (physical) address.

1. Select **Start**, type **cmd** in Start Search text box, then press **ENTER** to open the command prompt.

2. Enter the following command:

ipconfig /all

3. Your system's configuration information will display, as shown in Figure 2-11.

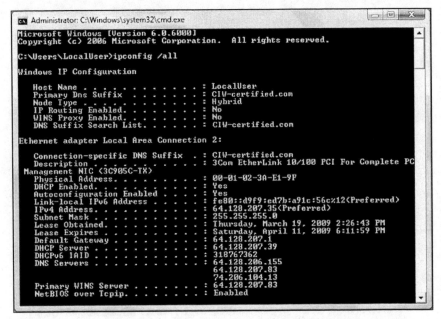

Figure 2-11: TCP/IP configuration — Windows Vista

4. Write your computer's adapter address (physical address), IP address, subnet mask and default gateway in the spaces provided.

Adapter address: _____

IP address: _____

Subnet mask: _____

Default gateway: _____

5. Close the command prompt window.

The *ifconfig* command — Linux/UNIX

The *ifconfig* (interface configuration) command is the Linux/UNIX equivalent of the *ipconfig* command. It displays the hardware and software configurations of the NIC.

The following is an example of using the *ifconfig* command:

```
ifconfig
```

The command yields the following results, depending on the NIC and network configuration:

```
eth0   Link encap:Ethernet HWaddr 00.A0.24.55.29.E8
       inet addr:192.168.3.11 Bcast:192.168.3.255 mask:255.255.255.0
       UP BROADCAST RUNNING MULTICAST MTU:1500 Metric:1
       RX packets:17 errors:0 dropped:0 overruns:0 frame:0
       TX packets:95 errors:0 dropped:0 overruns:0 carrier:0
       collisions:0 txqueuelen:100
       Interrupt:9 Base address:0x300

lo     Link encap:Local Loopback
       inet addr:127.0.0.1 Mask:255.0.0.0
```

```
UP LOOPBACK RUNNING MTU:3924 Metric:1
RX packets:22 errors:0 dropped:0 overruns:0 frame:0
TX packets:22 errors:0 dropped:0 overruns:0 carrier:0
collisions:0 txqueuelen:0
```

The *arp* command

To understand the *arp* command, you should review the information about Address Resolution Protocol (ARP) discussed earlier. ARP resolves software addresses to hardware addresses.

NOTE:
See **Optional Lab 2-4: Viewing the ARP cache.**

Assume that the following two hosts exist on a TCP/IP Ethernet network: Node1 and Node2. Node1 knows the IP address of Node2. However, Node1 cannot send data to Node2 unless Node1 knows the Ethernet (hardware) address of Node2. ARP resolves IP addresses to Ethernet addresses, as shown in Figure 2-12.

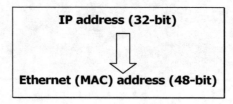

Figure 2-12: Resolving IP addresses to Ethernet (MAC) addresses

The *arp* command displays ARP information. It will show the physical (MAC) address of computers with which you have recently communicated. The command for viewing the ARP cache is as follows:

```
arp -a
```

NOTE:
You need to recognize this command and its use, but there is seldom any need to directly execute the *arp* command.

This command yields the following result:

```
Interface: 192.168.3.13
    Internet Address           Physical Address           Type
    192.168.3.11               00-60-83-7c-24-a2           Dynamic
    192.168.3.15               00-60-97-24-db-df           Dynamic
    192.168.4.12               00-aa-00-38-e7-c3           Dynamic
```

To delete an entry from the ARP cache, use the following syntax:

```
arp -d IP address
```

NOTE:
Every TCP/IP host will maintain its own ARP cache.

In this example, *IP address* identifies the entry you want to delete.

Network analyzers

Network analyzers, also called packet sniffers, allow network administrators to analyze data traversing a network. The data is "captured" by the network analyzer as it is transmitted across the network. After it has been captured, the data can be closely studied. For example, you can view the Ethernet header, which indicates the physical (MAC) addresses of both the source and the destination nodes.

Network analyzers can help an administrator troubleshoot and manage a network. Most network analyzers support several network protocols, such as TCP/IP and IPX/SPX. If you are viewing the packets on your network and notice a computer sending error messages, you can identify the computer and determine the problem. A free, powerful open-source network analyzer is Wireshark (*www.wireshark.org*).

A network analyzer can help troubleshoot and manage a network by providing the following services:

- **Monitoring network traffic to identify network trends** — This practice helps establish a network baseline. For example, you may notice that network traffic is heaviest in the morning when all users start their computers.

- **Identifying network problems and sending alert messages** — Problems (such as traffic exceeding a given parameter) can be predefined by the network administrator.

- **Identifying specific problems** — Problems might include error messages generated by a network device, which can then be repaired.

- **Testing network connections, devices and cables** — Network analyzers can send test packets over the network. The packets can be traced to discover faulty components or cables.

NOTE:
The open-source program Wireshark is a popular analyzer for both Linux and Windows systems. It is located at *www.wireshark.org,* and is primarily a packet sniffer.

Figure 2-13 shows the results of a packet capture using Wireshark.

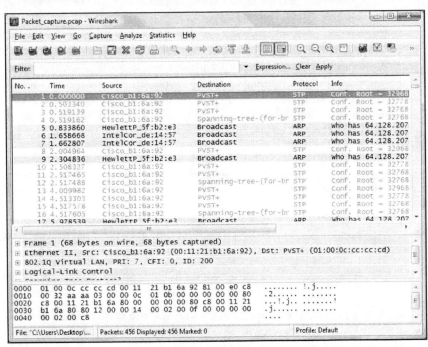

Figure 2-13: Wireshark packet capture

Troubleshooting considerations

OBJECTIVE
3.6.1:
Troubleshooting IP-enabled systems

As you troubleshoot connectivity problems on a LAN and to the Internet, consider the following:

- **DNS name resolution** — Have you entered the correct address for a DNS server? If you can ping an IP address but not a host name, there is a problem with DNS.

- **Hosts file configuration** — Is the hosts file accurate? Many systems check this file before going to a DNS server for name resolution.

- **Static versus dynamic IP addressing** — If you are adding a new host to a network, determine how the other hosts obtain an IP address. It is generally not wise to use both static and dynamic IP addressing on the same network because confusion can result if two nodes try to use the same address. Either configure all hosts to use DHCP or APIPA, or configure all hosts to use manually entered (static) IP addresses.

- **Default gateway and subnet mask** — Be sure that you have specified the correct IP address for the default gateway if you need to access the Internet. In addition, ensure that you have entered the correct subnet mask, because this information helps the system determine whether an address is local or remote.

OBJECTIVE
3.6.3: Client-side vs.
server-side in
troubleshooting

Using the diagnostic tools and interpreting your findings will help you determine whether the problem is on the client side or on the server side. For example, if you cannot ping another system on your network, you probably have a client-side connectivity problem. If you are able to ping your default gateway by IP address but not by name, there may be a problem with DNS (server-side) or there may be an incorrect entry in the hosts file (client-side). If you can ping your default gateway but cannot ping an address on the other side of the router, there may be a problem with the router.

If you can access the Internet (in other words, you already know that you have no connectivity problems) and you are suddenly unable to access your e-mail, check your account and password settings. After verifying these client-side issues, contact your ISP to see whether service is available. Occasionally, SMTP and POP servers are temporarily unavailable.

OBJECTIVE
3.6.4:
Troubleshooting
cable and ADSL
modems

Asymmetric Digital Subscriber Line (ADSL) and cable modem

Verifying the IP address, subnet mask and default gateway settings is especially important when troubleshooting Asymmetric Digital Subscriber Lines (ADSLs) and cable modems. Many ISPs offer static IP addresses to their **Digital Subscriber Line (DSL)** and cable customers, and you may be required to manually enter the IP addresses for the host and the gateway.

Digital Subscriber Line (DSL)
A high-speed direct Internet connection that uses all-digital networks.

cable modem
A device that allows computers to communicate over a network by modulating and demodulating the cable signal into a stream of data.

Cable and ADSL modems are designed for use with a single system. However, an entire home network can be connected through a **cable modem** by using an additional router. This router can be:

- A Windows or Linux system with one or two NICs, using software to translate addresses. Software can include Windows Internet Connection Sharing or the Linux *iptables* command.

- A dedicated router or firewall, such as those sold by Cisco Systems®/Linksys® (*www.linksysbycisco.com*) or NETGEAR, Inc. (*www.netgear.com*).

If you are using your own router and want to connect your modem to that router, you may need to use a crossover cable to establish the connection. You learned about crossover cables earlier in the course.

Sometimes cable and ADSL modems are reconfigured automatically by your ISP. Reconfiguration may include a new DHCP address, or even a new version of the operating system used on the modem. The operating system used for the cable modem is often referred to as firmware. Sometimes, a cable or ADSL modem will use a static IP address, so it is important to obtain information concerning your IP address either from the provider or from configuration information given at the time of installation.

As you troubleshoot connections, check for basic connectivity by pinging local IP addresses rather than DNS names; you want to discover basic connectivity first, then discover any problems with DNS resolution. You can then ping the default gateway. Simplifying your network may be necessary to test one element. For example, many home offices these days use a router to enable multiple systems to communicate with the Internet through a single cable/ADSL modem. If your network experiences problems, attach one of the workstations directly to the cable/ADSL modem. You may need to configure this workstation to use either DHCP (the most common option) or a static IP address, depending on your system provider. You can then determine whether the problem exists with the cable/ADSL modem.

Often, the best way to troubleshoot connectivity issues with these devices is to power them down, detach your connections, reattach your connections, and power them on again. You may want to wait one or two minutes before powering up the devices again. These devices reinitialize themselves when they are powered on, and your connectivity problems may disappear.

If you are still unable to access the Internet or your e-mail messages, contact your ISP. Service may be down, and many ISPs provide recorded messages informing you of service outages and their expected duration.

Communication Breakdown

Paul has been contracted to troubleshoot a problem with a cable modem connection for a small office. This office used seven Windows workstations and three Linux systems. One of the Linux systems acted as a router, which allowed the internal workstations to communicate with the Internet.

The connection has been working for a year, but suddenly all Internet access has failed. Office workers noticed the problem as soon as they tried to access the Internet to perform essential financial transactions for the company. The workers at the office have little knowledge of Internet connectivity, and have offered Paul a contract to fix the problem. Paul took the following steps:

- He used the ping utility to ensure that all local systems (systems in the office) could communicate with one another by IP address. His tests were successful, which showed that the systems could at least communicate on a basic level.

- Because the office network used a local DNS server, he then used the ping utility to confirm that all systems could communicate with one another by host name. This test was also successful, showing that DNS resolution was not the problem.

- Next, he used the ipconfig and ifconfig utilities to discover the default gateway. He noticed that the office was using reserved IP addresses that were statically configured. He then pinged the default gateway by IP address and host name. All tests showed that the default gateway (the Linux system) was responding. However, he still could not access the Internet from any of the systems.

- Paul then connected one of the workstations directly to the cable modem. He configured the system to use DHCP, which is what the cable modem required of any workstation or system attached to it. Still, no Internet access was available. These results suggested that the problem was either with the cable modem itself or with the ISP's network. He returned the network configuration of the office back to normal.

Paul knew that he could do little or nothing to resolve a problem with the ISP. However, he knew that he could still see whether the problem existed with the cable modem. Paul powered off the cable modem, waited a few minutes, and then powered it back on again. Internet access was restored. Paul checked the cable modem and found that it now had a different IP address, as well as a different version of the operating system. Apparently, a glitch had occurred after the ISP updated the software during the night. With Internet access restored to the office, Paul was able to collect his fee from a grateful customer.

Consider this scenario and answer the following questions:

- If rebooting the cable modem had not resolved the problem, what could Paul have done in regard to the ISP?

- Why did Paul take one of the workstations and connect it directly to the cable modem?

- Why was it important for Paul to configure the workstation to use DHCP in this particular instance? Is it possible that some cable or ADSL modems would require a fixed IP address instead? If so, where would Paul get this information?

Lesson Summary

Application project

How do you think the term "Request for Comments" originated? Investigate by locating, downloading and reading RFC 1000. Would you like to join the Internet Society (ISOC) and become a part of the standardization process? If so, contact ISOC (*www.isoc.org*) on the Web.

Must the loopback address be 127.0.0.1? No, but this address is recommended. To check your loopback address, locate and open the hosts file using your operating system's search feature. The loopback address is listed in the file. To test the loopback address, open the command prompt and enter the following command:

ping 127.0.0.1

You should receive a reply from your own computer (loopback), which means your NIC is configured properly for TCP/IP. Now enter the following command:

ping 127.34.34.100

This will also provide a successful reply. The entire 127 Class A address has been reserved for the loopback address. Exit the hosts file and close the command prompt.

Skills review

In this lesson, you studied the four layers of the Internet architecture model: network access, Internet, transport and application. You learned about RFCs, including the different states of protocols. You also defined common Internet protocols and matched them to their corresponding Internet layers. You learned about the routing process and about the routing protocols that are used to transfer packets from source to destination. You studied the key concepts of 32-bit IP addresses, including IP address structure, address classes, addressing rules and reserved addresses. You also studied subnet masks and learned about diagnostic tools used to troubleshoot TCP/IP networks.

Now that you have completed this lesson, you should be able to:

✓   3.1.5: Define the nature, purpose and operation essentials of Transmission Control Protocol/Internet Protocol (TCP/IP).

✓   3.2.4: Explain the routing process, including static routing versus dynamic routing, interior versus exterior routing protocols.

✓   3.2.5: Identify common TCP/IP network parameters, including IP address (static versus DHCP), subnet mask, default gateway, DNS information.

✓   3.3.1: Explain IP addressing and the concept of uniqueness, including IP address, subnet mask.

✓   3.3.2: Define IP address classes used on the Internet and determine valid IP addresses.

✓   3.3.3: Identify the uses of public and private IP addresses.

✓   3.3.4: Determine default subnet masks and describe the ANDing process.

✓   3.3.5: Define Classless Interdomain Routing (CIDR).

✓   3.3.6: Identify basic IPv6 concepts.

✓ 3.6.1: Identify issues to consider when troubleshooting IP-enabled systems, including DNS/name resolution, correct default gateway and subnet mask, hosts file configuration, DHCP versus static IP configuration.

✓ 3.6.2: Identify when to use various diagnostic tools for troubleshooting and resolving Internet problems, including ping, ipconfig, route, arp, traceroute, netstat, network analyzers (packet sniffers).

✓ 3.6.3: Distinguish between client-side problems and server-side problems when troubleshooting common services (e.g., e-mail and Web client connectivity issues).

✓ 3.6.4: Troubleshoot cable and ADSL modem connectivity.

Lesson 2 Review

1. Explain how the OSI/RM layers equate to the Internet architecture model layers.

   _____

   _____

   _____

   _____

2. Name the four maturity-level states through which a protocol must pass before it becomes a standard.

   _____

3. Define demultiplexing.

   _____

   _____

4. What type of routing is being used when a router is involved in communication between two computers that are not on the same network?

   _____

5. Routing Information Protocol (RIP) and Open Shortest Path First (OSPF) are examples of what type of routing protocol?

   _____

6. What provides structure to the approximately 4 billion possible Internet addresses.

   _____

7. Name the four types of broadcast addresses.

   _____

8. Name the three basic parameters that can be configured for a workstation on a TCP/IP network.

   _____

   _____

Lesson 2 Supplemental Material

This section is a supplement containing additional tasks for you to complete in conjunction with the lesson. These elements are:

- **Activities**
  Pen-and-paper activities to review lesson concepts or terms.

- **Optional Labs**
  Computer-based labs to provide additional practice.

- **Lesson Quiz**
  Multiple-choice test to assess knowledge of lesson material.

Activity 2-1: Reviewing TCP/IP suite protocols

In this activity, you will review what you have learned about TCP/IP (Internet) protocols. Match each protocol name on the left with the correct function on the right.

1. IP

   A. Broadcasts a request to translate an Internet (IP) address into a physical (MAC) address.

2. FTP

   B. Standard protocol for transferring e-mail messages.

3. DHCP

   C. Basic data transfer method used throughout the Internet. A connectionless protocol.

4. SMTP

   D. Protocol used for transporting HTML documents.

5. ARP

   E. Used for transferring files between computers.

6. HTTP

   F. Provides TCP/IP client systems (hosts) with address and configuration property information.

Understanding the protocols used by different operations can be helpful when troubleshooting communication failures.

Activity 2-2: Determining classes and valid IP addresses

In this activity, you will determine the class of each IP address and whether it is a valid IP address for a computer. If it is not a valid IP address, explain why in the spaces provided.

	IP Address	Class	Valid? Yes or No	Explanation
1.	192.23.111.8			
2.	10.1.1.256			
3.	148.108.62.95			
4.	127.0.0.1			
5.	245.255.123.49			
6.	100.54.100.90			
7.	162.34.0.0			
8.	127.65.18.191			
9.	1.1.1.1			
10.	208.152.84.255			
11.	225.37.257.34			
12.	255.255.255.255			

Activity 2-3: Determining default subnet masks

In this activity, you will determine the default subnet mask for each IP address. Write your answers in the spaces provided.

1. 17.223.13.22

_____

2. 194.10.99.2

_____

3. 211.34.126.10

_____

4. 152.4.202.69

_____

5. 128.156.88.1

_____

Optional Lab 2-1: Viewing port number assignments

In this optional lab, you will visit the IANA Web page that reports port assignments made by ICANN.

Note: Your computer must have Internet access for you to complete this lab.

1. Open any Web browser and go to ***www.iana.org/assignments/port-numbers***.

2. Review the port assignments, including both well-known and registered ports.

3. Go to ***www.iana.org/protocols/***. This page is more complex because it describes various parameters and protocols that help IP-based networks to function. To view information about a protocol, click on its title. Browse this page to view the Internet protocols and the RFCs that define them.

NOTE:
You should not make an application for any port numbers at this time.

4. Go to ***www.iana.org/protocols/apply/***. This page contains links to forms you can use to apply for port numbers. Click the links to view the forms for the following:

   • **Online Application for a System (Well-Known) Port Number** — This page provides a form that allows a company to request from ICANN and IANA a well-known port number for a specific service.

   • **Online Application for a User (Registered) Port Number** — This page provides a form that allows a company to request from ICANN and IANA a registered port number for a specific service.

5. When you are finished, close your browser.

In this lab, you learned more about port number assignments, and about how ICANN and IANA cooperate to regulate Internet communication.

Optional Lab 2-2: Determining a local or remote destination node

In this optional lab, you will use the *tracert* utility to determine whether the destination computer requires a router to forward a packet to another network.

Note: You can perform this lab only if you have a friend or family member with whom you can perform the lab steps concurrently. Your partner must also have completed Lab 2-1 to reconfigure his or her computer with a reserved IP address using the same Class C network address as did you. For example, your partner must also have specified an IP address of 192.168.3.X (where X is a number between 1 and 254, but different from the number you specified) and a subnet mask of 255.255.255.0. If you do not have a friend or family member with whom you can perform this lab, skip it and continue to the next optional lab.

Tech Note: The tracert replies displayed in this optional lab are based on computers configured with reserved IP addresses. Your replies will vary, depending on the IP addresses used by you and your partner. Your partner must be on the same network for this lab to succeed.

Tech Note: If you are behind a firewall, you may not be able to perform this optional lab successfully because many firewalls disable ICMP at the firewall.

1. Open a command prompt. At the prompt, enter the following:

    tracert [partner's IP address]

2. The response should resemble the following (depending on your partner's IP address):

    ```
    1   <10 ms  <10 ms  <10 ms  student7 [192.168.3.7]
    ```

    Only one hop was required because the packet went directly to the destination. A router was not required because the destination node was on the same network.

3. Trace a packet to a remote network. Identify a computer that is on a remote network. For example, if your IP address is 192.168.3.6, use the *tracert* command to trace the route to a computer with the IP address of 192.168.2.x or 192.168.4.x (where x is a variable, depending on your partner's address assignment). If you are connected to the Internet, you can enter the IP address or URL, such as *www.yahoo.com*. At the prompt, enter the following:

    tracert [remote IP address]

4. The response should resemble the following (depending on your default gateway and destination node):

    ```
    1   <10 ms  <10 ms  <10 ms  gateway [192.168.3.1]
    2   <10 ms  <10 ms  <10 ms  student7 [192.168.4.7]
    ```

    The first entry is the router (default gateway). The second entry is the destination host. Two hops were required because the packet destination was not on the local network. To access the remote network, the packet was directed to the default gateway, which routed the packet to the destination network.

5. Close the command prompt window.

Optional Lab 2-3: Using the tracert utility

In this optional lab, you will experiment with the *tracert* utility.

Tech Note: If you are behind a firewall, you may not be able to conduct this lab successfully because many firewalls disable ICMP at the firewall.

Note: This lab requires Internet connectivity.

1. Open a command prompt.

2. Use the *tracert* command to determine the path from your computer to your favorite location on the Internet. For example, enter the following:

   `tracert www.icann.org`

3. How many hops does it take to reach ICANN? What is the round-trip time? Compare *tracert* command output for paths from your computer with paths from computers in the United States (*www.ansi.org*) and in Europe (*www.iso.ch*).

4. If possible, disconnect your computer from the Internet. Run the *tracert* command to an Internet location, such as *www.icann.org*. What happens? Can you determine where the breakdown occurred? Write the result in the space provided.

   _____

   _____

5. Close the command prompt window.

Optional Lab 2-4: Viewing the ARP cache

In this optional lab, you will view the ARP cache, then add and delete ARP entries.

Note: You can perform this lab only if you have a friend or family member with whom you can perform the lab steps concurrently. Your partner must also have completed Lab 2-1 to reconfigure his or her computer with a reserved IP address using the same Class C network address as did you. For example, your partner must also have specified an IP address of 192.168.3.X (where X is a number between 1 and 254, but different from the number you specified) and a subnet mask of 255.255.255.0. If you do not have a friend or family member with whom you can perform this lab, skip it and continue to the lesson quiz.

1. Open a command prompt and enter the following:

   `arp -a`

2. View the entries in your ARP cache. If an entry does not exist for your partner's computer, create one by entering the following command at the command prompt:

   `ping [partner's IP address]`

3. View the ARP cache again by entering the following:

   `arp -a`

   An ARP entry should exist for your partner in the ARP cache.

4. Write your partner's ARP entry in the spaces provided. Include only the IP and physical addresses.

   Internet address: _____

   Physical address: _____

5. To delete an ARP entry use the *-d* option. At the command prompt, enter the following:

   `arp -d [partner's IP address]`

   Note: In Windows Vista, you may receive the following error message: "The ARP entry deletion failed: 87." This occurs if you do not have the administrative privileges required to purge the cache. To give yourself administrative privileges, right-click the **Command Prompt** *icon in the Start menu, select* **Run As Administrator***, then click* **Continue***. A new command prompt window will open with the word "Administrator" in the title bar. Enter the* **arp -d** *command again and it should work properly.*

6. View the ARP cache by entering the following:

   `arp -a`

   Your partner's ARP entry should no longer exist.

7. Close the command prompt window.

Lesson 2 Quiz

1. What is Transmission Control Protocol/Internet Protocol (TCP/IP)?

   a. A suite of protocols that allow computers running the same operating system to communicate
   b. A suite of protocols that allow computers from different vendors with various operating systems to communicate
   c. A single protocol that allows computers from different vendors with various operating systems to communicate
   d. A single protocol that allows computers running the same operating system to communicate

2. Which process determines the path that a packet will travel across a network?

   a. Resolving
   b. ANDing
   c. Routing
   d. Pinging

3. Which routing protocol is sensitive to such criteria as available bandwidth and security?

   a. Open Shortest Path First (OSPF)
   b. Routing Information Protocol (RIP)
   c. File Transfer Protocol (FTP)
   d. Transmission Control Protocol (TCP)

4. What is the default subnet mask for a Class B address?

   a. 255.255.255.255
   b. 255.255.255.0
   c. 255.255.0.0
   d. 255.0.0.0

5. Which of the following diagnostic tools helps determine connectivity between source and destination systems?

   a. The tracert command
   b. The ipconfig command
   c. The ping command
   d. The netstat command

Lesson 3: Internetworking Servers

Objectives

By the end of this lesson, you will be able to:

⚐ 3.4.1: Distinguish between HTTP and other Internet server types.

⚐ 3.4.2: Identify the functions and features of common Internet-based services, and identify protocols used by each, including file, print, HTTP, proxy, caching, mail, mailing list, instant messaging, media, DNS, FTP, news, certificate, directory, fax, transaction.

⚐ 3.4.3: Choose the correct server to fulfill a specific business/organizational need.

Pre-Assessment Questions

1. Which protocol is usually used when transferring HTML page content from a Web server to a client browser?

   a. HTTP
   b. NNTP
   c. MIME
   d. FTP

2. Which is the preferred protocol for transferring a 5-MB file between two systems over the Internet?

   a. HTTP
   b. NNTP
   c. MIME
   d. FTP

3. What is a directory server?

   _____

   _____

Overview of Internetworking Servers

NOTE:
You should have a general familiarity with the servers discussed in this lesson. The majority of the information in this lesson is beyond the scope of the CIW Foundations exam, but is extremely helpful for any IT professional.

Traditional networks are designed to store files in central sites and databases, and then present them to users at remote workstations. These files and databases that network users share are called network services. With the advent of the Internet, however, network services have become more distributed, or decentralized.

TCP/IP has allowed network services to become more accessible to the Internet. Common servers found on isolated networks and on the Internet include the following:

- File
- Print
- HTTP
- Proxy
- Mail

- Mailing list
- Media
- DNS
- FTP
- News

- Certificate
- Directory
- Fax
- Transaction

The following sections will discuss each of these server types.

File and Print Servers

NOTE:
File and print servers can be implemented locally, through a WAN or over the Internet.

Possibly the most common types of servers, file and print servers are a major factor in the increasing popularity of networks. These servers are often incorporated as one service (file and print) even if only one of the services is used on a server.

File server

OBJECTIVE
3.4.2: Common Internet services/protocols

File servers are network servers that store data files and programs. A file server is basically a remote disk drive that is shared by the network users. File servers are not the same as application servers: An application server runs programs and processes data; a file server stores files and programs. A file server can be any computer that shares a file, folder or entire disk drive with the network. It should be a powerful server capable of high speeds, security and data protection.

Print server

OBJECTIVE
3.4.2: Common Internet services/protocols

Network printers allow multiple users to send print jobs to the same physical printers. Without network printing capability, any user who wanted to print would need a printer physically attached to his or her computer, or would need to copy the document to a computer that had a printer attached. Because this arrangement would become cost-prohibitive in even small offices, most LANs use network-printing functions.

Line printer/line printer daemon (LPR/LPD)

print queue
A mechanism that stores print requests until they are passed to a printing device.

The Linux/UNIX network operating system can use the LPR/LPD printing protocol to submit print jobs to network printers. When a user submits a file for printing, the file is transmitted over the network in one direction (unidirectional). The LPR initiates commands and the LPD executes them. The commands manage the submission of print jobs to the printer, such as **print queue** management, and the transfer of print jobs from the print queue to the printer.

In the following lab, you will learn how to set up a computer as a file server. File sharing is an integral part of every network. Suppose you are the supervisor in a medical office. You may need to store patients' records in files on a single file server so that your employees can access those records. But you want to control access permissions to the files because some patient records are extremely confidential. How would you set up the file server so that your employees could access only certain files?

 Lab 3-1: Creating a file server

In this lab, you will create a shared folder on your computer to act as a file service so that other users on the same LAN can access and modify files stored in the folder.

1. Open **Windows Explorer** and create a new folder named *Shared* on drive C.

2. Right-click the **Shared** folder and click **Share**. This step displays the File Sharing dialog box (Figure 3-1).

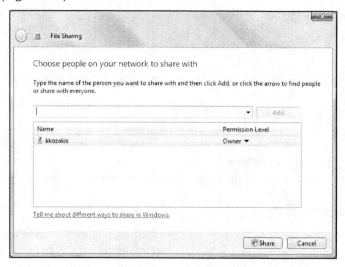

Figure 3-1: File Sharing dialog box

3. Click the drop-down arrow to the right of the empty text box, select **Everyone**, then click **Add**. This action specifies that anyone connected to the network can share the Shared folder.

4. Notice that Reader appears in the Permission Level column for Everyone. This means that a person can view your folder and its contents, but cannot add, modify or delete content. Click the arrow next to **Reader**, then select **Co-Owner**. This action specifies that everyone connected to the network can view, add, modify or delete the shared folder and its contents.

5. Click the **Share** button, then click **Done**. You can now "serve" files to other users over the network. Any files you put into the Shared folder are available to the network. The Shared folder icon should resemble Figure 3-2.

Figure 3-2: Shared folder named "Shared"

6. Double-click the **Shared** folder. Create a text document in the folder by right-clicking anywhere in the Shared folder window and selecting **New | Text Document**. Name the file with your name, such as *Sarah.txt*.

7. Open the text file, enter a line of text, then save and close the text file.

   At this point, other users on the same LAN can access the Shared folder on your hard disk drive as if it were a file server. For example, other users can view the contents of the folder, open the Sarah.txt file, modify it and then save it in the Shared folder. Other users can also copy and move files between the Shared folder and their own computers. Shared folders provide for a quick and efficient way to transfer files between computers on a LAN. Using shared folders is much simpler than sending documents by means of FTP or e-mail.

8. Close the **Windows Explorer** window.

Using a file server is similar to accessing folders on your own computer. The only difference is that you must access the folders through the network. You can also back up documents on a file server. The simplicity and ease of use of file servers make them extremely popular on LANs. Shared folders are commonly implemented on company LANs so that files are accessible to company employees and departments.

HTTP Server Essentials

OBJECTIVE
3.4.1: HTTP servers

OBJECTIVE
3.4.2: Common Internet services/protocols

The World Wide Web is a collection of computer systems running the HTTP service. (Remember that HTTP, on which the Web operates, is a TCP/IP application-layer protocol.) These computer systems (servers) act together as document delivery systems. Documents are delivered to systems running Web browsers (also called clients) as well as to user agents. These client systems request documents from HTTP servers, which are usually called Web servers. The documents that the server processes may be from a disk archive, or they may be created dynamically when the client requests them. The HTTP server and the Web browser are examples of client/server communications.

A Web browser is a software application that interprets and displays HTML documents. Worldwide interaction between the HTTP server and the Web browser also exemplifies the hyper-distributed networking involved in Web-based networking.

daemon
A Linux/UNIX program that is usually initiated at startup and runs in the background until required.

A Web site is a collection of documents and applications that create documents. The site is organized around a Web server process, which runs as a **daemon** process on Linux/UNIX systems and as a service on Windows systems. The Web server process binds to TCP Port 80 by default and listens for incoming requests from clients such as Web browsers. These requests are formed in a language called Hypertext Markup Language (HTML). The applications used by Web servers to create documents dynamically are called Common Gateway Interface (CGI) applications (or scripts).

Web server role

The HTTP (i.e., Web) server has access to a set of documents that it may return to a client in response to an appropriate request. These documents are located in a mass storage device, such as a hard drive, in a specific location that the server can read. These documents can be in a wide range of formats. For example, the server probably has access to a large collection of HTML documents as well as the associated image files in a range of formats. In addition, the server may be able to supply many other multimedia documents, such as sound files and video clips.

HTTP servers and MIME

An HTTP server can download any file type. Although a Web browser renders only certain types of images, HTTP can process a variety of file types. The **Multipurpose Internet Mail Extensions (MIME)** system allows HTTP and e-mail attachments to identify the files they must use. A version of MIME that encrypts MIME data, called **Secure MIME (S/MIME)**, is used for secure transmissions.

The different **MIME types** are classified under broad headings (text, image, application, audio and video), and then subclassified by exact type. For example, an HTML document has MIME type "text/html," whereas a plain text document has type "text/plain."

Whenever data is passed between a Web server and a browser, the data is labeled with its MIME type. The recipient uses the MIME type to render the information. For example, when a Web server sends an HTML document to a browser, it labels the document with its MIME type (text/html) so the browser can display the document properly. When a Web server sends an Adobe Acrobat file (application/x-pdf) to a browser, the browser will open the correct plug-in (namely, Adobe Acrobat Reader) to view the file. A plug-in is a program installed as part of the browser to extend its basic functionality.

When a Web browser requests a server resource, the server deduces the resource's MIME type from the extension part of the document name. For example, the server understands a request for the Uniform Resource Locator (URL) *http://www.machine.com/info.html* as referring to a document of type text/html, and labels the document with that type when it returns the document to the browser. The correspondence between file name extensions and MIME types may be hard-wired into the server, or may be configurable.

Images and MIME type

Similarly, if a Web server presents images, then it will use MIME to present them. If, for some reason, you need to present a non-standard image format — in other words, one that was not Graphics Interchange Format (GIF), Joint Photographic Experts Group (JPEG) or Portable Network Graphics (PNG) — then you will need to define a MIME type to accommodate the proprietary format.

File storage

You should store all files away from the Web server's root unless you need to create a virtual directory. A virtual directory is a folder that resides on the same server or another server and acts as if it resided on the server's root. It hides the actual location and name of the original folder. You will learn more about virtual directories later in this lesson.

Multipurpose Internet Mail Extensions (MIME)
A protocol that enables operating systems to map file name extensions to corresponding applications. Also used by applications to automatically process files downloaded from the Internet.

Secure MIME (S/MIME)
Secure version of MIME that adds encryption to MIME data.

MIME type
Identifies the contents of a file in the MIME encoding system using a type/subtype format; examples are image/jpg and text/plain.

NOTE:
A key point is the purpose of MIME and how it is used in HTTP and mail servers.

Naming the initial document

Although most servers allow you to define any name for the initial HTML document, most servers use *index.html*. So, when you want to create a page that will automatically render in a client's Web browser, you should discover the name that your server is configured to report. Other common initial document names include *welcome.html, main.html, default.htm, default.html* and *default.asp*.

Additional server considerations

NOTE:
This section on additional server considerations is important for you to understand. The topics covered are applicable to all servers, especially account access, permissions, logging and monitoring server and network bandwidth use.

Following is a brief discussion of issues concerning the use of an HTTP or other type of server.

HTTP servers and the operating system

HTTP servers work closely with the computer's operating system. One way to describe their interaction is that an HTTP server resides "on top of" the other services that form the operating system. Some servers, such as Apache server and Microsoft Internet Information Services (IIS), typically work on only one type of operating system. Other HTTP servers, such as Zeus and Sun Java System Web Server, provide versions that will work with a variety of operating systems.

Server security and operating system security

permissions
Instructions given by an operating system or server (or a combination thereof) that restrict or allow access to system resources, such as files, user databases and system processes.

Most Web servers can restrict files, folders and directories by establishing **permissions**. Permissions include the ability to read a file (read permission), create or delete a file (write permission), execute programs (execute permission) or deny access (no access). Operating systems can also establish permissions.

For example, the Linux operating system can restrict access to a certain resource, such as a file or directory. Apache server (or any other server) can restrict access to a specific resource. Operating system permissions generally take precedence over those granted by an HTTP server. Sometimes, the operating system and HTTP server permissions should be combined to ensure that a folder is secure.

NOTE:
You should know the basic permissions: read, write, execute and no access.

However, permissions can also become confused. CGI scripts and programs (files), for example, require execute permission. Therefore, the folder in which a script resides must have execute permission, as well. Naturally, you must determine whether both the Web server and the operating system allow execute permission. If the operating system forbids all executable program files in that folder, then the administrator must change this setting, even though the Web server has already given execute permission.

Access control

NOTE:
Access control is needed on any Web server containing sensitive information and is critical for secure areas of e-commerce sites. The server needs to validate the client, but the client also needs to validate the server in these situations. Refer to the discussion about certificates later in the lesson.

An important part of setting up and managing a Web server (or any other server type) is access control, which is similar to permissions. Most Web sites offer access to the general public; users do not need special permission to access such server resources. This type of access is often called anonymous access.

However, some sites need to restrict access to some or all of their server resources. An Access Control List (ACL) defines the permissions for a resource by specifying which users and groups have access to the resource. For example, the Web site may offer certain documents only to registered or paying users. Alternatively, the site may offer access to personal information, which must be supplied only to the owner of that information. The traditional method of restricting access to server resources is based on a database of permitted users, who must supply a password to access particular server information. The database of permitted users may be:

- Users with accounts on the host system. IIS, for example, uses the system account database on the host computer as its database of permitted users.

- A special database managed by the server itself (for example, the National Center for Supercomputing Applications [NCSA] server).

The second method separates people with permission to access Web server information from those with more global permission on the host system. Because thousands of users may be allowed to access information, the second method is much better for restricting access.

 Web servers that limit access to resources need a method for users to identify themselves; usually some form of password is required. Password-based access to the server is vulnerable to password sniffing, unless the server uses a method for exchanging encrypted passwords. Password sniffing is a method of intercepting the transmission of a password during the authentication process.

Access control and the server account

The access control restrictions discussed previously are enforced in the following two stages:

1. The Web server process checks to see whether certain actions are allowed, based on its configuration information.

2. The operating system enforces restrictions on actions that the Web server process can perform.

The operating system restrictions are based on the fact that the Web server process is owned by a user account on the host computer, and is subject to limitations imposed on that account. For example, if the Web server process is owned by an account called "http" and the http user does not have read permission in a certain directory, the server cannot access that directory, regardless of the server's internal configuration. In general, the restrictions imposed by the operating system are more reliable than those imposed by the Web server alone.

To take advantage of the security mechanisms provided by the operating system, the Web server process must be owned by an account with the fewest permissions needed for it to perform its task. In particular, the server should not be owned by a superuser or administrator account because a Web server process with these permissions is unconstrained by the operating system. For example, people use e-mail every day to communicate. Using an e-mail account requires a user name and password in conjunction with authentication (as you learned earlier, authentication is the ability to verify a person's identity). Remember that the Web server may demand permissions that the operating system may deny, especially when using CGI scripts.

Aliases and virtual directories

As part of their configuration options, most Web servers allow flexible mapping of URL path names to file names. This kind of mapping has various names, including virtual directories and aliases. Some of the advantages of flexible mapping of URL path names to file names include the following examples:

- The more flexible the mapping from URL path names to file names, the more freedom the administrator has to arrange files on the disk.

- If a set of documents may be reasonably accessed under several URL path names, all these URL path names can be mapped to the same file names.

For example, suppose you want a server to be able to supply a collection of documents called *doc1.html*, *doc2.html* and so forth, located in the directory */home/sales/docs*. The server root directory is */usr/local/etc/httpd*, but you want browsers to access the file *doc1.html* under the URL *http://www.CIW-certified.com/sales/doc1.html*. To allow this access, you must configure the server to map the URL path */sales/doc1.html* to the actual file path */home/sales/docs*, instead of to */usr/local/etc/httpd/docs/sales/doc1.html*.

Logging

Web servers and a majority of server types generate a log of the requests they handle. In addition to helping monitor correct server operation, these logs eventually contain information about who uses the server resources, which resources are most popular and how users initially find the site. The following three types of information are usually collected in server logs:

- **Access data** — Each time a client issues an HTTP command to the server, the command is logged.

- **Referrer data** — Part of the information transmitted by a browser to a server is the URL at which the browser is pointing when it makes the request. This information may be logged to indicate how users enter the site.

- **Error data** — Server errors (including improperly formatted HTTP requests, dropped TCP connections and access violations) are logged to help monitor server operations.

Monitoring server and network bandwidth use

Monitoring server and network bandwidth use is key to maintaining consistent performance. It allows network administrators to identify network bottlenecks in a timely manner. Bottlenecks usually occur when a server or network is flooded with traffic and cannot perform at acceptable levels.

Most network users are not tolerant of network servers that perform inconsistently — fast one day and slow the next. So the first objective is to bring about consistency in the performance. However, to detect inconsistencies, an administrator must have something to measure against, namely a baseline of normal network performance.

baseline
A recording of network activity, obtained through documentation and monitoring, that serves as an example for comparing future network activity.

A **baseline** is a recording of network activity, obtained through documentation and monitoring, that serves as an example for comparing future network activity. Baselines should be recorded when a network is running correctly. If problems are introduced to the network, the new network behavior can be compared with the baseline. Baselines can be used to determine bottlenecks, identify heavy traffic patterns, and analyze daily network use and protocol patterns.

The Windows Vista Reliability And Performance Monitor can determine a baseline for the number of packets per second sent to a system over a network. Reliability And Performance Monitor allows you to collect data for a particular variable over time. This baseline will allow you to determine the amount of network traffic sent to your system during normal traffic periods. It can also determine a baseline for processor (CPU) and memory use on the server.

During peak network traffic periods, or when performance is noticeably slower, Reliability And Performance Monitor can be used to collect data and compare it with the baseline. If the new data shows a significant increase in network traffic, processor or memory use, changes may be required. For instance, you may need to install a faster processor or more RAM on the server. You may need to increase your network bandwidth by upgrading the network from Ethernet to Fast Ethernet, or replace a problem hub with a switch.

Server and network monitoring software such as Reliability And Performance Monitor are essential to monitoring server and network bandwidth use.

Common Web servers

NOTE:
Additional information is provided about popular Web servers later in this lesson.

The most common Web servers include:

* Apache server (*www.apache.org*)

* Microsoft Internet information Services (IIS) (*www.microsoft.com*)

* Sun Java System Web Server (*www.sun.com*).

Originally, Apache server operated exclusively on Linux/UNIX systems. However, in 1998 it was ported to Windows servers. As of this writing, Apache servers represent almost half of those used on the Internet.

Each of these Web servers implements the topics covered in the preceding section, which includes account access, permissions and logging. All servers can be monitored to determine their system and network bandwidth use.

Server-side technologies

Web servers often run programs to help enhance a Web page or provide access to database servers. These programs are called server-side applications. Examples of server-side technologies include:

* **JavaServer Pages (JSP)** — Sun's solution. You can learn more about JSP at www.sun.com.

* **Active Server Pages (ASP) and .NET** — Microsoft's server-side scripting solutions. ASP is an older solution. You can learn more about ASP and .NET at www.microsoft.com.

* **PHP Hypertext Preprocessor (PHP)** — An open-source solution. You can learn more about PHP at www.php.net.

Each of these languages can be used to implement CGI.

Open Database Connectivity (ODBC)

data source name (DSN)
A text string that is used to reference the data source by application programs.

As you learned earlier, ODBC is a standard developed by Microsoft that allows databases created by various vendors to communicate with one another. ODBC is often used with server-side languages. It is also used by database servers. When creating an entry in ODBC, you need to register the database in ODBC and provide a **data source name (DSN)**, which contains all the necessary connectivity information. Specific information you need to provide includes the vendor's database driver, the name of the database, a user ID and the location of the database. Several types of DSN exist. The most common are the system DSN, which all users can employ, and a user DSN, which is designed for use only by a specific user.

Database Servers

OBJECTIVE
3.4.2: Common
Internet
services/protocols

A database is a file that stores information in a series of tables and columns. Tables in a database contain fields that allow data to be read and cross-referenced.

Many different types of databases exist, including flat file databases (for example, the Windows registry) and relational databases. A relational database allows you to manipulate information contained in tables and columns. All database servers present relational databases, and make it possible for remote individuals (for example, users with Web browsers) and hosts (for example, Web servers) to access the data. A database server can be installed on a dedicated system or on the same system as a Web server. In either case, a Web server is often configured to present HTML/XHTML pages that present information obtained from a relational database.

Database servers and Structured Query Language (SQL)

**Structured Query
Language (SQL)**
A language used to
create and
maintain
professional, high-
performance
corporate
databases.

All database servers use **Structured Query Language (SQL)** to create, maintain and query databases. Commands such as SELECT, FROM and JOIN can be used to create, maintain and manipulate tables. Often, a Web site administrator will need to use SQL to ensure that a Web page presents valid database information on a page.

Examples of database servers include:

- Oracle (*www.oracle.com*).

- IBM DB2 (*www.ibm.com*).

- Microsoft SQL Server (*www.microsoft.com*).

Proxy Servers

OBJECTIVE
3.4.2: Common
Internet
services/protocols

A proxy server is an intermediary between a network host and other hosts outside the network. Its main functions are to provide enhanced security, manage TCP/IP addresses and speed access to the Internet by providing caching server functions for frequently used documents.

In a network setting, a proxy server replaces the network IP address with another, contingent address. This process effectively hides the actual IP address from the rest of the Internet, thereby protecting the entire network.

Proxy servers can provide the following additional services:

NOTE:
You need to
understand that a
proxy server is often
used to cache Web
pages on larger
networks.

- **Caching of Web documents** — If corporate users access information on a Web server from the Internet, that information is cached to the local proxy server. This caching allows anyone on the corporate intranet to access the same information from the local system instead of repeatedly downloading the files from the Internet. This feature reduces the amount of network traffic produced on the Internet, which leads to improved performance for the corporate intranet and the Internet.

- **Corporate firewall access** — A proxy server can provide safe passage for corporate users to the Internet through a firewall, allowing protected use of HTTP and FTP. You will learn more about firewalls later in the course.

- **Filtering client transactions** — A proxy can control access to remote Web servers and their resources by filtering client transactions. Filtering is accomplished by limiting or denying access to specific URLs, specific host IP addresses, domain names, host or computer names, Web contents, and specific users. For example, you can deny access by anyone in a company to *http://www.nonsense.com* by specifying that URL in a proxy server's configuration. You can also deny access *from* a particular computer within a company, using the computer's name or IP address to limit access. In addition, you can deny access to an individual by specifying that person's user name.

- **Transaction logging** — Proxy servers generally support transaction logging. Network administrators can track client activity and customize which data to record. Some of the data that can be logged includes accessed URLs, dates and times, and the byte counts of all data that has been transferred. Information on routing and success of a transaction can also be logged and used to evaluate network performance.

- **Securing internal hosts** — A proxy server can help isolate internal systems so that they cannot be as easily attacked from systems based on the Internet.

Proxy server configuration

NOTE:
If you have time, open the Internet Options window of the Control Panel, then click the Connections tab. Next, click the LAN Settings button to open the window in which you can enter proxy settings. Similar windows are available in Mozilla Firefox and other browsers.

If your network uses a proxy server, you must ensure that all the clients are properly configured. For example, to browse the Web, you must enter the correct address of that proxy server into your browser. Otherwise, the proxy server will ignore any requests you make.

Furthermore, you must configure every application to work with your proxy server, including Web browsers, Telnet applications and FTP programs. Otherwise, not all applications will be able to access outside networks. Browsers from both Mozilla and Microsoft provide proxy server configuration, and you can obtain third-party programs that will allow almost any application to work properly with a proxy server.

Mail Servers

OBJECTIVE
3.4.2: Common Internet services/protocols

A mail server stores and/or forwards e-mail messages using several protocols, including SMTP, POP3 and IMAP. As you learned earlier, these three protocols all reside at the application layer of the OSI/RM.

Simple Mail Transfer Protocol (SMTP) is responsible solely for sending e-mail messages. In Linux/UNIX, the sendmail program activates in response to a command and sends the requested message.

 Do not confuse SMTP with the protocols that store and access mail. SMTP only sends the e-mail message. If you are using Linux/UNIX, the sendmail program uses SMTP to relay the message to the recipient. If you are using Windows, you will use a program such as Microsoft Exchange Server, or one from another vendor.

Two methods are used to store and access e-mail messages:

- **Post Office Protocol version 3 (POP3)** — POP3 servers store and forward e-mail messages to the host. For example, if you were to send an e-mail message, the message would be stored in the appropriate mail server until the recipient downloaded it from the server. The POP3 server responds to a request, asks for a password, and then forwards the messages immediately.

- **Internet Message Access Protocol (IMAP)** — IMAP handles messages in a more sophisticated manner because it allows a user to browse and manage files remotely, whereas a POP3 server forces a user to download files before reading, deleting or otherwise managing them.

Popular mail servers include Eudora Internet Mail Server, IBM Lotus Domino, Kerio MailServer and Microsoft Exchange Server.

Mail servers and MIME

NOTE:
Make sure you understand the function of MIME, and that it can be used on both HTTP and mail servers.

As you learned earlier, MIME is commonly used to transmit files with e-mail. For instance, you use MIME to attach a GIF image or a Microsoft Word document to an e-mail message. MIME identifies a file type, encodes the file and decodes it at the receiving end so it will display properly. MIME performs these steps by adding a header to each file. The MIME header contains the encoding method and the type of data contained within.

The identity of a file is determined by the MIME type. As discussed earlier, the different MIME types are classified under broad headings (text, image, application, audio and video), and then subclassified by exact type. E-mail typically uses MIME for non-text file transfers. For example, a GIF file is MIME type image/gif.

Whenever data is passed between an e-mail sender and recipient, the data is labeled with its MIME type. The recipient uses the MIME type to render the information. For example, when an e-mail client sends a QuickTime video to a recipient, it labels the file with its MIME type (video/quicktime) so the recipient can execute the file properly. The same procedure is used by a Web server to transmit files to browser clients.

Unusual documents or graphic formats may not be defined by MIME types. In this case, you must manually associate a file with the appropriate program. For example, you may receive a configuration (CFG) file type attachment that you cannot open; you may not have the program needed to run or read it, or a MIME type may not have been defined. In either case, you can save the file to your Desktop, right-click the file, and click the Open With option. Choose the proper application to run the file, and the file will execute. If you do not have the proper application, you need to install the application on your computer to run the file.

To learn more about MIME types, visit the MIME Information Page at *www.hunnysoft.com/mime.*

Problems with mail servers

Mail servers can experience various problems, including the following:

- A virus or worm attack, in which a program replicates itself on the computer system, usually through executable software, and causes system damage.

- A slowdown in which the e-mail server may be running low on RAM or disk space.

Sometimes, however, problems with other network devices can slow e-mail. For example, if you experience slow e-mail, a firewall or other intermediate device may be creating a bottleneck.

Instant Messaging (IM)

OBJECTIVE
3.4.2: Common Internet services/protocols

Instant messaging (IM) is a computer-based method of communication that typically runs as a service on a mail server. You can use IM to type and view messages sent to one or more recipients, and view the responses immediately. Unlike e-mail, which can be sent whether your recipient is online or not, instant messages can be sent only to contacts who are currently online — that is, logged on to an IM service.

To use IM, you must install a client on your system and then register for service. Instant messaging allows you to specify a list of contacts (known as a buddy list or a contact list) with whom you would like to communicate. When you log on to your IM service, the status (online or offline) of each of the contacts in your list will display. To open an IM session, you specify an online contact and open a window where you and your contact can type messages that both of you can see.

NOTE:
ICQ stands for "I Seek You." ICQ servers use the proprietary protocol ICQv5 for communication.

In June 1998, America Online (AOL) acquired Mirabilis.

Instant messaging became very popular in November 1996, when a company called Mirabilis introduced a free IM utility known as ICQ. When you logged on to your ICQ service, your client communicated with an ICQ server, sending it your IP address and the number of the port on your computer that is assigned to the ICQ client. Your client also sent the names of everyone on your contact list to the ICQ server. The ICQ server then created a temporary file with the connection information for you and the list of your contacts.

The server also reported those contacts who were logged on. The server sent a message back to your ICQ client with the connection information for your online contacts and displayed their status as "online." The server also sent a message to your online contacts, notifying them that you were online.

Today, several IM services, clients and servers are used. Yahoo!, MSN and AOL use their own proprietary protocols and clients. Instant messaging clients are available from a variety of sources, including the following:

- AOL Instant Messenger (*http://dashboard.aim.com/aim*)

- Miranda Instant Messenger (*www.miranda-im.org*).

- Yahoo! Messenger (*http://messenger.yahoo.com*)

- Windows Live Messenger (*http://download.live.com/messenger*)

- ICQ Instant Messenger (*www.icq.com*)

Pidgin is a multi-protocol instant messaging client for Linux, BSD, Mac OS X and Windows. It is compatible with AIM, ICQ, Windows Live Messenger, Yahoo!, Internet Relay Chat (IRC), Jabber, Gadu-Gadu and Zephyr networks. Pidgin allows you to perform IM with users at various other networks (such as AOL, Yahoo! and MSN) simultaneously. You can download Pidgin at *http://www.pidgin.im/*.

Mailing List Servers

OBJECTIVE
3.4.2: Common Internet services/protocols

A mailing list server is a standard SMTP server that can automatically forward an e-mail message to every member on a distribution list. Some mailing list servers, such as LISTSERV (*www.listserv.net* or *www.lsoft.com*), are designed for this purpose. Other SMTP servers, such as Microsoft Exchange Server, can be configured as mailing list servers.

NOTE:
Mailing lists are common. If you are a member of an organization, you may receive e-mail messages from a mailing list server. These messages are from the organization and usually contain news and useful membership information.

Another name for a mailing list server is "reflector." An autoresponder is not a mailing list server; rather, it is a technology you can enable on a Web server. You can configure a Web server to automatically use an SMTP server to answer an inquiry or order from a user.

A mailing list server allows people to work together even though their e-mail accounts reside on different e-mail servers across the Internet.

For example, suppose James establishes a mailing list server for a company project. The account to which everyone will send e-mail messages about this project will be project@company.com. This account and the distribution list both reside on the mailing list server. James' e-mail address, james@fender.com, is on the mailing list server's distribution list, as are the following: patrick@gibson.com, joseph@hamer.com, jill@40.com and susan@metallica.com. If Jill were to send an e-mail message to project@company.com, then James, Patrick, Joseph and Susan would receive exact copies of this e-mail message. In fact, the server would also send Jill a copy because she is also on the list of recipients. The server will forward this message to every person on the list James has configured, as shown in Figure 3-3.

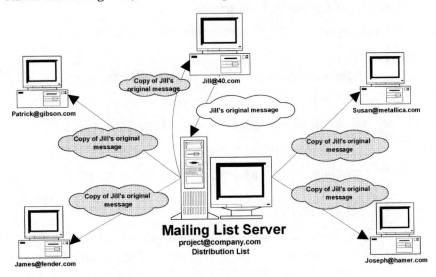

Figure 3-3: Mailing list server

In effect, a mailing list server allows you to imitate a newsgroup. The main difference is that any e-mail message you send does not remain persistent on a central server for a given time. Mailing lists have become popular because many users consider e-mail messages easier to manage than newsgroup postings.

Mailing List Manager (MLM)

The interface that allows you to configure a mailing list server is often called a Mailing List Manager (MLM). Using an MLM, you can customize the behavior of the mailing list server. For example, you can configure a moderated list, which means that a designated individual will screen all submissions before they are sent to everyone on the list.

Public and private mailing lists

You can create public or private mailing lists with a mailing list server. Examples of public mailing lists include the well-known LISTSERV and Majordomo groups. Topics covered by such lists range from aviation to zoology. You can configure a public mailing list server to allow anyone to join the list at any time.

NOTE:
Mailing list servers are configured to remove addresses differently. Each message usually contains instructions on how to be removed from the list.

The specific syntax and information requirements differ from one public mailing list server to another. Most servers allow users to join a mailing list automatically by having them send an e-mail message with the word "join" or "subscribe" in the body of the message or the header. Users can unsubscribe from a mailing list by sending an e-mail message with words such as "unsubscribe" or "remove" in the message or header.

Go to the LISTSERV Web site at *www.lsoft.com* to view a comprehensive list of the LISTSERV mailing groups.

In a business setting, mailing list servers are generally not configured to allow automatic subscriptions. Advanced mailing list servers also allow you to encrypt e-mail messages, giving you reasonable assurance that no one can read your messages without authorization.

Mailing list server vendors

Following are several popular mailing list server vendors:

- Sun Java System Messaging Server (*www.sun.com/software/products/messaging_srvr/*)

- LISTSERV (*www.listserv.net* or *www.lsoft.com*)

- Microsoft Exchange Server (*www.microsoft.com*)

- SparkLIST (*www.sparklist.com*)

Often, mailing list servers come bundled with other products.

OBJECTIVE
3.4.2: Common
Internet
services/protocols

**streaming audio
and video**
Audio and video
files that travel over
a network in real
time.

buffer
A cache of memory
used by a computer
to store frequently
used data. Buffers
allow faster access
times.

Media Servers

A media server offers **streaming audio and video** over a network. This type of server is suited for intranets as well as the Internet. More popular vendors include Microsoft Windows Media Services (*www.microsoft.com/windows/windowsmedia/*) and RealPlayer (*www.real.com*).

These servers are useful because businesses and other organizations use the Internet to conduct long-distance conference calls as personally as possible. Generally, these servers use UDP ports and **buffers** to achieve the effect of a real-time connection.

Remember that UDP is a connectionless protocol, so media servers must find some way to simulate a continuous connection. Some of the latest developments attempt to improve transmission quality by paralleling UDP streams. These strategies help enhance the illusion of a real-time connection.

OBJECTIVE
3.4.2: Common
Internet
services/protocols

DNS Servers

Invented by Paul Mockapetris in 1984, the Domain Name System (DNS) is a mechanism used on the Internet to translate host computer names into IP addresses. For example, CIW Certification has a Web server that can be accessed using the FQDN of *www.CIW-certified.com*. The same Web server can also be reached by entering the IP address *http://74.206.104.14*. Both the name and the IP address refer to the same Web server, but the former is much easier to remember. Without DNS, users would be forced to enter long numerical strings every time they needed access to any part of the Internet.

NOTE:
You need a general
understanding of
what DNS servers do
and when they are
appropriate as part
of a network. DNS
was introduced in
an earlier lesson.

DNS servers, also called name servers, contain the server application that supports name-to-address translation. You were introduced to DNS servers earlier in the course. Typically, the system on which the name server resides is called the name server system.

DNS is a decentralized system: It does not depend on one source for updates, and one server does not store all the data. Instead, DNS is a distributed database that exists on name servers across the Internet.

As you have already learned, the ICANN is responsible for DNS management.

Hosts file

Until DNS was implemented, a single file known as the hosts table was managed and updated by the Stanford Research Institute Network Information Center (SRI-NIC). Whenever network administrators needed the latest hosts table for their name servers, they downloaded it from the SRI-NIC FTP server. As the Internet grew, this file became very large and difficult to manage, and no longer provided an effective way to distribute name-to-address data.

The hosts file on your computer (which you were introduced to earlier in the course) is similar to the hosts table used earlier for the Internet. The hosts file is a simple text file that is referenced locally by applications and commands for name-to-address resolution. The format for entries is as follows:

```
Internet-address        official-host-name              aliases
```

For the hosts file to provide local diagnostics, the loopback address (127.0.0.1) must be included. After the loopback address is entered, you can add any IP address and corresponding host name that you require (the number sign [#] is used for comments). For example:

```
# List the loopback address.

127.0.0.1        localhost

# You can list as many IP-to-host addresses as you need.
# These entries will
# override your computer's DNS settings.

192.168.3.15        student15              patrick
```

In Windows Vista, the hosts file can be opened with Notepad. It is located at:

```
C:\Windows\System32\drivers\etc
```

DNS hierarchy

domain name space
The three-level domain name hierarchy (root-level, top-level and second-level domains) that forms the Domain Name System (DNS).

DNS is hierarchical and distributed. It consists of three levels — root-level, top-level and second-level domains — and is often referred to as the **domain name space**. Figure 3-4 illustrates the domain name space.

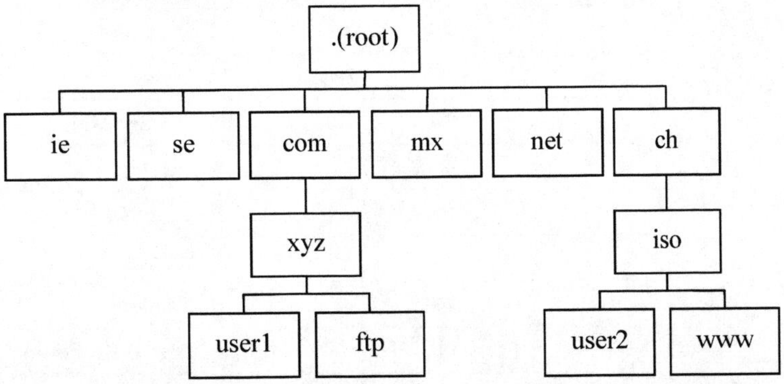

NOTE:
You need to understand DNS hierarchy.

Figure 3-4: Domain name space

Following is a description of each level in the DNS hierarchy.

Root-level domain

The root-level domain is the top of the hierarchy. It contains entries for each top-level domain. The root-level domain is updated daily and replicated on root domain servers across the Internet. It is expressed by a period (.). This period is usually removed from the end of domain names (for example, *www.company.com* instead of *www.company.com.*).

Top-level domain

The top-level domain is one level below the root-level domain. It consists of categories found at the end of domain names (such as .com or .uk). It divides domains into organizations (.org), businesses (.com), countries (.uk) and other categories. Each top-level domain has a master server that contains entries for all registered second-level domains (such as company.com).

The top-level Internet domains are described in Tables 3-1 through 3-3. The first seven domains are associated with the United States and are assigned by the Internet Network Information Center (InterNIC). However, the majority of top-level domains are country codes. Each country assigns domain names using its own standards. The third type of top-level Internet domains (shown in Table 3-3) is designated by category; these domains were recently approved by the ICANN.

Table 3-1: Top-level Internet domains — original

Top-Level Domain — Original	Description
com	Commercial organizations
edu	Educational institutions
gov	Government institutions
mil	Military
net	Network support centers (ISPs)
org	Other organizations (originally non-profit)
int	International organizations (rarely used; country codes are used instead)

Table 3-2: Top-level Internet domains — ISO country codes (samples)

Top-Level Domain —Country Code	Description
au	Australia
ca	Canada
ch	Switzerland
fr	France
ie	Ireland
mx	Mexico
se	Sweden
uk	United Kingdom
us	United States

Table 3-3: Top-level Internet domains — categories

Top-Level Domain — Category	Description
aero	Travel industry
biz	Businesses
coop	Cooperatives
info	Content and research-related sites
museum	Museums
name	Personal Web addresses
pro	Professional

Second-level domain

The second-level domain is one level below the top-level domain. Second-level domains include the businesses and institutions that register their domain names with the top-level domains (through their respective registrars).

Second-level domains include registered names such as the following:

- *iso.ch*

- *amazon.com*

Second-level domains can also be categories of top-level domains. For example, the United States domain (us) is further categorized into a second-level domain for each state, such as California:

- *ca.us*

Companies and academic institutions in the United Kingdom (and most other countries) are also categorized, as shown:

- *co.uk*

- *ac.uk*

Finally, second-level domains can be divided into subdomains. For example, a subdomain of the second-level domain *company.com* may be as follows:

- *sales.company.com*

A host computer of that subdomain may be identified as follows:

- *user1.sales.company.com*

DNS components

DNS consists of the following two key components:

- **Name server** — a server that supports name-to-address translation and runs the DNS service.

- **Name resolver** — software that uses the services of one or more name servers to resolve unknown requests. For example, if a host requests *www.novell.com*, and the DNS server does not have the name information, it will use name resolver software to ask another name server on the DNS hierarchy. DNS clients and servers use name resolver software.

In Linux/UNIX, the resolver is actually a group of routines that reside in the C library */usr/lib/libc.a.* In Windows, the TCP/IP properties contain a DNS section that must be configured with the IP addresses of the DNS servers.

DNS server types

DNS follows the standard client/server model: The client makes a request, and the server attempts to fulfill that request. DNS servers can fill several different roles, depending on the organization's needs. No matter what role the server takes, the client must specify the name server's domain name or IP address. The following server types are included in the DNS model:

- **Root server** — Root servers can identify all top-level domains on the Internet. If a client requests information about a host in another domain, any server (except a secondary server, which will be introduced shortly) can communicate that request to the root server. Most server administrators will never configure a root server.

- **Primary server** — A primary server is the authority for a domain and maintains the DNS databases for its domain. It is the first DNS server in a domain. Companies and ISPs that implement their own DNS and participate on the Internet require a primary server. Primary servers are also called master servers.

- **Secondary server** — A secondary server receives its authority and database from the primary server. Secondary servers are used by server administrators to provide fault tolerance, load distribution and easier remote name resolution for the primary DNS server. Secondary servers are also called slave servers.

zone file
A file containing a set of instructions for resolving a specific domain name into its numerical IP address. Found in DNS servers.

- **Caching-only server** — A caching-only server is one that does not contain its own **zone file**, but receives entries from other DNS servers.

- **Forwarding server** — A forwarding server is one that receives requests and then forwards them to other servers.

Linux/UNIX name daemon (named)

The name daemon allows a Linux/UNIX computer to function as a DNS server. The most common implementation of Linux/UNIX DNS is the Berkeley Internet Name Domain (BIND). Microsoft DNS is based on the BIND implementation, but does not adhere strictly to it. Linux/UNIX BIND servers are the most widely used DNS servers on the Internet.

DNS records

Every domain consists of DNS records. A DNS record is an entry in a DNS database (on a primary server) that provides additional routing and resolution information. Many different types of records can be configured, but only a few are needed for full address resolution and routing. Table 3-4 lists the most common DNS records.

Table 3-4: Common DNS records

DNS Record	Function
Name Server (NS)	Identifies DNS servers for the DNS domain.
Start Of Authority (SOA)	Identifies the DNS server that is the best source of information for the DNS domain. Because several backup DNS servers may exist, this record identifies the primary server for the specified DNS domain.
Address (A)	The most commonly used record; associates a host to an IP address. For example, you can establish an association between an IP address and a Web server by creating an address record.

Table 3-4: Common DNS records (cont'd)

DNS Record	Function
Canonical Name (CNAME)	Creates an alias for a specified host. For example, the name of a WWW server is *server1.company.com* (Web servers are commonly named WWW). A CNAME record creates a "WWW" alias to the *server1.company.com* host so it can also be accessed at *www.company.com*.
Mail Exchanger (MX)	Identifies a server used to process and deliver e-mail messages for the domain.

These records are the most widely used. Many other types of records are used with DNS for different functions.

DNS process example

NOTE:
See **Activity 3-1: Diagramming DNS server relationships**.

You work at company XYZ with the domain name *xyz.com*. You send an e-mail message to a person at the International Organization for Standardization (ISO), which has the domain name *iso.ch*. Before your computer sends the message, it needs the IP address of the *iso.ch* mail server. Following are the steps taken in this process:

1. Your computer sends a DNS request to your configured name server.

2. Your name server queries itself for the requested entry. If an entry does not exist in its cache, it will forward the request to the Internet's root servers.

3. A root server will send your name server the reference information for the requested domain's (*iso.ch*) primary and secondary name servers.

4. Your name server will query the *iso.ch* primary (or secondary) name server for the requested record. The request will be fulfilled with the *iso.ch* name server sending the requested IP address.

5. Your name server will provide your computer with your request's IP address.

The *nslookup* command

The *nslookup* command can be used to query Internet domain name servers to learn name-to-IP-address mappings. This command is used for any system (for example, a workstation or a server). The user has the option to request a specific name server to provide information about a given host or to get a list of all hosts in a given domain. The *nslookup* command is usually used at a command prompt or a Linux/UNIX terminal. By default, the *nslookup* command will query the default DNS server used by the system you are using.

NOTE:
You need to know how this command is used and be able to recognize the command output. The nslookup utility is commonly used to test communication with and operation of DNS servers.

You can use *nslookup* as a one-time command or as an interactive command. When used as a one-time command, it will return information for only one system or zone. Following is the syntax for using *nslookup* as a one-time command:

```
nslookup options address
```

Following is an example of a one-time use of *nslookup*:

```
nslookup www.CIW-certified.com
```

The output displays the following results, depending on your system's DNS configuration:

```
Server:    ns1.sprintlink.net
Name:          www.CIW-certified.com
Address:   74.206.104.14
```

You can also use *nslookup* interactively. At a command prompt or terminal, simply issue the following command:

```
nslookup
```

You will then be placed into an nslookup session, which allows you to make queries for multiple systems. You can also use an interactive session to list the contents of entire zones (if allowed), and to switch from your default DNS server to another DNS server (if allowed). Your command prompt or terminal will change from a standard prompt to the > (greater than) character. You can then issue commands to determine name resolution. Following is an example of a typical nslookup session:

```
>james
    Server:             192.168.2.5
    Address:   192.168.2.5#53

    Name:               james.stangernet.com
    Address:   192.168.2.5
                        www.CIW-certified.com
    Server:             192.168.2.5
    Address:   192.168.2.5#53

    Non-authoritative answer:
    Name:               www.CIW-certified.com
    Address:   74.206.104.14
    exit
C:\>
```

In the preceding session, the user searched for a system named james, which is contained in his server's DNS zone. If this name were not contained in the zone, an error message would be displayed. The second query was for the system named *www.CIW-certified.com*. Notice that the *exit* command allows you to end an nslookup session and return to your command prompt or terminal. In many systems, *nslookup* has been deprecated and replaced with commands such as *host* or *dig*.

The phrase "non-authoritative answer" can mean either of the following:

- The DNS server that returned this information is not authoritative for the system you have asked about (for example, it is a secondary DNS server). A primary DNS server that has not been appropriately configured may also return this message.

- The DNS server that has given this information has been configured as a secondary DNS server.

To obtain a list of all nodes in a given domain, such as *CIW-certified.com*, execute the following sequence of commands:

```
nslookup
```

```
> ls  CIW-certified.com
```

You must have permission to list the domain with the DNS administrator. If not, you will receive an error that says: "***Can't list domain: Bad error value."

In some operating systems (for example, Ubuntu Linux), the nslookup command has been deprecated in favor of the host and dig commands.

In the following lab, you will use the *nslookup* command for both a one-time and an interactive session. Suppose you are on the IT staff of a company that sells hair removal products through an electronic storefront, and you have been asked to test the operation of the default DNS server. You also want to obtain a list of all nodes in a particular domain. How would you use the nslookup utility to perform these tasks?

Lab 3-2: Using the nslookup utility

In this lab, you will use the nslookup utility.

Note: Your firewall may forbid nslookup queries.

1. Select **Start**, type **cmd** in Start Search text box, then press **ENTER** to open the command prompt.

2. Type **nslookup www.CIW-certified.com**, then press **ENTER** to issue a one-time command.

   Record the information you found in the space provided:

   _____

   _____

3. Type **nslookup** and press **ENTER** to begin an interactive session.

NOTE:
The *nslookup* command works for any server type, including FTP, HTTP and e-mail.

4. Conduct searches for the following systems:

   ```
   ftp.microsoft.com
   ftp.ubuntu.com
   www.bbc.co.uk
   ```

5. Type **exit** and press **ENTER** to end the session.

6. Close the command prompt window.

In this lab, you used the *nslookup* command. You issued a one-time command and conducted an interactive session.

FTP Servers

OBJECTIVE
3.4.2: Common Internet services/protocols

Most of the Internet server suites include an FTP server. However, you should always check to see whether an FTP server is included, or whether you need to obtain a separate FTP daemon or service. Even though FTP is one of the oldest protocols, it remains one of the most consistently used of all the servers discussed in this lesson.

NOTE:
You need a general understanding of what FTP servers do and how they can be a useful part of a network.

In most situations, if you have a file approaching 2 megabytes (MB), you should transfer it by means of FTP, because sending such a large file through a mail server slows that server and the network. In addition, if the mail server has difficulty transferring a large file, it will no longer forward that message. However, it will not delete the message; the message will remain in the e-mail server queue until a server administrator deletes it. With FTP, on the other hand, if a problem occurs with the file, you need only resend it. Thus, little administrative intervention is needed.

Also, e-mail servers will often silently drop e-mail attachments of various types. This fact alone makes e-mail servers inefficient methods for transferring and storing many files.

Logging and access control

FTP servers log all traffic (which is usually anonymous). You can consult the FTP server logs to determine the amount of traffic.

Although you can password-protect an FTP site, many administrators choose to allow anonymous access. To strengthen security, they ensure that no sensitive information is kept on the FTP server. One reason that FTP servers generally use anonymous logon access is that the protocol requires passwords to be sent unencrypted. This openness allows hackers to obtain passwords with special programs called packet sniffers, or protocol analyzers.

You will learn more about FTP server security later in the course.

News Servers

News servers use the Network News Transfer Protocol (NNTP). Like the standard office bulletin board, a news server allows users to post information in an easily accessible location. Using a news server, you can secure specific newsgroups, or (as in the case of the popular **Usenet** newsgroups) you can leave them open to the public. One of the most important uses for a newsgroup is to provide a forum for groups to communicate while developing projects.

A network news service consists of objects, both physical and virtual. A service can usually be configured to accept file attachments, which can allow members to exchange files as part of a public conversation. These files will remain persistent for a specified period, creating a message-based forum. The news server thus allows a company to document a project and enhance collaboration.

The newsgroup's name is also its network address, written in a hierarchy index form. For example, rec.sport.football.college is a **newsgroup** with the topic of college football, whereas rec.sport.soccer is about soccer. Both hierarchies begin with "rec" (recreation) and "sport" before subdividing into different names of sports.

To read a newsgroup, the user opens a news reader software program, such as that found in Microsoft Outlook Express or the Mozilla Thunderbird newsgroup news client. The news client locates the news server containing the newsgroup and requests access. After access is granted, the client can access the newsgroups on the news server.

When one newsgroup server communicates with another to gain access to the central newsgroup files, the action is called a newsfeed.

Most Internet newsgroups are generated and maintained by contributors. Generally, whoever maintains a newsgroup charges no access fees and has no formal means of enforcing standards for articles. Contributors often identify themselves only by an e-mail address.

OBJECTIVE
3.4.2: Common Internet services/protocols

Usenet (User Network)
A collection of thousands of Internet computers, newsgroups and newsgroup members using Network News Transfer Protocol (NNTP) to exchange information.

newsgroup
On Usenet, a subject or other topical interest group whose members exchange ideas and opinions. Participants post and receive messages via a news server.

NOTE:
You need a general understanding of the function of a news server.

Newsgroup policies

The news server helps organize resources with the emphasis on distributing and locating information rather than owning or controlling it. Following are the basic policies of this legacy:

- Usenet is a public collection of newsgroups originally developed in the university community, with rules and procedures based on academic freedom and peer review. For example, users can call for a vote on banning offensive material, but lack the means to enforce a ban.

- Public newsgroups have no restrictions on access. Private newsgroups are restricted to specific users. Secure newsgroups encrypt articles transmitted between users and servers. Usenet newsgroups are always non-secure, reflecting the academic culture of open dissemination.

- Moderated newsgroups carry only articles approved by a moderator. Unmoderated newsgroups operate without restrictions on content.

- Intranet and extranet newsgroups can help a company develop and track projects. Often, these groups are password-protected so that only specified users can gain access.

Newsgroup security

Secure Sockets Layer (SSL)
A protocol that provides authentication and encryption, used by most servers for secure exchanges over the Internet. Superseded by Transport Layer Security (TLS).

Many administrators use news servers to create secure newsgroups. You can achieve security by enabling user-specific password protection, or by means of a **Secure Sockets Layer (SSL)** session. Although both of these solutions are secure, an SSL session provides greater security. To enable an SSL session, you need to obtain a certificate that enables encryption. You can obtain a certificate from a company such as VeriSign, or configure and use a certificate server.

Certificate Servers

OBJECTIVE
3.4.2: Common Internet services/protocols

Transmitting information over the Internet can be risky. Information you send is passed from one computer to the next until it reaches its destination. During the transmission, other users can eavesdrop on the transmission or intercept your information, and even change the contents of your message.

key
A variable value, such as a numeric code, that uses an algorithm to encrypt and decrypt data. Some applications encrypt and decrypt with the same key, whereas other applications use a pair of keys.

Certificate servers validate, or certify, **keys**. Keys are strings of text generated from a complex series of encryption algorithms that allow you to secure communication for a company or group of users. Many Web servers, such as IIS, create keys that, after having been validated, can be applied to other servers, such as news servers, mail servers or Web servers. The purpose of this process is to create a way for people to communicate and be reasonably sure that others are not eavesdropping or assuming a false identity.

NOTE:
You need a general understanding of the role of certificates in security.

The nature of e-mail and newsgroup servers and protocols makes them susceptible to identity theft. Digital certificates help minimize this security risk by authenticating users before they transmit information. A digital certificate is a password-protected, encrypted data file containing message encryption, user identification and message text. It is used to authenticate a program or a sender's public key, or to initiate SSL sessions. It must be signed by a certificate authority (CA) to be valid.

Directory Servers

OBJECTIVE
3.4.2: Common
Internet
services/protocols

A directory server is a dedicated server that identifies all resources on a network. It makes these resources available to authenticated users. For example, a directory server allows a company to provide a directory of names, network services, e-mail addresses, department personnel, company contacts and address information to all users.

The most efficient solution does not include the storage of current company or individual contact list databases. Most employees do not update their own contact lists; such outdated information can affect accuracy and performance. The most effective way to improve access to such information is to use only one database and one access protocol.

NOTE:
You should understand the function of a directory server. In particular, you must be familiar with LDAP (presented later in this section).

For example, a directory server allows users to remotely access such information quickly from a central location because it allows them to query the database without affecting network performance. An administrator need only configure employee e-mail programs to query the database.

Many companies give their employees electronic address books that contain a centralized list of e-mail addresses and contact information. The IT department updates the address book so the latest version is always available. Thus, company employees can automatically access it using their e-mail programs.

Additional directory service uses

A directory service enables a company to reuse the information in its directory, keep management costs from increasing, and avoid re-entry of user information for every application that requires such information. A directory service can also help administrators manage applications and users, and can help users locate other users or e-mail addresses.

In addition, a directory service can help with the following procedures:

- Locating and managing all company accounts with the same directory.

- Allowing users, both inside and outside the network, to use the service. For example, an office in one city can store the directory information about all its members on one server. Users outside that office can also access the information, with permission.

- Maintaining a single database of e-mail contacts.

Directory service protocols

Two protocols serve as the basis for most directory services:

- X.500

- Lightweight Directory Access Protocol (LDAP)

X.500

X.500 is used to manage user and resource directories. It is based on a hierarchical system that can classify entries by country, state, city and street, for example. The X.500 protocol was designed to offer a global directory. It has had limited success on its own because it is complex and difficult to implement, but it has been the basis for many other directory services.

X.500 directories offer the following characteristics:

- **Scalability** — can be offered as a global database, but can also be divided into smaller databases for efficient management.

- **Synchronization** — can synchronize with other directories to ensure all data is current.

- **Replication** — can replicate with other X.500 directories, thereby making all database copies identical (for reducing retrieval time) and creating backup copies.

Lightweight Directory Access Protocol (LDAP)

NOTE:
LDAP may one day become an Internet-wide directory service.

LDAP was developed from X.500 at the University of Michigan. It is easier to implement than X.500 because it is based on TCP/IP, allowing communication on intranets as well as the Internet. LDAP uses a simplified X.500 directory structure and a simplified directory-access method.

Whereas the X.500 directory-access method is also called the Directory Access Protocol (DAP), the LDAP acronym incorporates "lightweight" to denote a simpler structure. Netscape Directory Server (NDS) uses the LDAP standard for its directory structure and its access method.

When Netscape adopted LDAP as its standard, the rest of the Web community followed. Eventually, the Internet may provide public "White Pages" for e-mail addresses and users with LDAP. The LDAP directory structure is hierarchical, similar to an X.500 directory.

Fax Servers

OBJECTIVE
3.4.2: Common Internet services/protocols

A fax server is an alternative to providing individual fax machines throughout a company location. For instance, many companies purchase a fax machine for each department in the company. For larger companies, this policy can result in dozens of machines. The fax machines must also be conveniently located for the employees.

A fax server provides a centrally located fax system for all company departments, and can save costs from purchasing dozens of individual fax machines. Fax servers consist of a bank of fax modems. These modems allow outgoing and incoming faxes to be processed by the next available fax modem.

Both internal and remote company employees can use the fax server. With the acceptance of digital signatures in electronic commerce (or e-commerce), documents can be signed and faxed without ever existing in paper form.

Because fax services do not consume large amounts of network resources, a fax service is often installed on a server running another service. For instance, fax services are often installed on company file servers.

Transaction Servers

OBJECTIVE
3.4.2: Common Internet services/protocols

When a transaction takes place, such as ordering office supplies over the Internet with a company credit card, a transaction server guarantees that all required databases are updated. It verifies that all parts of a transaction have taken place successfully. In some cases, this task is complicated. For example, the online merchant's database must reflect the transaction, as well as the credit card company's and, in some cases, the manufacturer's database.

Transaction servers are intended as client/server replacements for Customer Information Control System (CICS) mainframe servers. Transaction servers are Web-based and allow a network to provide a stand-alone solution or a bridging tool to mainframe servers. Some transaction servers, such as Microsoft Transaction Server, are designed to interact with Web-specific databases through the use of .NET.

A transaction server also comes preconfigured to connect to databases, thereby enabling the spontaneous transfer of information. Specifically built to enable a three-tier solution, transaction servers allow high-volume transactions with minimal network overhead.

If a transaction is unsuccessful because one of the databases fails, the server will execute preprogrammed actions, such as canceling the transaction.

Choosing Web Server Products

OBJECTIVE
3.4.3: Choosing servers

As a networking professional, you will need to make and justify decisions. Part of this decision-making process is learning what a company truly requires and then making the appropriate choices.

Following are descriptions of some industry-standard Internet servers. This list is not comprehensive and does not constitute an endorsement of any product. This discussion is intended to give you a sense of the available products.

Apache Web server

Apache Web server is a tested, well-accepted solution. It is considered extremely reliable. As of this writing, almost half of all Web sites deliver their information with this server. Originally designed to support Linux/UNIX, Apache now supports Windows systems as well (for example, Windows Server 2003 and Windows Server 2008). All versions are available free of charge.

open source
A peer-based development process describing organizations and products that provide free source code to the development community at large with the goal of developing better products; includes Apache Web server and Linux.

Apache Web server includes no formal support system (such as a customer support desk) because it has been developed by a not-for-profit, membership-based group called The Apache Software Foundation (*www.apache.org*). The Apache Web server is part of the **open-source** movement. However, you can obtain configuration and support information from many sources by entering the keyword "Apache" in your favorite search engine.

A downloadable version is available at the Apache HTTP Server Project site (*http://httpd.apache.org/*). The Apache Web server is not packaged with additional Internet services. You must obtain other server programs for news, FTP and so forth. However, many different developers have combined Apache Web server with other services. For example, XAMPP provides Apache Web server, as well as PHP, MySQL (a SQL server), Perl and FileZilla (an FTP server). You can learn more about XAMPP at *www.apachefriends.org/en/xampp.html.*

Microsoft Internet Information Services (IIS)

IIS is now in its seventh version, and includes HTTP, FTP, NNTP, SMTP, certificate, ASP, index (catalog) and transaction services.

IIS 6 operates only with Windows Server 2003 and Windows XP Professional. IIS 7 operates only with Windows Server 2008 and Windows Vista. Both are free of charge, but you must purchase a license for the appropriate Windows operating system. You can obtain a copy from the Microsoft Web site (*www.microsoft.com*).

One of the strengths of IIS is that it allows you to use a remote server to store and retrieve files. The remote server need not be a Web server itself, a fact that allows you to distribute the processing load evenly.

graphical user interface (GUI)
A program that provides visual navigation with menus and screen icons, and performs automated functions when users click command buttons.

Because IIS is a Microsoft product, you can obtain worldwide, fee-based support. You can also administer it from a **graphical user interface (GUI)** or through HTML forms. Additionally, you can issue commands from a DOS session.

Sun Java System Web Server

Sun Microsystems helped define the Web, and its servers are among the most tested. Additionally, its products support many platforms, including Sun Solaris, Windows, Linux, AIX and HP-UX.

The Sun Java System Web Server supports JavaServer Pages (JSP) technology and Java servlets. These interpreters allow you to use Java to connect to databases; in addition, you can implement other server-side scripting applications. For more information, consult the Sun Java System Web Server site (*www.sun.com/software/products/web_srvr/*).

Java software and Web servers

servlet
A small Java application that runs on a server.

Many Web servers use Java. Any time Java code is compiled and run solely on the Web server, it is known as a servlet. A Java **servlet** is an application that resides on a server. These applications can provide various services, including database connectivity. Servlets allow the following:

- Chaining, which allows output from one servlet to be given to another servlet, either on the local computer or on a remote computer

- Connections to databases

- Near-universal support on systems (for example, Windows, Linux, Solaris)

Java Virtual Machine (JVM)
The artificial computer that runs Java programs and allows the same code to run on different platforms.

In order for Java servlets and other applications to function, however, you must first install a **Java Virtual Machine (JVM)** on your system. You can obtain a JVM from various vendors. The standard JVM is available from Sun (*www.java.com*).

Content Management System (CMS)

Content Management System (CMS)
A server or series of servers that allows you to easily create, store and track all documents and information produced by an organization.

A **Content Management System (CMS)** is a server or series of servers that allows you to easily create, store and track all documents and information produced by an organization. A CMS resides on a server, and is designed to accept and organize content submissions. Large and small organizations alike use CMS systems to help ensure that employees can create and access information efficiently, and reduce duplication of effort and time wasted searching for content.

Benefits of using a CMS include:

- **Centralized management of content** — All information and work is stored and organized in one place, where it can be administered properly.

- **The ability to reuse content** — Once content is properly stored, that content can be reused in numerous ways to benefit the company.

- **Increased collaboration** — A CMS can capture institutional knowledge about products and procedures, and make it readily available.

Common CMS services

NOTE:
Role management, permission management and version control are essential elements of a CMS.

CMS services include the following:

- Role management

- Permission management

- Content publication

- Content editing

- Version control

- Indexing and searching

- Caching and replication

- Simplified backup

- Syndication

NOTE:
Additional CMS functions can include:
- Storage of discarded and previous versions of files.
- Publishing to e-commerce servers.
- Workflow reporting.

Figure 3-5 illustrates the typical functions and services provided by a CMS.

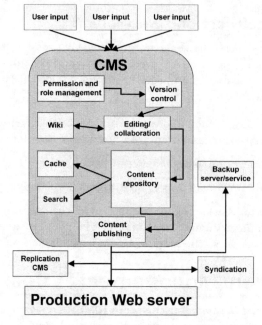

Figure 3-5: CMS services and functions

Each of these services will be discussed in the following sections.

Role management

A CMS requires companies to determine roles for each user. Following are examples of CMS roles:

- **Creators/owners/authors** — users who are able to generate and modify content. However, they often can work only on their own content, and not that of others.

- **Managers** — users who have been given all permissions over those who they supervise. Managers can alter or discard content, even if they do not own the content. Managers can define users on the system, as well as change content ownership, and create new projects and directories. Also called "supervisors" in some CMS applications.

- **Editors** — users who have the ability to make content changes.

- **Reviewers** — users who have the ability to leave comments or make suggestions about content changes, but are not allowed to make any changes.

- **Publishers** — users who have the ability to view content, but also to create comparison, or differential, documents to determine what has occurred over time.

- **Viewers** — users who can view content, but not alter it in any way. Depending upon the capabilities of the CMS, viewers may or may not be able to print or download content.

- **Administrators** — users who have full control over the system.

 Many of these terms vary from one CMS to another.

Permission management

Content available on a CMS can be made available to users on a granular basis. Certain files and directories can be provided to everyone, or to certain individuals, departments or job functions only.

Permissions can be managed in various ways, including:

- Directory services servers (Microsoft Active Directory, Open LDAP, Novell Directory Services).

- Public Key Infrastructure (PKI).

Content publication

A CMS is responsible for ensuring that content can be published to users based on the permissions that have been established. Therefore, some content may be available for everyone to read and edit, whereas other content may be restricted to certain users.

Content editing

A sophisticated CMS provides editing tools that make it easy for individuals to edit content. Most CMS implementations will allow users to edit simple HTML and text documents. More sophisticated implementations include tools that allow users to edit more complex content, such as audio and video.

Version control

A CMS can manage multiple submissions of the same document. Whenever two or more users edit the same document, a *race condition* is said to exist. This condition can cause important information and changes to be lost. If two or more users attempt to edit a file, the CMS will either lock out all but one user, or otherwise manage the submissions so that both sets of changes are integrated in alternative documents. As a result, all user submissions are saved. A CMS thus helps reduce the duplication of effort.

Another element of version control is the ability for the CMS to create backup copies of documents that have been edited. Users can refer to these copies and determine what changes have been made. A CMS can also create a special document called a *differential document*. This document allows users to trace the changes that have been made to the original document over time. The differential document provides a side-by-side comparison of documents, in which users can determine when ideas and concepts were introduced or removed from a file or resource.

 The practice of version control is also called revision control or versioning.

Finally, there may be times when it is necessary to have a document or even an entire site revert back to a previous version. This practice is often referred to as a *rollback*. Only certain users with specific roles can conduct rollbacks.

Indexing and searching

A CMS implementation makes a site easily searchable. Many companies will implement a CMS for this reason alone. Sometimes, searches are conducted through third-party services such as Google. However, most CMS servers include native search capability.

Caching and replication

A CMS is capable of creating copies of content and distributing them to additional servers. This strategy of load balancing ensures quick access to documents because information is distributed among multiple CMS servers. Caching content is usually done internally by the CMS, and helps ensure that often-used content is readily available.

Replicating and distributing content is separate from caching. Replication is a key tactic in ensuring scalability. Scalability is essential for large departments and companies that need to make sure content remains readily available.

Simplified backup

Because a CMS stores information centrally, this information can be readily backed up. The concept of backup differs from scalability. Scalability ensures that content remains available and accessible to users so that they can access it quickly. Backup ensures that content is still available despite a catastrophic event, such as a hard disk failure, a power supply failure, or an incident involving severe weather or vandalism.

Backup options include:

- Creating a tape backup.

- Sending files to a third-party for backup.

NOTE:
Syndication is important in many CMS implementations, not just for a CMS that is used to manage Web server content.

Syndication

The practice of syndication involves making content available via an RSS (Really Simple Syndication) or Atom feed, or via e-mail. Many CMS servers have the ability to syndicate content themselves or to make content available to various feed services, such as FeedBurner (*www.feedburner.com*) or FeedBlitz (*www.feedblitz.com*).

CMS as a workflow management tool

As you can see, a CMS is more than a place to store files. It is a workflow management tool that helps managers and executives ensure that users properly submit and manage content. As long as the company has properly defined roles for users, and the CMS has been properly configured to reflect these roles, the CMS server becomes a central tool that ensures content is updated properly and remains available to the correct individuals.

It is also common for companies to use a CMS to help manage the submission and editing of Web site pages and content.

You can store any content you want on a CMS, including:

- HTML files.

- PDF files.

- Spreadsheet documents.

- Word processing documents.

- Presentation slide shows.

- Multimedia (images, audio and video) files.

A CMS allows all of this content to be shared according to assigned permissions and roles, and also manages the editing of such content.

Requirements analysis

As you might suspect, implementing a CMS properly requires more than just installing a server and populating it with content. You will need to conduct a high-level analysis of your company's needs. This analysis involves determining server requirements, as well as your company's structure.

As you determine server requirements, consider the following:

- Number of users

- Projected server load

- Storage capacity

You will need to configure the CMS to support and enforce the job roles you have defined in your company. Consider the following:

NOTE:
Be aware of the importance of mapping department job roles and functions to CMS roles.

- **Mapping department job roles and functions to CMS roles** — You will find that the requirements of the Research and Development department will be far different than the requirements of the Human Resources department, for example. Work closely with department managers to determine exact job functions as you map the CMS roles to the actual job roles in your company. Create sample CMS roles, and ask the managers and their workers to confirm that the roles you have defined accurately reflect the job roles.

- **Existing resources** — You will likely need to connect your CMS to other company resources, including Web servers, databases, media servers, and file and print servers. Gather these requirements and create a network map to ensure that the implementation will go smoothly.

Managing a CMS

When managing a CMS, you will be faced with various issues, such as managing workflow, determining management roles and acquiring content. Following is a discussion of the most important issues.

Workflow management

One of the functions of a CMS is to provide notifications regarding document ownership and the state of a particular project. With one glance, an individual can review the progress of a particular document from creation through editing and publishing.

Workflow management also involves the ability for managers to approve key activities and essential steps as a project moves towards completion. A CMS has the ability to track these approvals to help guide the project along, and to help managers conduct a forensic analysis of past projects. A forensic analysis is a process in which managers investigate a past project to determine where the project succeeded, and what could have been done to overcome any challenges that occurred.

Content acquisition

The most time-intensive part of implementing a CMS is creating the content that goes into it. A CMS is designed to help users submit content as easily as possible. When working with a CMS, make sure that you consider the following issues:

- **Ease of submission** — How easy is the CMS to use? If the submission process requires special software or procedures that users consider difficult, you may find that the CMS does not suit your organization.

- **Time to create content** — Just because a CMS exists does not necessarily mean that it can be populated quickly. Create a submission schedule so that content can be acquired in a sustainable fashion.

A properly configured and managed CMS is the best way to capture the institutional knowledge of a particular organization. This is primarily because a CMS is designed to facilitate group participation and document editing. As you acquire content, make sure that you encourage the use of the following:

- **Peer-based editing** — Everyone should be encouraged to make constructive changes. The point of a CMS is to capture the wisdom of the entire organization, not just one individual or group of individuals. Collaboration between multiple workers on a document is critical to success.

- **Wikis** — A wiki enables individuals to freely communicate in a relatively open environment. Consider using a wiki to help create or modify a document, rather than focusing on trying to complete and perfect it with each edit.

Standard tagging

When information is submitted to a CMS, the information is marked. Marking the data allows it to be dated, then placed into a queue. The information is given a specific ID that allows the CMS to differentiate this information. The practice of marking this content is often called "tagging." Tagging content ensures that the content is published in an orderly fashion. Specifically, tagging ensures that new content:

- Does not conflict with separate submissions from other individuals. If potential conflicts occur, multiple submissions will be logged and stored.

- Is properly tracked so that previous versions can be used and compared with current content versions.

- Is logged.

Taxonomic and social tagging

Tagging involves using a technology to identify and rank information as being more or less useful. A CMS most often uses Extensible Markup Language (XML) to conduct tagging. Two types of tagging exist:

- **Standard** — A specified individual or group of individuals, considered expert(s) in the related field, determines content relevance and accuracy. The strength of this form of tagging is that experts can apply their expertise to the process. Weaknesses include the fact that individuals can become overwhelmed; and individuals can become biased, which may cause information to be tagged in a way that is not useful to the majority of the organization. Traditional tagging is often referred to as applying a taxonomy, or weighting content.

- **Social** — All users, or a defined group of users (non-experts), have the ability to weigh in on content. The strength of social tagging is that it is much easier to determine what the majority of end users need. Weaknesses include the fact that particular documents or tasks that are unpopular still need to be used and read. Just because a document is not popular does not necessarily mean that it is unimportant. Social tagging is often referred to as applying a folksonomy, or crowdsourcing.

Hybrid arrangements also exist, in which socially tagged content is reviewed by an acknowledged expert or group of experts. This final review helps ensure that content is properly categorized and used.

Template creation and management

A CMS often uses templates to standardize the document-creation process and ensure a consistent look and feel for all content created.

Templates ensure:

- A consistent look and feel for all documents. This includes standard branding.
- That all parties receive standard information and instructions for each document being edited.

Often, a CMS will contain templates of various document types, including:

- Non-disclosure agreements (NDAs).
- Non-compete agreements.
- Contracts relevant to the particular business.
- Slide show presentations for marketing, sales, or research and development.
- Marketing slicks.
- Web site layouts.

Localization

Localization is the practice of either translating documents to another language, or otherwise altering wording and other content to better suit a particular culture or system of values. Localization concerns include:

- **On the fly localization** — the ability to localize a Web page to various languages through an end-user request.
- **Character sets** — Standard character sets can include UTF-8 (Unicode), the Universal Character Set (ISO/IEC 10646) and various language-specific character sets.
- **Language direction** — Some languages are read right to left (RTL), whereas others are read left to right (LTR).

Personalization and portals

Personalization involves customizing content on the fly for a particular user or type of user. Using various technologies, it is possible to personalize a user's CMS experience. Technologies can include:

- **Role-based customization** — As a user logs in, interface elements are made available or omitted depending upon the user's role and permissions.
- **User-set preferences** — A user is often allowed to set preferences, default directories and other settings based on permissions.

It is possible to enforce custom environments and record preferences using cookies and login scripts.

When content has been sufficiently personalized, the CMS is said to have turned a Web site into a portal (as opposed to a static Web site).

In many cases, an administrator may decide to convert a personalized page created by a CMS into a static page that always remains available. Such pages are said to be "baked" because they are now always static. The advantage of a baked page is that the CMS does not have to constantly generate this page from scratch at every user request. In many cases, a baked page is created to reduce the CMS workload.

When a CMS creates a new page dynamically, that page is said to be "fried."

CMS and the content life cycle

The life cycle of content in a CMS is somewhat circular. Content is generated, edited and published; then it is reviewed and re-created; and then it is republished after quality user input and testing. The key to a successful content life cycle is to make sure that this user input is captured properly.

A simplified life cycle includes the following stages:

- **Creation** — the development of all content that goes into the CMS. Includes the submission of content, as well as all peer-based evaluation and editing work. Also called acquisition.

- **Management** — The CMS and administrators organize and prioritize content based on permissions and job roles. Also involves workflow management steps and reporting, as well as placing content into individual repositories and databases.

- **Delivery** — includes publishing content to Web servers, e-commerce servers, wikis and syndication services. Content is published according to predetermined rules that specify which users are allowed to read various types of content.

- **Evaluation** — determines how existing content needs to be changed or if it needs to be discarded. Content deletion is often referred to as content destruction.

- **Re-development** — Existing content is altered and then reintroduced to the CMS.

Figure 3-6 illustrates the typical life cycle of content in a CMS.

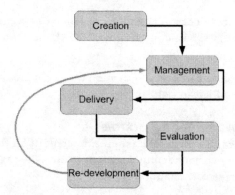

Figure 3-6: CMS content life cycle

CMS security concerns

Security problems can occur if one person uses another person's workstation or browser. It is common for most users to set browsers to automatically log in under a particular profile. As a result, security can be compromised. For example, suppose that Mary has configured her browser to automatically log in under her profile when she goes to the URL for the CMS. Then, suppose that Todd uses Mary's workstation to log in to the same CMS at a later time. Todd will be using Mary's permissions, and not his own.

You can solve such problems by making sure that automatic login features are not enabled, and by educating users to make sure they check the profile they are using whenever they log in to the CMS.

Types of CMS

Various types of CMS exist. The two most common are:

- Web CMS.

- Enterprise CMS.

Web CMS

Perhaps the most common type of CMS is Web CMS, which is designed specifically to manage the submission of content onto one or more Web servers. A Web CMS has the following responsibilities and features:

- Tools that allow occasional users of HTML and other languages to create relatively sophisticated Web pages

- Workflow management capabilities

- The ability to cache and compare previously created pages

- Content syndication

 Another term for Web CMS is portal.

Enterprise CMS

An enterprise CMS serves more than just the organization's Web servers. Additional systems that the CMS can manage include:

- Human resources.

- Shipping and delivery.

- Payment and invoice systems.

- Customer relations.

- Sales management.

CMS vendors and products

Examples of CMS vendors and products include the following:

- Joomla (*www.joomla.org*)

- Microsoft SharePoint Server (*www.microsoft.com/cmserver/default.mspx*)

- Open Source CMS (*www.opensourcecms.com*)

- Light CMS (*www.speaklight.com*)

- Drupal (*http://drupal.org*).

- Mambo (*www.mamboserver.com*)

For more information about CMS implementations, visit the following resources:

- The CMS Wire Portal (*www.cmswire.com*)

- CMS Watch (*www.cmswatch.com*)

- CMS Matrix: (*http://cmsmatrix.org*)

- The Content Management System entry at Wikipedia (*http://en.wikipedia.org/wiki/Content_management_system*)

- CMS Review (*www.cmsreview.com*)

In the following lab, you will conduct research about CMS implementations. Suppose your fast-growing organization is considering the possibility of implementing a CMS. Your IT supervisor has assigned you to obtain information about CMS implementations, determine the benefits and drawbacks of a CMS, and present your findings at next week's manager's meeting for discussion. Where can you find information that would help you complete your research?

 Lab 3-3: Researching CMS implementations

In this lab, you will conduct research about CMS implementations. As you visit various Web sites, you will learn more about typical CMS terms, features and servers.

1. Open a Web browser and go to ***http://aplikacja.info/cmswiki***. Browse the site to learn more about specific CMS features and functions.

   Search for the following terms:

   - Personalization

   - Life cycle

   - Permissions

   - Baked

   - Fried

2. Go to ***www.templatemonster.com/cms-blog-templates.php*** to review templates that you can use in a CMS.

3. Review the following CMS provider Web sites:

   - Joomla (*www.joomla.org*)

   - Microsoft SharePoint Server (*www.microsoft.com/cmserver/default.mspx*)

   - Drupal (*http://drupal.org*).

   - Mambo (*www.mamboserver.com*)

4. Visit the following Web sites to investigate some of the latest CMS news and developments:

   - The CMS Wire Portal (*www.cmswire.com*).

   - CMS Watch (*www.cmswatch.com*)

- CMS Matrix: (*http://cmsmatrix.org*)

5. Close your browser.

In this lab, you learned more about typical CMS terms, features and servers.

Case Study

Keeping E-Mail Addresses Current

Lars is the e-mail administrator for a medium-sized company that operates offices in Stockholm, Buenos Aires and Singapore. These offices communicate daily and must continue to do so as efficiently as possible. Because of the high rate of turnover as well as the distances between the offices, users cannot easily obtain current e-mail addresses for their associates.

Lars recommends to Chen, the IT administrator, that they implement a directory server using the Lightweight Directory Access Protocol (LDAP). Lars' reasons are as follows:

- LDAP enables clients to query a database quickly over long distances without affecting network performance.

- The database, which would be managed by Lars, would provide a centralized, current listing of the associates in each of the offices.

- By configuring employee e-mail programs to query the database, Lars can ensure that employees will have instant access to current associate e-mail information.

*   *   *

Consider this scenario and answer the following questions:

- Can you think of any additional benefits to using a directory server and LDAP?

- Would any other server types or protocols be as effective as Lars' proposed solution?

Lesson Summary

Application project

Which particular software products are used at your company? Two popular Web servers are Apache and Microsoft IIS. Research both Web server products on the Internet to determine the best product for your company. Influencing factors include:

- Your current network operating system.

- The costs involved.

- Ask questions such as the following:

- Will the Web server provide interoperability within the company's existing infrastructure?

- If you already have a Web server, would it be difficult to migrate the current Web server to a new Web server?

Skills review

In this lesson, you learned about the major types of internetworking servers. Specifically, you studied file, print, HTTP, proxy, mail, mailing list, media, DNS, FTP, news, certificate, directory, fax and transaction servers. You learned about how each server uses different protocols from the TCP/IP suite, and how each server performs a different function to enhance business on TCP/IP networks. You also learned about Content Management System (CMS) implementations, and the creation and management of CMS content.

Now that you have completed this lesson, you should be able to:

✓ 3.4.1: Distinguish between HTTP and other Internet server types.

✓ 3.4.2: Identify the functions and features of common Internet-based services, and identify protocols used by each, including file, print, HTTP, proxy, caching, mail, mailing list, instant messaging, media, DNS, FTP, news, certificate, directory, fax, transaction.

✓ 3.4.3: Choose the correct server to fulfill a specific business/organizational need.

Lesson 3 Review

1. What three types of information are usually contained in server logs?

   _____

2. What is a proxy server?

   _____

   _____

3. Define a mailing list server.

   _____

   _____

4. What do media servers do?

   _____

5. Domain Name System (DNS) servers are composed of what two key components?

   _____

6. What protocol does a news server use?

   _____

7. What is the primary benefit of using a certificate server?

   _____

8. What is the primary purpose of a Content Management System (CMS)?

   _____

   _____

9. Describe the CMS content life cycle.

   _____

   _____

Lesson 3
Supplemental Material

This section is a supplement containing additional tasks for you to complete in conjunction with the lesson. These elements are:

- **Activities**
  Pen-and-paper activities to review lesson concepts or terms.

- **Optional Labs**
  Computer-based labs to provide additional practice.

- **Lesson Quiz**
  Multiple-choice test to assess knowledge of lesson material.

Activity 3-1: Diagramming DNS server relationships

In this activity, you will diagram the relationships among DNS root servers, primary or master servers, and client systems. Use the space provided to draw the relationships.

Include the following components from the DNS model in your diagram, and be sure to indicate all potential relationships among the components:

A. Root server

B. Primary server

C. Secondary server

D. Client

Activity 3-2: Recommending the appropriate server

For this activity, read the following scenarios, and then consider the server type you would recommend. Write and explain your answer in the space provided.

1. You are the administrator of a small company that requires extensive security. Although security is a concern, you must also consider the costs associated with obtaining certificates. Which server would you recommend?

   _____

   _____

   _____

2. After noticing that your company's access to the Internet is slowing, you determine that you need to provide a way to ease the burden on your HTTP server. What type of server would help you accomplish this goal?

   _____

   _____

   _____

3. You want to provide your employees with an electronic address book that contains a centralized list of e-mail addresses and contact information. You want to ensure that the latest version is always available when you update the address book. What type of server would allow employees to remotely access this information quickly without affecting network performance?

   _____

   _____

   _____

Optional Lab 3-1: Viewing installed services

In this optional lab, you will view the installed services on your system.

1. Open the **Control Panel**, click **Classic View** if necessary, then double-click **Programs And Features**.

2. In the left pane, click the **Turn Windows Features On Or Off** link. This action opens the Windows Features window, which displays installed Windows Vista features, as shown in Figure OL3-1.

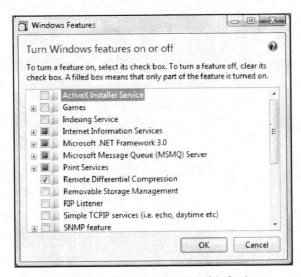

Figure OL3-1: Installed Windows Vista features

3. Scroll through the list of features. Installed features are identified by a check mark. A filled (shaded) check box indicates that only some of the available selections for a feature group have been installed.

4. Close the **Windows Features** window.

5. Redisplay the **Control Panel**, then double-click **Network And Sharing Center**. Click the **View Status** link to the right of Local Area Connection, then click the **Properties** button. This action opens the Local Area Connection Properties dialog box, which displays the network protocols, services and clients to which you are connected, as shown in Figure OL3-2.

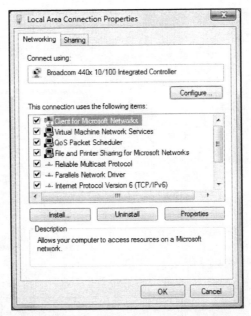

Figure OL3-2: Local Area Connection Properties dialog box — network protocols, services and clients

6. Scroll through the list of network components. The installed services are indicated by the icon of a computer with a hand under it.

7. Close all open dialog boxes and windows.

8. Right-click an empty area of the taskbar, then select **Task Manager** to display the Windows Task Manager.

9. Click the **Services** tab to display a list of the services installed on your computer and their current status. Your services list should resemble Figure OL3-3.

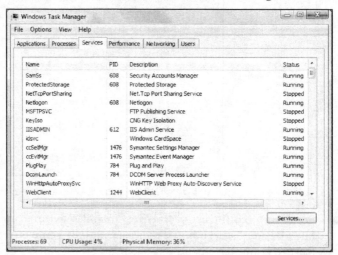

Figure OL3-3 Windows Task Manager — Services tab

10. Scroll through the list of services. Services with a status of Running are currently running on your computer.

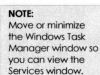

NOTE:
Move or minimize the Windows Task Manager window so you can view the Services window.

11. Click the **Services** button to display the Services window (Figure OL3-4). The Services window provides more details about your installed services and allows you to configure additional options.

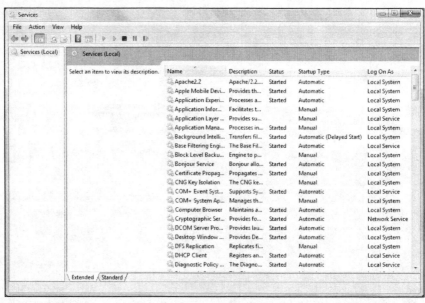

Figure OL3-4: Services window

12. Scroll through the list of services. You can configure services to start automatically when Windows starts or to start manually as needed, or you can disable services.

13. Close all open windows.

Lesson 3 Quiz

1. What two servers are often incorporated as one service?

    a. HTTP and directory servers
    b. Mail and mailing list servers
    c. File and print servers
    d. News and media servers

2. How does the HTTP server interact with TCP/IP?

    a. HTTP enables multi-person text input, which allows many individuals to access and read the same message.
    b. HTTP validates keys used to decode encryption algorithms.
    c. HTTP allows many users on a network to access the same files.
    d. HTTP listens on Port 80 for incoming requests from clients, such as Web browsers.

3. Instructions given by a server that restrict or allow access to system resources are called:

    a. passwords.
    b. permissions.
    c. file access protocols.
    d. rules.

4. The protocol that identifies a file type, encodes the file using the file type, and decodes it at the receiving end to display properly is called:

    a. Simple Mail Transfer Protocol (SMTP).
    b. File Transfer Protocol (FTP).
    c. Post Office Protocol (POP).
    d. Multipurpose Internet Mail Extensions (MIME).

5. You are a mail administrator and you receive complaints that users can receive mail but cannot send it. Which mail server should you troubleshoot?

    a. SMTP server
    b. IMAP server
    c. POP3 server
    d. NNTP server

Lesson 4:
Hardware and Operating System Maintenance

Objectives

By the end of this lesson, you will be able to:

- 3.1.2: Identify power requirements for international travel.

- 3.7.1: Identify maintenance issues for common system elements, including IRQs, DMA, I/O cards, NICs, motherboards, SCSI, IDE/ATA, serial ATA (including hard drives).

- 3.7.2: Connect common peripherals, including parallel, serial, USB, FireWire devices (e.g., printers, hard drives, scanners), CD-ROM/DVD.

- 3.8.1: Obtain proper licensing for operating systems and associated applications.

- 3.8.2: Recover from application failures.

- 3.8.3: Restart the system and identify common boot problems.

- 3.8.4: Explain why a hard drive must be partitioned and formatted.

- 3.8.5: Identify common file systems (e.g., NTFS, FAT, Ext3, ReiserFS).

- 3.8.6: Manage basic file and directory permissions.

- 3.8.7: Use common file system management tools, including Convert, Chkdsk, Disk Cleanup, Disk Defragmenter.

- 3.8.8: Delete temporary files manually and by using operating-system-specific methods.

- 3.8.9: Back up and restore files to prevent data loss, including digital tapes, CDs.

- 3.8.10: Identify ways to remotely manage and troubleshoot workstations.

Pre-Assessment Questions

1. The situation in which two or more devices share a configuration setting is called:

   a. a high-level format.
   b. a low-level format.
   c. a power spike.
   d. a resource conflict.

2. What is the name of the smallest storage allocation unit managed by an operating system?

   a. Cluster
   b. Cylinder
   c. Partition
   d. Root

3. What is direct memory access (DMA)?

   _____

   _____

Basic Hardware and System Maintenance

Periodically, all computer components experience (or appear to experience) failure. Before replacing components or obtaining the services of a qualified computer technician, you can often fix a problem yourself by performing one of the following simple tasks (depending on the component):

- Check that the component is plugged in.

- Check that the component is turned on.

- Check that all components are connected in order to operate properly (for example, ensure that the keyboard is connected to the computer).

You should also perform periodic preventive maintenance (PM) in order to avoid component failures. Preventive maintenance procedures typically include device cleaning, general maintenance and testing.

Device cleaning

NOTE:
See **Optional Lab 4-1: Removing dust from a PC.**

One of the primary reasons for cleaning a system is to remove accumulated dust. Dust acts as a heat insulator. Excessive dust can cause components to overheat and fail. Dust, dirt and other foreign matter can cause excessive wear on physical components. If a system is missing slot covers, for example, replace them. They will help reduce dust and make your system last longer.

If you need to remove dust from internal system components (such as the motherboard and adapter boards), use a soft brush and a static-free vacuum. You can also use compressed air to remove dust.

 WARNING! *Before conducting preventive maintenance on any device, turn off the device and unplug the power cord. Leaving power applied to the computer or peripheral can be a shock hazard and can cause component failure.*

General maintenance and testing

planned maintenance
Any scheduled maintenance procedures, including preventive maintenance.

General maintenance means taking care of any minor problems that you discover during **planned maintenance**. For example, if you find a worn cable while cleaning a computer, you should replace the cable at that point, rather than waiting for it to fail. Other general maintenance procedures include checking items that you know can cause system problems, such as disk fragmentation. (Disk fragmentation will be discussed in detail later in this lesson.)

You should verify basic system operations after completing preventive maintenance procedures to make sure that your system is in good working order.

In the following sections, we will discuss common system components in detail, including installation, removal and configuration procedures that you may need to perform.

OBJECTIVE
3.7.1: System component maintenance

motherboard
The main circuit board in a computer, on which the microprocessor, physical memory and support circuitry are located.

Motherboard

The **motherboard** is the main circuit board in a computer, on which the microprocessor, physical memory and support circuitry are located. All system devices (such as the keyboard; the mouse; and serial, parallel and Universal Serial Bus (USB) devices) connect directly or indirectly to the motherboard. Many motherboards use a multi-layer construction, which means that there are internal traces in addition to those on the top

trace
Thin conductive path on a circuit board, usually made of copper.

and bottom of the board. The internal **traces** are delicate and easily damaged, so care must be taken when handling motherboards.

The motherboard must be fastened to the system chassis. Usually, you will fasten the motherboard using small plastic or metal tabs that plug into the motherboard, and then onto holes in the chassis. When fastening the motherboard, take care not to allow any metal to improperly connect and ground the motherboard. The motherboard should not touch any metal object, except through proper connections (for example, to the power supply). In addition, make sure that all parts are fastened tightly to the motherboard, and that excess dust does not build up.

IRQs, I/O Addresses and DMA

OBJECTIVE
3.7.1: System component maintenance

resource conflict
A situation in which two or more devices share a configuration setting.

interrupt request (IRQ)
A hardware line over which devices can send interrupt signals to the processor.

In some cases, you need to provide parameters when you install devices in your computer. Though there are a few exceptions, most devices will require unique configuration values. Some of these are set by the system and cannot be changed. For those that can be set or modified, you must avoid introducing **resource conflicts** (also known as device conflicts). When you install a network device adapter, you must determine which system resources are already in use so that you can identify available resources for the installed device.

In a personal computer, communication is controlled through interrupts. **Interrupt requests (IRQs)** are hardware lines that are used to identify when a device wants to communicate with the processor and to notify a device that the processor wants the device's attention. This arrangement ensures that only one device at a time can communicate with the processor. For example, when a printer has finished printing, it sends an interrupt signal to the computer so the computer can decide what processing task to perform next.

Modern computers contain 16 IRQs, numbered 0 through 15. If your system will not boot properly or you cannot hear sound from your sound card, an IRQ resource conflict may have occurred.

I/O address
A memory location that allows resources to be allocated to a system device.

direct memory access (DMA)
A process that allows devices to bypass controllers and directly access memory.

An **I/O address** is a memory location that allows the system processor and system devices to communicate. Most devices will have at least one unique input/output (I/O) address.

Direct memory access (DMA) is the process by which a device can directly address system memory, bypassing the processor. DMA is most often used by hard disk controllers, but can also be used by other peripherals. DMA is different from programmed input/output (PIO), which requires that all data first pass through the processor. PIO is now considered obsolete.

Electronic communication

You must understand how computers communicate, both internally and with one another. To understand computer communication, you need to understand how to convert values among three numbering systems:

- Decimal (base 10)

- Binary (base 2)

- Hexadecimal (base 16)

Understanding the function of general mathematics in relation to your computer hardware is essential.

Binary numbering

A computer understands only two values, 1 (one) and 0 (zero). All system elements, including memory locations, and the subtle shades and hues displayed on your monitor, are defined as strings of 1s (ones) and 0s (zeros).

The number system recognized by computers is known as the binary system and is based on powers of 2. You designate binary positions by using either the 1 or the 0 in each value. You also read binary values from right to left, instead of left to right. Table 4-1 shows how binary values increment.

Table 4-1: Binary numbering

Power Notation	Decimal Equivalent	Binary Value
2^0	1	1
2^1	2	10
2^2	4	100
2^3	8	1000
2^4	16	10000
2^5	32	100000
2^6	64	1000000
2^7	128	10000000
2^8	256	100000000

Figure 4-1 represents the first nine binary values.

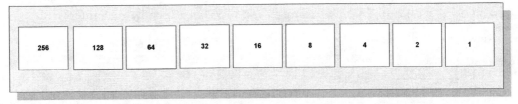

Figure 4-1: Representing numbers to ninth binary placeholder

Figure 4-1 does not represent all the binary positions. It includes only the first nine binary positions. To obtain further binary positions, you would multiply 256 by 2 to obtain the decimal equivalent of the tenth binary position, which is 512. To learn further values, you can multiply 512 again by 2, and so forth.

Converting decimal values into binary

Any number, either decimal or hexadecimal, can be converted into binary. To convert decimal numbers into binary, use the preceding figure as an example and read the 1 and 0 entries. Always read binary values from right to left. Always add the positions marked with a 1. For example, if you want to represent the decimal number of 2 in binary, you would write the following:

   10

In the previous example, the "0" in first binary position tells you to skip the first value, which represents the decimal number of 1. You then move on to the second value, which represents the decimal number of 2. The "1" informs you that you should count that number when adding. To represent the number 5 in binary, you would enter the following:

101

In the previous example, you count the first binary position (1), skip the second (2), and count the third (4). You then add the two values (1 and 4) to get the decimal sum of 5. The numbers 10 and 33 are represented, respectively, by the following binary numbers:

1010
100001

The binary representation of the decimal number 100,000 would be:

11000011010100000

As you can see, representing 100,000 requires 17 binary values:

65536	32768	16384	8192	4096	2048	1024	512	256	128	64	32	16	8	4	2	1
1	1	0	0	0	0	1	1	0	1	0	1	0	0	0	0	0

Add all the values represented by a 1, and you will get the decimal number 100,000.

Bytes and bits

The smallest unit for binary numbers is known as a bit. A bit represents a single binary value, either 1 or 0. However, when referring to storage, you more commonly refer to data being stored in bytes. A byte is a group of 8 bits. A byte can represent any decimal value between 0 and 255.

A byte is still a very small amount of data. You will more commonly see references to kilobits (Kb), kilobytes (KB), megabits (Mb), megabytes (MB), gigabits (Gb) and gigabytes (GB). Table 4-2 lists storage values you will probably encounter.

Table 4-2: Storage values

Unit	Description
Bit	A single binary digit.
Nibble	4 bits, or one half of a byte.
Byte	8 bits, the standard unit for measuring memory, file size and so forth.
Word	The amount of data that a microprocessor can handle at one time. Usually, this is 16 bits (or 2 bytes).
Kilobit (Kb)	1024 bits.
Kilobyte (KB)	1,024 bytes, or "one-thousand" bytes. This number may seem counterintuitive, but computers consider the number 1,024 to be one-thousand.
Megabit (Mb)	1,024 kilobits.
Megabyte (MB)	"1 million" bytes. More precisely, 1,024 kilobytes, or 1,048,576 bytes.
Gigabit (Gb)	1,024 megabits.
Gigabyte (GB)	"1 billion" bytes. More precisely, 1,024 MB, or 1,073,741,824 bytes.

NOTE:
Make sure that you understand the difference between bits and bytes. Remember that computers regard 1,024 bytes as a kilobyte. This will seem strange to some who might expect a kilobyte to equal exactly 1,000 bytes.

Other prefixes are used to describe larger byte values, but they are beyond the scope of this course.

To give you an idea of how storage expectations have changed over the years, the original IBM PC included 64 KB of memory, and its operating system (MS-DOS 1.0) could support a maximum of 640 KB of memory. Systems now typically include 2 GB of memory (and are upgradeable to 4 GB), and most current PC operating systems can support up to 4 GB of total system memory in a 32-bit system environment (and up to 128 GB in a 64-bit system environment).

legacy adapter board
An older, non-Plug-And-Play adapter board.

*Sometimes, you will have to use your understanding of binary to configure **legacy adapter boards**. For example, some devices have to set the device address in binary through switch settings or jumpers.*

Hexadecimal numbering

NOTE:
Hexadecimal is known as a "base-16" language because it repeats the same pattern every 16th digit.

The hexadecimal numbering system uses the digits 0 through 9, and the letters A through F. Thus, the numbers 0 through 9 are the same in both decimal and hexadecimal. However, the decimal number 10 is known as "A" in hexadecimal. The decimal number 15 is hexadecimal number F. However, the decimal number 16 is known in hexadecimal as 10, and the hexadecimal equivalent of the decimal number 17 is 11. The hexadecimal number 1A is the equivalent of 26. The pattern continues, so that the number 42 is 2A, and so forth. This scheme allows relatively small hexadecimal numbers to represent very large decimal numbers.

Each hexadecimal digit represents the value of a 4-bit binary number. With this knowledge, you can convert hexadecimal values into binary and into decimal. Table 4-3 contains a summary of equivalent values in decimal, hexadecimal and binary.

Hexadecimal values are sometimes written with a lowercase "h" following the number to prevent users from confusing them with a decimal value. For example, you might see an address expressed as 0060h.

Table 4-3: Comparing decimal, hexadecimal and binary values

NOTE:
This table is designed to make you understand how hexadecimal works.

Decimal	Hexadecimal	Binary*
0	0	0000
1	1	0001
2	2	0010
3	3	0011
4	4	0100
5	5	0101
6	6	0110
7	7	0111
8	8	1000
9	9	1001
10	A	1010
11	B	1011
12	C	1100
13	D	1101
14	E	1110
15	F	1111

Table 4-3: Comparing decimal, hexadecimal and binary values (cont'd)

Decimal	Hexadecimal	Binary*
16	10	10000
17	11	10001
18	12	10010
19	13	10011
20	14	10100
21	15	10101
22	16	10110
23	17	10111
24	18	11000
25	19	11001
26	1A	11010
27	1B	11011
42	2A	101010
43	2B	101011
50	32	110010
100	64	1100100
1000	3E8	1111101000
1,000,000	F4240	1111010000100 1000000

* Beginning with four digits, and continuing upward.

Tech Tip

Windows operating systems have a calculator program called calc.exe that can convert decimal values into hexadecimal and binary. However, you may sometimes need to convert these values without the aid of a calculator.

Memory address locations and ranges are commonly expressed in decimal values. Memory and disk utilities that let you directly view content will typically use hexadecimal as a viewing option, with hexadecimal sometimes the only option available.

Converting from hexadecimal into binary and decimal

Converting from hexadecimal into binary requires that you represent each individual hexadecimal value as binary. Each hexadecimal value equals four binary digits. For example, the binary equivalent of the hexadecimal number 3DC would be as follows:

3	D	C
0011	1101	1100

Thus, the binary equivalent of the hexadecimal value of 3DC is 001111011100. Properly ordering each value or group of values is important during the conversion process. To convert this value into decimal, you would place the three groups of binary numbers next to one another in the same order as each hexadecimal value, then add only the binary values marked with a 1, as follows:

2048	1024	512	256	128	64	32	16	8	4	2	1	
0	0	1	1	1	1	0	1	1	1	0	0	= 988

Thus, the decimal equivalent of the hexadecimal value 3DC is 988.

Converting from binary into hexadecimal

NOTE:
See **Activity 4-2:
Converting decimal,
binary and
hexadecimal values**
to give you more
practice converting
among these
numbering systems.

To convert from binary into hexadecimal, it is easiest to first group the binary numbers into groups of four, then turn each group of four into decimal numbers. Make sure you begin grouping values from right to left. If you end up with a last group containing fewer than four digits, do not worry. This happens because you need not count the very last digits to the left if they are all 0s.

Next, add each group of four binary digits and convert each group into a decimal number. Finally, convert each of these decimal numbers into a hexadecimal number.

ASCII

American Standard Code for Information Interchange (ASCII) defines a standard code for storing text (letter and number) values. The original ASCII was a 7-bit standard that defined 128 values for letters, numbers, punctuation and control characters. Most systems now support the 8-bit ASCII extended character set, which includes another 128 characters.

More recently, another encoding standard, known as Unicode, has come into common use. Unicode is an international 16-bit encoding standard that can represent the 65,536 characters that can be used in major world languages.

Communication basics

To begin understanding how computers communicate, you need to understand the terms serial and parallel, and how they relate to communication. Regardless of whether a computer is communicating internally or with a remote system, all communication occurs as either serial or parallel. Figure 4-2 illustrates serial communication.

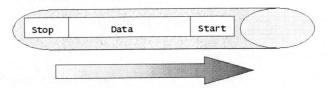

| Stop | Data | Start |

Figure 4-2: Serial communication

Serial communication

COM
PC serial ports are
referred to as
numbered COM
(communication)
ports. COM ports
have a maximum
transmission speed
of roughly 115 Kbps.

Serial communication occurs one bit at a time over a single line. You can move only one bit at a time because a single line can have only one value, either on or off (1 or 0). Data, in the form of bits, moves through a serial communication channel as a datastream. Serial communication is used with devices attached to a computer's serial (**COM**) (communication) port, for modem communication and for network communication. The universal serial bus (USB), as its name implies, also uses serial communication, and allows rates of 12 Mbps (USB 1.0/1.1) or 480 Mbps (USB 2.0). When USB 3.0 becomes commercially available (targeted for 2010), it will be able to support rates of 5 Gbps (5,000 Mbps).

 The term "bits per second" (bps) refers to how many ones or zeros a data path or data port can handle. The term "bytes per second" (Bps) describes how many 8-bit blocks a data path or data port can handle. The equivalent of 12 Mbps in megabytes per second is 1.5 MBps. The equivalent of 480 Mbps in megabytes per second is 60 MBps.

Parallel communication

In parallel communication (Figure 4-3), the computer is moving several bits at a time. In a PC, this typically means moving 8 bits (a byte) or 16 bits (a word) at a time. Parallel communication requires a separate line for each data bit, as well as additional control lines to manage the data transfer. Parallel communication is used with devices connected to a computer's parallel port and the internal system buses. PC parallel (**LPT**) ports are 8-bit parallel ports. The original speed for LPT ports was 500 Kbps, although higher data rates are available.

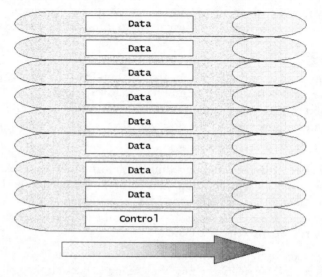

Figure 4-3: Parallel communication

IRQ, I/O address and DMA assignments

Table 4-4 lists standard IRQ, I/O address and DMA assignments. I/O address values are given in hexadecimal notation. A blank cell indicates that no standard resource assignment exists for that device.

Table 4-4: Standard resource assignments

Device	IRQ	I/O Address Range	DMA Channel
System timer	0	0040 – 0043	
Keyboard controller	1	0060 – 006F	
Real-time clock	8	0070h – 0071h	
COM1	4	03F8h – 03FFh	
COM2	3	02F8h – 02FFh	
COM3	4	03E8h – 03EFh	
COM4	3	02E8h – 02EFh	
LPT1	7	0378h – 037Fh	
LPT2	5	0278h – 027Fh	
PS/2 mouse port (motherboard)	12	0060h – 006F	

Table 4-4: Standard resource assignments (cont'd)

Device	IRQ	I/O Address Range	DMA Channel
Primary hard disk controller (primary SATA)	14	01F0h – 01F7h	Auto, if available
Secondary hard disk controller (secondary SATA)	15	0170h – 0178h	Auto, if available
Math co-processor (if present)	13	00F0h – 00FFh	

Viewing and changing resource assignments

NOTE:
Lab 4-1: Viewing resource assignments will demonstrate the Device Manager in Windows Vista that you can use to resolve resource conflicts.

You will usually not need to change a resource assignment. If you do, however, you can use the Windows Vista Device Manager. In Linux, you would do so by viewing files in the /proc/ directory. For example, consider the following Linux command:

> /proc/interrupts

This command yields a text file you can open in any word processor to view the current IRQ settings.

Consider the following Linux command:

> /proc/iomem

This command yields a text file containing I/O addresses.

In the following lab, you will view resource assignments on your system using the Windows Vista Device Manager. Suppose that you have just installed a new printer on your Windows Vista system in your home office, but print tests have failed. You suspect a resource conflict. How would you determine which system resources are already in use in order to identify available resources for your new printer?

 Lab 4-1: Viewing resource assignments

In this lab, you will view resource assignments on your system.

1. Open the **Control Panel** and display it in **Classic View** if necessary.

2. Double-click **System**, then click the **Device Manager** link in the left pane to open the Device Manager (Figure 4-4). You can use the Device Manager to view and adjust various resource settings, as necessary.

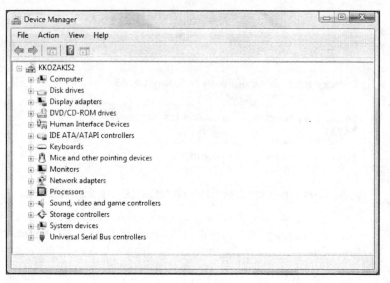

Figure 4-4: Device Manager

3. Double-click **IDE ATA/ATAPI Controllers**, then double-click your hard drive
    controller (for example, *NVIDIA nForce Serial ATA Controller*) to display its Properties
    dialog box. Click the **Port 0** tab. Notice that DMA Mode displays in the Transfer Mode
    drop-down list (Figure 4-5).

Figure 4-5: Hard drive controller properties — Port 0

4. Deselect **Let BIOS Select Transfer Mode**, then display the **Transfer Mode** drop-
    down list. Notice that PIO Mode is the other option you can choose.

    *Tech Note: If your system has a standard Serial ATA drive that is not working properly,
    you would probably need to switch the transfer mode setting to PIO Mode. If you have
    a hard drive that uses DMA, a setting of PIO Mode would cause hard drive problems.*

5. Close the drop-down list without changing the device setting.

6. Click the **Resources** tab and scroll through the Resource Settings list. Notice the
    resource settings that display for the I/O ranges and IRQ (Figure 4-6). Also notice

that No Conflicts displays in the Conflicting Device List area, indicating that your system does not have a resource conflict.

Figure 4-6: Viewing resource settings

Note: You must have administrator privileges to change network resource settings on your system.

7. Close all dialog boxes and windows.

Mass Storage Device Interfaces

OBJECTIVE
3.7.1: System component maintenance

interface
A communication channel between two components.

To communicate with a motherboard, a mass storage device (for example, a hard drive or a USB flash drive) must be connected to that motherboard through an **interface**. The two most common interfaces used to connect mass storage devices in modern computers are

- Serial Advanced Technology Attachment (SATA).
- Small computer system interface (SCSI).

Serial ATA (SATA)

Integrated drive electronics (IDE), also known as Advanced Technology Attachment (ATA), was formerly the standard electronics interface used to connect mass storage devices to the motherboard. Serial ATA (SATA) provides faster speeds than standard ATA. SATA is currently the *de facto* standard for PC-based drives. SATA devices are connected using a cable that somewhat resembles a small Category 5 Ethernet cable.

Small computer system interface (SCSI)

bus
An electronic pathway that conducts signals to connect the functional components of a computer.

SCSI (pronounced "skuzzy") was originally adopted by Apple Computer as an expansion **bus** standard. Eventually, SCSI gained popularity in the personal computer marketplace, especially for applications requiring large hard disks. However, the serial ATA (SATA) interface is the most popular for modern PCs.

SCSI is a parallel interface standard that allows you to connect multiple devices to a single interface adapter in a daisy chain configuration. You can attach a SCSI cable from the SCSI port on your computer to another SCSI device, then attach that SCSI device to a second SCSI device, and so on up to 127 devices. This grouping can include a mix of internal and external devices. SCSI devices include:

- Hard disk drives.

- Printers.

- Scanners.

- Tape drives.

- A wide variety of other peripherals.

A SCSI daisy chain must be terminated at both ends and only at the ends. Termination is the most common problem associated with SCSI devices.

Network Interface Card (NIC)

You were introduced to NICs earlier in the course. Each network device must have a NIC (also known as a network adapter card). Figure 4-7 shows a typical peripheral component interconnect (PCI) network adapter that is already installed. The network adapter makes the physical connection between the device (such as a computer) and the network cabling. When selecting a network adapter, you must choose an adapter that is supported by both your computer and your network.

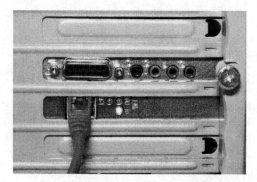

Figure 4-7: Installed network adapter

The network adapter is essentially a translator between the computer and the network. Networks transmit data serially, or one bit at a time. The network adapter converts the data from the computer into a format appropriate for transmission over the network.

The network adapter component that handles data transmission is called the transceiver. You were introduced to transceivers earlier in the course. All modern networking devices (for example, Ethernet cards, modems, mobile phones) use a transceiver. It ensures that the appropriate data format is being used when transmitting information. Most NICs have more than one transceiver, with each attached to the different connectors available on the back of the card.

OBJECTIVE
3.7.2: Common
peripherals

peripheral port
A socket on a
computer into
which a peripheral
device is
connected.

**PS/2-style
connector**
The six-pin mini-DIN
connectors
introduced with the
IBM PS/2.

Common Peripheral Ports

Peripheral ports are the sockets on the back panel of the computer into which input and output devices connect to the computer. Newer computers provide many ports. If a port is unavailable for a particular device, you must install an expansion board that includes the port you need.

Newer systems have **PS/2-style connectors** for the mouse and keyboard (Figure 4-8). Most new systems also have monitor adapter circuitry built into the motherboard and a permanent monitor connector. Some systems have embedded sound card and game controller support.

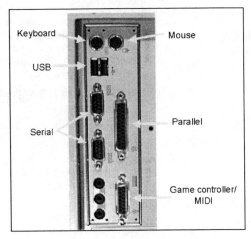

Figure 4-8: Peripheral ports

You will typically see one or two serial ports and one parallel port. In addition, modern systems have one or two USB ports on the back. Some systems have USB ports on the front of the system as well, to provide easy access.

Standard port use

PS/2-style keyboard and mouse ports are used as keyboard and pointing device connectors only. The mouse port should be more accurately considered a pointing device port because of the variety of pointing devices in common use. Pointing devices include mouse devices, trackballs and touch-sensitive pads, all of which connect to the PS/2 mouse port.

Many manufacturers now color-code ports and connectors on new systems. This color-coding makes it easier for users, specifically home users, to set up their own systems.

NOTE:
Make sure that you
are aware that USB
is the standard
printer interface.
The fastest parallel
port interface is 2
MBps, which is faster
than standard USB.
Still, standard USB is
more efficient in its
data transfer.

The standard ports listed in Table 4-5 support several different types of devices. For example, a serial port can support a modem, a serial printer, a serial mouse or a digital camera interface.

Table 4-5: Standard port use

Port	Use Guidelines
First serial port (COM1)	If you are using a serial mouse, it should always be connected to COM1. If you have a PS/2 mouse, COM1 is available for use by any serial device. It is possible to print through a serial port, including COM1. Regardless of the COM channel you use, serial communications are enabled by a universal asynchronous receiver-transmitter (UART). The most common UART is 16550A.
Second serial port (COM2)	COM2 can support any serial devices, but a potential configuration concern exists: Hardware-configured internal modems typically default to using COM2 and would therefore conflict with any other device connected to COM2. It is possible to print through a serial port, including COM2.
Parallel port (IEEE 1284)	The parallel port is usually used for connecting a local printer, but other devices operate through a parallel port, including network adapters and disk controllers. The IEEE 1284 standard supports five different modes: -Compatibility (150 KBps) -Nibble (50 KBps to 150 KBps) -Byte (up to 500 KBps) -Enhanced parallel port (500 KBps to 2 MBps) -Extended capability (up to 2 MBps — uses DMA) You may need to enter a system's complementary metal oxide semiconductor (CMOS) to choose the most appropriate mode. Sometimes, you may need to choose a mode supported by your system and the peripheral device.
USB port	A serial interface. The USB port can physically support any USB device. It is often used for printers, scanners, keyboards, mouse devices and external hard drives. USB hubs allow a single-system USB port to support multiple devices, up to 127 peripherals. Two USB standards exist: -USB 1.0/1.1 -USB 2.0, also called high-speed USB High-speed USB is backward-compatible with USB 1.0. However, USB 1.0 does not support USB 2.0 devices. USB 2.0 supports speeds of up to 480 Mbps (60 MBps). USB 1.0 supports speeds up to 12 Mbps (1.5 MBps), although an earlier 1.0 version supported only 1.5 Mbps (less than 300 Kbps).
Game port	The game controller port often serves as the Musical Instrument Digital Interface (MIDI) connector. This port can connect MIDI-compliant digital music devices, such as digital keyboards.
FireWire (IEEE 1394)	A serial interface. FireWire is used for various devices that require high throughput, including external disk drives, digital and Web cameras, and network connections. IEEE 1394 devices support transfer rates from 100 to 400 Mbps with projected speed enhancements expected to make transfer rates much higher. As with any interface type, IEEE 1394 ports can be added using PCI adapters. IEEE 1394 ports can support up to 63 peripherals.

Troubleshooting port and cabling problems

Make sure that cables are properly inserted into the proper ports. Check all cables associated with a problem device and make sure they are securely plugged in. Table 4-6 lists common problems related to ports and cables, and their solutions.

Table 4-6: Common port and cabling problems and solutions

Cable/Port	Problem	Cause/Solution
Serial	Mouse fails when modem is turned on. Mouse is jittery, or modem intermittently fails.	IRQ conflict. Change either the mouse or the modem port. Secure the cable into both the modem and computer.
Parallel	Slow or no printing.	Verify that the correct IEEE 1284 mode is chosen. Secure the cable on both the printer and the computer.
USB	USB 2.0 device performing slowly or not at all.	Ensure that you have a cable that supports USB 2.0 speeds. Verify that the cable is secure.
IEEE 1394 (FireWire)	The connection is intermittent.	Verify that the cable is secure.
SCSI	No communication, or communication in at least one device is intermittent after adding a new device.	Verify termination on the SCSI chain.

In the following lab, you will identify a number of the most common peripheral ports. Suppose you are a musician with an interest in digital music editing and home studio equipment. You just bought new software that enables you to use your computer to record music you compose on your synthesizer. You need to connect the synthesizer to your computer by means of a MIDI cable. Can you recognize the MIDI port on your computer?

 Lab 4-2: Identifying common peripheral ports

In this lab, you will identify common peripheral ports.

1. Look at the back panel of your PC, and identify each of the peripheral ports you see. Do you have the following ports? If so, how many? Write your answers in the spaces provided.

   PS/2: _____   USB: _____

   Serial: _____   Game: _____

   Parallel: _____   FireWire: _____

2. Open your system and display the internal components. Identify SATA cables, hard disk drives, CD-ROM drives, various adapter boards and so forth.

3. Use a static-free vacuum or can of compressed air to blow dust out of the system.

Power Requirements

OBJECTIVE
3.1.2: International power

Electricity is measured according to different standards in North America and in Europe, and computing and networking equipment is manufactured to different standards, depending on where the equipment will be used.

If you travel to Europe and take your laptop or notebook computer that was designed for use in the United States, you will need a special plug adapter in order to plug into an electrical receptacle in England, for example. The notebook computer's power supply will automatically convert the power.

Optical Discs

OBJECTIVE
3.7.2: Common peripherals

Optical discs are optical storage devices that store data on a reflective metal surface that is accessed by a laser beam. Optical discs include:

- Compact discs (CDs), including CD-ROMs, CD-Rs and CD-RWs.

- Digital video discs (DVDs).

- Blu-ray Discs (BDs).

Data is written to an optical disc by burning depressions into the metal surface of the disc. These depressions are called pits; the flat areas on the metal surface are called lands. A land reflects laser light from the disc surface into a sensor and is interpreted as the binary digit 1. A pit scatters laser light from the disc surface into a sensor and is interpreted as the binary digit 0.

CD-ROM characteristics

A compact disc read-only memory (CD-ROM) is an optical storage device from which data can be read only. In other words, data cannot be written to a CD-ROM. CD-ROM drives use common mass storage interfaces. The most common type of CD-ROM device has a SATA interface, but SCSI and USB versions are also available.

Table 4-7 lists key features of CD-ROMs, which have become a popular storage and distribution medium.

Table 4-7: CD-ROM features

NOTE:
Review the CD-ROM features and compare them with those of hard disks.

Feature	Description
Storage capacity	Up to 1 GB of data.
Reliability	Not affected by magnetic fields because it is an optical medium. Does not degrade over time because the data is burned into the surface by a laser beam.
Durability	Much more durable than their predecessors, floppy disks. Avoid scratching the surface of a CD-ROM; data in the affected sectors may be destroyed. Can also be physically damaged by high heat.
Performance	CD-ROM drives now surpass many hard disks in performance, which has improved dramatically in the past few years.
Security	Commercially distributed CD-ROMs are a read-only medium. After the data has been written to the CD-ROM, it cannot be changed.
Mixed-media support	In addition to digital data, a CD-ROM can contain audio, image and video content, and can play audio CDs.
Cross-platform compatibility	The current ISO 9660 data format (High Sierra format) standard is supported by Windows operating systems, MS-DOS, Linux/UNIX, the Apple Macintosh operating system and others.

Writable CDs

Writable CD devices allow you to create, or "burn," your own data and audio CDs. You can create your own distribution CDs, copy selected files or folders from your hard disk, and duplicate existing CD-ROMs and audio CDs.

WARNING! *You should always adhere to copyright regulations. It is illegal to make copies of copyrighted material, which includes both software distribution CDs and audio CDs. You are sometimes granted a limited right to make backup copies, or you may obtain copy permission from the copyright holder. Make sure that you do not violate copyright restrictions when copying any CD.*

Writable CDs are available in the following two formats:

NOTE:
The difference between a CD-R and CD-RW is in the medium.

- **CD-recordable (CD-R)** — a write-once format. After the data has been written to the CD-R, it cannot be modified.

- **CD-rewritable (CD-RW)** — a rewritable format. You can write data to it multiple times, similar to hard disks. Only CD drives that support multi-read capability can read CD-RWs.

 Some early CD-RW drives were known as erasable CD drives, or CD-E drives. According to specifications, you should be able to rewrite over the same spot on a CD-RW nearly 1,000 times.

Live CD

A live (or bootable) CD is a CD that contains a bootable computer operating system on the medium itself. You can use a live CD to run an operating system on a computer that lacks a hard disk drive. Most live CDs are based on Linux, and most Linux distributions now come on live CDs.

Live CDs can be used to:

- Install a Linux distribution on a hard drive.

- Test operating system and hardware compatibility.

- Test an operating system distribution before installing it on a hard drive.

- Provide a secure platform where files cannot be permanently modified.

- Repair or restore a computer system.

- Recover data.

Live USB

Live (or bootable) USB flash drives are similar to live CDs in that they also contain bootable computer operating systems on the medium itself. However, live USB devices can also write changes and save settings back onto the USB device. Because of this, you can store applications and personal files on a live USB and use it on multiple systems.

A live USB can provide a measure of security because you can carry the device with you and store it in a secure location. However, a USB device is easy to misplace or can be easily stolen, so you need to make sure you back up and encrypt your data before transferring it to a live USB.

DVD characteristics

NOTE:
DVDs are sometimes referred to as digital versatile discs.

Digital video discs (DVDs) were designed and developed for use with applications in both video and data storage. They work in much the same way as CD-ROMs: Data is stored in pits and lands. However, DVDs have a much higher storage capacity the pits are smaller, and DVDs use a higher track density than CD-ROMs do.

MPEG-2
Current video compression standard.

Most DVD drives use a SATA interface, although USB and IEEE versions are available and have become common. The physical removal and replacement procedures for internal devices are the same as for other SATA mass storage devices. DVD drives are Plug-And-

Play devices, but typically come with other software in addition to the required device drivers. For example, they often include **MPEG-2** decoding software and a media player so you can play DVDs on your computer.

The initial DVD standard provided 4.7 GB of storage capacity. Current DVD standards support dual-layer discs with a storage capacity of 8.5 GB. Also, a double-sided disc standard supports 9.4 GB when writing to one side of the DVD or 17 GB total when writing to both sides of the DVD. The current transfer rate is 1.3 MBps for all formats, with an access time ranging from 150 to 200 milliseconds (ms).

DVD drives are backward-compatible; those that support the newer standards can also support the initial DVD standard. DVD drives can also read CD-ROMs and CD-RWs, and play audio CDs.

Writable DVD (DVD-RW)

NOTE:
Writable DVD is becoming more common on high-end home computer systems.

Although writable DVDs are not commonly seen on standard corporate desktops, specifications exist for them. Currently, four different writable DVD standards exist. Table 4-8 describes these standards and their storage capacities.

Table 4-8: Writable DVD standards

Standard	Storage Capacity	Description
DVD-R	4.7 GB per side	Write-once standard currently in use. The standard was released in 1997. Supported by most DVD drives.
DVD-RAM	4.7 GB per side	Write-once standard currently in use. The standard was released in 1997. The least expensive format, but has only limited support.
DVD-RW	4.7 GB per side	A rewritable standard. Most DVD drives are designed to read this standard. Very few DVD-RW devices are available.
DVD+RW	8.5 GB per disc	A rewritable standard. Few DVD drives are designed to read this standard. Very few DVD+RW devices are available.

Blu-ray Disc characteristics

NOTE:
Technically, the laser used by Blu-ray Discs is blue-violet. In any case, the name is derived from the laser used to read and write data from the medium.

Blu-ray, also known as Blu-ray Disc (BD), is a high-definition optical disc storage medium that is designed to be the successor to DVDs. Blu-ray Discs were introduced in 2006 and have the same physical dimensions as standard CDs and DVDs. Approximately 200 consumer electronics, personal computer, recording media, video game and music companies form the Blu-ray Disc Association (BDA), an industry consortium that develops and supports Blu-ray Disc technology.

Current DVDs use a red laser to read and write data to the disc. Blu-ray uses a blue laser, which has a much shorter wavelength, enabling it to store much more data on the disc compared to DVDs. Single-layer BDs can hold up to 25 GB of data, and dual-layer BDs can hold up to 50 GB. A 50-GB BD can hold over nine hours of high-definition video or 23 hours of standard-definition video. Most current BD players include a BD/DVD/CD-compatible optical head, which makes them backward-compatible with DVDs and CDs.

Blu-ray Disc-recordable

There are two types of Blu-ray Disc-recordable optical disc formats:

- **BD-R** — a write-once format

- **BD-RE** — a rewritable format

Optical disc drive maintenance

OBJECTIVE
3.7.1: System
component
maintenance

CD, DVD and BD drives of all types are vulnerable to contamination. Keep the drives closed when they are not in use, and check all discs for foreign matter before inserting them into the drive. Commercial products are available for cleaning disc surfaces. CDs, DVDs and BDs should be handled only by the edges, and care must be taken to avoid scratching the disc surface.

Commercial cleaning kits are available to clean the internal laser. Never directly touch or try to manually clean the laser.

Brush away or vacuum accumulated dust without contaminating the disc carrier area or laser. Verify that the data and power cables are securely mounted.

NOTE:
Try this technique
using your own
system.

If an optical disc drive will not open because of a malfunction or power loss, it is possible to eject a disc manually from the drive. Locate the small hole on the face of the drive near the Open/Close button. Straighten a paper clip, place it (or another thin instrument) into the hole and press hard to eject the disc manually.

When an optical disc drive fails completely, you will generally need to replace the drive.

TV Tuner Card

TV tuner card
A computer
component that
enables television
signals to be viewed
on a computer
monitor.

A **TV tuner card** is a computer component that you can use to watch television programs on a computer monitor. Most TV tuner cards also function as video-capture cards, which means that they can record television programs onto a hard disk. TV tuner cards are designed to plug directly into expansion slots in your computer.

There are four kinds of TV tuner cards:

- **Analog TV tuners** — output a raw video stream for real-time viewing. Generally broadcast as an MPEG stream.

- **Digital TV tuners** — output a raw video stream for real-time viewing. Generally broadcast as an MPEG-2 stream.

- **Hybrid tuner** — can be configured to act as either an analog tuner or a digital tuner.

- **Combo tuner** — a card with two separate tuners, one analog and the other digital. You can watch an analog stream while recording a digital stream, or vice versa.

There are also external TV tuner cards available for mobile phone handsets, to enable users to watch mobile TV.

HDMI Connections

**HDMI (High-
Definition
Multimedia
Interface)**
A compact
audio/video
interface for
transmitting
uncompressed
digital data.

High-Definition Multimedia Interface (HDMI) is an audio/video interface that is used to transmit high-definition digital video and high-resolution digital audio data. HDMI consists of 19 wires wrapped in a single cable that resembles a USB wire. HDMI is able to carry a bandwidth of up to 5 Gbps.

HDMI supports any TV or PC video format, including standard, enhanced, and high-definition video, and up to eight channels of digital audio. It is commonly used for high-definition televisions (HDTVs) and home theater systems that have surround-sound audio. Every new HDTV has at least two HDMI inputs, and other devices such as digital video recorders (DVRs), DVD players, Blu-ray players, game consoles and personal computers include HDMI outputs to deliver audio and video.

Digital Video Interface (DVI)
A video interface technology that carries uncompressed digital video data to a display.

NOTE:
Visit www.datapro.net/techinfo/dvi_info.html to learn more about DVI.

Modern personal computers and video graphics cards use the **Digital Video Interface (DVI)**. DVI is a video interface technology that maximizes the quality of flat-panel LCD monitors and digital projectors. Until recently, the DVI standard was the digital transfer method used for enhanced-definition television (EDTV), high-definition television (HDTV), Plasma displays, and other high-end video displays for televsion, movies and DVDs. HDMI is now replacing DVI as the technology of choice.

An HDMI video signal is electronically compatible with a DVI signal, making HDMI backward-compatible with DVI. This means that a DVI source can run an HDMI monitor, or vice versa, by means of a suitable adapter or DVI/HDMI cable.

HDMI is a far superior technology to the analog cables most people still use for their television audio/video. With an analog interface, a clean digital signal is translated into a less precise analog signal, sent to the television, then converted back to a digital signal to display on the screen. With each conversion, the digital signal loses integrity, which can distort the picture quality. HDMI preserves the source digital signal by eliminating the digital-to-analog-to-digital conversion. However, to preserve the integrity of the digital signal and prevent degradation, HDMI cables should not run longer than 15 feet (5 meters).

To replicate what HDMI provides with a single cable using analog cables, you would need to connect three component-video cables and six analog audio cables. A single HDMI cable replaces the tangle of multiple analog cables, making the process of setting up a home theater system, for example, much simpler, while delivering superior output.

For more information about HDMI, visit the following sites:

- *www.hdmi.org*

- *www.wisegeek.com/what-is-hdmi.htm*

- *www.tech-faq.com/hdmi.shtml*

Mobile Computing

mobile computing
A person's ability to use technology in non-stationary positions and in transit.

Mobile computing refers to a person's ability to use technology while "on the go." Devices that enable a user to engage in mobile computing include:

- Notebook computers.

- Personal digital assistants (PDAs), such as Palm Pilot, etc.

- Mobile phones.

- Smartphones, such as BlackBerry, iPhone, etc.

- Portable media players, such as iPod, Zune, etc.

These types of devices (and more) are becoming very popular as the technology becomes more widely (and affordably) available. People today are trying to juggle more activities with their limited time, so these devices are very useful because:

- They are portable.

- They can connect to each other via the Internet.

- They allow data storage.

- They contain enough processing power to perform tasks that you can also perform using your computer.

However, the very features that make mobile computing devices useful also make them a security risk to users when these devices contain proprietary or confidential data. Major features of mobile computing devices that can cause risk to the user include:

- **Their small size** — The devices can be easily misplaced, lost or stolen.

- **Weak user authentication mechanisms** — The user can disable authentication or it can be easily compromised.

- **Their ease of interconnectedness** — Users can easily connect to users with malicious intentions, in some cases without even knowing it.

The following sections will introduce common mobile computing devices and associated technologies.

PDAs

A personal digital assistant (PDA) is a handheld mobile computing device. Most PDAs have color screens and audio capabilities, and can access the Internet, intranets and extranets. Older PDAs typically had softkeys, a directional pad, a thumb keypad and/or a numeric keypad for entering data. Modern PDAs generally use a touch screen for entering data, a memory card slot for storing data, and a WiFi or Bluetooth connection for wireless connectivity. Some PDAs also include a USB port for USB flash drives. Popular PDA brands include Palm, Visor, Psion and RIM.

A sample PDA is shown in Figure 4-9.

Figure 4-9: Sample PDA device

Bluetooth

Bluetooth
A standard for short-range radio signals that is used to form personal area networks (PANs).

Bluetooth is a wireless protocol that is used to exchange data over short distances. Bluetooth allows you to form a personal area network (PAN), which is a computer network that is used to communicate among computer devices that are in close proximity to one another, such as desktop computers, laptop computers and mobile devices. By embedding a Bluetooth chip and receiver into devices, these devices can communicate with each other without the need for cables.

NOTE:
Bluetooth
technology is
named for King
Harald Blatand
("Bluetooth") of
Denmark, who
united Denmark
and part of Norway
into a single
kingdom in the late
900s (hence the
inspiration for the
name: uniting
devices through
Bluetooth).

There are currently three classifications for Bluetooth devices. Table 4-9 lists the signal strength and range for each class.

Table 4-9: Bluetooth classifications

Bluetooth Class	Signal Strength	Range
Class 1	1 milliwatt	Up to 33 feet (10 meters)
Class 2	10 milliwatts	Up to 33 feet (10 meters)
Class 3	100 milliwatts	Up to 328 feet (100 meters)

Bluetooth is not designed to replace wireless LAN technologies because its range is too limited. Its main purpose is to simplify the process of connecting computer devices within a confined area, such as a home.

To learn more about Bluetooth, visit *www.bluetooth.com*.

Smartphones

smartphone
A mobile phone
that includes PC-like
functionality.

A **smartphone** is a mobile phone that includes PC-like functionality. There is no industry standard definition for a smartphone. In general, smartphones contain powerful processors, plenty of memory, large (relatively) screens, and operating system software.

Smartphone functionality can include:

- Fully featured media players.

- Digital photo and video cameras.

- E-mail and instant messaging capabilities.

- High-speed mobile Internet access.

- Global positioning system (GPS) capabilities.

Among the most popular smartphone brands are iPhone and BlackBerry.

iPhone

The iPhone is a smartphone introduced by Apple, Inc. (*www.apple.com*) in 2007. The iPhone uses a touchscreen for data input; it does not contain a keypad. The user can display a virtual keyboard and keypad in the touchscreen as needed. The absence of a physical keypad allows the iPhone's touchscreen to be much larger than screens that similar-sized mobile phones can provide.

The iPhone device provides Internet connectivity, WiFi connectivity, Bluetooth connectivity, digital cameras and fully functioning media players. Later models also include GPS capabilities. iPhones are "locked"; that is, they use the mobile phone service of a specific provider only. In the United States, that provider is AT&T.

Figure 4-10 shows a sample a sample iPhone.

Figure 4-10: Sample iPhone

To learn more about iPhones, visit *www.apple.com/iphone/*.

BlackBerry

A BlackBerry is a mobile communication device that is considered to be a smartphone and a personal digital assistant (PDA). It was developed by the Canadian company Research In Motion (*www.rim.com*) and is very similar to Apple's iPhone. The BlackBerry device provides Internet connectivity, e-mail capabilities, text messaging, an address book, a calendar, a day-planner, an alarm clock and mobile phone service. Some models provide WiFi connectivity, Bluetooth connectivity, a digital camera, GPS functionality and a fully functioning media player. BlackBerrys utilize a built-in QWERTY keyboard that is designed for "thumbing," or using only the thumbs to type.

Figure 4-11 shows a sample BlackBerry.

Figure 4-11: Sample BlackBerry

To learn more about the BlackBerry device, visit *www.rim.com*.

Portable media players

A portable media player is a device that can connect to a PC to download and play MP3 audio files. Some portable media players can also allow the user to watch movies, surf the Web, play games and store images. Some include WiFi connectivity. Among the most popular brands are iPod, iPod Touch and Zune.

iPod

An iPod is a portable media player launched by Apple, Inc., in 2001. iPod devices play MP3 audio files and can hold anywhere from a few hundred to ten thousand songs. Users can connect an iPod to a Windows or Macintosh personal computer and synchronize the songs available on the iPod to those available on the PC. iPod uses an Apple application called iTunes to enable communication between the iPod and the PC. Newer iPod models store songs using flash memory, which does not lose its contents when the user turns off the power.

Figure 4-12 shows a sample iPod.

Figure 4-12: Sample iPod

To learn more about iPods, visit *www.apple.com/itunes*.

iPod Touch

The iPod Touch is a portable media player launched by Apple, Inc., in 2007. iPod Touch includes WiFi connectivity and uses a touchscreen display, similar to an iPhone. You can use iPod Touch to play songs, watch movies, surf the Web, play games and store images.

To learn more about iPod Touch, visit *www.apple.com/ipodtouch*.

Zune

The Zune portable media player is Microsoft's answer to Apple's iPod. You can use Zune devices to download online music, video and podcasts, as well as display images and receive FM radio signals. You can also use the Zune portable media player to download songs, music videos and TV shows from the Zune Marketplace online store. Zune devices have WiFi connectivity and can be synced with Windows PCs running the Windows XP,

Windows Vista or Windows 7 operating system. Zune is not compatible with Linux or Mac OS X.

To learn more about Zune, visit *www.zune.net*.

Memory Stick

Memory Stick is a removable flash memory device that is used to store data for portable computing devices. Memory Stick was launched by Sony (*www.sony.com*) in 1998. Memory Sticks provide an easy way to transfer large amounts of data from portable devices to PCs, and vice versa. Modern Memory Sticks can hold as much as 32 GB of data and are used to store a wide variety of digital content, from photos and computer data to music and video images.

Figure 4-13 shows a sample Sony Memory Stick.

Figure 4-13: Sample Sony Memory Stick

To learn more about the Memory Stick, visit *www.high-techproductions.com/memorystick.htm*.

Secure Digital (SD) cards

A Secure Digital (SD) card is a memory card designed specifically for use in portable devices. SD cards are used extensively in devices such as digital cameras, mobile phones, media players, PDAs, GPS receivers and video game consoles. SD cards are about the size of a postage stamp, and are available in a variety of transfer speeds and storage capacities. Standard SD cards can hold anywhere from 4 MB to 4 GB of data. High-capacity SD cards (SDHCs) can hold anywhere from 4 GB to 32 GB of data. You can use SD cards to store and transfer images, songs, video and other digital data from a portable device to a PC.

People commonly use SD cards to organize their collection of music and images. Some people prefer to store data on smaller-capacity SD cards to better organize and categorize their files, whereas others place all of their files on a higher-capacity SD card. It is important to keep backup copies of your files on a PC in case the SD card(s) are damaged or lost.

Figure 4-14 shows a sample SanDisk SD card.

Figure 4-14: Sample SanDisk SD card

MiniSD and microSD cards

In addition to the standard SD card, there are the miniSD and microSD cards. The miniSD card is about 37 percent of the size of a standard SD card, and the microSD card is about one-quarter the size of a standard SD card. Both cards were developed to meet the constantly changing industry demands for smaller mobile devices. Both cards are incompatible with standard SD card slots, but can be connected to SD slots via a special adapter.

Both cards have a storage capacity of up to 2 GB. The microSD card is used primarily with mobile handsets, hand-held GPS devices, portable audio players, video game consoles and expandable USB flash memory drives.

To learn more about SD cards of all types, visit *www.sdcard.org.*

Google Android

Android is an operating system developed by Google for mobile devices and handsets. Android is based on the Linux kernel and, as of October 2008, most (but not all) of the code has been made available as open source. Android utilizes a custom virtual machine that was designed to optimize memory and hardware resources in a mobile environment. Developers can write applications for Android in the Java programming language. The applications will run on the virtual machine environment that runs on top of the Linux kernel.

Because Android is open source, developers who need to create custom applications for mobile devices can now do so without the need to purchase special software. As of this writing, not many devices support Android, but this is expected to change quickly as developers add new, innovative technologies and emerge to provide new services for mobile device users.

To learn more about Android, visit *www.android.com.*

Other mobile device operating systems include:

- BlackBerry Operating System.

- Windows Mobile.

- Palm OS.

- Symbian.

- Linux.

- J2ME (Java ME).

Netbooks

netbook
A more compact, Web-oriented version of the standard laptop PC; relies on the cloud-computing model in which the Internet is used for remote access to Web applications.

A **netbook** computer is a more compact, Web-oriented version of a standard PC-based notebook (i.e., laptop) computer. Because netbooks rely heavily on the Internet for remote access to Web applications, they are ideally suited for the cloud-computing model that has emerged over the past few years. Figure 4-15 shows a sample netbook.

Figure 4-15: Sample netbook

Netbooks and cloud computing

In many ways, cloud computing relies on thin clients like Web browsers, and no longer requires the more complex elements common to traditional computers. People who remember the pre-PC days remember working with thin clients called mainframe terminals. In many ways, netbooks and cloud computing bring back the thin client terminal model, but in a much more powerful, satisfying way.

This time, however, the netbook is a far more capable machine that allows individuals to focus on doing what most people want to do: check e-mail, browse the Web, send instant messages to friends, run standard applications, and access software and features that are hosted on remote systems. Although most netbooks cannot accommodate large database installations or applications such as AutoCAD, they are ideally suited for accessing their cloud-computing equivalents.

Netbooks, peripherals and memory

A netbook usually does not have all of the standard peripheral ports that a standard notebook computer offers. Netbooks rely on wireless network connections, usually foregoing the traditional wired connections completely. Many netbooks do not have a USB, FireWire or CD-ROM drive; they are completely reliant on the Internet to transfer files. Even five years ago, this dependence would have been a problem, but Internet access has become much more available.

Many netbooks do not use a traditional hard disk. Instead they use a solid-state drive or even a Secure Digital (SD) card. The netbook may have smaller storage capacity, but the use of alternative drive types and the elimination of peripherals create a much smaller computer that has very low power consumption and heat output. Lower heat output helps obviate the need for internal fans, which increase power usage and cost.

Netbook advantages

The resulting device is often easier to use and maintain, and it usually has longer battery life. In fact, many users regard netbooks as "green" alternatives to standard PC notebooks, because fewer resources are required to create and maintain them. Furthermore, the relative simplicity of a netbook usually makes it cost less to manufacture, a fact usually reflected in the lower cost of a netbook.

Many operating systems will run on netbook computers, including various versions of Windows and Linux. Netbooks used Intel-based PCs at the beginning. Many manufacturers are now introducing Advanced RISC Machine (ARM) and PowerPC (PPC) architectures in an effort to further reduce power consumption and increase computing speeds.

Prominent netbook manufacturers include:

- ASUS International (*www.asus.com*)

- HP (*www.hp.com*)

- Dell (*www.dell.com*)

- Acer (*www.acer.com*)

- Lenovo (*www.lenovo.com*)

Client Operating System Management

As an IT professional or as an individual computer user, you may need to perform system management tasks to maintain your client operating system. In the remaining sections of this lesson, we will discuss the importance of:

- Obtaining proper operating system and software licensing.

- Identifying common file systems.

- Using common file system management tools.

- Using utilities to perform maintenance and recover from application failures.

- Troubleshooting software, including identifying common boot problems.

- Identifying ways to remotely manage and troubleshoot workstations.

Software Licensing

OBJECTIVE
3.8.1: OS and
application
licensing

When you purchase operating system or application software, you are actually purchasing the right to use the software under certain restrictions imposed by the copyright owner (for example, the software publisher). These restrictions are described in the license agreement that accompanies the software.

Typically, these restrictions state that you have the right to load the software onto a single computer and make one backup copy. If you install, copy or distribute the software in ways that the license prohibits, such as allowing a friend or colleague to load the software on his or her computer, you are violating federal copyright law. It is imperative that you understand and adhere to the restrictions outlined in the license.

When you load operating system or application software, the license agreement typically displays during the installation process. You must indicate that you have read and understood the agreement before the installation procedure will allow you to continue.

NOTE:
Consider the importance of using only properly licensed operating system and application software to avoid legal, technical and software maintenance problems.

Apart from legal consequences, using unlicensed software can also mean:

- No documentation.

- No warranties.

- No technical product support.

- Greater exposure to software viruses.

- Corrupt discs or defective software.

- Ineligibility for software upgrades.

Partitions and Logical Drives

OBJECTIVE
3.8.4: Hard drive partitioning/ formatting

When installing an operating system on a new computer or after recovering from a hard disk failure, you will need to prepare the hard disk before it can be used. Disk preparation includes the following three fundamental steps:

1. Partition the hard disk, using applications such as fdisk in Linux or Device Manager in Windows Vista.

2. Create logical drives, using fdisk or Device Manager.

3. Format the logical drives, using applications such as mkfs in Linux or Device Manager in Windows Vista.

Disk partitioning

A partition is a way of dividing a hard disk's total storage space. You will typically partition a hard disk as either:

- **A primary partition only** — A primary partition is required if you want to use a hard disk as the system's boot drive, which is the drive that will be used for system startup. A hard disk can be configured with multiple primary partitions, although the default is generally to partition the hard disk as a single primary partition.

- **A primary partition and an extended partition** — You can create an extended partition if space remains after you recreate the primary partition. A hard disk can have only one extended partition.

Figure 4-16 illustrates a drive with a primary and an extended partition.

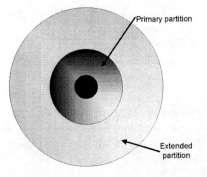

Figure 4-16: Disk partitions

active partition
A logical partition that contains the files necessary to boot an operating system. This partition is read first at boot time. If no active partition exists, or if the operating system files are corrupted or missing, the computer will report error messages.

The primary partition being used for startup must be identified as the **active partition**. This identification forces the system to read the initial load programs from that partition. A hard disk can be configured with multiple primary partitions, but only one partition can be identified as the active partition. The default, in most situations, is to partition the hard disk as a single primary partition.

Logical disk drives

A disk partition must be assigned a logical drive identifier (drive ID or drive letter) before it can be recognized by an operating system. A primary partition is treated as a single logical drive. An extended partition can be divided into multiple logical drives, as shown in Figure 4-17.

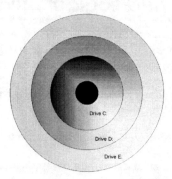

Figure 4-17: Logical disk drives

The system drive will be identified as Drive C. Drive IDs D through Z are available for assignment. Drives A and B can be used as drive IDs for floppy disk drives only.

Logical disk drives are not the only devices that need logical drive IDs. CD drives, DVD drives and other devices that are used for interactive storage must be assigned drive IDs. Drive IDs are also used to identify connections to shared file resources in a network environment.

Logical drive format

root directory
Topmost hard disk directory (folder).

After a logical disk drive is defined, it must be formatted. The format process prepares the logical drive for use by the operating system. Any attempts to write to or read from a logical drive that has not been formatted will generate an error. The format procedure creates the file system **root directory** and the files used to track disk space use.

Logical drive format is known as a high-level format. This distinguishes logical drive format from the low-level format that is sometimes required to prepare a hard disk for use. A hard disk must be prepared through low-level format before disk partitions can be defined. Low-level format is primarily the responsibility of the hard disk manufacturer, and hard disks ship already formatted.

File System Types

After you have created partitions and logical drives, you must format the primary partitions and the logical drives so the operating system can use them.

cluster
A group of sectors used as the basic unit of data storage.

The format process creates the drive's file system by adding information about how files should be stored on the drive to organize and manage disk storage. For example, the file allocation table (FAT) file system supported by MS-DOS and all Windows family operating systems uses a file allocation table to track **cluster** use. Because it is responsible for tracking space use, the file system also sets the maximum amount of space that can be managed as a single unit (a logical drive).

The file system you choose will depend on the operating system you are running. Table 4-10 describes the most common file systems for computers and the operating systems supported by each.

NOTE:
Make sure you understand the FAT32 and NTFS formats.

Table 4-10: Computer file systems

File System	Operating System Support	Description
FAT32	Windows 2000 Windows XP	Provides support for logical drives and primary partitions with greater than 2-GB capacity.
NTFS 5.0	Windows 2000	Offers support for large hard disks. Offers a variety of important features, including the ability to assign access permissions to files, and to compress files "on the fly" to conserve disk space. Instead of the file allocation table, it uses the master file table (MFT), an actual file that provides information about files and folders stored on disk. Offers the ability to encrypt files, disk quotas that allow disk space to be limited by partition, and enhanced logging. Supersedes FAT32 as the preferred file system for Microsoft Windows operating systems.
NTFS 5.1	Windows XP Professional Windows XP Home Edition Windows Server 2003	Enhancement of NTFS 5.0. Includes all the benefits of 5.0, and adds more efficient memory management, read-only NTFS partitions and hard links. Recommended for systems that have disks larger than 32 MB. Volumes formatted in earlier versions of NTFS cannot provide the same benefits as NTFS 5.1.
NTFS 5.2	Windows Vista Windows Server 2008	Enhancement of NTFS 5.1 specifically to support Windows Vista and Windows Server 2008. Integrates Transaction NTFS, which ensures that multiple file operations (creations, moves, deletions) occur as one atomic event (i.e., they all succeed or they all fail) to ensure complete reliability.
Ext3	Linux	Used by default in Ubuntu Linux. A journaling file system, which allows it to recover more quickly from system errors.
Ext4	Linux	A journaling file system that is the successor to ext3. Includes 64-bit storage limits and other performance improvements. Ext4 supports volume sizes up to 1 exabyte (1,000,000,000 GB) and file sizes up to 16 terabytes (1,000 GB). Ext4 also provides extents, which are ranges of contiguous physical blocks that reduce fragmentation and improve large file performance. For more information, consult *http://kernelnewbies.org/Ext4*.
ReiserFS	Linux	The Reiser file system (ReiserFS), created by Hans Reiser, is somewhat newer than Ext3 and uses more sophisticated algorithms for storing information. A journaling file system. For more information, consult *www.kernel.org/pub/linux/utils/fs/reiserfs*.
Reiser4	Linux	The successor to ReiserFS. Provides more efficient journaling and support of small files. Also provides faster directory handling for directories with a large number of files. Supports encryption and compression, and offers database transaction support. For more information, consult *www.kernel.org/pub/linux/utils/fs/reiser4*.

In the following lab, you will view drive partition information. As previously mentioned, the ability to view drive partitions on a computer is very important, especially if you need to add a logical drive ID to a newly added device. Suppose you want to add a DVD drive to your Windows system. You will need to assign a logical drive ID to the device. How would you choose and assign the proper drive ID? What utility could you use to view your system's volume and drive partition information?

 Lab 4-3: Viewing drive partitions using Disk Management

In this lab, you will use the Windows Vista Disk Management utility to view drive partition information.

1. Click **Start**, right-click **Computer**, then click **Manage** to display the Computer Management window.

2. In the left pane of the window, click **Disk Management** to display your system's volume and partition information (Figure 4-18).

Figure 4-18: Disk Management — volume and partition information

3. Review the partition structure that exists. From this window, you can format disks and change the file system type.

4. Close the **Computer Management** window.

File System Management Tools

You use file system management tools to maintain your hard disk and data in order to ensure that your system operates at peak efficiency. These tools also help prevent hardware problems and data loss. In the following sections, we will discuss file and directory permissions, and then discuss the purposes and uses of the Convert, Disk Defragmenter, Chkdsk, Disk Cleanup, Backup and Restore utilities.

OBJECTIVE
3.8.6: File and
directory
permissions

File and directory permissions

One of the primary benefits of an NTFS file system is that it allows you to secure resources. NTFS allows you to set **permission bits** on system resources (for example, files and directories). With NTFS, you can protect files so that only certain users or groups of users can read them. One group of users may be able to execute applications in a directory, whereas another group may have full access to it. The security provided by a user-based file system such as NTFS can have drawbacks, however. Consider the following potential problems:

permission bit
A file or directory attribute that determines access. Permission bits include read, write and execute permissions.

- If permissions are applied improperly, you may take security for granted.

- Improperly set permissions can disable or damage an operating system.

Convert utility

Information about the files on an NTFS volume and their attributes is stored in the master file table (MFT). In Windows Vista and Windows XP, a partition or logical drive can be converted from FAT32 into NTFS by using the Convert utility. The Convert utility uses the following syntax:

OBJECTIVE
3.8.7: File system
management tools

```
convert drive /FS:NTFS [/v]
```

Replace *drive* with the letter of the drive you are converting into NTFS. The */v* option stands for verbose and prints information about the success of the operation to the screen. In Windows Vista and Windows XP, if a partition can be locked, the conversion will occur immediately, without a restart. However, Windows Vista and Windows XP still require you to restart the system before boot and system partitions can be converted.

In the following lab, you will learn how to view NTFS permissions. NTFS allows you to secure resources, such as files and directories. Suppose you work as an IT technician at a company, and you need to divide the execute permissions for files or applications among different groups of employees. Applying permissions appropriately helps ensure security as well as the smooth functioning of the various systems. Assuming your company uses NTFS, what utility should you use to view NTFS permissions for various files and applications?

 Lab 4-4: Viewing NTFS permissions

In this lab, you will view NTFS permissions for directories and files.

1. Open **Windows Explorer** and make Drive C the active drive.

   Note: Drive C should be an NTFS drive. If it is not, select another drive that is NTFS, or use the Convert utility.

2. Use the appropriate commands to create a new folder and a text file on Drive C.

3. Right-click the folder you created, click **Properties**, then click the **Security** tab. The NTFS permissions that are assigned by default to this resource display in the Properties dialog box (Figure 4-19).

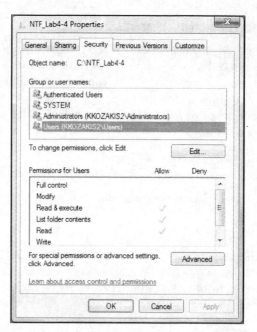

Figure 4-19: Properties dialog box — Security tab

4. Close the **Properties** dialog box.

5. Right-click the text file you created, click **Properties**, then click the **Security** tab to view its NTFS permissions.

6. Close the **Properties** dialog box and **Windows Explorer**.

Disk Defragmenter utility

OBJECTIVE
3.8.7: File system
management tools

Over time, as files are created and deleted, a partition can become severely fragmented. Fragmentation is one of the leading preventable causes of poor performance. Contiguous files provide good performance because the disk drive read/write heads do not have to jump from location to location. You can use the Disk Defragmenter utility to defragment hard disks and put fragmented files back together in a contiguous format.

In Windows Vista, the Disk Defragmenter utility runs in the background only when your computer is idle. You use the Task Scheduler to determine when and how often Disk Defragmenter is to run. By so doing, your hard disk is automatically defragmented on a regular basis. By default, Disk Defragmenter defragments files smaller than 64 MB only. If you want to defragment files on Drive C that are larger than 64 MB, you need to enter the following command at the command prompt and add the *–w* parameter:

```
defrag c: -w
```

In the following lab, you will learn how to defragment a hard disk using the Disk Defragmenter utility. Suppose your boss needs you to install a new spreadsheet application for an important new project. You install the application correctly, but find that your system now tends to start up sluggishly or exhibit other aspects of poor performance. You suspect that your hard disk may require defragmenting because you have installed and worked with many new files and programs over the past several months.

Lab 4-5: Defragmenting hard disks

In this lab, you will defragment your hard disk.

1. Select **Start | All Programs | Accessories | System Tools | Disk Defragmenter** to open the Disk Defragmenter (Figure 4-20). Notice that you cannot select a drive to defragment in this window. If you want to defragment any drive other than C:\, you must execute the *defrag* command from the command prompt.

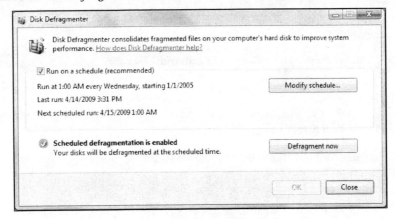

Figure 4-20: Disk Defragmenter

2. Click the **Modify Schedule** button to display the Disk Defragmenter: Modify Schedule dialog box (Figure 4-21). You use this dialog box to specify how often to defragment your disk, as well as the day of the week and time that the process should execute.

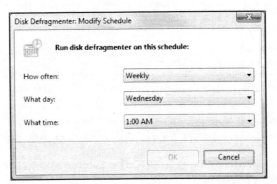

Figure 4-21: Disk Defragmenter: Modify Schedule dialog box

3. Close the **Disk Defragmenter: Modify Schedule** dialog box.

NOTE:
You may want to allow the defragmentation process to execute for a few minutes in case it actually completes in that amount of time.

4. In the Disk Defragmenter, click the **Defragment Now** button. This action starts the defragmentation process. Because the process may take from several minutes to several hours to complete, click the **Cancel Defragmentation** button to suspend the process, then close the **Disk Defragmenter**.

Chkdsk utility

OBJECTIVE
3.8.7: File system
management tools

You can use the Chkdsk utility in Windows to create and display a status report for a disk based on its file system. You can also use Chkdsk to list and correct errors on the disk, and to display the status of the disk in the current drive.

Chkdsk examples

NOTE:
Experiment with the
Chkdsk utility using
the commands (or
similar commands)
shown in this
example.

Consider the following command:

```
chkdsk
```

This syntax will yield a status report showing any errors discovered in the current partition.

Now consider the following command:

```
chkdsk g:
```

This syntax will yield a status report showing any errors discovered in the partition you specified (in this example, G).

Next, consider the following command and option:

```
chkdsk g: /f
```

This syntax will yield a status report showing any errors discovered in the partition you specified (in this example, G) and will fix the errors.

Checking a disk in Linux/UNIX

In Linux or UNIX, you use the *fsck* command to check disk partitions. The *fsck* command performs the same function as the Chkdsk utility in Windows systems. For example, if you want to check the first partition on the first hard drive, you would enter:

```
fsck /dev/hda1
```

Disk Cleanup utility

OBJECTIVE
3.8.7: File system
management tools

Operating systems generate temporary files that you should periodically delete to conserve disk space. In some cases, deleting temporary files and directories will help you recover from application failures and from failed application installations. Common locations of temporary files in Windows Vista include:

OBJECTIVE
3.8.8: Deleting
temporary files

- C:\$WINDOWS.~Q\DATA\Documents and Settings*user_name*\Local Settings\Temp.

- C:\$WINDOWS.~Q\DATA\Documents and Settings*user_name*\Local Settings\Temporary Internet Files.

- Directories and subdirectories created by installation programs.

NOTE:
Temporary files are
often referred to as
"temp" files.

You can delete temporary files manually by right-clicking them and clicking Delete, or you can use the Windows Disk Cleanup utility.

The Disk Cleanup utility enables you to recover the disk space used by temporary files, unused applications, files in the Recycle Bin, files you downloaded as part of Web pages and files created when Chkdsk attempted to recover lost file fragments.

In the following lab, you will learn how to use Disk Cleanup to delete temporary files that waste important disk space. Suppose your co-workers have asked for your help with minor performance problems they are having on their Windows systems. After questioning them, you learn that most of them have never deleted the cache of temporary files on their hard disk drives. So you decide to teach them as a group how to use the Disk Cleanup utility. After their lesson, you instruct them all to use this cleanup method at least once a week.

 Lab 4-6: Deleting temporary files

In this lab, you will delete any temporary files residing on your system.

1. Select **Start | All Programs | Accessories | System Tools | Disk Cleanup** to display the Disk Cleanup: Drive Selection dialog box (Figure 4-22).

Figure 4-22: Disk Cleanup: Drive Selection dialog box

Note: If you have only one hard disk and the disk is not partitioned, the Disk Cleanup: Drive Selection dialog box will not appear. Instead, when you click the Disk Cleanup command, the Disk Cleanup dialog box shown in Figure 4-23 will appear.

NOTE:
In Step 2, Disk Cleanup will scan the system after you click OK. The scan may take several minutes to complete.

2. Specify the drive you want to clean up, then click **OK**. The utility will calculate how much disk space will be recovered, then display the Disk Cleanup dialog box shown in Figure 4-23. You use the Disk Cleanup dialog box to select the types of files to remove when the utility executes. To view a list of eligible files, click any of the items in the list box to select it, then click the **View Files** button. Notice that downloaded program files, temporary Internet files and thumbnails are specified to be deleted by default.

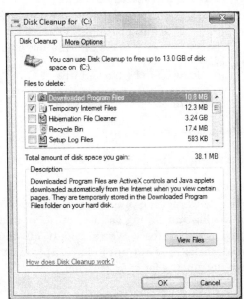

Figure 4-23: Disk Cleanup dialog box

restore point
A snapshot of a computer's settings at a particular point in time. Also known as a system checkpoint.

3. You can also use the More Options tab to specify to remove optional Windows components and programs that you do not use, as well as all saved system **restore points** except for the most recent one.

Note: A computer automatically creates restore points at regular intervals. If you experience problems, you can restore your computer settings to their most recent restore point (in other words, the point at which your computer was functioning with no errors or problems).

4. On the Disk Cleanup tab, click **OK**, then click **Delete Files** to execute the disk cleanup process. When the process is finished, all utility dialog boxes will automatically close.

OBJECTIVE
3.8.7: File system management tools

Backup and Restore utilities

Even the best ongoing maintenance schedule cannot prevent a hard disk drive from wearing out or accidents from occurring. Keeping a current backup of all data files is essential to ensuring that data can be recovered if a hard disk drive fails. When you back up data, you store copies of folders and files to a source other than your computer's hard disk. Depending on file size and available hardware, storage sources can include writable CDs, writable DVDs and network server hard disks.

All files and folders have archive properties that identify when the file or folder needs to be backed up. New files and existing files that have been modified have their archive attributes set to "on," indicating that they are ready for backup the next time data is backed up. Each time a file is backed up, the archive attribute is set to "off," indicating that the most recent version of the file has been backed up.

Backing up and restoring data in Linux/UNIX

You can use the *dump* command to back up files and directories on Linux and UNIX systems. You can then use the *restore* command to restore the backed-up data, if needed.

Backing up data in Windows Vista

NOTE:
Before performing a backup, you should think about the data you want to back up and the location in which you want to store the backed-up information.

In Windows Vista, you can use the Backup And Restore Center to back up data. The first time you conduct a backup operation, you will be prompted for information before starting the backup process. This information is used to complete the following steps:

1. Select the file types to be backed up.

2. Select a file location or storage media for the backed-up data.

3. Specify backup options.

4. Initiate the backup.

NOTE:
In **Optional Lab 4-3: Using a cloud-computing backup solution,** you can back up files to the Web using a cloud-computing service called Box.

In the following lab, you will learn how to back up data in Windows Vista. Suppose you and another co-worker are preparing copy for your company's Web site. Your tasks consist of writing and editing large amounts of information, in both text and table format, to be posted to the company Web site as HTML documents. This project is scheduled to take several weeks, so you want to back up your work on a regular basis. How can you store these documents for safe-keeping?

Lab 4-7: Backing up data in Windows Vista

OBJECTIVE
3.8.9: Backup and
restore procedures

In this lab, you will back up selected files using the backup procedure in Windows Vista.

Note: The backup procedure is very time-consuming and requires that your system have access to a writable CD drive, writable DVD drive or network drive in which to store the backed-up data. You cannot back up data to the same drive on which your data resides; you must back up your files to a different drive. You also cannot back up data to a tape drive, CD-ROM drive or USB flash drive. If you do not have a writable CD or DVD, or you do not have access to a network share, skip this lab and continue to the next section.

1. Select **Start | All Programs | Accessories | System Tools | Backup Status And Configuration** to display the Backup Status And Configuration dialog box.

2. Click **Set Up Automatic File Backup** to display the Back Up Files dialog box. You use this dialog box to specify where you want to save your backup. You can specify to save your backup to a hard disk, writable CD, writable DVD or network share. If you have a writable CD, insert it into your CD-R/RW drive. If you do not have a CD-R/RW drive, you can specify to back up data to a network share.

3. Select the appropriate option button, specify the appropriate drive in the drop-down list, then click **Next**.

4. You will now be prompted to specify which file types you want to back up, as shown in Figure 4-24. It is recommended that you back up all file types selected in the dialog box, which is the default. For the sake of time, deselect all check boxes except for one of your choice.

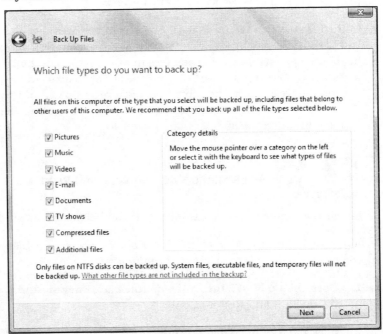

Figure 4-24: Specifying file types to back up

5. Click **Next**. You will be prompted to specify how often to create a backup. Notice that you can specify to automatically run the backup utility daily, weekly or monthly, as well as the day and time.

6. Accept all default settings and click **Save Settings And Start Backup**. If this is the first time you have executed a backup, Windows will create a new, full backup now. Notice that Windows creates a shadow copy of the files you specified to back up. A shadow copy is a point-in-time copy of your files. This feature allows you to restore previous versions of your files and folders, if need be.

7. When the backup finishes successfully, click the **Close** button to close the Back Up Files dialog box.

8. Open **Windows Explorer** and display the contents of the CD-R/RW or network drive to which you backed up the data. You should see a folder containing the backed-up data. Expand this folder and all of its subfolders so you can see the backup files. Backed-up data is stored as .zip files (with a maximum size of 200 MB each).

9. Close **Windows Explorer**. Notice that the Backup And Restore Center displays on your screen. After you perform a backup, the Backup And Restore Center is updated to show when the backup was performed and where it was stored. Notice that you can use the Backup And Restore Center to back up your entire PC, rather than only the file types you specified. The next time you perform a backup, only files that have been modified from the time you performed the previous backup will be backed up.

10. Close the **Backup And Restore Center**.

Restoring data in Windows Vista

If backup data needs to be accessed, you can restore the data using the Backup And Restore Center. By default, the files are restored to their original locations and existing files are not overwritten. However, using advanced options, you can specify that the files be restored in an alternative location of your choice.

In the following lab, you will learn how to restore data that has been backed up. Suppose you have been compiling a list of potential customers for your opt-in online marketing business, backing up the list each night after you finish the day's work. Your most recent day's work, however, was lost due to a power spike caused by an electrical malfunction. You need to recover the data from the most recent backup, which was the previous night. Restoring data allows you the option of overwriting existing files, and enables you to place restored files in a specific location on your system.

Lab 4-8: Restoring data in Windows Vista

In this lab, you will restore the data that you backed up in the previous lab.

Note: You must have completed Lab 4-7 before you can complete this lab. If you did not complete Lab 4-7, skip this lab and continue to the next section.

1. Open the **Control Panel**, then double-click **Backup And Restore Center** to display the Backup And Restore Center.

2. Click the **Restore Files** button to display the Restore Files window. You can choose to restore files from the latest backup or files from an older backup. Ensure that **Files From The Latest Backup** is selected, then click **Next**.

3. You can now choose to restore specific files or folders by selecting the Add Files or Add Folders button (or you can click the Search button to search for the backed-up

data). Click the **Add Folders** button to display the Add Folders To Restore dialog box. Select the backup folder that you want to restore, click the **Add** button, then click **Next**.

4. Specify the location where you want to restore the files (a folder on the system, a network share or another disk), then click **Next**.

5. When the restore procedure is finished, click **Finish**.

Troubleshooting Software

Software troubleshooting refers to solving any problems other than those caused by system hardware. Software problems can have a number of causes, including bugs, corrupted files, incompatibilities and virus infections.

Discerning between hardware and software problems can sometimes be difficult. Hardware failures often initially appear to be software-related; they can be symptoms of a software problem, such as a corrupted device driver.

One of the best ways to avoid software problems is to keep your software up to date. Operating system manufacturers often issue regular updates to correct known problems. Microsoft refers to these updates as service packs. Application program manufacturers will also sometimes release updates that fix known problems. Often, the main justification for the release of a new software version is to fix known bugs.

In the following sections, you will study software problems as they are exhibited during the operating system boot process and when applications fail.

Operating system boot problems

Following is a brief discussion of boot problems that can occur in workstations.

Error: No operating system

You may sometimes receive an error indicating that no operating system is present. If this happens, perform the following steps:

1. Make sure that there is no floppy disk inserted in the floppy disk drive.

2. Perform a cold boot of the system (i.e., turn your computer off and back on again) to ensure that an operating system is present. Sometimes, completely powering down the system and restarting it can solve a temporary problem that appears to be a disk failure.

Table 4-11 lists some other common boot-problem error messages and their solutions.

Table 4-11: OS boot problem errors

Error Message	Problem	Solution
-Bad or missing command interpreter **-Missing ntldr (Windows)** **-Kernel not available (Linux)**	Operating system files are missing. Operating system files can be lost through disk corruption, file corruption or file deletion. System startup failure can also be caused through user actions — for example, by making changes to the system registry, which is a database in which Windows stores configuration information.	Use a boot disk, if available. Refer the problem to a help desk technician if a boot disk is not available. System reinstallation may be necessary. You may also be able to restore the system using system recovery features found in many operating systems. If changes were made to the system registry, you may be able to start up in Safe mode (which is a basic configuration that is primarily used for system troubleshooting and repair) and correct the registry. Otherwise, you may need to reinstall the operating system and restore data from backups. See the Tech Tip following this table.
Hard disk or controller failure	This message indicates a hardware failure, but the problem can initially look like a software failure.	Boot from a CD-ROM and try to access the hard disk and controller. You will need to get the failing component replaced by a trained technician.

Depending on the nature of the edits to the registry, Windows Vista may be able to correct the error. Press F8 to interrupt startup, as you would to start up in Safe mode, and select the Last Known Good Configuration option. This action will revert to the previous configuration and may allow you to start the operating system.

Occasionally you will not be able to find a cause for the system failure. In such cases, repair the system and monitor its performance. If the failure does not occur again, it could have been caused by a transient event such as a power spike.

Blue screen of death (BSOD)

The technical name for the BSOD is the stop screen. The term "blue screen of death" refers to a blue screen that displays during startup in Windows, which indicates that a critical operating system failure has occurred during startup. This failure may be caused by a transient condition, so one of the first solutions to try is to restart the system. Also, try starting up using the Last Known Good Configuration option.

If a system has been working properly and starts experiencing BSOD failures during startup, you need to determine whether the system can start up at all. Try starting up in Safe mode rather than Normal mode. If you can start in Safe mode, the problem may be one or more corrupted files or configuration settings. Restore from backups and test. If you still cannot start the system in Normal mode, reinstall the operating system.

If the problem occurs during a new installation, a component (for example, a NIC or a video driver) is probably not compatible with Windows. You will probably not be able to install Windows to run properly on the system.

If a BSOD appears during startup, the system will store the information on the screen in a dump file. In Windows Vista, dump files are located in the C:\Windows\Minidump folder. You can read more about how to parse (in other words, read) Windows blue screens at *http://technet.microsoft.com/en-us/library/cc750081.aspx.*

System lockup

If a system locks up often, consider the following solutions:

- If possible, determine what application was running at the time of the lockup. The application may be incompatible with the operating system or with a hardware component.

- Look for IRQ conflicts.

- Check log files for indications of a related problem.

When recovering from a lockup, you may need to power down your system manually by pressing and holding down the power key for five seconds. Otherwise, Windows may not surrender control of the system to the actual computer.

Application failures

Application failures can take several forms in an operating system. An application may not load, or it may crash under certain conditions. After most application errors, you should try to quit the application (if it did not quit automatically) and attempt to duplicate the error. If you can consistently duplicate the error, the problem probably lies with the application. If the error does not occur at the same point or in the same fashion, the problem is probably in the operating system or a device driver.

 Some manufacturers list known problems on their Web sites. Others do not publish the problems, but may provide bug and other problem information through technical support. Some manufacturers charge for telephone support. Many manufacturers that charge for telephone support still provide free support by e-mail.

Next, try restarting the operating system to initialize the system and clear errors caused by transient conditions. Attempt to duplicate the error after system restart; if you cannot, the error was probably caused by a transient condition.

In the following sections, we will discuss some of the more common application failures.

Application will not start

When an application will not start, consider the following causes and solutions:

- System random access memory (RAM) may have gotten too low, in which case you must free up system memory. Shut down applications running on the system.

- The current logon environment may have crashed, even though it may appear to be running properly. In all Windows systems, the logon environment is made possible by explorer.exe and other applications. Sometimes, this application will fail to execute properly. First, try logging off the system and logging back on. If doing so does not solve the problem, restart the system. To determine whether the problem is specific to your account, log on as another user and try to launch the application. If it launches in the other logon environment, review the settings for the problem account. If the problem continues, reinstall the application.

- Some applications will not load properly unless you have additional privileges. Verify your permissions.

- System RAM may get too low because application crashes will not surrender the RAM they have been using to the operating system. Restart the system.

- Some applications will not run unless your system is using a certain resolution or color level. Verify or change system resolution to solve the problem.

NOTE:
See **Optional Lab 4-2: Using the Windows Vista Event Viewer.**

System log

Viewing the system log is an effective way to determine the reason or reasons for an application's failure to launch. In Windows systems, use Event Viewer to see log entries generated by the application.

In Linux/UNIX systems, the log file is called messages, and resides off the /var/log/ directory. You can also open the /var/log/messages file using various applications, including text editors such as vi. You can also use the *cat* command to view the entire file, as shown in the following syntax:

```
cat /var/log/messages
```

However, you may not want to read the entire log file. To read only the last 10 lines of the log file, use the *tail* command instead of the *cat* command.

Windows protection errors

Windows protection errors may sometimes occur on a system. Such an occurrence also indicates a problem with internal (operating system) management and security. Windows protection faults are often caused by device drivers that were not written specifically for your operating system. They can also be caused by applications or utilities that attempt to bypass the operating system and directly access local system hardware. Make sure you are using the most recent driver version for your operating system. Some errors can be corrected by reinstalling the operating system, but this solution means that the computer cannot be used while the operating system is being installed and configured.

Application installation and loading failures

Application installation and loading failures can include the following situations:

- An application will not load into memory.

- An application causes an illegal operation, resulting in the BSOD.

- An application will not install at all.

Table 4-12 provides information about the most common application installation and loading failures, as well as proposed solutions.

Table 4-12: Application installation and loading errors

Failure	Solution
Incompatible application	Make sure that the application or application version is compatible with the operating system. Otherwise, find a compatible version of the application.
Lack of administrative privileges	Linux and Windows systems often require a user with full administrative privileges to install some applications. Log off and log back on as the administrator to the system. If the system belongs to a Microsoft domain, and the local administrator has been limited, log on as the domain administrator.
Registry busy or corrupt	The area of the Windows registry pertinent to the application may be locked or busy. Use Task Manager to ensure that no other applications are currently running (Task Manager provides information about programs and processes running on your computer. Press CTRL+ALT+DEL, then click the Start Task Manager button to open Task Manager). If the registry is corrupt, you may need to restore it from a backup.
Media failure	The local or remote drive containing the installation medium may not be available or may be unrecognized. Ensure that the drive and/or network connection is working properly.

Table 4-12: Application installation and loading errors (cont'd)

Failure	Solution
Failed service	Start or restart the service (or daemon in Linux/UNIX). You may need to restart the entire system, or log off and log back on.
Application dependency	Some applications require certain services and additional applications and libraries before installation can occur. Install all dependencies, and then install the application. In Linux, for example, an application may not run because of a problem with the X Window environment. You may need to edit the X Window configuration files (for example, the files and subdirectories in the /etc/X11 directory).
Hardware failure	The application depends on a device, such as a NIC, that is somehow unavailable. Check the device.
Leftover files from a previous (failed) installation	Regardless of your operating system, temporary files exist in a directory with permissions that forbid the current user from deleting them. Delete the files and/or directories. You may need to consult system documentation to learn where temporary files are stored for the application and specific operating system.
Insufficient drive space	An application may fail to run or install if your hard drive is full. Many applications generate log files and other files in temporary folders. If no space is available, the application will crash. Clear some space and try again.

Remote Management and Troubleshooting

OBJECTIVE
3.8.10: Remote
workstation
management

As an IT Professional, you may periodically need to manage and troubleshoot workstation problems from a remote location. The following sections will review several tools you can use to access workstations from remote locations.

 The tools discussed in the following sections were explained in detail in the CIW Internet Business Foundations course. The following discussion will summarize the information presented previously in that coursebook.

Telnet

Telnet is a TCP/IP suite protocol that allows you to establish a remote connection with a server and then use that computer to gather the information you need. Essentially, you are logging on to the server and accessing information as if you were sitting at it.

To use Telnet, you need an account and a password on the host computer. You can use Telnet to access some public servers (such as public libraries and government resources) using a generic password.

A Telnet command resembles the following:

```
Microsoft Telnet> open cals.evergreen.edu
```

NOTE:
In Linux/UNIX
systems, all
commands are
case-specific. For
example, typing
"Telnet" will yield an
error message.

The result of this request is an invitation to log on to The Evergreen State College system, in which you could search for a book, for example.

Secure Shell (SSH)

Secure Shell (SSH), sometimes known as Secure Socket Shell, is a protocol that you can use to gain secure access to a remote computer and then execute commands to administer the system. Many client types use the SSH protocol, which features a Telnet-like interface. In the past, SSH was used only on UNIX-based systems. However, an SSH server can be installed on any Windows platform using Cygwin (*www.cygwin.com*), a program that simulates the Linux environment for Windows systems.

NOTE:
If you want,
download and
install Cygwin.
Doing so will install a
series of programs
that will provide a
Linux/UNIX emulator
that you can run like
an application on
your Windows
system.

SSH clients exist for almost any operating system (for example, Macintosh, Windows or Linux/UNIX). All SSH sessions are encrypted. However, sending encrypted authentication information across unsecured channels is potentially harmful. Configuring SSH to authenticate users with public keys rather than passwords is recommended, but does not occur by default with SSH. The latest version of the SSH protocol is SSH2. Many users now prefer SSH over Telnet. Figure 4-25 shows a sample SSH session.

```
root@albion.stangernet.com: /root
login as: root
root@albion's password:
Last login: Sun Mar  7 15:28:53 2004 from winxp.stangernet.com

[root@albion root]# mkdir config_files
[root@albion root]# cd config_files/
[root@albion config_files]# cp /etc/passwd .
[root@albion config_files]# cp /etc/shadow .
[root@albion config_files]# cd ..
[root@albion root]# tar -cvf backup.tar config_files/
config_files/
config_files/passwd
config_files/shadow
[root@albion root]# ls -lh backup.tar
-rw-r--r--    1 root     root          10K Mar  7 15:33 backup.tar
[root@albion root]# gzip backup.tar
[root@albion root]# ls -l backup.tar.gz
-rw-r--r--    1 root     root         1422 Mar  7 15:33 backup.tar.gz
[root@albion root]# /etc/rc.d/init.d/sshd status
/bin/bash: /root/.bashrc/:: Not a directory
sshd (pid 32387 32226 711) is running...
[root@albion root]# /etc/rc.d/init.d/httpd status
/bin/bash: /root/.bashrc/:: Not a directory
httpd (pid 21734 21733 21732 21731 21730 21729 21728 21727 801) is running...
[root@albion root]#
```

Figure 4-25: Sample SSH session

NOTE:
The "Not A
Directory" error is
caused by a
mistaken entry in a
file named bashrc.
The entry is referring
to a non-existent
directory.

The preceding figure shows a session in which a user logged on to a remote system named *albion.stangernet.com*. The user logged on as root (the administrative account in most systems), then backed up important configuration files (including the /etc/passwd and /etc/shadow files, which contain user authentication information). The user then archived these files and compressed them using the gzip program. Finally, the user checked the status of the SSH and HTTPD daemons.

Virtual Network Computing (VNC)

**Virtual Network
Computing (VNC)**
A program that
allows you to
control a computer
at a remote
location.

Virtual Network Computing (VNC) is a program that allows you to control a computer at a remote location. VNC consists of two components:

- **The server** — This component listens on a specific port (for example, TCP 5800 on Windows systems) and allows clients to connect to it. Authenticated users can log on and see the server display on their remote computers. Unlike Telnet or SSH, VNC provides a full GUI display.

- **The viewer** — This component allows users to see the remote system's logon environment.

The server and the viewer do not need to be running the same operating system.

VNC can be used in a variety of ways. In an office, for example, a systems administrator can use VNC to diagnose and fix problems on a co-worker's computer, or can access and administer server computers without having to work from the server room. Help desk staff might also use VNC to troubleshoot a computer problem for remote employees, or to install software on remote systems.

Remote Desktop

Remote Desktop is a Windows service you can use to gain access from your computer to a Windows session that is running on another computer. For example, you can connect to your work computer from home and gain access to all your applications, files and network resources, as if you were using your computer at work. If you leave programs running at work, when you get home you can display your work Desktop on your home computer, with the same programs running.

When you connect to your computer at work, Remote Desktop automatically locks it to prevent others from accessing your applications and files. When you return to your computer at work, you can unlock it by pressing CTRL+ALT+DEL.

Remote Desktop also allows multiple users to participate in active sessions on a single computer. Users can leave their applications running while other users log on to the computer. Remote Desktop will preserve the state of each user's Windows session.

In addition, Remote Desktop enables you to switch from one user to another on the same computer. For example, suppose you are working at home and have logged on to your computer at work to access a file. While you are working, a family member asks to use your home computer. You can disconnect Remote Desktop, allow the other user to log on to complete his or her task, and then reconnect to your computer at work, continuing where you left off.

Remote Assistance

Remote Assistance is a Windows feature that allows a user to seek assistance from another person in a remote location. This feature involves allowing a trusted person at the remote location to connect to your computer and view your screen. Remote Assistance is used in conjunction with Windows Live Messenger (or e-mail), enabling the remote person to offer real-time assistance via instant messaging.

When you accept a connection from a remote assistant, your Desktop displays on the remote computer. The remote person can send you directions for performing a task, then you can perform the task and the results will display on both your computer and the remote computer. This capability allows for instant feedback. Your remote partner can also take control of your computer. However, you have the option to decline any assistance. You retain control of your computer unless you specifically relinquish that control to the person assisting you. Remote Assistance requires both computers to be running the same version of Windows.

Network Maintenance in Adverse Conditions

Nevine is an archeologist who is spending six months at an archeological site in southern Egypt. She has become known as the IT administrator after setting up a small computer network (using the Windows Vista operating system) in the main tent. Due to the frequent desert winds that blow across the Sahara and deposit dust practically everywhere, Nevine realizes she needs to set up a preventive maintenance program to keep the small network working properly.

Nevine decides to immediately perform the following tasks:

- She asks her colleagues to help seal the tent as much as possible to prevent dust from infiltrating the chamber containing the network devices.

- She checks all computers to ensure that slot covers completely cover all slot openings.

Next, Nevine decides to implement the following preventive maintenance program:

- Back up user data to high-capacity storage disks on a daily basis.

- Run the Chkdsk utility on a weekly basis to check for and correct physical disk errors.

- Run the Disk Cleanup utility on a weekly basis to delete temporary files and conserve disk space.

- Run the Disk Defragmenter utility on a quarterly basis to defragment the hard disk drives.

- Clean all adapter boards and input devices with a static-free vacuum and compressed air on a quarterly basis to remove accumulated dust.

*   *   *

Consider the following questions:

- What additional maintenance activities could Nevine implement to ensure that the small network continues to work properly?

- How often should she perform these tasks?

Lesson Summary

Application project

When you have time, attempt to restart your computer in Safe mode (press the F8 key during the reboot process).

When your Desktop displays, note the differences in the Desktop between Normal mode and Safe mode. What are the differences?

Open the Display Settings dialog box (right-click the Desktop, click Personalize, then click the Display Settings link). What is your screen resolution? Open Windows Explorer and attempt to access a network drive. What happens? Restart your computer in Normal mode.

Skills review

In this lesson, you learned about the basic hardware and system maintenance procedures that you should perform to minimize component failure and system problems. You learned about the maintenance issues associated with motherboards, IRQs, I/O addresses, DMA, SATA disk drives and SCSI devices. You were introduced to peripheral ports, and you learned about optical discs, TV tuner cards and HDMI connections. You also learned about mobile computing devices and associated technologies.

You also studied the basics of managing a client operating system. You learned about the importance of software licensing and preparing a hard disk for use. You reviewed the characteristics of several file system types, and you learned how to use file system management tools and troubleshooting software. Finally, you learned how to remotely manage and troubleshoot workstations.

Now that you have completed this lesson, you should be able to:

✓ 3.1.2: Identify power requirements for international travel.

✓ 3.7.1: Identify maintenance issues for common system elements, including IRQs, DMA, I/O cards, NICs, motherboards, SCSI, IDE/ATA, serial ATA (including hard drives).

✓ 3.7.2: Connect common peripherals, including parallel, serial, USB, FireWire devices (e.g., printers, hard drives, scanners), CD-ROM/DVD.

✓ 3.8.1: Obtain proper licensing for operating systems and associated applications.

✓ 3.8.2: Recover from application failures.

✓ 3.8.3: Restart the system and identify common boot problems.

✓ 3.8.4: Explain why a hard drive must be partitioned and formatted.

✓ 3.8.5: Identify common file systems (e.g., NTFS, FAT, Ext3, ReiserFS).

✓ 3.8.6: Manage basic file and directory permissions.

✓ 3.8.7: Use common file system management tools, including Convert, Chkdsk, Disk Cleanup, Disk Defragmenter.

✓ 3.8.8: Delete temporary files manually and by using operating-system-specific methods.

✓ 3.8.9: Back up and restore files to prevent data loss, including digital tapes, CDs.

✓ 3.8.10: Identify ways to remotely manage and troubleshoot workstations.

Lesson 4 Review

1. What are the two formats supported for writable compact discs (CDs)?

   _____

2. What steps must you perform to prepare a hard disk for use?

   _____

   _____

3. Why is it important to periodically defragment a partition on which files are frequently created, modified and deleted?

   _____

   _____

4. What is the purpose of the Disk Cleanup utility?

   _____

   _____

5. What are some of the problems associated with using unlicensed software?

   _____

   _____

6. What is the term for an audio/video interface that can transmit high-definition digital video and high-resolution digital audio data in a single cable?

   _____

   _____

7. What is a smartphone?

   _____

   _____

Lesson 4
Supplemental Material

This section is a supplement containing additional tasks for you to complete in conjunction with the lesson. These elements are:

- **Activities**
  Pen-and-paper activities to review lesson concepts or terms.

- **Optional Labs**
  Computer-based labs to provide additional practice.

- **Lesson Quiz**
  Multiple-choice test to assess knowledge of lesson material.

Activity 4-1: Reviewing CD and DVD maintenance issues

In this activity, you will review CD and DVD maintenance issues. Consider corrective and preventive measures you can undertake to resolve the following CD-ROM and DVD maintenance issues. For each issue, write your answer in the space provided.

1. **Issue:** CD/DVD drive is contaminated.

   Solution:_____

   _____

   _____

2. **Issue:** CD/DVD is defective.

   Solution:_____

   _____

   _____

3. **Issue:** Internal laser is contaminated.

   Solution:_____

   _____

   _____

4. **Issue:** CD or DVD drive door will not open because of a malfunction or lost power.

   Solution:_____

   _____

   _____

Activity 4-2: Converting decimal, binary and hexadecimal values

In this activity, you will convert values among the decimal, binary and hexadecimal numbering systems.

Note: Do not use a calculator at first.

1. What is the hexadecimal value of 100011010? Make sure to focus on the process of determining this value, rather than just obtaining the value.

   _____

   _____

   _____

Version 2.0

2. Convert the hexadecimal value found in Step 1 into decimal.

_____

_____

_____

_____

_____

_____

3. How would you represent the hexadecimal value of 2DF in binary?

_____

_____

_____

_____

4. Convert the following number into both binary and hexadecimal: 91364

_____

_____

_____

_____

5. Check your work. If you have access to a Windows computer, you can do this using the Calculator program. In the program, select **View | Scientific** to display scientific functions, as shown in Figure A4-1. Doing so will allow you to easily convert among decimal, binary and hexadecimal.

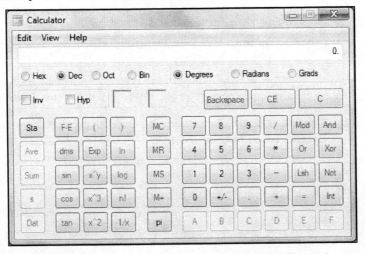

Figure A4-1: Windows Calculator program — Scientific mode

Optional Lab 4-1: Removing dust from a PC

In this optional lab, you will remove dust from a PC.

1. Turn off your system, if necessary.

2. Unplug the power cable from the unit.

3. Obtain either a can of compressed air or a static-free vacuum cleaner. Also, obtain a small brush. Do not use a standard vacuum cleaner because these produce large amounts of electrostatic discharge (ESD) that can damage your system.

4. Remove the case cover.

5. If possible, take the opened case outside to remove dust. Doing so ensures that the room you are working in will not get dusty. However, make sure that you do not expose the system to any dangerous conditions (for example, rain). Also, make sure that you put the system in a secure place so that it cannot fall, get hit by falling objects or otherwise become damaged.

6. As you remove dust, pay special attention to the following components:

   - CD/DVD drives

   - The area surrounding the CPU

   - Power connectors

7. Make sure that all components (for example, adapter cards) are still properly attached to the system and that no component is out of place. Sometimes, moving the PC can loosen components.

8. Replace the case cover.

9. Turn on the system to make sure that it still works properly.

Optional Lab 4-2: Using the Windows Vista Event Viewer

In this optional lab, you will use the Windows Vista Event Viewer to view information about hardware or software problems that your system may have encountered.

1. Open the **Control Panel**, double-click **Administrative Tools**, then double-click **Event Viewer** to open the Event Viewer (Figure OL4-1).

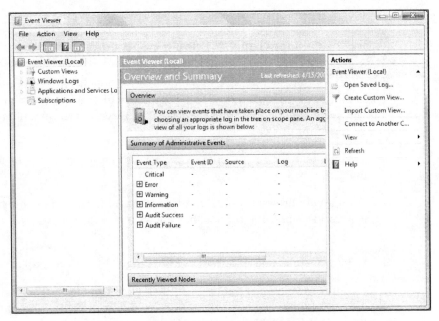

Figure OL4-1: Event Viewer

2. In the left pane, expand **Windows Logs**, click **Application**, then scroll through the log in the center pane. The Application log contains events logged by applications, including application errors. Notice that some entries in the Level column are marked Error and Warning, indicating potential application errors.

3. In the left pane, click **Security**, then scroll through the log in the center pane. The Security log records events such as resource use, and valid and invalid logon attempts.

   Note: You will not be able to view the Security log unless you have administrator privileges.

   Note: The Security log may not contain any items if no events took place that would be considered a security problem. If you have enabled logon auditing, attempts to log on to your system are recorded in the Security log. Invalid logon attempts will display as security failures.

4. In the left pane, click **System**, then scroll through the log in the center pane. The System log contains events recorded by Windows system components, such as device drivers. The System log will contain a record of any driver or system component that fails to load during startup.

5. Close all windows.

The Event Viewer can be very helpful in resolving any application failures you encounter by providing possible reasons for the failure.

Optional Lab 4-3: Using a cloud-computing backup solution

Software as a Service (SaaS), commonly referred to as cloud computing, is a powerful model that uses multiple server-side computers to create a solution. In this optional lab, you will use a cloud-computing service called Box to back up a data file and send the file to a recipient (in this case, to yourself).

1. Create a text document, enter some text into it, then save it to your Desktop as *ciw.txt*.

2. Open a Web browser and go to **http://box.net**. The Box home page will appear. Box is a cloud-computing service that allows users to access and share content across the Web.

3. Enter the requested information in the Sign Up Now section, then click **Continue**.

4. Click **Lite**, which is a free service, then click **Continue**. The Welcome To Box: Create A New Folder dialog box will appear, as shown in Figure OL4-2. You use this dialog box to specify a folder name in which to place your data files.

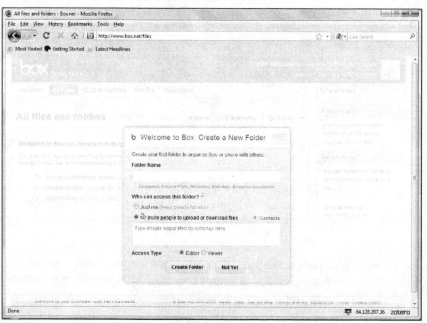

Figure OL4-2: Welcome To Box: Create A New Folder dialog box

5. In the Folder Name text box, type **Backup**. Ensure that the **Editor** access type is selected, then click the **Create Folder** button.

6. A message box will display informing you that your folder has been created. Click the **Take Me There** button. This action will display your empty Backup folder, as shown in Figure OL4-3.

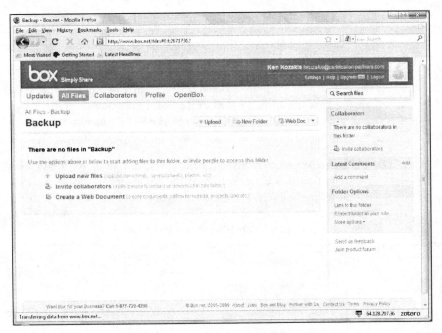

Figure OL4-3: Empty Backup folder in Box

7. You are now ready to upload files to Box to create your backup. Click the **Upload New Files** link. The Upload Files dialog box will appear.

8. Click the **Add Files** button to display the Select Files To Upload dialog box. Navigate to your Desktop, select *ciw.txt*, then click **Open**. In the Upload Files dialog box that appears, click the **Upload** button. These actions will upload *ciw.txt* to your Box folder, Backup. Your screen should resemble Figure OL4-4.

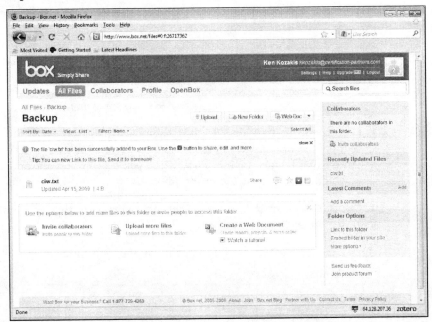

Figure OL4-4: Backup folder containing ciw.txt

At this point, you have now effectively backed up your file to a remote location. But with Software as a Service (SaaS) applications, you have the ability to do more with your backup file than simply store it. You have the ability to:

- Send this file to a person.

- Make this file available to other users who have logged into the Box service.

9. Next, you will send your backed up file to a person (in this case, to yourself) via e-mail. Click the **Link To This File** link to display the Link To This File dialog box. You can share the URL that displays in the Web Address To Share This File text box with non-Box users via e-mail or IM so that they can also access the file.

10. Click the **Send Link** button. Enter your Gmail or Windows Live Hotmail e-mail address that you created in *Internet Business Foundations, Lesson 6: E-Mail and Personal Information Management,* then click the **Send** button. You will receive an e-mail message containing the URL for *ciw.txt*, as shown in Figure OL4-5. You can then click the URL to download and view the file.

Figure OL4-5: Recipient of shared file

11. Click the **Link To This File** link, then click the **Unshare** button. This action specifies that people who have access to *ciw.txt* will no longer have access. Click the **Okay** button to unshare the file. Now, when you try to open *ciw.txt* from the e-mail account to which you sent the file in the previous step, you will be unable to do so.

12. Click the **Logout** link in the upper-right portion of the screen to log out of Box, then close your Web browser.

In this lab, you used a cloud-computing application to back up a file and send it to a recipient.

Lesson 4 Quiz

1. Which of the following describes the location through which a processor transfers data and commands to a device?

    a. DMA channel
    b. I/O address
    c. IRQ assignment
    d. PIO channel

2. Which of the following electronic interfaces used to connect mass storage devices to the motherboard is currently the de facto standard for PC-based drives?

    a. IDE
    b. SATA
    c. SCSI
    d. USB

3. What type of problem may be caused by accumulated dust?

    a. Electrostatic discharge
    b. Heat
    c. Power spike
    d. Resource conflict

4. In order to guarantee complete reliability, which file system must you use to ensure that multiple file operations (creations, moves, deletions) occur as one atomic event on a Windows computer?

    a. NTFS 5.2
    b. NTFS 5.1
    c. FAT32
    d. Ext4

5. Which of the following Windows utilities would you use to rearrange files into contiguous structures to improve system performance?

    a. Chkdsk
    b. Convert
    c. Disk Cleanup
    d. Disk Defragmenter

Lesson 5: Network Security and Personal Privacy Protection

Objectives

By the end of this lesson, you will be able to:

⚲ 3.5.1: Identify typical attacks on clients and procedures to counter each attack type.

⚲ 3.5.2: Recognize and avoid social engineering attacks.

⚲ 3.5.3: Distinguish among symmetric, asymmetric and hash encryption.

⚲ 3.5.4: Define authentication principles, including password resetting, password aging.

⚲ 3.5.5: Describe Virtual Private Networks (VPNs) and the purposes of remote access protocols, including Point-to-Point Tunneling Protocol (PPTP), Layer 2 Tunneling Protocol (L2TP).

⚲ 3.5.6: Distinguish among the following security zones: DMZ (including dual-homed and triple-homed firewalls), VLAN, intranet, extranet.

⚲ 3.5.7: Define fundamental PKI concepts.

⚲ 3.5.8: Identify the purpose of an uninterruptible power supply (UPS), and list common concerns and configuration parameters.

⚲ 3.11.1: Define phishing and pharming, and identify ways to avoid becoming a victim.

⚲ 3.11.2: Identify ways to avoid anti-social activity, including online stalking and cyberbullying.

⚲ 3.11.3: List symptoms and ramifications of spending too much time on the Internet and on gaming.

⚲ 3.11.4: Use encryption technology to secure communications (e.g., e-mail encryption, password generators, password managers).

Pre-Assessment Questions

1. What type of attack occurs when a host or system cannot perform properly because another system on the network is using all its resources?

   a. Back-door attack
   b. Denial-of-service attack
   c. Man-in-the-middle attack
   d. Trojan attack

2. Which of the following encryption methods uses a public key and private key pair?

   a. Hash encryption
   b. PGP
   c. Asymmetric-key encryption
   d. Symmetric-key encryption

3. What is the name for a mini-network that resides between a company's internal network and an external network (for example, the Internet)?

Importance of Network Security

hacker
An unauthorized user who penetrates a host or network to access and manipulate data.

Although the primary motivation for connecting systems is to share information and resources, this connectivity also makes systems and data vulnerable to unwanted activity. Connectivity always implies risk. A **hacker** can conduct many different attacks using many different methods. However, you can protect a network against unwanted entry by recognizing and implementing security techniques.

Defining security

In relation to networking, security is best defined as a set of procedures designed to protect transmitted and stored information, as well as network resources. Security involves defending and protecting assets.

As an end user, you should understand how to recognize a security incident, then understand whom to contact in case of a suspected problem. This lesson will explain these steps. You should also understand essential security concepts, including common threats and attacks, authentication, encryption, firewalls and security zones.

This lesson also discusses issues related to Internet users' personal privacy and personal protection. The Internet has grown rapidly in enabling users to engage in many personal activities such as social networking, shopping and entertainment. With this growth comes new challenges and risks as some individuals take advantage of these Internet activities for illicit purposes. This lesson will address personal security issues such as personal information privacy, Internet fraud, identity theft, online stalking, cyberbullying and Internet addiction.

Viruses and Worms

OBJECTIVE
3.5.1: Security attack types

virus
A malicious program that replicates itself on computer systems, usually through executable software, and causes irreparable system damage.

Computer viruses are perhaps the most well-known attack type. A **virus** is a malicious program designed to damage network equipment, including stand-alone computers. A virus requires an explicit action on the part of an individual or a workstation in order to spread. Viruses can spread in many ways, including the following:

- **E-mail** — Unsuspecting users may attach infected documents and programs, and then send the programs to other users. Often, an unsuspecting e-mail recipient may open an infected attachment; an attachment that contains a virus is sometimes disguised as a legitimate application or image. If the e-mail recipient double-clicks this file, the virus will infect the recipient's system, and may also spread to other users.

- **Disks** — In the past, floppy disks were the primary means of spreading viruses. Increasingly, however, removable USB drives have become common methods of spreading viruses.

New viruses appear daily. You can learn about the latest virus attacks from many sources, including the following:

NOTE:
Viruses attack individual systems and are only considered a network concern because they can use the network's communication path to spread.

- Symantec (*www.symantec.com*)

- CERT® (*www.cert.org*)

- McAfee (*www.mcafee.com*)

Virus types

Many types of viruses exist, including the following:

NOTE:
Macro viruses are often passed as documents attached to e-mail messages.

- **Macro/script** — a small program written in macro code for word processing or spreadsheet applications such as Microsoft Word or Excel. When the infected file is opened, the macro is executed.

- **File infecting** — attaches itself to executable programs (or is itself executable) and is activated when the user launches the program. If you receive an executable program from an unknown source, scan the program using anti-virus software before running it.

- **Boot sector** — copies itself to the boot sector of hard drives, allowing itself to be loaded into memory each time a system is started. After being loaded into memory, a boot sector virus may replicate itself on other drives and may completely erase the drives it accesses.

- **Stealth** — attempts to avoid detection by redirecting hard-disk-drive read requests from the virus-scanning software or by manipulating directory structure information. This manipulation causes the virus-scanning program to miss the stealth virus in its scanning process, leaving the virus on the system.

- **Polymorphic** — contains programming code enabling it to execute differently each time it is run. Because it appears as a different process each time, this virus avoids being detected by virus-scanning software.

- **Retro** — specifically attacks anti-virus software. Often included with other virus types. The virus code contains a retro virus portion that disables the virus-detection software, allowing another portion of the virus code to attack the operating system, applications or stored files.

Worms

A worm is a malicious program that can spread from system to system without direct human intervention. It is similar to a virus except that it automatically replicates.

Virus protection software

The best defense against a virus is to regularly run an industry-recognized, currently updated anti-virus program. Anti-virus software identifies and removes viruses from your computer. Anti-virus applications work as follows:

NOTE:
Most systems provide some level of virus protection through the BIOS.

signature database
In an anti-virus program, a collection of viruses, worms and illicit applications that are listed as security threats.

- The anti-virus application uses a **signature database**, which is a collection of viruses, worms and dangerous programs.

- The application scans the system for viruses and dangerous programs. The scan can include hard drives and system memory.

- The application notifies you of an infection.

- The application may be able to remove the virus.

Anti-virus programs are sold by companies such as McAfee (*www.mcafee.com*) and Symantec (*www.symantec.com*). Programs are also available as freeware and shareware from the TUCOWS Web site (*www.tucows.com*).

Removing viruses

It is important to understand that anti-virus applications do not necessarily remove all infections they detect. Virus removal may require you take additional actions, including:

- Manually editing the system registry.
- Removing files.
- Shutting down the system.

In many cases, the virus or worm will have affected important system files that cannot be repaired while the system is still running. You must create a specialized boot disk for the system. You then reboot the system using this boot disk, which has additional anti-virus applications installed. You can then use these applications to rid the system of the virus.

Repairing damage

Even if an anti-virus application can remove a virus or worm, it may not be able to repair files damaged during the incident. The anti-virus application may also not be able to remove files deposited by the virus. As you consider ways to recover from a virus infection, remember that anti-virus applications cannot work miracles.

Updating the signature database

For anti-virus programs to work, it is essential to keep them current. Update the signature database often — even the best anti-virus programs cannot protect systems if their anti-virus files are outdated. In many cases, daily updates are advisable. During times when a worm or virus has stormed the Internet, even hourly updates might better protect your system.

User education

Perhaps the most effective action that an administrator can take to prevent viruses from infecting his or her company's systems is to teach network users about the potential consequences. Informing users of the potential for damage and lost productivity can motivate them to implement the following recommended practices.

- If you receive an executable program from someone you do not know, do not open it.
- If you receive an executable program from someone you know, scan it before running it.
- If you suspect a virus or detect unusual activity on your system, inform the IT department immediately.

Overview of Network Attack Types

OBJECTIVE
3.5.1: Security attack types

Viruses and worms may be the most well-known attack types, but they are not necessarily the most common nor the most destructive. Table 5-1 lists other common types of attacks waged against network resources. You will learn more about these attacks throughout this lesson. This list is provided now to familiarize you with the terms.

Table 5-1: Network attack types

packet sniffing
The use of protocol analyzer software to obtain sensitive information, such as user names and passwords.

replay attack
An attack in which packets are obtained from the network or a network host, then reused.

account lockout
A legitimate practice in which a user account is automatically disabled after a certain number of failed authentication attempts.

dictionary program
A program specifically written to break into a password-protected system. It has a relatively large list of common password names that it repeatedly uses to gain access.

Attack	Description
Spoofing	Spoofing (also known as a masquerade attack) involves altering or generating falsified or malformed network packets. A host (or a program or application) pretends it is another entity on a network. The entity under attack is convinced it is dealing with a trusted host, and any transactions that occur can lead to further compromise.
Man in the middle	An attack in which the attacker places him- or herself physically in the middle of a connection in order to obtain information. Includes **packet sniffing** and **replay attacks**.
Denial of service (DOS)	DOS is a type of attack waged by a single system on one or more systems. DOS attacks involve crashing a system completely, or occupying system resources (for example, CPU cycles and RAM) in order to render the system non-functional. DOS can also involve causing legitimate system features and tools to backfire. For example, many operating systems provide for **account lockout**. If account lockout is enabled, a malicious user can purposely and repeatedly disable logon capability for user accounts. As a result, users will be unable to access any network services.
Distributed denial of service (DDOS)	DDOS involves the use of multiple applications found on several network resources to crash one or more systems, denying service to a host. DDOS is often used to consume a server's data connection.
Brute force	A brute-force attack involves repeated guessing of passwords or other encrypted data, one character at a time, usually at random. It can also involve physical attacks, such as forcing open a server room door or opening false ceilings.
Dictionary	Dictionary attacks involve repeated attempts to guess a password. They are a type of brute force attack, but use a file, called a **dictionary program**, containing a long list of words (instead of random values) to repeatedly guess user names and passwords.
Back door	A back-door attack involves code inserted secretly into an application or operating system by developers; the code opens a networking port that allows illicit access into the system. Usually, only the developers know the password, but in many cases these passwords become publicly known.
Buffer overflow	A buffer overflow is a condition that occurs when a legitimate application (or part of one) exceeds the memory buffer allocated to it by the operating system. Buffer overflows can occur due to inadvertent flaws written into program code. All applications must use a memory buffer. Sometimes, however, applications can place too much information into a buffer, resulting in a buffer overflow. Applications that do not carefully check the size of information before processing it are especially vulnerable to overflows.
Trojan	A trojan is malicious code that is disguised to appear as a legitimate application. For example, a seemingly harmless game might, in fact, also contain code that allows a hacker to defeat a system's security.
Social engineering	Social engineering involves attempts to trick legitimate employees or individuals into revealing company information or changing system settings so the attacker can gain access to a network. Social engineering attacks include phishing and pharming, which you will learn about later in this lesson.

Never use any techniques or software described in this course to attack systems you do not own. Furthermore, if you ever simulate any attacks for your own research purposes, be sure to use a completely isolated network.

Avoiding attacks

You can avoid attacks by taking the following steps:

digital signature
An electronic stamp added to a message that uniquely identifies its source and verifies its contents at the time of the signature.

- **Install stable updates** — Make sure that your applications and operating systems use the latest, stable versions. All updates should originate from trusted sources (for example, the vendor that sold you the product). Verify that updates are, in fact, updates and not trojans. For example, check for a file's **digital signature**. These solutions help avoid buffer overflow and trojan-based attacks. Updates can also help eliminate back-door attacks, provided that the company has found all existing back doors and has not introduced new ones.

- **Use encryption** — Encryption is a security technique to prevent access to information by converting it into a scrambled (unreadable) form of text. If you encrypt network transmissions, you can avoid man-in-the-middle attacks. You will study encryption in more detail shortly.

- **Be suspicious of information requests** — Social engineering experts rely on naive users and confusion. If you receive a request by telephone or e-mail, verify the nature of the request before divulging information. For example, reveal sensitive information only to a trusted IT worker in the presence of your manager or other appropriate individual.

- **Remain informed** — The most secure organizations take the time to inform their employees regularly about the latest attacks.

Defeating Attacks

Table 5-2 summarizes key security concepts that can be used to defeat attempts to gain illegitimate access. These services are also described in the OSI/RM.

Table 5-2: OSI/RM security services

digital certificate
A password-protected, encrypted data file containing message encryption, user identification and message text. Used to authenticate a program or a sender's public key, or to initiate SSL sessions. Must be signed by a certificate authority (CA) to be valid.

Service	Description
Authentication	Proves identity upon presentation; for example, a user account logon name and password.
Access control	Grants various levels of file or directory permissions to users.
Data confidentiality	Provides protection of data on a system or host from unauthorized access. For example, remote users logged on to a system may be unaware that their transactions are being monitored. To ensure confidentiality, they may use some form of encryption to prevent others from understanding their communication.
Data integrity	Provides protection against active threats (such as man-in-the-middle attacks) that attempt to alter messages before they are sent or received. The integrity service prevents or recognizes such an attempt, giving the system time to recover or stop it.
Non-repudiation	Provides proof that a transaction has occurred. Repudiation occurs when one party in a transaction denies that the transaction took place. The other party may use a means of non-repudiation to prove that the transaction actually did occur. For example, a sales receipt provides a means of non-repudiation. Another example: A Web server is able to prove that a transaction has occurred by showing a log file or a cached copy of a client's **digital certificate**.

Updates

Make sure that you update your system and all applications with the latest, stable updates. Do not make the mistake of updating only the operating system (for example, simply using Windows Update or Ubuntu Linux Update Manager). You must also update individual applications (for example, Mozilla and SSH applications).

Authentication

OBJECTIVE
3.5.4:
Authentication
principles

NOTE:
Kerberos (Windows and Linux/UNIX) enables mutual authentication, in which the client is authenticated by the server and the server is authenticated by the client.

smart card
A credit card that replaces the magnetic strip with an embedded chip for storing or processing data.

As you learned earlier, authentication is the ability to determine a user's true identity. To communicate effectively, users in enterprise networks must ensure that they are actually communicating with the person they want to address. However, IP spoofing, falsified e-mail messages, social engineering and other techniques all intervene to defeat the authentication process.

Networks can employ the following three methods to prove a user's identity and achieve authentication:

- **What you know** — the most common form of authentication; involves the use of passwords. When you log on to a computer network, you are often asked for a password. A password is something you know.

- **What you have** — requires you to use a physical item, such as a key, for authentication. An example is a building entry card. If you have a card (which you pass over a scanner), you will be granted access to the building. In this case, the authentication is based on possessing the card. The most powerful example of this technology type is a **smart card**.

- **Who you are** — involves biometrics, which is the science of connecting authentication schemes to unique physical attributes. Examples of this method include the use of fingerprints, visual and photographic identification, and physical signatures. More sophisticated methods include retinal scans, facial maps, voice analysis and digital signatures. Each method attempts to validate an individual's claim concerning his or her identity.

 The term "strong authentication" describes extensive steps, including the use of encryption, to ensure authentication. Strong authentication is a combination of what you know, what you have and who you are.

Passwords

Passwords are one of the core strengths of computer and network security, and are part of the "what you know" authentication method. If the password is compromised, the basic security scheme or model is affected. To enforce good password practice, you need to require passwords and to help users choose strong passwords (you will learn about strong passwords shortly).

Because so many different operating systems exist, no universal standard can be adopted for the ideal password. However, strong passwords generally include at least three of the following four types of content:

- Uppercase letters

- Lowercase letters

- Numbers

- Non-alphanumeric characters, such as punctuation

Strong passwords should also adhere to the following guidelines:

- Repeat letters or digits in the password.

- Do not use common names or nicknames.

- Do not use common personal information (for example, date of birth, spouse's or children's names, etc.).

Essentially, you must think like a hacker: Avoid strategies that may allow others to discover your password (for example, using your date of birth as your password, or writing your password on paper and leaving it in plain view).

Password aging

NOTE:
Setting password-aging parameters is not the same as setting account lockout parameters, which are discussed in the next section.

Password aging relates to the frequency with which users must change their passwords. Following are password-aging concepts used in most operating systems:

- **Maximum password age** — the amount of time a user can keep an existing password.

- **Minimum password age** — the amount of time a user must keep a password before changing it.

- **Password history** — determines the number of passwords that the operating system will remember. If a user chooses a password that resides in the password history database, the operating system will force the user to choose another password.

- **Minimum password length** — the lowest acceptable number of characters for a password.

- **Password complexity** — requires the use of non-alphanumeric characters and/or uppercase letters in a password. The resulting security gain is often small because many users will resort to practices such as using *password01*, *password02* and *password03* to avoid this restriction. Although this technique does not offer optimal security, it is more secure than using the same password continually.

- **Encryption options** — for example, Linux allows the use of MD5 (theoretically non-recoverable) or 3DES passwords. Windows operating systems offer similar options for encrypting passwords.

Password aging is an important concept to implement because it can make password cracking with dictionary and brute-force attacks more difficult. For setting the maximum password age, most organizations assign a value of between 30 and 90 days. Requiring more frequent changes can complicate the system or create problems: If users are asked to change their passwords more than once every 30 days, they may write down their passwords in order to remember them. As you learned earlier, others can discover a written password.

Tech Tip

When choosing password-aging elements, compare the estimated security gain with the increase in difficulty for users. If the burden on users exceeds the value of the additional security, consider very carefully whether the measure is worthwhile.

Account lockout

Account lockout is the primary tool used to thwart password guessing. It works by disabling accounts after a specified number of invalid passwords have been entered. This technique is especially useful for preventing remote brute-force or dictionary-based password attacks. Generally, account lockout should be set up to occur after three to five invalid logon attempts.

NOTE:
Make sure you
understand the
importance of
account reset.

Account reset

Account reset provides the option of automatically resetting the account after a specified interval. This option is valuable because valid users can forget their passwords, especially when password changes are required. Large organizations, especially, must often allow accounts to reset automatically after a given interval. Even an interval as short as 15 minutes will generally prevent the effective use of a brute-force password attack. One drawback to requiring manual account reset is that it allows for a possible denial-of-service (DOS) attack. An attacker can disable users accounts by launching a password-guessing program.

Linux and strong passwords

By default, Linux systems use six-character passwords and also reject any password that resembles a dictionary password (in other words, any text string that looks too much like a word found in a standard dictionary). As a result, you need to use a password such as *8igMo$ne!* instead of *bigmoney*. However, you can enforce more stringent password requirements. For example, many Linux systems administrators prefer a password of eight characters and require two non-alphanumeric characters.

Managing passwords

OBJECTIVE
3.11.4: Securing
communications

Most people need to remember multiple passwords to engage in various computing activities. You need passwords to log on to a network, an FTP site, e-mail clients, online shopping accounts, online bank accounts and so forth. For security, you should have different passwords for each account. If you have only one password for all your accounts, and someone learns your password, all your accounts could become compromised.

password manager
A software
application you can
use to store and
manage multiple
passwords.

You can use a **password manager** software application to help you store and manage your passwords. Many password managers can also store bank PINs, credit card numbers and personal information. With a password manager, you only need to remember one password — the master password needed to access the password manager — in order to gain access to your other passwords. This master password must be strong enough to resist brute-force or dictionary attacks. If someone learns your master password, all your protected passwords (and other information) will be compromised.

NOTE:
Password managers
are also known as
"password vaults"
and "password
databases."

There are three types of password managers:

*   **Desktop** — stores passwords on a local hard drive

*   **Portable** — stores passwords on a mobile device, such as a PDA or smartphone

*   **Web-based** — stores passwords on a Web site whose purpose is to securely store login information for users

There are many password manager applications from which to choose. Among them are the following:

*   KeePass (*http://keepass.info*)

*   LastPass (*https://lastpass.com*)

*   SurfSecret KeyPad (*www.surfsecret.com/business-products/keypad.shtml*)

*   TurboPasswords (*www.chapura.com/passwordmanager.php*)

*   Password Safe (*http://passwordsafe.sourceforge.net*)

- RoboForm (*www.roboform.com*)

- AnyPassword (*www.anypassword.com*)

An example password manager: KeePass

An example of a popular password manager is KeePass. KeePass is a free, open-source solution that runs on Windows, Apple and Linux/UNIX operating systems. Like many password managers, KeePass stores all of your information in a database that is encrypted. KeePass supports the AES and Twofish encryption algorithms. KeePass also includes a password generator, which you will learn about next.

Using password generators

password generator
An algorithm that receives input from a random or pseudo-random number generator and automatically generates a password.

Because it is important to use strong passwords that are immune to brute-force and dictionary attacks, you may want to consider using a **password generator** to provide strong passwords for you. A password generator is an algorithm that receives input from a random or pseudo-random number generator and then automatically generates a password.

There are many password-generating software programs available on the Internet. However, using them does raise a security concern — if the connection to the password generation site's program has been compromised, your generated password may also be compromised.

Some examples of secure password generators include the following:

- KeePass (*http://keepass.info*)

- LastPass (*https://lastpass.com*)

- JpassGen (*http://sourceforge.net/projects/jpassgen/*)

Digital certificates

As you learned earlier, a digital certificate is a small file that provides authoritative identification. Digital certificates verify the sender's identity. A trusted third party, known as the certificate authority (CA), is responsible for verifying the legitimacy of the digital certificate. After you receive a legitimate digital certificate from a person or host (for example, a Web or e-mail server), you can be reasonably sure that you are communicating with the proper party. Effectively, a digital certificate is the equivalent of an identification card (for example, a passport or a driver's license), because it proves the identity of an individual or company over the Web.

X.509
The standard used by certificate authorities (CAs) for creating digital certificates.

Digital certificates use the **X.509** standard. This standard ensures that certificates contain the following data about the certificate owner:

- Name, company and address

- Public key

- Certificate serial number

- Dates that the certificate is valid

- Identification of the certifying company

- Digital signature of the certifying company

Digital certificates contain digital signatures to ensure that a message has not been altered during transmission from the sender. The typical implementation of a digital signature is as follows:

1. Tina reduces her message using a hash algorithm, then encrypts the message with her private key. She has created an encrypted file that contains a distinct signature. This digital signature is an encrypted digest of the text that is sent with the text message.

2. Sarah receives the message and decrypts the digital signature with Tina's public key. This decryption allows Sarah to verify the digital signature by re-computing the signature's hash value and comparing it with the received signature's hash value. If the values match, then the message has not been altered, and is authenticated.

You will learn more shortly about the encryption and keys mentioned in this process.

non-repudiation
The security principle of providing proof that a transaction occurred between identified parties. Repudiation occurs when one party in a transaction denies that the transaction took place.

Authentication requires a digital certificate verified by a CA. Digital certificates are used for **non-repudiation**, which is the ability to prove that a transmission has been sent by the sender and received by the recipient. (You were introduced to non-repudiation earlier.) Sending a message with a digital certificate guarantees that the sender cannot later deny having sent the transmission, and the recipient cannot deny having received the transmission.

OBJECTIVE
3.5.7: PKI concepts

Public Key Infrastructure (PKI)

Public Key Infrastructure (PKI) refers to a series of CAs that enable users to manage public encryption. PKI CA servers are repositories for managing digital certificates. The primary goal of PKI is to enable the secure creation and management of digital certificates. In addition to authenticating the identity of the entity owning a key pair, PKI also provides the ability to revoke a key if it is no longer valid. A key becomes invalid if, for example, a private key is cracked or made public. If you need a certificate for a server (for example, a Web or e-mail server), you will use PKI.

Table 5-3 describes essential terms that relate to certificates generated through PKI.

Table 5-3: Certificate terms

Term	Description
Certificate policy	A set of rules and procedures that describe the ways in which employees in an organization should use digital certificates.
Certificate Practice Statement (CPS)	A formal explanation of how a CA verifies and manages certificates.
Certificate expiration	The end of a certificate's expected life cycle. All certificates have valid beginning and end dates coded inside them (for example, October 31, 2011). Expiration occurs when the certificate end date has arrived. All certificates created by PKI have a specific life cycle.
Certificate revocation	The practice of invalidating a certificate before the end of its expected life cycle. Reasons for revocation may include: -Employee termination. -Employee reassignment. -Changing the company name. -Changing the DNS name of a server. -A compromised CA.

NOTE:
All certificates created by PKI have a specific life cycle.

Table 5-3: Certificate terms (cont'd)

Term	Description
Suspension	The practice of temporarily invalidating, or deactivating, a key for a specific length of time. The key can be reactivated. However, if the certificate expires during a period of suspension, a new key will need to be generated.
Renewal	The practice of renewing a key before it expires. Keys that have been revoked or that have already expired cannot be renewed.
Destruction	The practice of eliminating all public and private keys; effectively eliminates an identity from PKI.
Certificate Revocation List (CRL)	A list of certificates that are no longer considered valid. Users must manually download and then check this list.
Online Certificate Status Protocol (OCSP)	A real-time protocol that allows users to check for revoked certificates.

Encryption

OBJECTIVE
3.5.3: Encryption types

You were introduced to the concept of encryption earlier. Encryption is the primary means to ensure privacy across the enterprise. This technique is often used to assist authentication efforts, as well. Currently, you can choose from three encryption models:

- Symmetric-key encryption

- Asymmetric-key encryption

OBJECTIVE
3.11.4: Securing communications

- Hash encryption

Symmetric-key encryption is the most familiar form of encryption, but for enterprise-wide communication, asymmetric-key and hash encryption are also used.

Encryption always implies the use of algorithms. At the networking level, algorithms often create keys, or text strings that scramble and unscramble information. The following sections will introduce the three types of encryption and their algorithms.

Symmetric-key (private-key) encryption

NOTE:
Symmetric-key encryption is most commonly used when passing data between two secure systems on the same network.

In symmetric-key, or private-key, encryption, one key is used to encrypt and decrypt messages. Even though symmetric-key encryption is a simple process, all parties must know and trust one another completely, and have confidential copies of the key. The first transmission of the key is crucial. If it is intercepted, the interceptor knows the key, and confidential material is no longer protected. Figure 5-1 illustrates symmetric-key encryption.

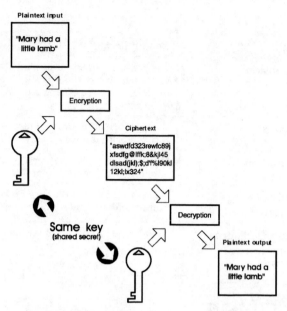

Figure 5-1: Symmetric-key encryption

An example of a symmetric key is a simple password you use to access your automated teller machine or to log on to your ISP.

Symmetric algorithms
You can create a symmetric key with many different algorithms. The three most common symmetric algorithms are:

- Data Encryption Standard (DES).

- Triple DES.

- Advanced Encryption Standard (AES).

Data Encryption Standard (DES)
DES is an encryption standard that encrypts data using a 56-bit key. The same key is used to encrypt and decrypt the data. The advantages of DES are that it is fast and simple to implement. However, key distribution and management are difficult because DES relies on a single-key model.

DES has been in production use for more than 30 years, so many hardware and software implementations use the DES algorithm. The U.S. National Institute of Standards and Technology (NIST) formally adopted DES in 1977. DES and its cousin, Triple DES, remain the standard form of encryption for many companies and organizations. Another name for the Data Encryption Standard is the Data Encryption Algorithm (DEA).

Triple DES
Standard DES is considered sufficient for normal information. For sensitive information, some users employ a technique called Triple DES. In this case, the message is first encrypted using a 56-bit DES key, then decrypted with another 56-bit key, and finally encrypted again with the original 56-bit key. The Triple DES thus effectively has a 168-bit key.

Because of the several levels of encryption, Triple DES also thwarts man-in-the-middle attacks. Normal DES is fast, and Triple DES is faster than other symmetric algorithms. The biggest advantage of Triple DES is its ability to use existing DES software and hardware. Companies with large investments in the DES encryption algorithm can easily implement Triple DES.

 Encrypting and decrypting data requires nothing more than passing the data through an algorithm. The process for encryption is essentially identical to the process for decryption.

NOTE:
The FineCrypt application, profiled in Lab 5-2, uses AES by default.

Advanced Encryption Standard (AES)

Most security experts believe that DES and Triple DES no longer meet security requirements. The NIST began the process of determining a successor to DES. Among other requirements, the symmetric algorithm chosen for AES had to:

- Allow the creation of 128-bit, 192-bit and 256-bit keys.

- Provide support for various platforms (e.g., smart cards; 8-bit, 32-bit and 64-bit processors).

- Be as fast as possible.

The NIST chose the Rijndael algorithm out of several finalists. It allows the creation of 128-bit, 192-bit or 256-bit keys. It is a block cipher, which means it encrypts messages in blocks, 64 bits at a time. The developers were especially interested in making an algorithm that could perform quickly on various platforms, including asynchronous transfer mode (ATM) networks, Integrated Services Digital Network (ISDN) lines and even high-definition television (HDTV).

 Any of the previously mentioned algorithms can be used for symmetric encryption. Remember that both parties involved in the encryption process (the sender and the recipient) must agree ahead of time on the symmetric algorithm to be used.

Symmetric encryption: Benefits and drawbacks

The benefits of symmetric-key encryption are its speed and strength. These features allow you to encrypt a large amount of information in less than a second.

The drawback of symmetric-key encryption is that all recipients and viewers must have the same key, and all users must have a secure way to retrieve the key. To pass information across a public medium such as the Internet, users need a way to transfer this password key among themselves. In some cases, the users can meet and transfer the key physically. However, network users cannot always meet with one another in person.

password sniffing
A method of intercepting the transmission of a password during the authentication process. A sniffer is a program used to intercept passwords.

Another drawback is that hackers can compromise symmetric keys by using a dictionary program, engaging in **password sniffing**, or simply snooping through a desk, purse or briefcase.

In the following lab, you will learn how to apply symmetric-key encryption. Suppose your boss sends you overseas to implement the new expansion phase of your company's sales operations. You communicate with your boss by means of e-mail, primarily because it affords greater security and confidentiality, and it allows both of you to create and retain written records of your communication. You both must ensure that competitors and other outsiders cannot understand the documents you send across the Internet, so you decide to use symmetric-key encryption technology to prevent electronic snooping and unauthorized access.

Lab 5-1: Applying symmetric-key encryption

In this lab, you will use a symmetric-key algorithm to encrypt a file.

1. Copy the FineCrypt installation binary (fcinst.exe) from the C:\CIW\Network\Lab Files\Lesson05 folder to your Desktop. If necessary, download FineCrypt from *www.tucows.com* or from *www.finecrypt.net*.

2. On your Desktop, double-click **fcinst.exe**, then click **Run** to display the FineCrypt installation Wizard.

3. Perform the steps necessary to install the application. Accept the license agreement and all defaults, then click **Install**. When the installation is complete, click **Finish**.

4. Minimize all open windows on your Desktop, if necessary.

5. Create a text file named ***aes_yourname.txt*** (where *yourname* is your first and last name), write a message, then save and close the file.

6. Right-click ***aes_yourname*.txt**, then select **FineCrypt | Encrypt With Password**.

7. If you have just installed FineCrypt, a wizard will appear. This wizard is designed to inform you about features that FineCrypt provides. Click **Next** as many times as necessary to finish the presentation, then click **Finish**.

8. Right-click ***aes_yourname*.txt** and select **FineCrypt | Encrypt With Password** again. The FineCrypt: Enter Passphrase dialog box will appear (Figure 5-2).

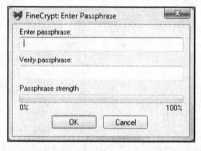

Figure 5-2: FineCrypt: Enter Passphrase dialog box

9. Enter a passphrase of your choice in the Enter Passphrase and Verify Passphrase text boxes. Make sure that this passphrase uses between eight and sixteen characters. To ensure that you do not forget the passphrase, write it in the following space:

_____

10. Click **OK** to close the dialog box.

11. In the Encrypt dialog box, click ***aes_yourname*.txt**, then click the **Encrypt** button at the top of the dialog box. This action creates a new file named *aes_yourname.fca* on your Desktop. The file icon shows a lock with a key (Figure 5-3).

aes_yournam
e.fca

Figure 5-3: Encrypted file

At this point, you could transfer your encrypted file to another user. However, the other user must know your encryption password to be able to open the file. Determining how to securely communicate the password across a network is an inherent limitation of symmetric-key encryption.

In this lab, you used the FineCrypt application's AES encryption algorithm to encrypt a text file.

Asymmetric-key (public-key) encryption

NOTE:
The Windows Encrypted File System (EFS) is based on asymmetric-key encryption.

Asymmetric-key encryption uses a key pair in the encryption process rather than the single key used in symmetric-key encryption. A key pair is a mathematically matched key set in which one key encrypts and the other key decrypts. Key A encrypts that which Key B decrypts; and Key B encrypts that which Key A decrypts.

An important aspect to this concept is that one of these keys is made public, whereas the other is kept private, as shown in Figure 5-4. Hence, asymmetric encryption is also called public-key encryption. The key that you publish is called a public key, and the key you keep secret is the private key. Initially, you can distribute either key. However, after one key of the pair has been distributed, it must always remain public, and vice versa. Consistency is critical.

Figure 5-4: Public-key encryption

An example of asymmetric-key encryption is as follows: To send a secret message to David, you encrypt the message with David's public key, and then send the encrypted text. When David receives the encrypted text, he will decrypt it with his private key. Anyone who intercepts the message cannot decrypt it without David's private key.

Although private and public keys are mathematically related to one another, determining the value of the private key from the public key is extremely difficult and time-consuming.

Asymmetric-key algorithms
The two most common asymmetric-key algorithms are:

- Rivest, Shamir, Adleman (RSA.)

- Digital Signature Algorithm (DSA).

NOTE:
RSA (www.rsa.com) is one of the best known companies in the field of cryptography. The RSA Web site contains an extensive amount of information about cryptography and security. This coursebook can discuss only a few of RSA's contributions.

RSA algorithm

RSA (named for developers Ron Rivest, Adi Shamir and Leonard Adleman) is a public-key encryption system created in 1977. The RSA algorithm is used in several commercial operating systems and programs, including Windows family operating systems. It is also included in existing and proposed standards for the Internet and the World Wide Web.

Digital Signature Algorithm (DSA)

DSA was introduced by NIST and is available openly. It is used to sign documents. Although it functions differently from RSA, it is not proprietary and has been adopted as the standard signing method in GNU Privacy Guard (GPG), the open-source alternative to Pretty Good Privacy (PGP), which you will learn about shortly.

Asymmetric encryption: Benefits and drawbacks

For communication over the Internet, the asymmetric-key system makes key management easier because the public key can be distributed while the private key stays secure with the user.

The primary drawback of asymmetric-key encryption is that it is quite slow, due to the intensive mathematical calculations that the program requires. Even a rudimentary level of asymmetric encryption can require a great deal of time. Consequently, many applications use asymmetric-key encryption to encrypt only the symmetric key that encrypts the body of the message.

Hash (one-way) encryption

NOTE:
A common use of hash encryption is in remote logon authentication. Some authentication methods pass a hash of the user's password rather than the password itself for logon validation.

Hash encryption typically uses a hash table that contains a hash function. This table determines the values used for encryption. A table of hexadecimal numbers is used to calculate the encryption.

Hash encryption is used for information that will not be decrypted or read. (Hash decryption is theoretically and mathematically impossible.) For example, two different entities may need to compare values without revealing the information. Hash encryption allows someone to verify but not copy information, and is commonly used by e-mail programs and SSL sessions.

Although permanent encryption may seem illogical, there are many uses for encryption that cannot be decrypted. For example, an automated teller machine (ATM) does not actually decrypt the personal identification number (PIN) entered by a customer. The magnetic stripe has the customer's code encrypted one-way. This one-way encryption is the hash code. The automated teller machine calculates the hash on the PIN that the customer enters, which yields a result. This result is then compared with the hash code on the card. With this method, the PIN is secure, even from the ATM and the individuals who maintain it.

Hash algorithms

Hash encryption uses complicated mathematical algorithms to achieve effective encryption. The two standard hash algorithm families in current use are:

- Message Digest (MD2, MD4 and MD5).

- Secure Hash Algorithm (SHA).

Message Digest (MD2, MD4 and MD5)

The Message Digest (MD) algorithms are a group of hash functions that take any length of data and generate a unique fingerprint of certain length (generally 128 bits). The process is one-way because you cannot generate the message back from the signature, and the fingerprints are unique because no two messages will have the same hash.

MD algorithms are used to generate unique one-way fingerprints of e-mail messages, certificates and other items to ensure content integrity.

MD4 and MD5 are faster than MD2. MD4 produces a 128-bit hash. However, it was susceptible to attacks that could reverse-engineer the hash codes. Therefore, it is now considered broken and is no longer used. MD5 is stronger than MD4, produces a 128-bit hash and is the most commonly used algorithm. You can learn more about MD5 in RFC 1321.

Secure Hash Algorithm (SHA)

Secure Hash Algorithm (SHA) is also known as Secure Hash Standard (SHS). SHA was developed by NIST and the U.S. National Security Agency (NSA), and it is used in U.S. government processing. It can produce a 160-bit hash value from an arbitrary-length string.

SHA is structurally similar to MD4 and MD5. Although it is about 25 percent slower than MD5, it is much more secure. It produces message digests that are 25 percent longer than those produced by the MD functions, making it more secure against attacks.

Pretty Good Privacy (PGP) and GNU Privacy Guard (GPG)

When individuals want to communicate securely over long distances, they generally use combinations of the encryption schemes described previously. Perhaps the most popular high-technology encryption programs for e-mail and text files are Pretty Good Privacy (PGP) and GNU Privacy Guard (GPG).

GPG is the open-source version of PGP and was originally designed for UNIX systems. Both PGP and GPG can be used on Windows, Macintosh and Linux/UNIX systems. You can learn more about PGP at *www.pgp.com*, and you can learn more about GPG at *www.gnupg.org*. The remainder of this discussion applies to both applications.

PGP/GPG functionality

PGP and GPG use symmetric-key encryption to scramble the original message you want to send. Next, they use asymmetric-key encryption to encrypt only the symmetric key you just used. Finally, they use hash encryption to sign the message and ensure that no one can tamper with it.

This combination employs the strengths of each encryption method. Asymmetric encryption is quite slow, but PGP, GPG and methods such as SSL use it only to encrypt the symmetric key, not the actual message. Because symmetric-key encryption is so fast, it encrypts the message itself. Hash encryption then signs the message efficiently.

To use an application such as PGP or GPG, you must first generate a key pair. You must then publish your public key, which you can give to anyone. However, you must keep your private key completely secret. If you back up your private key, you must be sure to store it in a secret locked location. If anyone were to obtain this key, that individual would be able to read all your secret information.

NOTE:
You need to understand what a firewall does and when one should be used.

Network-level protocols and encryption

Network-level protocols and algorithms establish a secure channel at the network layer, providing privacy, integrity and authentication. For example, VPN protocols usually operate independently of the packet contents. The protocols handle the packets, and the data portion (payload) of each packet is encrypted. The function of the protocols is to deliver the packets to a destination. The protocols handle authentication just enough to identify the recipient when identification is required. SSL sessions and **Kerberos** are also vital network-level encryption methods.

Firewalls

A firewall is a secure computer system placed between a trusted network and an untrusted one, such as the Internet. On one side of a firewall is your company's production network, which you supervise, control and protect. The other side contains a public network (such as the Internet) over which you have no control.

The term "firewall" comes from a safety technique used in building construction. Wherever a wall separates sections of a building, such as different businesses or apartments, it is made as fireproof as possible. This measure protects the occupants and property throughout the building if one unit catches fire.

In computer networking, a network firewall acts as a barrier against potential malicious activity, while still allowing a "door" for people to communicate between a secured network and the open, unsecured network. The most common location for a firewall is between a corporate LAN and the Internet. This site is vital to the enforcement of your security policy.

Essential firewall functions

A firewall controls access to your private network (for example, your LAN or intranet). It can also create secure intranet domains. Furthermore, it is the primary means of enforcing your security policy, greatly simplifying the tasks of determining threats and using countermeasures. Without such a point for monitoring and controlling information, a systems or security administrator would have an excessive number of places to monitor.

A firewall can further enhance privacy by "hiding" your internal systems and information from the public. A firewall also enforces logging and provides alarm capacities. Finally, a firewall simplifies the authentication process.

Firewalls allow users from a protected network to access a public network while simultaneously making the protected company's products and services available to the public. Before you implement your firewall, you should know which services your company requires, and which services will be available to both internal and external users. The availability of services on both sides of the firewall largely determines which firewall functions you will use.

Potential firewall functions include:

- Filtering packets.

- Detecting intrusions.

- Providing enhanced password authentication.

- Logging and reporting.

- Permitting encrypted access (with a VPN).

You can use these functions in a variety of combinations. Sometimes they will be used on individual computers, but most often they will be combined. Logging and reporting, for example, occur at various levels. Together, these functions form your firewall's building blocks.

Internal firewall

NOTE:
Internal firewalls are also known as enclave firewalls.

Internal firewalls are standard firewalls, but reside inside your company's internal network. Internal firewalls are meant to protect sensitive departments and divisions. They can be used in the following ways:

- To protect sensitive systems, such as those in human resources or accounting departments

- To isolate networks that still need Internet connectivity, but which use software whose behavior might cause problems with other resources in the company

Personal firewall

Personal firewalls are available for personal computers. They offer protection for an individual system instead of protecting an entire network. Such tools can detect and respond to attacks. For Windows systems, personal firewall tools include.

- Comodo Internet Security (*http://personalfirewall.comodo.com*).

- ZoneAlarm (*www.zonealarm.com*).

- Sunbelt Personal Firewall (*www.sunbeltsoftware.com*).

- Online-Armor (*www.tallemu.com*).

To create a personal firewall in Linux, you can use the *iptables* command (for kernels 2.3 and higher).

Personal firewalls offer many of the firewall features listed in this lesson, such as packet filtering, intrusion detection, and logging. When used in conjunction with anti-virus software, a personal computer is very secure, provided that you update the anti-virus and personal firewall software frequently.

Packet filtering

Packet filtering is the use of a router or firewall to inspect each packet for predefined content. Although packet filtering does not provide error-proof protection, it is almost always the first line of defense. Engineers usually filter packets at the external router, which discards certain types of activity entirely.

Packet filtering is also inexpensive, mainly because most routers can perform this task. A router is necessary to connect your network to the Internet, so by using your router to perform packet filtering as well, you can gain functionality with little additional cost.

Packet filtering works at the data link, network and transport layers of the OSI/RM. Implementation requires instructing the router to filter the contents of IP packets based on the following fields in the packet:

- Source IP address

- Destination IP address

- TCP/UDP source port

- TCP/UDP destination port

For example, if you want to protect your network from a group of attackers, configuring a packet filter to block all connections from that group might be the best solution. Such a configuration is recommended because packet filters are generally included on routers and firewalls.

Proxy server

Proxy servers are very important to firewall applications because a proxy replaces the network IP address with a single IP address. Multiple systems can use this single IP address. A proxy server provides the following services:

- **Hiding network resources** — Hackers will see only one IP address instead of all exposed systems.

- **Logging** — A proxy server can log incoming and outgoing access, allowing you to see the details of successful and failed connections.

- **Caching** — A proxy server can save information obtained from the Internet (for example, Web pages). This cache contains copies of information found on the Internet. Internal Web clients, for example, that access the Internet through the proxy will see these copied (or cached) pages, and will thus not need to access the Internet to view them. A proxy server will regularly check these copies to see whether sites or pages have been updated. It will also automatically purge old information after a certain length of time. A common proxy server problem occurs when the server returns old information. In such cases, the administrator must purge the existing cache, or set the proxy server to update its cache more often.

Application-level gateway

An **application-level gateway** acts as a proxy between the Internet and your internal system at the application level. An application-level gateway firewall receives an outbound network packet and transmits it for the internal system. Inbound traffic works in a similar way.

Application-level gateways create a complete break between your internal and external systems. This break gives your firewall system an opportunity to examine all transmissions before passing them into or out of your internal networks.

An application gateway can serve as an SMTP firewall. In that case, external inbound e-mail messages would be received from the Internet at the firewall's external port. The firewall can then verify the source of the e-mail messages and scan all attachments for viruses before transmitting the mail to the internal network.

Although this process is rather complex, it is often necessary; neither source verification nor virus-scanning capabilities are built into SMTP specifications. Still, an application-level gateway provides the appropriate technology to implement this type of security.

 When you or your organization uses an application-level gateway, you must configure each of the clients to function with this gateway.

Most firewall systems today are combinations of packet-filtering and application-level gateways. They examine packets individually, and they use predetermined rules. Only packets that engage in acceptable activities (as defined by your security policy) are allowed into and out of the network.

Network Address Translation (NAT)

You were introduced to **Network Address Translation (NAT)** earlier in the course. NAT is the practice of hiding internal IP addresses from the external network. The internal IP addresses are usually the reserved IP addresses that the ICANN recommends using for internal address schemes.

 You learned about reserved IP addressing earlier in the course. RFC 1918 outlines the reserved addresses. These addresses are ideal because Internet routers are configured not to forward them. These packets cannot traverse the Internet unless they are translated using NAT.

Following are two ways to provide true NAT:

- Configure "masquerading" on a packet-filtering firewall.

- Use a proxy server to conduct requests from internal hosts.

When a firewall or router is configured to provide NAT, all internal addresses are translated to public IP addresses when connecting to an external host. When packets return from an external host, they are translated back so the internal network host can receive them.

Accessing Internet services

If Internet access is required and a network is located behind a proxy server or firewall, you may have problems accessing Internet services that use less-common ports. For example, most proxy servers and firewalls already allow HTTP. Difficulties may occur when you require additional services, such as e-mail, FTP and program downloads.

To avoid these common problems, perform the following tasks:

- Make sure the network has access to all Internet-related protocols used by the company. Examples include HTTP (TCP port 80), SSL (TCP port 443), FTP (TCP port 20, 21), Telnet (TCP port 23), POP3 (TCP port 110), SMTP (TCP port 25) and NNTP (TCP port 119). For certain services, such as FTP, you will need all ports above 1023 (in other words, the registered, dynamic or ephemeral ports). Each of these ports must be "opened" at the firewall or proxy server to allow traffic using that port.

- Make sure that the IP addresses assigned to the computers in your network have permission to access the Internet.

After the required ports are opened at the firewall, further rules can be applied to block ports by IP address. This capability allows administrators to regulate the services that can be accessed over the Internet by individuals or by departments.

Troubleshooting additional problems

If you experience additional access problems behind a firewall, consider the following issues:

- Verify that you are using the correct IP address and subnet mask.

- Check your default gateway and verify that the computer can communicate with systems on the same subnet.

- Verify DNS resolution.

- After you have confirmed IP information and DNS resolution, try to use multiple protocols on the Internet. Check e-mail, Web, Telnet and FTP services to determine which services are available and which are not.

- The corporate firewall may not allow home-based account access to the corporate e-mail server. For example, suppose that a user can access his or her e-mail account from work but cannot access this same e-mail account from home. If you can confirm the user's basic connectivity (in other words, that the user can communicate on the Internet), you may suspect that the corporate firewall is blocking the e-mail connection. The only resolution is for the employee to use a separate e-mail account and check e-mail from work. Ask the IT department to reconfigure the firewall to allow outside connections to the remote employee.

- Often, a firewall can cause a bottleneck. For example, suppose that delivery time has increased for messages that are sent to people outside work. In this case, the company's firewall is serving as a bottleneck, slowing e-mail delivery to outside addresses.

Firewall Topologies

Most enterprise security professionals consider the firewall to be the "choke point" through which all traffic must pass. Enterprise networks use various models to implement that choke point, depending on their needs and available resources. Each model is designed to create a matrix of filters and points that can process and secure information. The four common firewall implementations are:

- **Packet filter** — the most simple and, consequently, the most popular of the common topologies.

- **Dual-homed bastion host** — a firewall with two NICs. Requires all traffic to pass through a **bastion host**.

- **Triple-homed bastion host** — a firewall with three NICs. Requires all traffic to pass through a bastion host

- **Screened subnet (back-to-back firewalls)** — uses an additional packet-filtering router to achieve another level of security

Packet filter topology

A packet filter firewall topology inspects only Internet addresses and port numbers after analyzing network header fields. Packet filtering offers the following advantages:

- This strategy can filter much unwanted traffic.

- It is inexpensive, but still provides a significant degree of protection.

Figure 5-5 shows a diagram of a packet-filtering router.

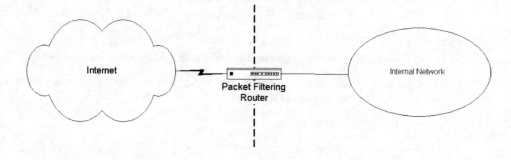

Figure 5-5: Packet-filtering configuration

Packet filtering has the following potential drawbacks:

- The degree of safety it offers depends greatly on the expertise of the people who implement the filters.

- The security of your entire network depends primarily on a single device; if a hacker defeats the packet filter, your network will no longer have a firewall in place.

- A packet filter cannot implement effective logging and alarms.

Dual-homed bastion host

Another commonly used firewall topology is the dual-homed bastion host. A dual-homed bastion host is a firewall with two NICs. The first NIC faces the public network, and the second NIC faces the private network. Benefits of a dual-homed bastion host are:

- Firewall software processes all requests and filters all traffic.

- It is inexpensive to implement.

This type of firewall has two drawbacks:

- Only a single system separates your network from the public network.

- You are not able to create a DMZ.

Figure 5-6 illustrates a dual-homed bastion host.

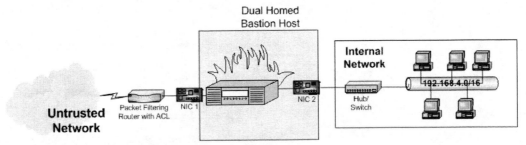

Figure 5-6: Dual-homed bastion host

Triple-homed bastion host

The triple-homed bastion host, also called a three-homed firewall, is also quite popular. The triple-homed bastion host often separates the Internet, the internal network and the DMZ.

The main advantage of a triple-homed bastion host is that Internet traffic avoids the company's internal network, which keeps the internal computers safe from the public.

Figure 5-7 illustrates a three-homed firewall.

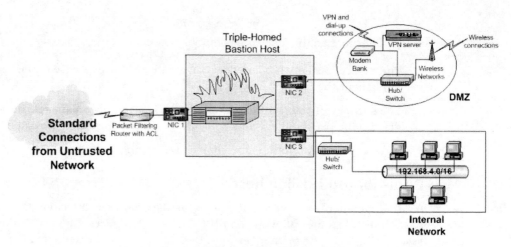

Figure 5-7: Triple-homed bastion host

Screened subnet (back-to-back firewalls)

NOTE:
The screened
subnet is a common
configuration. It is
often seen on sites
supporting
e-commerce.

Another commonly used firewall topology is the screened subnet, also called back-to-back firewalls. It is the most secure of the four general implementations, mainly because all publicly accessible devices, including modem pools and other resources, are placed in a secure isolated network. In this configuration, the DMZ functions as a secure isolated network positioned between the Internet and the internal network (Figure 5-8).

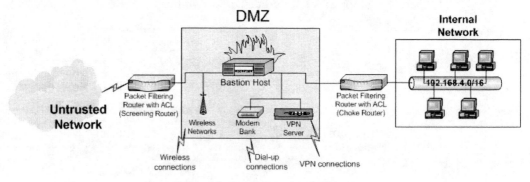

Figure 5-8: Screened-subnet firewall

This configuration uses external and internal routers. Each is configured so that its traffic flows only to or from the bastion host. This arrangement prevents any traffic from directly traversing the subnetwork, or DMZ. The external router uses standard filtering to restrict external access to the bastion host, and rejects any traffic that does not come from the bastion host.

Security Zones

OBJECTIVE
3.5.6: Security zones

Security zones refer to specially designated groupings of services and computers. Security zones can be created by a firewall, a router or a switch. In this section, you will learn about four types of security zones:

*   Demilitarized zone (DMZ)
*   Intranets
*   Extranets
*   Virtual LANs (VLANs)

Demilitarized zone (DMZ)

NOTE:
Another name for a demilitarized zone is a demarcation zone.

A DMZ is a mini-network that resides between a company's internal network and the external network (for example, the Internet). The DMZ is not part of the company's internal network, nor is it fully part of the untrusted network.

The DMZ can be created by using a firewall with three NICs:

- One NIC connects to the trusted network.
- One acts as the gateway to the DMZ.
- One is addressable by the Internet.

A DMZ can also be created by using two routers and a firewall. One router, called a screening router, receives traffic from the Internet. The firewall then filters traffic. A second router, often called the choke router, filters traffic before it passes to the trusted network.

A DMZ is used as an additional buffer to further separate the public network from your internal private network. Many systems administrators place Web, DNS and e-mail servers in a DMZ for convenience. The benefit of this practice is that the firewall provides some protection but allows traffic to enter the network. However, a DMZ is not a completely secure zone; any server in a DMZ is less protected than it would be if it resided in the internal network. DMZs are an integral component of triple-homed bastion hosts and screened subnets, both of which will be presented later in this lesson.

Intranet

As you learned earlier, an intranet is a security zone available only to authorized organization employees. It is a private network; only company employees can have access to it. An intranet is, in many ways, a miniature private version of the Internet. It is a network that uses the same protocols as the Internet (HTTP, NNTP, FTP and so forth). However, it is completely isolated from Internet traffic. Intranets are often essential networks that allow companies to:

- Enable employees to share information with one another.
- Bridge older equipment (for example, mainframes and legacy call centers) to newer technologies (for example, database-driven Web sites and VoIP connectivity).
- Obtain human resources information.
- Connect to remote systems by means of a secure gateway.

Extranet

An extranet is a private network that allows selected access to outsiders only after they provide authentication information. These outsiders might be a specific group of users from a partner company, or a group of individuals from various locations who are allowed access to certain resources for a specific business purpose.

Network and security professionals often limit extranet access according to the following parameters:

- **User name and password (or other authentication credentials)** — Access is given only after authenticating with a particular host (for example, a firewall or Web server).
- **Time** — The given authentication information will be valid only for a specific time.

- **Specific locations** — In some cases, extranet administrators will allow access only from specific IP addresses or host names.

Extranet connections should be encrypted to avoid man-in-the-middle attacks.

Virtual LAN (VLAN)

You were briefly introduced to VLANs earlier in the course. A virtual local area network (VLAN) is a logical grouping of hosts, made possible by a network switch and most newer routers. Generally, a VLAN is not implemented by a firewall. In a VLAN, a group of hosts can be created regardless of where they are physically connected to a LAN. Members of this group will then compete with one another for network access, regardless of their physical locations.

VLANs are useful in the following ways:

- **Security** — If you place hosts that receive or transmit sensitive traffic inside a VLAN, malicious users will have more difficulty sniffing network traffic. Because a VLAN can help you create a group of computers, you can also use a VLAN to apply an access policy that, for example, prohibits all traffic other than HTTP, POP3 and SMTP from entering or leaving that group.

- **Performance** — A VLAN can help reduce traffic in parts of your network. For example, if several systems are causing too much traffic for a particular segment, a VLAN can be created to isolate these systems. A VLAN can also be used to balance network load between segments.

- **Ease of administration** — The ability to separate a logical grouping of systems from their physical location makes it possible to keep a user's workstation in the same physical location, but have the workstation participate in a new group of workstations pertinent to the user's tasks. In short, a user can belong to a new department, but remain in the same physical location.

A VLAN is not a complete security solution. It supplements firewalls and other measures.

OBJECTIVE
3.5.5: VPNs and remote access

extranet
A network that connects enterprise intranets to the global Internet. Designed to provide access to selected external users.

NOTE:
The availability of secure, encrypted communication is typically the key factor in determining whether to implement a VPN.

tunneling protocol
A protocol that encapsulates data packets into another packet.

Virtual Private Network (VPN)

A virtual private network (VPN) is a configuration that allows secure communication across long distances, usually for a company **extranet**. It can extend the corporate LAN to the Internet, providing secure worldwide connectivity. In a VPN, the Internet is often the corporate network backbone, thereby eliminating the dichotomy of inside network and outside network, as well as the need to maintain many networks. VPNs are appropriate for any organization requiring secure external access to internal resources. For example, a VPN is appropriate for companies whose facilities are spread over long distances but need to communicate as if they were located together. VPNs are also important because they allow companies to embed non-Internet protocols within TCP/IP.

VPNs and tunneling

All VPNs are **tunneling protocols** in the sense that their data packets or payloads are encapsulated or tunneled into the network packets. Encryption occurs at the source and decryption occurs at the destination. For example, suppose that you administer the network of a company with two offices, one in Washington, D.C., and the other in Sydney, Australia. If your company network runs IPX/SPX, and you need to create a connection between offices using the Internet, you can use a VPN and "tunnel," or encapsulate, IPX/SPX within TCP/IP. You can encapsulate other protocols, as well.

Security fundamentals (for example, authentication, message integrity and encryption) are very important to VPN implementation. Without such authentication procedures, a hacker can impersonate anyone and then gain access to the network. Message integrity is required because the packets can be altered as they travel through the public network. Without encryption, the information may become truly public.

VPN protocols and standards

Following are descriptions of the protocols that a VPN is most likely to use.

Point-to-Point Tunneling Protocol (PPTP)

Point-to-Point Tunneling Protocol (PPTP) is a popular VPN tunneling protocol. PPTP is designed to establish a private channel between communicating systems (usually a client and a server computer) on a public network such as the Internet. The protocol encapsulates data and information/control packets using the Internet Generic Record Encapsulation protocol version 2 (GREv2). PPTP works only on IP.

Point-to-Point Tunneling Protocol (PPTP)
A protocol that allows users and corporations to securely extend their networks over the Internet using remote access

Layer 2 Tunneling Protocol (L2TP)

Layer 2 Tunneling Protocol (L2TP) is an Internet Engineering Task Force (IETF) standard tunneling protocol. It is primarily used to support VPNs over the Internet for non-TCP/IP protocols. For instance, both Apple networks and Novell networks can create VPNs over the network using L2TP. It is a combination of PPTP and Cisco's Layer 2 Forwarding (L2F) protocol. The primary advantage of L2TP is that it is supported by more vendors than PPTP.

IP Security (IPsec)

IP Security (IPsec)
An authentication and encryption standard that provides security over the Internet. It functions at Layer 3 of the OSI/RM and can secure all packets transmitted over the network.

IP Security (IPsec) is another IETF standard that provides packet-level encryption, authentication and integrity for VPNs. IPsec is not a protocol; rather, it is a standard. IPsec is more flexible than L2TP and PPTP because you can specify different authentication methods. Using IPsec, you can:

- Use digital certificates to authenticate the sender of data.

- Use asymmetric-key (public-key) encryption to encrypt the data. This encryption is accomplished by means of the Internet Security Association Key Management Protocol (ISAKMP), which allows the receiving device to obtain a public key and authenticate the sending device using a digital certificate.

Remote access server (RAS)

Do not confuse VPNs with another remote protocol technology known as remote access server (RAS). With RAS, users employ dial-up modems from their laptop or home computer to connect and log on to a RAS. The RAS host is usually located on a company network; after the user logs on to the remote access server, he or she gains access to the company network, e-mail and Internet.

callback
A process in which a remote access server returns a call to a remote client that has logged on in order to authenticate that client.

The main difference between a VPN and RAS is that with RAS, users connect to the private network using traditional dial-up modems instead of connecting over the Internet. RAS offers security through a **callback** feature. Callback requires a user to log on to a RAS. After logging on, the user is disconnected. The RAS calls the user back to ensure the call was made from an authorized computer.

Security Audit

An audit is a review of the state of the network. Ideally, an audit should be conducted by a party who is not responsible for maintaining the network on a daily basis; a disinterested party might be more likely to discover overlooked security problems. Also, if the systems administrator is responsible for an audit, he or she may be more interested in covering up errors or ignoring them rather than fixing them. The auditor should report findings not only to the systems administrator but also to upper management so that they can ensure that problems will be resolved.

During the auditing process, an auditor should perform the following tasks:

- Conduct a "status quo" analysis, in which the auditor identifies common patterns for the network being audited.

- Conduct a risk analysis, which examines potential network problems.

- Make recommendations about the results of the audit.

As a novice networking professional, you will probably not be assigned to conduct an audit. However, you should know about audits and why they are necessary.

Uninterruptible Power Supply (UPS)

OBJECTIVE
3.5.8: Uninterruptible
power supply (UPS)

**uninterruptible
power supply (UPS)**
A power supply that
uses a battery to
maintain power
during a power
outage.

An **uninterruptible power supply (UPS)** is a device that allows your computer to keep running for at least a short time when the primary power source is lost. As such, a UPS provides a measure of security by protecting data and networks in the event of a power outage. It also provides protection from power surges.

With a UPS, AC line voltage feeds into a charger that keeps the battery backup charged at all times. The computer is powered from the battery, not from the AC line, so there is no need to switch over if power is lost. Generally, if a power outage occurs, the UPS will keep the computer running long enough for you to save data and shut down the computer properly. If power is out for an extended length of time, the UPS can initiate a system shutdown before battery power is lost, thereby eliminating (or at least minimizing) data loss. A UPS will also smooth power irregularities and provide clean, stable power. Figure 5-9 illustrates a UPS.

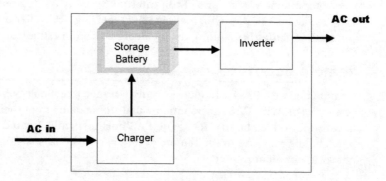

Figure 5-9: Uninterruptible power supply (UPS)

One major concern when selecting a UPS is its power rating in watts. Be sure that the UPS provides enough power to support the devices that you plan to connect. Connecting more than one computer to a UPS is usually not recommended except on UPS systems designed for that purpose. Connecting multiple systems increases the UPS power requirement. Also, only one of the systems will be able to monitor the UPS status signals.

Choosing systems for UPS

You must decide which computers to protect with UPS systems. Protecting all computers may not always be practical. However, you should protect mission-critical systems, including network servers and any other systems that provide data or services to a network. If a computer system must be kept running or if you must guarantee that a computer will be shut down correctly if power is lost, you should provide UPS support for that computer.

Configuring UPS

You can configure a UPS to specify the number of minutes it will provide power to the system. However, be careful not to specify to shut down a system in a time frame longer than the UPS itself can remain operational. For example, if you specify a system shutdown 45 minutes after a power loss, but the UPS can only remain operational for 30 minutes, you may lose data and services.

A UPS can also be configured to shut down entire systems automatically, shut down only certain components automatically (for example, monitors) or place components into minimal power-use mode until you manually shut down the system.

Personal Privacy and the Internet

Most Internet users assume that their use of the Internet is implicitly private and anonymous. However, all browsers collect information about the users that enter search queries, such as their IP addresses, information about the their browser or computer systems, and so forth. Therefore, it is difficult to keep your personal information confidential.

Furthermore, unscrupulous individuals use the Internet to perpetrate acts of fraud. Internet scammers employ various techniques to try to elicit your personal information, which they can use to commit fraud or identity theft to benefit financially, and some of these techniques can be difficult to detect.

Internet privacy

Internet privacy
The ability to control what information you reveal about yourself over the Internet, and to whom (or what) you reveal it.

anonymizing tools
Internet components and application features that make the user's Internet activity untraceable.

Internet privacy refers to the ability to control what information you reveal about yourself over the Internet and to whom (or what) you reveal it. In an effort to keep personal information private, or to prevent their Internet activities from being traced, users can enable **anonymizing tools** to engage in anonymous Web browsing.

Anonymizing tools serve to make a person's activity on the Internet untraceable. Such tools include:

- **Browser privacy mode features** — enable anonymous Web browsing, in which no cache or history of your browsing sessions are kept.

- **Proxy servers** — provide a degree of anonymity because only the information on the server is visible to outsiders.

- **VPN servers** — provide a degree of anonymity because only the information on the server is visible to outsiders.

- **Anonymizer Web sites** — serve as proxy sites in that the site will retrieve a Web page for you, but the site you visit will only receive information about the proxy site, not you.

These tools essentially prevent Web sites (browsed by the user) from obtaining personally identifiable information.

The advantages to using anonymizers are that users can:

- Minimize the risk of retribution for conducting research or speaking out about controversial topics.

- Protect search histories from observation.

- Prevent identity theft.

However, anonymizers can also be used to avoid the consequences of engaging in illicit online behavior.

Browser privacy mode

NOTE:
Privacy mode is sometimes referred to as "porn mode" because it can be used to hide a person's illicit browsing history.

When you browse the Web, browsers store information about the sites you visit in history, and they keep images, videos and text within cache. Some current Web browsers now include a feature called privacy mode, in which no cache or history of your browsing sessions are kept. This allows you to browse the Internet without storing data that could be retrieved at a later date, and effectively hides your browsing habits from others.

You can choose to enable privacy mode as soon as you open your browser so that your entire browsing session remains anonymous. This setting is useful on public computers. You can also enable privacy mode at any time during a browsing session. In this case, a new browsing window will appear in which to conduct anonymous browsing. Your existing window (and all open tabs) will be disabled until you close the private browsing window. Once you close the private window, your original window will reopen with your original session(s) intact.

The following popular Web browsers include the privacy mode feature:

- **Mozilla Firefox** — The privacy mode feature is available in Firefox 3.1; it is not available in previous versions of Firefox. However, if you run a previous version of Firefox, you can download the Firefox add-on Stealther 1.0 to achieve similar results.

- **Microsoft Internet Explorer** — The privacy mode feature is called InPrivate and is available in Internet Explorer 8; it is not available in previous versions of IE. InPrivate is composed of three subfeatures:

  o InPrivate Browsing allows you to enable privacy mode.

  o InPrivate Blocking informs you about Web sites that can track your browsing history and lets you block such activity.

  o InPrivate Subscriptions allows you to choose which Web sites to subscribe to or block.

- **Google Chrome** — The privacy mode feature is called Incognito. You can enable or disable Incognito on each open tab in the browser. Therefore, you can use some tabs to surf publicly, and others to surf Incognito. Because the tabs are separate instances of the browser, they do not interfere with one another.

- **Apple Safari** — The privacy mode feature is called Private Browsing. Private Browsing was introduced in Safari 2.0, the first operating system to support privacy mode.

You can also use Web sites that provide anonymizer services to thwart tracebacks, hide your online identity and bypass proxy servers. There are several Web sites that provide anonymizer services:

- Anonymizer (*www.anonymizer.com*)

- Anonymize.NET (*http://anonymize.net/*)

- Merlet (*www.merletn.org/uk/anonymizer*)

- Privacy Center (*www.ultimate-anonymity.com*)

- Change IP Country (*http://anonymizer.nntime.com/*)

Ethics of anonymous browsing

Because anonymous browsing hides your identity, you can use it to minimize risk if you engage in online behavior that may be potentially dangerous. For example, you can use anonymous browsing in certain countries with repressive regimes to expose human rights abuses, or communicate about sensitive or prohibited subjects without fear of reprisal. On the other hand, you can use it for something as innocuous as keeping a surprise event or gift a secret.

However, people can also engage in anonymous browsing for unethical or illegal purposes. For example, people who engage in illegal activities such as online fraud or child pornography could use it to prevent law enforcement agencies from tracing their online activities. Employees or students could use it to surf inappropriate Web sites while at work or school, and hide their activities from employers and teachers. Essentially, anonymous browsing allows a person to browse the Web without leaving behind any incriminating evidence.

Without the fear of reprisal, people may be more apt to engage in unethical or illegal online activity, secure in the knowledge that they can keep their activities anonymous and minimize the risk of being caught.

Internet fraud

Internet fraud
Scam or other deceptive practices committed via the Internet, usually for the purpose of monetary gain or identity theft.

Internet fraud refers to scams that are conducted via Internet services. With the explosive growth of the Internet and e-commerce, online scammers try to present fraudulent schemes that appear as legitimate services and product offerings that one would expect to see on legitimate e-commerce Web sites. You can avoid becoming the victim of Internet fraud (and other types of fraud) by adhering to this old adage: "If it seems too good to be true, it probably is."

Internet fraud mirrors other types of fraud in which criminals engage over the phone or through the mail. A healthy dose of skepticism when considering offers will help prevent most people from becoming victims of Internet fraud.

There are many types of Internet fraud. Some of the more prevalent include the following:

- **Auction and retail scams** — These scams offer popular products that are likely to attract many consumers. The consumer is asked to send money for a product, but receives nothing or an inferior product in return. In many cases, the inferior product is a stolen item, a counterfeit item or a reworked item.

- **Business opportunity scams** — These scams promise consumers that they can make thousands of dollars a month by going into business for themselves in a "work-at-home" venture. The consumer is asked to send money for a "startup kit" containing the materials and information necessary to get their home-based business up and running. However, they usually receive nothing or information that is, for all intents and purposes, worthless.

- **Investment scams** — These scams occur when a cyber-criminal tries to manipulate securities markets for their own gain. For example, the criminal tries to pass false information about a thinly traded stock to cause a dramatic increase in the price of the stock. Then they immediately sell their own holdings of the stock to gain a substantial profit before the stock price falls back to its usual low level. Other buyers of the stock become victims of the scheme when the price falls.

- **Credit card scams** — These scams occur when a cyber-criminal obtains the credit card number of another person and uses the number to place orders for goods or services online.

- **Purchase scams** — These scams occur when a buyer (many times from another country) will spam merchants and request that they send merchandise to their location. The spammer will provide credit card information to which the merchant can charge for the cost of the goods. After several weeks or months, the merchant will receive a chargeback from the credit card processor and lose all the funds. Well-known examples of this type of fraud are reshipping scams in which merchants are tricked into shipping goods to countries with weak legal systems. The goods are paid for with stolen or fake credit cards, and the original shipper gets stuck with the bill.

- **Money transfer scams** — These scams occur when a person receives an offer to work with a foreign company to help the company transfer money through the person because it is too cumbersome (supposedly) to do it through other channels. The cyber-criminals will then send fake checks or money orders to the victim, hoping to receive real monies from the victim in return.

- **Dating scams** — These scams occur when the cyber-criminal develops an online relationship with a victim, eventually persuading the victim to send money.

For more information about Internet fraud, and to view examples and case studies of Internet fraud, visit the following sites:

- Wikipedia's article "Internet Fraud" at *http://en.wikipedia.org/wiki/Internet_fraud/*

- The United States Department of Justice's article "Internet and Telemarketing Fraud" at *www.usdoj.gov/criminal/fraud/internet/*

- ScamBusters.org's articles "Internet Fraud" at *www.scambusters.org/PWwebsites.html* and *www.scambusters.org/PWwebsites2.html*

For information about how to avoid Internet fraud, visit the following sites:

- The Federal Bureau of Investigation's Internet Fraud page at *www.fbi.gov/majcases/fraud/internetschemes.htm*

- The U.S. Securities and Exchange Commission's article "Internet Fraud: How to Avoid Internet Investment Scams" at *www.sec.gov/investor/pubs/cyberfraud.htm*

- The National Consumers League's article "Internet Fraud Tips" at *www.fraud.org/tips/internet/*

Identity theft

identity theft
Fraud committed in
your name by
someone else who
has illicitly gained
access to your
personal
information.

Identity theft occurs when someone uses your personal information to commit fraud in your name without your knowledge. The perpetrator typically uses your name, Social Security number, credit card number or other financial account information to commit fraud. By the time you become aware that you are the victim of identity theft, your credit may be overextended, you may receive calls from debt collectors or, in rare cases, you may even be arrested for a crime you did not commit.

If you find out that you are the victim of identity theft, you should immediately file a complaint with the Federal Trade Commission (*www.ftccomplaintassistant.gov*), file a police report, place a fraud alert on your credit reports, and close accounts that you know you did not open.

Identity thieves use a variety of methods to obtain personal information about you, including the following:

- **Dumpster diving** — They search your trash looking for bills or statements containing financial information.

- **Skimming** — They steal credit card numbers while under the guise of processing your card for payment.

- **Phishing** — They send e-mails or make telephone calls in an effort to make you reveal personal information.

- **Address changing** — They complete a change of address form to divert your bills and statements to their location.

- **Stealing** — They steal mail, wallets, purses and so forth to obtain information.

Following are steps you can take to prevent identity theft:

- Check your monthly statements and periodically review your credit report to ensure that nothing is amiss.

- Refrain from divulging personal information to someone unless he or she is known and trusted.

- Refrain from entering personal information into a Web form that is not protected with SSL (denoted by "https" in the URL).

- Keep your Social Security card in a secure location, such as a safe or safety deposit box. Do not carry it with you.

- Shred bills, statements and documents that contain your personal information.

Phishing

OBJECTIVE
3.11.1: Phishing and
pharming

OBJECTIVE
3.5.2: Social
engineering attacks

Phishing is a form of social engineering that attempts to gather personal and financial information from unsuspecting victims. Typically, phishers send users legitimate-looking e-mail that appears to come from a well-known and trustworthy Web site. The e-mail message prompts recipients to visit a fake Web site that looks identical to the legitimate Web site. The users are then asked to update personal information, such as passwords, or credit card, Social Security or bank account numbers, which the legitimate organization already has. The phisher can then use the information entered into the fake Web site for malicious purposes.

Pharming

Pharming is the act of installing malicious code on personal computers or servers that redirects Internet traffic from a legitimate Web site to an identical-looking bogus Web site. Pharmers can then prompt users for their user names and passwords in an attempt to acquire their personal information in order to access their bank accounts, and commit identity theft or other kinds of fraud in the users' names. Unlike phishers, who approach their targets one by one, pharmers can victimize a large number of computer users simultaneously because no conscious action is required on the part of the users.

Anti-phishing software

Phishing scams that lead to identity theft are a serious and growing problem. You can help avoid phishing scams by installing anti-phishing software. An anti-phishing program is designed to identify phishing content contained in Web sites and e-mail messages. It often takes the form of a toolbar that is integrated with your Web browser and e-mail client. You can use the information provided by the toolbar to detect fake Web sites that are masquerading as legitimate sites. Many anti-phishing programs maintain a database in which they keep a list of fake Web sites.

One of the most popular and effective anti-phishing devices is the Netcraft Toolbar, shown in Figure 5-10.

Figure 5-10: Netcraft Toolbar

When you install the Netcraft Toolbar, you become a member of the Toolbar community. Members of the community are able to report phishing Web sites that they encounter, and Netcraft adds the culprits to a list. When other members of the community attempt to access any of those sites, they will be prevented from doing so.

The Netcraft Toolbar provides other services as well, such as:

- Displaying each site's hosting location, including its country of origin.

- Flagging suspicious URLs containing characters that have no valid purpose.

- Ensuring that browser navigation controls display in all windows so that pop-up windows cannot hide the controls.

The Netcraft Toolbar is available for both Microsoft Internet Explorer and Mozilla Firefox. To learn more about the Netcraft Toolbar, visit *http://toolbar.netcraft.com*.

Other examples of anti-phishing software include the following:

- PhishTrap (*www.phishtrap.com*)

- Avira Premium Security Suite (*www.avira.com*)

- Phishtank (*www.phishtank.com*)

- Gralicwrap (*www.gralicwrap.com*)

- Kaspersky Internet Security (*www.kaspersky.com*)

- ESET Smart Security (*www.eset.com*)

In the following lab, you will use the Netcraft Toolbar to block a phishing site. Suppose you receive an e-mail message from what appears to be your credit card company. You are prompted to click a link called Billing Center, and when you do, you are routed to a Web page that asks for your credit card number, personal identification number (PIN),

Social Security number and bank account number. How can you ensure that the Web page is legitimate and avoid becoming the victim of a phisher's scheme to commit identity theft?

OBJECTIVE
3.11.1: Phishing and
pharming

Lab 5-2: Using the Netcraft Toolbar

OBJECTIVE
3.5.2: Social
engineering attacks

In this lab, you will use the Netcraft Toolbar to block a phishing site.

1. Start **Firefox**. Go to ***http://toolbar.netcraft.com*** to display the Netcraft Toolbar home page.

2. Click the **Download Netcraft Toolbar** button. In the Netcraft Anti-Phishing Toolbar box, click the **Firefox** icon. In the Software Installation dialog box that appears, click **Install Now** to begin the installation process.

NOTE:
If you were
downloading the
Netcraft Toolbar into
Internet Explorer,
you would click the
Internet Explorer 6+
icon at Step 2.

3. In the Add-Ons dialog box that appears, you will be prompted to restart Firefox. Click the **Restart Firefox** button. When Firefox redisplays, you will see the Netcraft Toolbar at the top of your screen.

4. **Firefox:** Now you will practice blocking a phishing attack. Go to ***http://toolbar.netcraft.com/phish_mail*** to display the Practice Blocking A Phishing Site page, as shown in Figure 5-11.

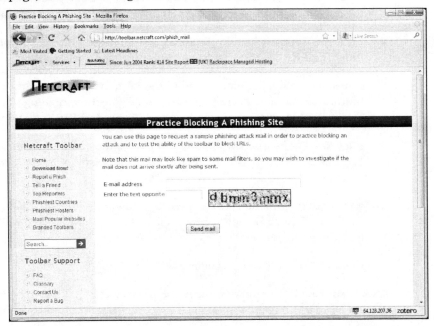

Figure 5-11: Practice Blocking A Phishing Site page

NOTE:
Make sure you enter
a live e-mail address
at Step 5.

5. Enter your live e-mail address and the specified CAPTCHA text in the appropriate fields, then click the **Send Mail** button.

Note: You cannot use your class.com e-mail address for this step. Use your e-mail address from Gmail, for example, so you can retrieve the message from Netcraft.

6. Start your e-mail client and open the e-mail from Netcraft Toolbar. Your phishing e-mail message should resemble Figure 5-12.

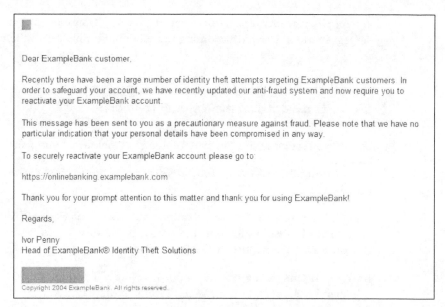

Dear ExampleBank customer,

Recently there have been a large number of identity theft attempts targeting ExampleBank customers. In order to safeguard your account, we have recently updated our anti-fraud system and now require you to reactivate your ExampleBank account.

This message has been sent to you as a precautionary measure against fraud. Please note that we have no particular indication that your personal details have been compromised in any way.

To securely reactivate your ExampleBank account please go to:

https://onlinebanking.examplebank.com

Thank you for your prompt attention to this matter and thank you for using ExampleBank!

Regards,

Ivor Penny
Head of ExampleBank® Identity Theft Solutions

Copyright 2004 ExampleBank. All rights reserved.

Figure 5-12: Phishing e-mail from Netcraft Toolbar

7. Click the ***https://onlinebanking.examplebank.com*** link in the message. A Phishing Site Detected dialog box will appear, informing you that the page you are trying to visit has been blocked by the Netcraft Toolbar. Click **Yes** to visit the site. Notice that the page prompts you to provide credit card account and PIN information.

8. Click the **Netcraft** logo in the Netcraft Toolbar, then select **Report | Report A Phishing Site**. The Report Suspicious URL page will appear.

9. Enter the requested information at the bottom of the form, then click the **Report URL** button. This action submits the URL as a possible phishing site to the Netcraft Toolbar community, then displays the Thank You For Your Report page.

   Note: The Thank You For Your Report page indicates that the URL is already blocked because URLs from fictional, as well as real, phishing attack e-mails are blocked automatically.

10. Redisplay the phishing e-mail message and click the URL again. In the Phishing Site Detected dialog box that appears, click **No**. A message page will appear informing you that the phishing site was blocked by Netcraft Toolbar.

11. Close all open tabs and windows.

This lab demonstrated how you can use the Netcraft Toolbar to be forewarned and submit a report about possible phishing URLs. Did you find this anti-phishing device useful?

Personal Protection and the Internet

Maintaining a healthy balance between entertainment media and other activities in their children's lives has always been a challenge for parents. Because Internet use is so prevalent, preventing children and teenagers from engaging in inappropriate online behavior makes this challenge even more difficult. Many adults find themselves facing similar challenges when using the Internet for entertainment and social networking purposes.

This section will focus on some major Internet-based challenges that Internet users face:

- Online stalking
- Cyberbullying
- Internet addiction

Online stalking

Online stalking occurs when a person ("stalker") stealthily pursues, harasses and/or preys upon another person using online venues such as e-mail, chat rooms and social networking sites. The stalker often (but not necessarily) meets the victim in an online venue, and often (but not always) gains his or her trust before perpetrating harassment activities.

Many online stalkers eventually spy on, monopolize, harass or threaten their victims through e-mail, IM, chat rooms and so forth, and they generally continue to e-mail or IM their victims even after they are asked to stop. In some cases, online stalkers have been known to commit crimes ranging from assault to far worse.

Some online stalkers attempt to cover their inadequacy or incompetence by bullying people they perceive as competent and popular in an attempt to control and subjugate them. Others establish relationships online where they feel more confident, then feel slighted or angry when a relationship is not reciprocated or perceived in the same way by the other person. Still others use the anonymity of the Internet to establish false identities strictly for the purpose of gaining a person's trust in order to eventually victimize him or her. Clearly, caution is always advised when dealing with people on the Internet that you do not know in person.

To prevent yourself from becoming a victim of online stalking or to stop an online stalker, practice the following techniques:

- **Use blind carbon copy (BCC) on mass e-mail messages** — Use BCC to protect your privacy and that of the people on your mailing list. By using BCC, you can send an e-mail message to many, even hundreds of people at once, and only the sender's name/address (you) and the recipient's name/address will be visible to each individual recipient. If your message is intercepted by an online stalker (or if one of your recipients happens to be an online stalker), then the stalker will not see the rest of the names/addresses on your list and will be unable to contact your friends.

- **Learn to recognize online stalkers, and then avoid them** — If you join a chat room and befriend a person who, over time, demands more of your time and acts hurt or jealous when you are not available, for example, you may have identified a stalker. Cease all communication with such people immediately.

- **If a stalker continues to send you e-mails or IMs, ignore them** — If you answer a stalker at all, even to ask him or her to stop, then the stalker knows that you are engaging with him or her and will persist. For example, if you receive an IM from a stalker, simply drag the IM window off your Desktop so it is no longer visible. The stalker may still send you IMs, but you cannot see them and thus do not respond, and eventually (hopefully) the stalker may become get bored and move on.

- **Be wary of people you meet online** — Although valuable friendships can certainly begin in online venues, the reality is that you do not know the actual identity of any person you meet online. A person may or may not be who he or she claims to be. Use caution when communicating with any friends or acquaintances online. Do not provide personal information to others in online venues, especially if you know your communication is not private. And it is rarely advisable to arrange an in-person meeting with someone you have met online; if you do this, be sure to advise a trusted person (a parent, relative or good friend) of the details of your arranged meeting — or better yet, bring someone along.

- **Report activities that make you feel uncomfortable, harassed or threatened** — If you find yourself in a situation where you are being stalked online, report it immediately. Tell trusted persons such as parents, guardians, relatives, teachers or good friends. Keep a written record of all incidents of harassment, including copies of e-mails or other exchanges. If you feel threatened, contact the police.

Cyberbullying

cyberbullying
Willful harm inflicted on others through the use of information and communication technologies.

OBJECTIVE
3.11.2: Avoiding anti-social activity

We are all familiar with the schoolyard bully who took lunch money, started fights or taunted us or others for no apparent reason. The Internet has spawned a new kind of tormenter: the cyberbully. **Cyberbullying** refers to the deliberate behavior of an individual or group to cause harm to others, through the use of computers or other electronic devices.

The Internet enables users to harass others in relative anonymity. Cyberbullies are often teenagers who are consumed by anger, fear or frustration, and they choose to victimize someone to torment them or boost their own egos. Some cyberbullies simply are bored and have too much time at their disposal, and they victimize others for fun or to elicit reactions. However, cyberbullies are not limited to teenagers; many adults use the anonymous venue of the Internet to take out their frustrations on others by behaving in ways that they would not behave in face-to-face exchanges. In addition, teens are not the only ones who may suffer from cyberbullying; any individual can fall victim to a cyberbully.

Cyberbullies often send hurtful e-mail messages to victims, or to others about a victim, that insult the victim's physical appearance, friends, sexuality, sense of fashion and so forth. Cyberbullies may also create a Web site in which the victim is targeted by insults and false innuendos.

Popular online applications such as MySpace (*www.myspace.com*), Facebook (*www.facebook.com*) and Twitter (*http://twitter.com*) offer users an outlet to share random thoughts and post photos that could potentially be seen by millions of people. This kind of exposure can subject a person to cyberbullying. According to CyberBullying.us, 33 percent of all youths have been victimized by a cyberbully. In extreme cases, teens have killed each other or committed suicide after being victimized by cyberbullying.

Preventing cyberbullying

In many school districts in the United States, schools have attempted to get involved by punishing cyberbullies for actions that have taken place off-campus. But schools have to be very careful that they do not exceed their authority or violate the students' rights to free speech. Some schools have been sued for attempting to prevent or punish cyberbullying. It is very important that parents participate in trying to stop or prevent cyberbullying because most cyberbullying activities are perpetrated from home.

Steps that can be taken to prevent or stop cyberbullying include the following:

- Schools can educate students about cyber-ethics and the consequences of illicit online activities.

- Parents can enforce consequences if their teens engage in cyberbullying, such as restricting or removing their Internet or IM accounts or activities.

- Schools and parents can teach teens about ways that they may become unintentional cyberbullies (e.g., inadvertently sending a message to the wrong recipient) and ways to prevent this.

- Schools and parents can teach teens to be accountable for their actions and not allow cyberbullying (or any kind of bullying) to occur.

- Schools and parents can teach teens to watch for cyberbullying activities among their peers, refuse to participate in them and discourage others from participating.

The following Web sites are among the many that provide resources for victims of cyberbullying and their parents:

- BullyingUK (*www.bullying.co.uk*)

- Cyberbullying.us (*www.cyberbullying.us*)

- Bully Beware Productions (*www.bullybeware.com*)

- WiredKids, Inc. (*www.stopcyberbullying.org*)

Internet addiction

OBJECTIVE
3.11.3: Internet
addiction

The Internet is an important educational tool, and it provides many resources for information and outlets for entertainment. Unfortunately, many users spend so much time involved with online games, social networking, blogging, instant messaging and so forth that they are missing out on real-world experiences. Internet addiction among individuals of all ages and types is a growing concern.

For many people, the Internet is an escape from troubled or painful situations. Children and teens who have poor social or coping skills are particularly at risk for developing inappropriate or excessive online habits. People of all ages may use the Internet to combat boredom at first, then find themselves hooked on activities that they have trouble controlling their desire for. Many adults fall victim to Internet addictions involving online gaming, shopping, auctions, gambling and pornography.

People who are addicted to the Internet may:

- Spend time online at the expense of sleep and relationships with friends and family.

- Look for attention and companionship from strangers they meet in online chat rooms.

- Send instant messages to friends rather than develop face-to-face relationships, which can impact how they learn to interact with their peers.

- Avoid real-world problems and spend their time in the imaginary world of an online game where they can be or experience things they cannot in real life.

Preventing Internet addiction

People can use the Internet to help with school or work projects and assignments, to communicate with peers and family online, and to relax. But if a child, teen or adult is using the Internet excessively to the exclusion of other worthwhile activities, there are steps that parents, loved ones, friends or users themselves can take to prevent or end Internet addiction:

- **Demonstrate a caring attitude** — If you see someone you care about exhibiting changes in behavior, such as fatigue, social withdrawal, declining grades or work performance, etc., let them know that you have noticed the changes and are concerned about their welfare.

- **Develop an Internet-usage time schedule** — Parents can talk with children or teens about the Internet activities in which they engage. Establish rules about Internet use, and create a time schedule together to monitor its usage.

- **Learn tools you can use to monitor Internet use** — Parents should learn how to check history folders and Internet logs, and install filters to block inappropriate Web sites. By doing so, you can maintain some control over what your children or teens can access and monitor what they are viewing online.

- **Encourage non-Internet-related activities** — Help loved ones find other activities that might capture their interest. If there is an online topic in which someone you know is interested, try to find an offline equivalent for it. Try to get them to participate in outdoor activities or activities that will help them develop new skills.

- **Do not let the Internet infiltrate all aspects of life** — Protect your family and protect yourself as well. Do not allow computers in your children's or teens' bedrooms. Do not let your kids or loved ones use computing devices while riding in the car, but encourage conversation instead. Reserve "offline" time for your family and for yourself, to encourage real-world activities.

- **Get help if needed**— If you find that you or a loved one or friend has developed an addiction to Internet activity, consider turning to resources that can help. Online resources such as the Center for Internet Addiction Recovery (*www.netaddiction.com*) provide services such as information, diagnosis, treatment and support for various types of Internet addiction. You can also find local support groups for Internet addiction by searching online for services in your area.

Case Study

A Call That Went Awry

Ramona received an e-mail message marked as "High" importance from her bank. The message contained an urgent plea to call an account manager immediately and provided the number at the bottom of the message. When Ramona called the number, the recipient identified himself as the account manager who sent the message and told Ramona that someone was trying to electronically access funds from her account. In order to take steps to find out who was trying to access her funds, the account manager requested that Ramona confirm her identity by providing some personal details.

In her eagerness to stop the unknown perpetrator from accessing her funds, Ramona confirmed to the account manager her name, address, date of birth, PIN number, password and other personal information in answer to the account manager's queries. During the call, Ramona asked if she could change her PIN number and password, and the account manager verbally accommodated her request.

Ramona did not hear from the account manager again and assumed that the problem had been resolved. She confirmed this by checking her account and noticing nothing amiss. However, when she received her next credit card statement, she found that almost US $10,000 in purchases had been charged to her account, reaching her account limit.

Ramona immediately called the police and told them what happened. The desk sergeant with whom she spoke said that she needed to take up her complaint with her credit card company and wished her well. Ramona immediately called her credit card company, and persuaded them to freeze her account and investigate the purchases.

*   *   *

Consider this scenario to determine what Ramona could have done differently to prevent this identity theft from happening. Answer the following questions:

- Should Ramona have immediately called the number for the account manager given in the e-mail? If she had checked to see that it matched the number of her bank, what do you think she would have discovered?

- What questions could Ramona have asked at the beginning of the call to ensure she was talking to a bona fide bank employee?

- What information is safe to provide over the phone and what information should Ramona have withheld?

- How long do you think it took to resolve the problem? Do you think Ramona was forgiven the debt? If not, what else can she do to resolve this situation?

Lesson Summary

Application project

You can apply a digital certificate to your e-mail for encryption between co-workers and various contacts. To encrypt your e-mail, you can retrieve a digital certificate from an Internet certificate authority, such as VeriSign. Access the VeriSign Web site (*www.verisign.com*) and read the instructions for obtaining digital certificates, called digital IDs.

As a network administrator, you can purchase multiple digital IDs for your network users to ensure e-mail confidentiality. What is the cost of one VeriSign digital ID? How much would it cost to buy 500 digital IDs? If you decide to register and download digital IDs for all your network users (each user would have his or her own private key), you must be sure that all users have the public keys for all co-workers and contacts to whom they will send encrypted messages. Public keys can be downloaded from VeriSign (a database contains the public keys of all registered certificates) or sent by e-mail to each user.

After a user has loaded the public key for the destination e-mail account user, he or she can send encrypted e-mail messages that can be decrypted only by the destination e-mail account (because only the destination user has the private key). Does your company need secure e-mail? Would this security policy be beneficial? Is secure e-mail a cost-effective means of security for your company?

Skills review

In this lesson, you learned about network security threats, the common attacks waged against network resources and the most familiar attack, computer viruses. You also learned about authentication principles and the three major types of encryption. You learned about network-level protocols that provide privacy, integrity and authentication at the network layer. You learned about firewalls and security zones, and how they enable a business to protect itself from outside parties. You also studied Internet privacy issues, including anonymous Web browsing, Internet fraud, identity theft and phishing. Finally, you learned about Internet-based challenges that require personal protection measures for users of all ages: online stalking, cyberbullying and Internet addiction.

Now that you have completed this lesson, you should be able to:

✓   3.5.1: Identify typical attacks on clients and procedures to counter each attack type.

✓   3.5.2: Recognize and avoid social engineering attacks.

✓   3.5.3: Distinguish among symmetric, asymmetric and hash encryption.

✓   3.5.4: Define authentication principles, including password resetting, password aging.

✓   3.5.5: Describe Virtual Private Networks (VPNs) and the purposes of remote access protocols, including Point-to-Point Tunneling Protocol (PPTP), Layer 2 Tunneling Protocol (L2TP).

✓   3.5.6: Distinguish among the following security zones: DMZ (including dual-homed and triple-homed firewalls), VLAN, intranet, extranet.

✓   3.5.7: Define fundamental PKI concepts.

✓   3.5.8: Identify the purpose of an uninterruptible power supply (UPS), and list common concerns and configuration parameters.

✓ 3.11.1: Define phishing and pharming, and identify ways to avoid becoming a victim.

✓ 3.11.2: Identify ways to avoid anti-social activity, including online stalking and cyberbullying.

✓ 3.11.3: List symptoms and ramifications of spending too much time on the Internet and on gaming.

✓ 3.11.4: Use encryption technology to secure communications (e.g., e-mail encryption, password generators, password managers).

Lesson 5 Review

1. Name the virus type that executes differently each time it is run.

   _____

2. What is authentication, and what is its primary purpose?

   _____

   _____

   _____

3. What is the primary technique of ensuring privacy across the enterprise?

   _____

4. Which encryption technique is designed to be used for information that will not be decrypted or read?

   _____

5. What is the purpose of a firewall?

   _____

   _____

6. What is a bottleneck?

   _____

   _____

7. Why is the screened subnet the most secure of the four general firewall topologies?

   _____

   _____

8. What is identity theft?

   _____

   _____

9. Name three major challenges that constitute inappropriate use of the Internet, and from which users should be protected?

   _____

Lesson 5
Supplemental Material

This section is a supplement containing additional tasks for you to complete in conjunction with the lesson. These elements are:

- **Activities**
  Pen-and-paper activities to review lesson concepts or terms.

- **Lesson Quiz**
  Multiple-choice test to assess knowledge of lesson material.

Activity 5-1: Reviewing passwords

In this activity, you will review the elements of strong passwords and resolve a scenario in which passwords have become compromised.

1. Write down the elements of strong passwords and the guidelines they should follow.

_____

_____

_____

_____

_____

_____

_____

_____

_____

2. You suspect that several passwords have been compromised. Currently, users are required to change passwords every six months. What steps should you take?

_____

_____

Passwords are one of the core strengths of computer and network security. If the password is compromised, the basic security scheme or model is affected. To enforce good password selection, you need to require passwords and to help users choose strong passwords. In addition, password aging is an important parameter to implement because it can make password cracking with brute-force and dictionary attacks more difficult.

Activity 5-2: Distinguishing between proxy servers and firewalls

In this activity, you will determine whether the network requirements in the following scenarios are best met by a firewall, a proxy server, or both. For each scenario, write your answer in the space provided.

1. You are setting up a Web server as part of your network. Your network is configured with registered IP addresses, and users will be able to connect to remote Web sites directly. You need to limit traffic to HTTP traffic.

    _____

2. You are setting up Internet access for your network. Your ISP has given you two public IP addresses. One address will be used to configure a public Web server. All users must share the remaining address for Internet access.

    _____

3. You are setting up Internet access for your network. You do not want your local IP addresses to be visible on the network, and you need to limit traffic to World Wide Web and FTP transfers only.

    _____

Most direct Internet-access solutions include both firewall and proxy server protection, often combined in a single multi-function device.

Lesson 5 Quiz

1. A network attack in which repeated attempts are made to guess user names and passwords using a file containing a long list of words is called:

   a. a back-door attack.
   b. a brute-force attack.
   c. a dictionary attack.
   d. a man-in-the-middle attack.

2. A network-level protocol that uses tunneling to encapsulate data packets into network packets is called:

   a. non-repudiation.
   b. Pretty Good Privacy (PGP).
   c. remote access server (RAS).
   d. virtual private network (VPN).

3. A server whose primary goal is to enable the secure creation and management of digital certificates is called:

   a. a certificate authority (CA).
   b. Data Encryption Standard (DES).
   c. Public Key Infrastructure (PKI).
   d. Virtual Network Computing (VNC).

4. The practice of hiding internal IP addresses from the external network is called:

   a. information caching.
   b. Network Address Translation (NAT).
   c. packet-sniffing.
   d. spoofing.

5. A computer that holds various firewall components and services, and is connected to a public network is called:

   a. a bastion host.
   b. an intranet.
   c. an extranet.
   d. a virtual LAN (VLAN).

Appendixes

Appendix A: Objectives and Locations*
Appendix B: Movies*
Appendix C: Works Consulted*

Appendix found on Companion CD-ROM

CIW Foundations Glossary

account lockout — A legitimate practice in which a user account is automatically disabled after a certain number of failed authentication attempts.

active partition — A logical partition that contains the files necessary to boot an operating system. This partition is read first at boot time. If no active partition exists, or if the operating system files are corrupted or missing, the computer will report error messages.

ActiveX — An open set of technologies for integrating components on the Internet and within Microsoft applications.

adapter — A device that provides connectivity between at least two systems.

Advanced Research Projects Agency (ARPA) — A U.S. Department of Defense agency that created the first global computer network.

Advanced Research Projects Agency Network (ARPANET) — A computer network, funded by ARPA, that served as the basis for early networking research and was the backbone during the development of the Internet.

Ajax — A programming methodology that uses a number of existing technologies together and enables Web applications to make incremental updates to the user interface without the need to reload the browser page.

anonymizing tools — Internet components and application features that make the user's Internet activity untraceable.

anti-virus software — Software that scans disks and programs for known viruses and eliminates them.

applets — Small programs written in Java, which are downloaded as needed and executed within a Web page or browser.

application programming interface (API) — A set of universal commands, calls and functions that allows developers to communicate with an application or operating system.

Application Service Provider (ASP) — A company that provides applications and services (over the Internet) to individual or enterprise subscribers that would otherwise need to provide those applications and services on their own servers.

application-level gateway — A firewall component that inspects all packets addressed to a user-level application; uses proxies to control and filter traffic on a connection-by-connection basis. Also provides authentication.

assignment — The appointment of a specific resource to a specific task.

assumption — A factor that is considered to be real or certain for planning purposes.

asymmetric encryption — An encryption method in which two keys (a private key and a public key) are used to encrypt and decrypt a message. Also known as public-key encryption.

attachment — A file that is sent with an e-mail message.

attenuation — The weakening of a transmission signal as it travels farther from its source.

AU — Audio file format used by UNIX servers, the majority of Web servers. Most Web browsers can read AU.

Audio Interchange File Format (AIFF) — High-quality audio format developed by Apple Computer.

Audio Video Interleave (AVI) — Standard Windows file format for video files.

authentication — The process of verifying the identity of a user who logs on to a system, or the integrity of transmitted data.

back end — A series of systems that fulfill requests made by a client. Back-end systems can include mainframes and servers containing information databases.

backbone — The highest level in the computer network hierarchy, to which smaller networks typically connect.

bandwidth — The amount of information, sometimes called traffic, that can be carried on a network at one time. The total capacity of a line. Also, the rate of data transfer over a network connection; measured in bits per second.

baseline — A recording of network activity, obtained through documentation and monitoring, that serves as an example for comparing future network activity.

bastion host — A computer that houses various firewall components and services, and is connected to a public network such as the Internet.

binary file — A file containing data or instructions written in zeros and ones (computer language).

BitTorrent — A peer-to-peer file sharing protocol used for distributing large amounts of data.

blackhole list — A published list of IP addresses known to be sources of spam.

block-level element — A markup element that affects at least an entire paragraph.

blog — Short for "Web log." A collection of personal thoughts posted on a public Web site. Blogging is the act of adding entries to a blog.

Bluetooth — A standard for short-range radio signals that is used to form personal area networks (PANs).

Boolean operator — A symbol or word used in Internet searches to narrow search results by including or excluding certain words or phrases from the search criteria.

bottleneck — A point in network communication at which information is processed more slowly. Also, any element (a hard drive, I/O card or network interface card) that slows network connectivity rates.

brand — A concept or collection of symbols associated with a product, service or person.

browser e-mail — E-mail programs such as Outlook Express and Opera Mail that come bundled with a Web browser and with which they may be integrated.

buffer — A cache of memory used by a computer to store frequently used data. Buffers allow faster access times.

bus — An electronic pathway that conducts signals to connect the functional components of a computer.

business logic — The coding (usually in SQL) necessary to create relationships in the data stored in a database.

business-to-business (B2B) — An e-commerce model in which a Web-based business sells products and/or services to other businesses.

business-to-consumer (B2C) — An e-commerce model in which a Web-based business sells products and/or services to consumers or end users.

byte — A measurement of memory needed to store one 8-bit character.

cable modem — A device that allows computers to communicate over a network by modulating and demodulating the cable signal into a stream of data.

call center — A centralized office used for the purpose of processing a large volume of requests by phone.

callback — A process in which a remote access server returns a call to a remote client that has logged on in order to authenticate that client.

CAPTCHA (Completely Automated Public Turing Test to Tell Computers and Humans Apart) — A test that uses a word-verification graphic designed to differentiate humans from automated senders during online transactions.

Carrier Sense Multiple Access/Collision Detection (CSMA/CD) — The LAN access method used by Ethernet. Checks for network access availability with a signal.

Cascading Style Sheets (CSS) — A technology that allows greater style definition and formatting control of HTML elements. Formatting can be placed within the HTML or called remotely from an external style sheet.

change management — The process, tools and techniques that help people implement changes to achieve a desired outcome.

character set — The group of symbols used to render text on a page.

client — An individual computer connected to a network. Also, a system or application (such as a Web browser or user agent) that requests a service from another computer (the server) and is used to access files or documents.

client-side script — Code embedded into an HTML page and downloaded by a user; resides on the client and helps process Web form input. Common client-side scripting languages include JavaScript and VBScript.

cloud computing — A computing paradigm in which users are able to access software and services over the Internet instead of from their desktops.

cluster — A group of sectors used as the basic unit of data storage.

coax — Short for coaxial cable. High-capacity two-wire (signal and ground) cable; inner wire is the primary conductor, and the metal sheath serves as the ground.

codec — A compression/ decompression algorithm used by modern video and audio player plug-ins.

collective intelligence — The ability of a group to exhibit a greater degree of intelligence by solving problems collaboratively compared to the intelligence of an individual member.

COM — PC serial ports are referred to as numbered COM (communication) ports. COM ports have a maximum transmission speed of roughly 115 Kbps.

common field — A field contained in two or more database tables that forms a connection between the tables.

Common Gateway Interface (CGI) — A program that processes data submitted by the user. Allows a Web server to pass control to a software application, based on user request. The application receives and organizes data, then returns it in a consistent format.

Concurrent Versions System (CVS) — A tool that allows programmers to control different versions of the pieces of a program as those pieces are developed.

constraint — A factor, such as budget or time, that limits a project manager's options.

consumer-to-consumer (C2C) — An e-commerce model in which individual consumers sell their pre-owned products or personal services to other consumers.

contact center — A call center that allows consumers to contact agents via avenues other than by telephone.

Content Management System (CMS) — A server or series of servers that allows you to easily create, store and track all documents and information produced by an organization.

convergence — The integration of telephony and data technologies.

cookie — A text file that contains information sent between a server and a client to help maintain state and track user activities. Cookies can reside in memory or on a hard drive.

crowdsourcing — A problem-solving model in which a task ordinarily performed by one person is outsourced to a large group or community in order to obtain and analyze large amounts of data.

customs — National departments responsible for controlling items entering and leaving the country.

cyberbullying — Willful harm inflicted on others through the use of information and communication technologies.

daemon — A Linux/UNIX program that is usually initiated at startup and runs in the background until required.

data — Information being stored, usually in a database.

data source name (DSN) — A text string that is used to reference the data source by application programs.

database — A collection of data that can be sorted and searched using search algorithms.

database administrator — An individual who is responsible for the maintenance and security of an organization's database resources and data.

database management system (DBMS) — A program used to store, access and manipulate database information.

dead link — A hyperlink that, when clicked, sends a Web site visitor to a page or resource that does not exist on the server.

decryption — The process of converting encrypted data back to its original form.

deep URL — A URL that includes a path past the domain into the folder structure of a Web site.

dictionary program — A program specifically written to break into a password-protected system. It has a relatively large list of common password names that it repeatedly uses to gain access.

digital certificate — A password-protected, encrypted data file containing message encryption, user identification and message text. Used to authenticate a program or a sender's public key, or to initiate SSL sessions. Must be signed by a certificate authority (CA) to be valid.

digital signature — An electronic stamp added to a message that uniquely identifies its source and verifies its contents at the time of the signature.

Digital Subscriber Line (DSL) — A high-speed direct Internet connection that uses all-digital networks.

Digital Video Interface (DVI) — A video interface technology that carries uncompressed digital video data to a display.

direct memory access (DMA) — A process that allows devices to bypass controllers and directly access memory.

disk cache — Storage space on a computer hard disk used to temporarily store downloaded data.

dithering — The ability for a computer to approximate a color by combining the RGB values.

document type declaration (<!DOCTYPE>) — A declaration of document or code type embedded within an HTML, XHTML, XML or SGML document; identifies the version and nature of code used. Denoted by the <!DOCTYPE> tag at the beginning of the document.

Document Type Definition (DTD) — A set of rules contained in a simple text file that defines the structure, syntax and vocabulary as it relates to tags and attributes for a corresponding document.

domain name — An IP address represented in words.

domain name server — A server that resolves domain names into IP addresses.

domain name space — The three-level domain name hierarchy (root-level, top-level and second-level domains) that forms the Domain Name System (DNS).

Domain Name System (DNS) — A system that maps uniquely hierarchical names to specific Internet addresses.

dynamic — Always changing.

Dynamic HTML (DHTML) — A combination of HTML, script, styles and the Document Object Model (DOM) that provides Web page interactivity.

e-mail client — An e-mail program that is independent of any specific Web browser, and that you can use to send e-mail messages.

electronic commerce (e-commerce) — The integration of communications, data management and security capabilities to allow organizations and consumers to exchange information related to the sale of good and services.

Electronic Data Interchange (EDI) — The inter-organization exchange of documents in a standardized electronic format directly between participating computers.

emoticon — A combination of characters that, when read sideways, helps convey emotion in an e-mail message.

emulator — A type of software that imitates a computer then allows non-native software to run in a foreign environment. Sometimes also a hardware device.

Encapsulated PostScript (EPS) — File format used for importing and exporting graphics.

encryption — A security technique designed to prevent access to information by converting it into a scrambled (unreadable) form of text.

end-user license agreement (EULA) — A legal contract between the author of software and the end user that defines how the software can be used.

event handler — A line of code that allows a language to respond to a specific event or user input.

event-driven — Reacting to particular user actions or the browser's completion of a specific task.

Extensible Hypertext Markup Language (XHTML) — The current standard authoring language used to develop Web pages and other electronically displayed documents. XHTML requires stricter code syntax than HTML.

Extensible Markup Language (XML) — A markup language that describes document content instead of adding structure or formatting to document content. A simplified version of SGML.

Extensible Stylesheet Language (XSL) — A style language that provides formatting instructions for XML documents.

extranet — A network that connects enterprise intranets to the global Internet. Designed to provide access to selected external users.

Extreme Programming (XP) — A software development methodology that is designed to be very responsive to the customer's changing requirements.

field — A category of information in a database table.

File Transfer Protocol (FTP) — An Internet protocol used to transfer files between computers; allows file transfer without corruption or alteration.

firewall — A security barrier that controls the flow of information between the Internet and a private network. A firewall prevents outsiders from accessing an enterprise's internal network, which accesses the Internet indirectly through a proxy server.

fixed-width font — A font in which every character, including the space character, has equal width. In proportional-width fonts, letters such as I and J have less width than M or B.

folksonomy — The practice of categorizing online content through tags.

foreign key — A field in a related database table that refers to the primary key in the primary table.

frame — A scrollable region of a Web page in which other pages can be displayed; a single element of a frameset. Each frame has its own URL.

frameset document — A Web page that defines a set of adjacent frames in which other Web pages are displayed.

front end — A client that acts as an interface to a collection of servers (for example, mainframes or PC-based servers). A Web browser is a typical front-end client.

fully qualified domain name (FQDN) — The complete domain name of an Internet computer, such as www.CIW-certified.com.

Gantt chart — A horizontal bar chart that graphically displays project tasks and durations.

gateway — A node on a network that serves as a portal to other networks.

GNU Privacy Guard (GPG) — An open-source version of PGP, used for encrypting and decrypting e-mail messages, that does not use patented algorithms.

graphical user interface (GUI) — A program that provides visual navigation with menus and screen icons, and performs automated functions when users click command buttons.

Graphics Interchange Format (GIF) — A graphical image file format commonly used in HTML documents.

greenfield — A project that lacks any constraints imposed by prior development.

hacker — An unauthorized user who penetrates a host or network to access and manipulate data.

hash — A number generated by an algorithm from a text string. Also known as a message digest.

hash encryption — An encryption method in which hashes are used to verify the integrity of transmitted messages. Also known as one-way encryption

HDMI (High-Definition Multimedia Interface) — A compact audio/video interface for transmitting uncompressed digital data.

header — A block of information attached to a piece of data. The first part of a network packet. Can contain network addressing information or additional information that helps computers and applications process data.

help desk technician — An individual who diagnoses and resolves users' technical hardware and software problems.

hexadecimal — A base-16 number system that allows large numbers to be displayed by fewer characters than if the number were displayed in the regular base-10 system. In hexadecimal, the number 10 is represented as the letter A, 15 is represented as F, and 16 is represented as 10.

home page — The first Web page that displays when you access a domain.

hop — One link between two network devices; the number of hops between two devices is considered a hop count.

host — A computer that other computers can use to gain information; in network architecture, a host is a client or workstation.

hosts file — A file that contains mappings of IP addresses to host names.

hub — A device used to connect systems so that they can communicate with one another.

hyperlinks — Embedded instructions within a text file that link it to another point in the file or to a separate file.

hypertext link — Highlighted or underlined text in a Web page that, when clicked, links the user to another location or Web page.

Hypertext Markup Language (HTML) — The traditional authoring language used to develop Web pages for many applications.

Hypertext Transfer Protocol (HTTP) — The protocol for transporting HTML documents across the Internet.

I/O address — A memory location that allows resources to be allocated to a system device.

identity theft — Fraud committed in your name by someone else who has illicitly gained access to your personal information.

illicit server — An application that installs hidden services on systems. Illicit servers consist of "client" code and "server" code that enable the attacker to monitor and control the operation of the computer infected with the server code.

image map — A Web page image with clickable regions that are defined as "hot spot" hyperlinks to other pages or page sections.

index — A catalog of the contents of a database. Each entry identifies a unique database record.

Information Technology (IT) — The management and processing of information using computers and computer networks.

infrared — A spectrum of light used for communication between various network-enabled devices.

inline images — Images rendered in a Web page.

instant messaging (IM) — A computer-based method of communication in which users can type and view messages sent to one or more recipients, and view the responses immediately.

Integrated Services Digital Network (ISDN) — A communication standard for sending voice, video or data over digital telephone lines.

interactive — The characteristic of some hardware and software, such as computers, games and multimedia systems, that allows them to respond differently based on a user's actions.

interface — A communication channel between two components.

Internet — A worldwide network of interconnected networks.

Internet Control Messaging Protocol (ICMP) — A subset of Internet Protocol that is most often used to determine whether a computer can communicate with the rest of the network.

Internet fraud — Scam or other deceptive practices committed via the Internet, usually for the purpose of monetary gain or identity theft.

Internet Message Access Protocol (IMAP) — A protocol that resides on an incoming mail server. Similar to POP, but is more powerful. Allows sharing of mailboxes and multiple mail server access. The current version is IMAP4.

Internet privacy — The ability to control what information you reveal about yourself over the Internet, and to whom (or what) you reveal it.

Internet Protocol (IP) — The data transmission standard for the Internet. Every computer connected to the Internet has its own IP address, which enables a packet of data to be delivered to a specific computer.

Internet Service Provider (ISP) — An organization that maintains a gateway to the Internet and rents access to customers on a per-use or subscription basis.

interoperability — The ability of one computer system to communicate with another; often refers to different operating systems working together.

interrupt request (IRQ) — A hardware line over which devices can send interrupt signals to the processor.

intranet — An internal network based on TCP/IP protocols, accessible only to users within a company.

IP address — A unique numerical address assigned to a computer or device on a network.

IP Security (IPsec) — An authentication and encryption standard that provides security over the Internet. It functions at Layer 3 of the OSI/RM and can secure all packets transmitted over the network.

Java — An object-oriented programming language developed by Sun Microsystems that is fully cross-platform functional.

Java Virtual Machine (JVM) — The artificial computer that runs Java programs and allows the same code to run on different platforms.

Joint Photographic Experts Group (JPEG) — A graphical image file format commonly used for photographs.

junction table — A database table containing foreign-key fields that refer to the primary-key fields from the primary tables in a many-to-many relationship.

Kerberos — A proprietary key management scheme between unknown principals who want to communicate securely. Uses symmetric algorithms

and acts as a trusted third party that knows the identities of the organizations asking to communicate, but does not reveal them.

kernel — The essential part of an operating system; provides basic services; always resides in memory.

key — A variable value, such as a numeric code, that uses an algorithm to encrypt and decrypt data. Some applications encrypt and decrypt with the same key, whereas other applications use a pair of keys.

keyword — A word that appears on a Web page and is used by search engines to identify relevant URLs. Some words, such as "the" or "and," are too common to be used as keywords.

Layer 2 switch — A device that forwards traffic based on MAC addresses.

Layer 3 switch — A device that connects networks.

legacy adapter board — An older, non-Plug-And-Play adapter board.

legacy model — A model that, because of its age, may not support modern technologies without manipulation or upgrades.

Lightweight Directory Access Protocol (LDAP) — A protocol that allows a network entity to access a directory service listing.

link rot — The phenomenon in which hyperlinks on a Web site gradually become invalid as referenced Web page content, links and page locations change.

list server — A server that collects and distributes information from an authorized group of participants, called a listserve group.

listserve group — Users who subscribe to an e-mailing list through a list server.

LiveScript — The Netscape-developed scripting language that was the predecessor to JavaScript.

local area network (LAN) — A group of computers connected within a confined geographic area.

lossless compression — A type of data file compression in which all original data can be recovered when the file is decompressed.

lossy compression — A type of data file compression in which some file information is permanently eliminated.

LPT — Line printer port. PC parallel ports are referred to as numbered LPTs.

Mail Delivery Agent (MDA) — An e-mail server program that receives sent messages and delivers them to their proper destination mailbox.

Mail User Agent (MUA) — A messaging component used as a stand-alone application by the user.

mailing list server — An e-mail server that regularly sends e-mail messages to a specified list of users.

malware — Abbreviation for malicious software. Malware is software designed to harm computer systems.

many-to-many relationship — In databases, a relationship in which one record in Table A can relate to many matching records in Table B, and vice versa.

markup language — A series of commands used to format, organize and describe information on a Web page.

mashup — A Web page that integrates content and scripts from multiple Web sites to create new applications.

media — Any material that allows data to flow through it or be stored on it; includes hard and floppy disks, wire, cable, and fiber optics.

Media Access Control (MAC) address — The hardware address of a device connected to a network.

Message Transfer Agent (MTA) — A messaging component that routes, delivers and receives e-mail.

meta search engine — A search engine that scans Web pages for <meta> tag information.

metalanguage — A language used for defining other languages.

microformat — A data format that adds human-readable metadata to existing code so that the data can be processed by other software.

milestone — The end of a stage that marks the completion of a task or series of related tasks, resulting in a key deliverable.

MIME type — Identifies the contents of a file in the MIME encoding system using a type/subtype format; examples are image/jpg and text/plain.

mobile computing — A person's ability to use technology in non-stationary positions and in transit.

modem — Abbreviation for modulator/ demodulator. An analog device that enables computers to communicate over telephone lines by translating digital data into audio/ analog signals (on the sending computer) and then back into digital form (on the receiving computer).

motherboard — The main circuit board in a computer, on which the microprocessor, physical memory and support circuitry are located.

Moving Picture Experts Group (MPEG) — High-quality video file compression format.

MPEG-1 Audio Layer 3 (MP3) — Popular compression standard for audio files; retains most of the sound quality of the source.

MPEG-2 — Current video compression standard.

Multipurpose Internet Mail Extensions (MIME) — A protocol that enables operating systems to map file name extensions to corresponding applications. Also used by applications to automatically process files downloaded from the Internet.

Multistation Access Unit (MAU) — The network device that is the central connection point for Token Ring networks.

Musical Instrument Digital Interface (MIDI) — A standard computer interface for creating and playing electronic music. It allows computers to re-create music in digital format for playback.

narrowband — A specific set of frequencies established for wireless communication (usually for voice). Communicates at lower rates than broadband.

National Science Foundation (NSF) — An independent agency of the U.S. government that promotes the advancement of science and engineering.

needs analysis — Determining a customer's needs by acquiring information, processing and evaluating the information, then creating a plan of action to address the needs.

netbook — A more compact, Web-oriented version of the standard laptop PC; relies on the cloud-computing model in which the Internet is used for remote access to Web applications.

network — A group of two or more computers connected so they can communicate with one another.

Network Address Translation (NAT) — The practice of hiding internal IP addresses from the external network.

network engineer — An individual who manages and maintains a network infrastructure.

network interface card (NIC) — A circuit board within a computer's central processing unit that serves as the interface enabling the computer to connect to a network.

Network News Transfer Protocol (NNTP) — The Internet protocol used by news servers that enables the exchange of newsgroup (Usenet) articles.

network operating system (NOS) — An operating system that manages network resources.

newsgroup — On Usenet, a subject or other topical interest group whose members exchange ideas and opinions. Participants post and receive messages via a news server.

node — Any entity on a network that can be managed, such as a system, repeater, router, gateway, switch or firewall. A computer or other addressable device attached to a network; a host.

non-repudiation — The security principle of providing proof that a transaction occurred between identified parties. Repudiation occurs when one party in a transaction denies that the transaction took place.

object — An element on a Web page that contains data and procedures for how that item will react when activated. On a Web page, an object is typically a multimedia presentation.

object-based — Similar to object-oriented programming languages, but does not allow for inheritance from one class to another.

object-oriented — A style of programming that links data to the processes that manipulate it.

object-oriented programming (OOP) — Programming concept based on objects and data and how they relate to one another, instead of logic and actions; C++ and Java are OOP languages.

OCx — Optical carrier levels; defines the transmission speeds used in SONET/SDH.

Ogg Vorbis (.ogg) — A free, open-source alternative to the MP3 compression format for audio files; creates smaller, faster downloading files.

one-to-many relationship — In databases, a relationship in which a record in Table A can have multiple matching records in Table B, but a record in Table B has only one matching record in Table A.

one-to-one relationship — In databases, a relationship in which each record in Table A can have only one matching record in Table B, and vice versa.

online stalking — To pursue stealthily, harass and/or prey upon another person using online venues such as chat rooms, e-mail, social networking sites, etc. The stalker may also meet the victim in an online venue and may gain his or her trust before perpetrating harassment activities.

ontology — The study of how a particular knowledge domain, or system, is organized. An ontology is the product of an ontological study.

Open Buying on the Internet (OBI) — An open-technology standard used by organizations to exchange data in a common format; an alternative to EDI.

open source — A peer-based development process describing organizations and products that provide free source code to the development community at large with the goal of developing better products; includes Apache Web server and Linux.

Open Systems Interconnection (OSI) reference model — A layered network architecture model of communication developed by the International Organization for Standardization (ISO). Defines seven layers of network functions.

open-source license — A "copyleft" license that removes restrictions on the use and distribution of the licensed product.

order tracking — The ability to determine progress on delivery of a product. Businesses often provide order-tracking support to end users via Web browsers and e-mail clients.

P2P — A peer-to-peer network on the Internet.

packet — Data processed by protocols so it can be sent across a network.

packet sniffing — The use of protocol analyzer software to obtain sensitive information, such as user names and passwords.

password generator — An algorithm that receives input from a random or pseudo-random number generator and automatically generates a password.

password manager — A software application you can use to store and manage multiple passwords.

password sniffing — A method of intercepting the transmission of a password during the authentication process. A sniffer is a program used to intercept passwords.

patch — Programming code that provides a temporary solution to a known problem, or bug.

patent — A set of exclusive rights granted to an inventor for a fixed period of time upon disclosure of the invention.

pay per click (PPC) — An Internet marketing technique that enables you to list your site high in search engine rankings by advertising on keywords that describe your product or service.

PC repair technician — An individual who installs, modifies and repairs personal computer (PC) hardware components.

peer-to-peer network — A network in which each computer has both server and client capabilities.

peripheral port — A socket on a computer into which a peripheral device is connected.

permission bit — A file or directory attribute that determines access. Permission bits include read, write and execute permissions.

permissions — Instructions given by an operating system or server (or a combination thereof) that restrict or allow access to system resources, such as files, user databases and system processes.

Personal Digital Assistant (PDA) — A small, handheld computer used for personal information management.

personal information management (PIM) program — A tool used to schedule appointments and meetings, store contact information, and manage tasks.

planned maintenance — Any scheduled maintenance procedures, including preventive maintenance.

plenum — Space between building floors; usually contains air and heating ducts, as well as communication and electrical wires.

plug-in — A program installed in the browser to extend its basic functionality. Allows different file formats to be viewed as part of a standard HTML document.

podcast — The use of audio or video digital-media files that are distributed through Web feeds to subscribed users.

Point-to-Point Protocol (PPP) — A protocol that allows a computer to connect to the Internet over a phone line.

Point-to-Point Protocol over Ethernet (PPPoE) — A protocol that implements PPP on top of the Ethernet architecture to connect an entire network to the Internet.

Point-to-Point Tunneling Protocol (PPTP) — A protocol that allows users and corporations to securely extend their networks over the Internet using remote access servers. Used to create VPNs.

pop-under window — A small browser window that appears behind the browser window you are viewing.

pop-up window — A small browser window that appears in front of the browser window you are viewing.

port — A logical opening in an operating system or protocol stack that allows the transfer of information. Not the same as a TCP or UDP port.

Portable Document Format (PDF) — A file format that can be transferred across platforms and retain its formatting; designated by the file name extension .pdf.

Post Office Protocol (POP) — A protocol that resides on an incoming mail server. The current version is POP3.

presence — A status indicator that conveys a person's willingness and ability to engage in communications.

presencing — The ability for a device to automatically track and report the user's location and availability.

presentation responsibilities — The forms in which the data and business logic are presented on your screen. Presentation responsibilities include XHTML and HTML forms, and application-specific interfaces such as Web browsers.

Pretty Good Privacy (PGP) — A method of encrypting and decrypting e-mail messages. It can also be used to encrypt a digital signature.

primary key — A field containing a value that uniquely identifies each record in a database table.

print queue — A mechanism that stores print requests until they are passed to a printing device.

program management — The process of managing multiple interdependent projects to improve the performance of an organization.

project — A sequence of tasks that must be accomplished within a certain time frame to achieve a desired result.

project management — The practice of applying skills and processes to activities in order to meet deadlines and achieve desired results.

project schedule — A document that lists the planned dates for performing tasks and meeting goals defined in a project plan.

proprietary software — Software that is the legal property of an entity.

proxy server — A server that mediates traffic between a protected network and the Internet. Translates IP addresses and filters traffic.

PS/2-style connector — The six-pin mini-DIN connectors introduced with the IBM PS/2.

query — A question posed by a user to a database to request database information. The database returns the query results based on the criteria supplied by the user in the query.

QuickTime — A plug-in developed by Apple Computer for storing movie and audio files in digital format.

QuickTime Movie (MOV) — Standard file format for Apple QuickTime; uses the .mov, .moov or .qt file name extension.

Rapid Application Development (RAD) — An iterative software development methodology that uses prototypes to help define customer requirements.

record — A collection of information in a database table consisting of one or more related fields about a specific entity, such as a person, product or event.

relational database — A database that contains multiple tables related through common fields.

relationship — A connection between two or more database tables that is based on a field that the tables have in common.

relative URL — A URL that gives an abbreviated path to a resource using the current page as a starting position.

replay attack — An attack in which packets are obtained from the network or a network host, then reused.

Request for Comments (RFC) — A document published by the IETF that details information about standardized Internet protocols and those in various development stages.

reseller — A company that adds some value to an existing product or ser vice, then sells it to the public or to another company.

resource — A person, department or device needed to accomplish a task.

resource conflict — A situation in which two or more devices share a configuration setting.

restore point — A snapshot of a computer's settings at a particular point in time. Also known as a system checkpoint.

Return On Investment (ROI) — Profit earned as a result of a project relative to the value of resources required to complete it.

Rich Text Format (RTF) — Portable text file format created by Microsoft that allows image insertion and text formatting; an almost universal format.

root directory — Topmost hard disk directory (folder).

root-level server — A server at the highest level of the Domain Name System.

router — A device that routes packets between networks based on network-layer addresses; determines the best path across a network. Also used to connect separate LANs to form a WAN.

RSA — A popular, proprietary public-key encryption algorithm.

rule — In a style sheet, a format instruction that consists of a specified selector and the properties and values applied to it. Also a line or lines; the word is related to "ruler," a tool of measurement that can be used to draw straight lines.

sans-serif — A font style that does not use decorative strokes at the tips of characters. Includes the Arial font family.

scope — The goals and tasks of a project, and the work required to complete them.

scope creep — Gradual increases in project scope that can undermine the success of a project.

screen saver — A graphic or moving image that appears on your screen when your computer is idle.

search engine — A powerful software program that searches Internet databases for user-specified information.

search engine optimization (SEO) — The process of improving the volume and quality of traffic to a Web site by structuring content to improve search engine ranking. A specific activity of Internet marketing.

Secure Copy (SCP) — A program used with Secure Shell (SSH) to transfer files between systems.

Secure Electronic Transactions (SET) — An Internet protocol that uses digital certificates to secure financial transactions.

Secure MIME (S/MIME) — Secure version of MIME that adds encryption to MIME data.

Secure Shell (SSH) — A protocol and command interface that provides secure access to a remote computer.

Secure Sockets Layer (SSL) — A protocol that provides authentication and encryption, used by most servers for secure exchanges over the Internet. Superseded by Transport Layer Security (TLS).

security analyst/consultant — An individual who examines an organization's security requirements and determines the necessary infrastructure.

security manager — An individual who manages the security measures used to protect electronic data.

segment — Part of a larger structure; common term used in networking.

selector — In a style sheet, any element to which designated styles are applied.

semantic Web — A Web 2.0 implementation by which Web data is contextualized with the addition of machine-readable metadata.

SEO analyst — An individual who determines the visibility of Web sites across multiple clients and search engines.

serif — A font style that uses characters with small decorative additions at the outermost points of the characters, called strokes. Includes the Times and Times New Roman fonts.

server — A computer in a network that manages the network resources and provides, or serves, information to clients.

server administrator — An individual who manages and maintains network servers.

server-side script — Code that resides on a server to help process Web form input. Server-side CGI scripts are commonly written in Perl.

servlet — A small Java application that runs on a server.

shared domain — A hosting service that allows multiple entities to share portions of the same domain name.

shell — A command-based interface that allows a user to issue commands.

signature database — In an anti-virus program, a collection of viruses, worms and illicit applications that are listed as security threats.

Simple Mail Transfer Protocol (SMTP) — The Internet standard protocol for transferring e-mail messages from one computer to another.

site map — A brief, hierarchical representation of a Web site that enables visitors to quickly identify areas of the site and navigate to them.

Small-Screen Rendering (SSR) — A browser technology developed for wireless devices that reformats Web pages to display on 176-pixel-wide mobile phone display screens.

Smalltalk — A programming language that pioneered object-oriented programming. Not popularly used in Web development.

smart card — A credit card that replaces the magnetic strip with an embedded chip for storing or processing data.

smartphone — A mobile phone that includes PC-like functionality.

snail mail — Slang term for the standard postal service.

social networking — The grouping of individuals with common interests or goals into specific groups or communities.

socket — The end point of a connection (either side), which usually includes the TCP or UDP port used and the IP address. Used for communication between a client and a server.

soft phone — A software application that enables a PC or PDA to function as a telephone using VoIP technology.

Software as a Service (SaaS) — A software distribution model in which the software is hosted by a service provider and licensed for use by the user.

spam — Unsolicited and unwanted e-mail messages; the online equivalent of junk mail.

spam filter — An e-mail client program that identifies and filters out spam messages before they reach the e-mail Inbox.

spim — Spam that is delivered through instant messaging.

spread spectrum — Technologies that consist of various methods for radio transmission in which frequencies or signal patterns are continuously changed.

spyware — A software application secretly placed on a user's system to gather information and relay it to outside parties, usually for advertising purposes.

SSH File Transfer Protocol (S/FTP) — A file transfer protocol that allows the encryption of transmissions using the Secure Shell (SSH) protocol.

SSL/TLS-enabled FTP (FTPS) — FTP that runs on an SSL/TLS-secured connection.

stakeholder — A person or group with an interest in a project, and with the power to exert influence (either positive or negative) over the project and affect results.

standard — A definition or format that has been approved by a recognized standards organization.

Standard Generalized Markup Language (SGML) — A metalanguage used to create other languages, including HTML and XHTML.

Statement Of Work (SOW) — A contract to initiate a project; the contract contains project goals and specifies how those goals will be met.

streaming audio and video — Audio and video files that travel over a network in real time.

streaming media — A continuous flow of data, usually audio or video files, that assists with the uninterrupted delivery of those files into a browser.

Structured Query Language (SQL) — A language used to create and maintain professional, high-performance corporate databases.

switch — A device that connects either individual systems or multiple networks. A Layer 1 switch connects individual systems.

symmetric encryption — An encryption method in which the same key is used to encrypt and decrypt a message. Also known as private-key encryption.

Synchronous Optical Network (SONET) — High-speed fiber-optic system used as a network and Internet backbone. The European counterpart is the Synchronous Digital Hierarchy (SDH).

T1 — A digital carrier that transmits data at a speed of 1.544 Mbps.

table — A collection of data about a limited topic, organized into rows and columns in a database.

Tagged Image File Format (TIFF) — Commonly used graphic file format, developed by Aldus Corporation; uses the .tif or .tiff file name extension.

tags — Pieces of code, enclosed in angle brackets, that tell the HTML interpreter how to process or display text.

task — A unit of work that must be accomplished during the course of a project.

Telnet — The Internet standard protocol for remote terminal connection service.

text messaging — A method of person-to-person communication in which users type short text messages from mobile phones.

text-level element — A markup element that affects single characters or words.

TinyURL — A free Web service that generates short aliases for long URLs.

token passing — The LAN access method used by Token Ring networks. A data frame, or token, is passed from one node to the next around the network ring.

top-level domain — The group into which a domain is categorized, by common topic (company, educational institution) and/or geography (country, state).

trace — Thin conductive path on a circuit board, usually made of copper.

trackback — A method by which a blogger receives notification when other bloggers link to his or her blog entry.

transceiver — A device that transmits and receives digital or analog signals.

Transmission Control Protocol/Internet Protocol (TCP/IP) — A suite of protocols that turns data into blocks of information called packets, which are then sent across the Internet. The standard protocol used by the Internet.

Transport Layer Security (TLS) — A protocol based on SSL 3.0 that provides authentication and encryption, used by most servers for secure exchanges over the Internet.

trojan — A program disguised as a harmless application that actually produces harmful results.

troll — Web user who publishes negative comments or submits feedback simply to annoy or anger.

trouble ticket — A record of a problem related to a service provided by an ISP or ASP. Used to record receipt of a complaint and track resolution of the problem.

tunneling protocol — A protocol that encapsulates data packets into another packet.

TV tuner card — A computer component that enables television signals to be viewed on a computer monitor.

typosquatting — The unethical practice of registering domain names very similar to those of high-volume sites in hopes of receiving traffic from users seeking the high-volume site who mistakenly enter an incorrect URL in their browsers.

Unicode — A universal character set designed to support all written languages, as well as scholarly disciplines (e.g., mathematics).

unified communications (UC) — A business trend that seeks to simplify and integrate all forms of communication. Also, a set of technologies that enable voice to be converted into text, and vice versa.

Uniform Resource Identifier (URI) — A standardized method of referring to a resource using a text string.

Uniform Resource Locator (URL) — A text string that specifies an Internet address and the method by which the address can be accessed.

uninterruptible power supply (UPS) — A power supply that uses a battery to maintain power during a power outage.

update — A file or collection of tools that resolves system liabilities and improves software performance.

Usenet (User Network) — A collection of thousands of Internet computers, newsgroups and newsgroup members using Network News Transfer Protocol (NNTP) to exchange information.

user agent — Any application, such as a Web browser, mobile phone, PDA or help engine, that renders HTML for display to users.

user name — A unique name or number that identifies you when logging on to a computer system or online service. In an e-mail address, the part before the @ symbol.

vector graphics — Resizable images that are saved as a sequence of vector statements, which describes a series of points to be connected.

viewer — A scaled-down version of an application; designed to view and print files.

virtual domain — A hosting service that allows a company to host its domain name on a third-party ISP server.

virtual local area network (VLAN) — Logical subgroup within a LAN created with software instead of hardware.

Virtual Network Computing (VNC) — A program that allows you to control a computer at a remote location.

Virtual Reality Modeling Language (VRML) — A three-dimensional graphic authoring language.

virtualization — A software technology that enables you to run multiple virtual operating systems and applications on a single physical computer.

virus — A malicious program that replicates itself on computer systems, usually through executable software, and causes irreparable system damage.

Visual Basic — The Microsoft graphical user interface (GUI) programming language used for developing Windows applications. A modified version of the BASIC programming language.

Visual Basic Script (VBScript) — Scripting language from Microsoft derived from Visual Basic; used to manipulate ActiveX scripts.

Voice over IP (VoIP) — A technology that converts voice into data packets for transmission over a packet-switched IP network. Allows the use of the Internet for real-time voice and video traffic.

Waterfall model — A development process in which the development phases flow from one to the other sequentially.

Waveform (WAV) — Windows standard format for audio files.

Web 2.0 — A concept referring to the changing trends in the use of WWW technology and Web design that have led to the development of information-sharing and collaboration capabilities.

Web analytics — The practice of collecting data and studying user behavior in an attempt to increase market share and sales.

Web application developer — An individual who develops primarily server-side Web applications.

Web application framework — A set of software tools or code that is commonly used in the creation and management of online applications.

Web architect — An individual who creates the overview plan of a Web site's development.

Web browser — A software application that enables users to access and view Web pages on the Internet.

Web feed — A data format for delivering Web content that is updated frequently.

Web marketing manager — An individual who develops and implements plans to exploit the Internet for marketing and sales opportunities.

Web page — An HTML document containing one or more elements (text, images, hyperlinks) that can be linked to or from other HTML pages.

Web site — A World Wide Web server and its content; includes multiple Web pages.

Web site analyst — An individual who analyzes Web site statistics to determine the site's effectiveness.

Web site designer — An individual who is responsible for the organization and appearance of a Web site.

Web site manager — An individual who manages a Web development team.

Web-based e-mail — Free e-mail service from a provider such as Windows Live Hotmail or Yahoo! in which you request a user name. You can access your e-mail from any computer that has access to the Internet.

Webcast — An audio and/or video Web event that is distributed over the Internet.

Webinar — An interactive Web-based seminar or training session.

What You See Is What You Get (WYSIWYG) — (pronounced whiz-ee-wig) A user-friendly editing format in which the file being edited is displayed as it will appear in the browser.

wide area network (WAN) — A group of computers connected over an expansive geographic area so their users can share files and services.

wideband — A large set of frequencies capable of carrying data at higher rates (for example, 1.544 Mbps). Usually carries digital signals. Includes DSL and cable Internet access.

wiki — A page or collection of Web pages that can be viewed and modified by anybody with a Web browser and access to the Internet.

wireless access point (AP) — A device that enables wireless systems to communicate with each other, provided that they are on the same network.

Wireless Application Protocol (WAP) — A standard protocol that wireless devices use to access the Internet.

Wireless Markup Language (WML) — A markup language that presents the text portions of Web pages to wireless devices.

wizard — A tool that assists users of an application in creating documents and/or databases based on styles and templates. Also a tool that guides users step-by-step through a software installation process.

World Wide Web (WWW) — A set of software programs that enables users to access resources on the Internet via hypertext documents.

worm — A self-replicating program or algorithm that consumes system resources.

X.509 — The standard used by certificate authorities (CAs) for creating digital certificates.

x.org — A windowing system used with UNIX and all popular operating systems.

xDSL — Collectively, the variations of Digital Subscriber Line (DSL), which include ADSL, RADSL and HDSL.

XMLHttpRequest — An application programming interface (API) that is used to transfer XML and other text data between a Web server and browser.

zone file — A file containing a set of instructions for resolving a specific domain name into its numerical IP address. Found in DNS servers.

Index

H.323, 2-9
hacker, 5-3
half duplex, 1-48
handshaking, 1-24
hash encryption, 5-19
HDMI, 4-22
header, 1-22, 1-48
hexadecimal, 1-49
hexadecimal numbering system, 4-7
high-capacity SD card (SDHC), 4-27
High-Definition Multimedia Interface (HDMI), 4-22
high-level format (logical drive), 4-32
high-speed network, 1-29
historic (protocol state), 2-6
hop, 2-11
host, 1-11
hosts file, 2-20, 2-22, 3-17
hosts table, 3-17
host-to-host layer, 2-4
HTML, 3-6
HTTP, 2-7, 2-9
HTTP 1.0, 2-8
HTTP 1.1, 2-8
HTTP server, 3-6
hub, 1-28, 1-32
hybrid topology, 1-13
Hypertext Markup Language (HTML), 3-6
Hypertext Transfer Protocol (HTTP), 2-7, 2-9
I/O address, 4-4
IANA, 2-13
IBM DB2, 3-11
ICANN, 2-13, 2-14
ICMP, 1-26, 2-7
IDE, 4-13
identity theft, 5-35
IEEE, 1-31, 1-48
IEEE 1284 (parallel port), 4-16
IEEE 1394 (FireWire), 1-31, 4-16
IEEE 802, 1-48
IEEE 802.11 family, 1-53
IEEE 802.11n, 1-54
IEEE 802.2, 1-48
IEEE 802.3, 1-51
IEEE 802.3ab, 1-51
IEEE 802.3ae/u 10-Gigabit Ethernet, 1-52
IEEE 802.3an amendment, 1-53
IEEE 802.3u, 1-51
IEEE 802.3z, 1-51
IEEE 802.5, 1-53
IESG, 2-5
IETF, 2-5, 5-30
ifconfig command, 2-33
IGMP, 2-7
IIS, 3-10
IM, 3-14
IMAP, 3-13
indexing, in CMS, 3-32
indirect routing, 2-10
Industry Standard Architecture (ISA), 1-31
informational (protocol state), 2-6
infrared, 1-4
infrastructure mode, wireless, 1-40
initialization, 2-21
instant messaging (IM), 1-5, 3-14
Institute of Electrical and Electronics Engineers (IEEE), 1-31, 1-48
integrated drive electronics (IDE), 4-13
Integrated Services Digital Network (ISDN), 1-35
interface, 4-13

interface serial number, 1-49
interior routing protocol, 2-11
internal firewall, 5-21
International Organization for Standardization (ISO), 1-17, 3-21
International Telecommunication Union (ITU), 1-47
Internet addiction, 5-41
Internet architecture, 2-3
Internet Assigned Numbers Authority (IANA), 2-13
Internet backbone, 1-29
Internet Control Message Protocol (ICMP), 1-26, 2-7
Internet Corporation for Assigned Names and Numbers (ICANN), 2-13
Internet Engineering Steering Group (IESG), 2-5
Internet Engineering Task Force (IETF), 2-5, 5-30
Internet Exchange Point (IXP), 1-29
Internet fraud, 5-34
Internet Group Management Protocol (IGMP), 2-7
Internet layer, Internet architecture, 2-4
Internet Message Access Protocol (IMAP), 3-13
Internet Network Information Center (InterNIC), 3-18
Internet privacy, 5-32
Internet Protocol (IP), 1-25, 2-7
Internet Protocol (IP) network, 2-9
Internet Protocol (IP) telephony, 1-5
Internet Security Association Key Management Protocol (ISAKMP), 5-30
Internet Service Provider (ISP), 1-5
Internetwork Packet Exchange/Sequenced Packet Exchange (IPX/SPX), 1-26
InterNIC, 3-18
interoperability, 1-15
interrupt request (IRQ), 4-4
intranet, 5-28
investment scam, 5-34
IP, 1-25, 2-7
IP network, 2-9
IP Security (IPsec), 5-30
IP telephony, 1-5
IP version 4 (IPv4), 2-19
IP version 6 (IPv6), 2-20
ipconfig command, 2-31
iPhone, 4-24
iPod, 4-26
iPod Touch, 4-26
IPsec, 5-30
IPv4, 1-25, 2-19
IPv6, 1-25, 2-20
IPX, 1-26
IPX/SPX, 1-26
IRQ, 4-4
ISAKMP, 5-30
ISDN, 1-35
ISO, 1-17, 3-21
ISP, 1-5
ITU, 1-47
iTunes, 4-26
IXP, 1-29
Java, 3-29
Java Virtual Machine (JVM), 3-29
JavaServer Pages (JSP), 3-10, 3-29
J-carrier system, 1-56
Joint Photographic Experts Group (JPEG), 3-7
JPEG, 3-7
JSP, 3-10, 3-29
JVM, 3-29
KaZaA, 1-10
Kerberos, 5-20
kernel, 1-16

Companion CD-ROM Contents

The *Network Technology Foundations* companion CD-ROM contains the following files needed to complete the course labs:

💿 Network_Self-Study_Companion_CD
📁 Answers	📁 Appendix	📁 Lab Files

📂 Answers
📄 ANSWERS_Activity.pdf	📄 ANSWERS_OptionalLab.pdf	📄 ANSWERS_Quiz.pdf
📄 ANSWERS_CourseAssessment.pdf	📄 ANSWERS_PreAssessment.pdf	📄 ANSWERS_Review.pdf
📄 ANSWERS_Lab.pdf		

📂 Appendix
📄 Appendix_A.pdf	📄 Appendix_C.pdf
📄 Appendix_B.pdf	

📂 Lab Files
📁 Lesson01
📁 Lesson05

📂 Lab Files\Lesson01
📄 jre-1_5_0_06-windows-i586-p.exe
📄 phex_3.0.2.100.exe

📂 Lab Files\Lesson05
📄 fcinst.exe